DOSSIER

EDWARD JAY EPSTEIN

DOSSIER

THE
SECRET
HISTORY
OF
ARMAND
HAMMER

RANDOM HOUSE

NEW YORK

Copyright © 1996 by E. J. E. Publications, Ltd., Inc.

All rights reserved under International and Pan-American
Copyright Conventions. Published in the United States by
Random House, Inc., New York, and simultaneously in Canada by
Random House of Canada Limited, Toronto.

Grateful acknowledgment is made to the William Morris Agency,
Inc., for permission to reprint excerpts from *Hammer* by
Armand Hammer. Copyright © 1987 by Dr. Armand Hammer.
Reprinted by permission of the William Morris Agency,
Inc., on behalf of the author.

Library of Congress Cataloging-in-Publication Data

Epstein, Edward Jay.
Dossier: the secret history of Armand Hammer/Edward Jay Epstein.
p.   cm.
Includes bibliographical references (p. 387) and index.
ISBN 0-679-44802-0 (alk. paper)
1. Hammer, Armand, 1898–1990. 2. Businessmen—United States—
Biography. 3. Capitalists and Financiers—United States—
Biography. 4. Statesmen—United States—Biography. 5. United
States—Relations—Soviet Union. 6. Soviet Union—Relations—United
States. I. Hammer, Armand, 1898–1990. II. Title.
HC102.5.H35E67   1996
338.092—dc20   95-43146
[B]

Random House website address: http://www.randomhouse.com/

Printed in the United States of America on acid-free paper

2 4 6 8 9 7 5 3

FIRST EDITION

Frontispiece: *Passports,* Betty O. Epstein

Book design by Carole Lowenstein

For my mother

Behind every great fortune there is a crime.

—BALZAC

CONTENTS

PART THREE: THE OIL TYCOON

EPILOGUE

DOSSIER

PROLOGUE

London,
Sept 6, 1990

Peter Lotz.

<u>Will</u>

Dear Peter, All my instructions with regard to Bettye Murphy and her daughter Victoria are hereby revoked. Also my instructions with regard to Graziosa (Mrs Martha Kaufman (Hilary Gibson) are also revoked My instructions with regard to you Peter, remains the same ($50,000)

In case of my death the ballance in Graziosa should go to the Armand Hammer Foundation.

Armand Hammer

Three months before his death, Hammer made a handwritten revision of his will, cutting off two mistresses and his illegitimate daughter. Funds in a secret bank account that not even his closest associates were aware of were to be channeled to the foundation that supported his museum.

THE
DEATH
MARCH

NOTHING FOCUSES THE MIND LIKE A DEATH SENTENCE.

Armand Hammer received the grim news from his doctors in Los Angeles on October 12, 1990. Three days earlier, he had been in Virginia, at Albemarle Farms, the estate of the industrialist John Kluge. He was a guest at a weeklong bird shoot to which one hundred of the richest people in America had been invited. Lavish accommodations were provided, and prize pheasants had been flown in from England. The announced purpose of this event was to raise money to fund research to find a cure for cancer. In the midst of the first night's banquet, Hammer was forced to leave the table because of acute stomach and chest pains. His doctor, who traveled with him, initially thought it was something he ate and gave him medication and purges. But the pain intensified. He had trouble breathing and could not sleep. The next morning, while the other moguls went out to shoot pheasants, Hammer was carried aboard his private Boeing 727 jet and flown to his home in Los Angeles. At 6:45 P.M. on October 11, he was rushed to the emergency room of the UCLA Medical Center—an institution to which Hammer had donated generously.[1]

X rays showed massive damage to Hammer's shoulder and clavicle bones. Two consulting doctors noted a "diffuse moth-eaten pattern" of destruction and were in no doubt as to its cause: advanced cancer of the bone marrow. Hammer had been trained as a doctor, and he understood what this meant. His worst fear had come to pass: a cancer he had believed was in remission had spread out of control. He also knew that he could not withstand the debilitating radiation treatment for it. He was a ninety-two-year-old man severely weakened by chronic anemia, bronchitis, prostate enlargement, kidney ailments, and an irregular heartbeat. The prognosis was that he would die within a year.

When doctors had detected the multiple myeloma more than a year earlier, Hammer believed he could beat it. In 1981, President Reagan had appointed him chairman of the President's Cancer Panel, and Hammer had committed himself to raising $1 billion to battle the disease. He had stamped his name on a host of research stations: the Armand Hammer Center for Cancer Biology at the Salk Institute, the Armand Hammer Cancer Research Laboratory at Stanford University, the Julius and Armand Hammer Health Sciences Center at Columbia University, and the Armand Hammer Center for Advanced Studies in Nuclear Energy and Health. He had offered a $1 million Armand Hammer Cancer Prize to the scientist who found a cure. In an appearance on *The Bill Cosby Show,* he announced that the discovery of such a cure was imminent.

But in battling his own cancer, Hammer could not wait for science. He began using an herbal preparation from the jungles of Mexico that he took in a *té negro,* or black tea, three times a day. He confidently explained to his doctors that it contained an "antiplasterion" that would prevent the cancer cells from spreading (and in their medical reports they duly noted the mysterious black tea, which they were not allowed to analyze). Even though such unlicensed medicine was illegal to import, he arranged for security guards from his company, Occidental Petroleum, to fly it in on company planes in five-gallon containers. The *té negro* had seemed to work, and that summer he began to speak of his mortality conditionally, saying to associates "if I die" instead of "when I die."[2]

In October, after reviewing the X rays, Hammer realized that the *té negro* had failed. This seemed humiliating, and he made attempts to ensure that the public would never know that the disease he had in his hubris proclaimed victory over had beaten him. He instructed his doctors not to tell anyone, not even his only son, that he had cancer. His death certificate would state another cause of death, his casket would be sealed, and his UCLA hospital records would be purged of any references to cancer.

Hammer now had only weeks in which to put his affairs in order. When he had taken over Occidental Petroleum in 1956, it was nearly bankrupt, and he had transformed it into an international powerhouse by making deals with foreign governments for oil concessions. Now Occidental was the fourteenth largest industrial company in the United States. Though he owned less than 1 percent of Occidental's stock, he was the chairman, and he ran the company as if it were his fiefdom. He used the corporate treasury for his philanthropic activities. Occidental donated money to buy works of art for, and to exhibit, the Armand Hammer Collection. The company subsidized the Armand Hammer Conference on Peace and Human Rights, which was held every year in different cities. It financed Armand Hammer Productions, which produced films and books about Hammer's global activities. Occidental also paid for Hammer's annual celebrity-studded birthday party, his personal lawyers, his bodyguards, and his Boeing 727. And although he would not be able to dictate its corporate policy from the grave, he had taken measures to ensure that in the foreseeable future his name would be identified with his creation. At a cost of nearly $100 million, he had Occidental erect a permanent memorial to him adjacent to its world headquarters on Wilshire Boulevard—the Armand Hammer Museum of Art and Cultural Center—in which would be displayed in perpetuity the Leonardo da Vinci drawings he had renamed the Codex Hammer.

Though Hammer knew he had little time left, there was one deal that he wanted to complete before he died. It was code-named Elders of Zion. Hammer had chosen this cryptonym half-facetiously. His partners included Robert Maxwell, who owned a multibillion-dollar media empire, including Macmillan Publishing Company in the United States and the Mirror Newspaper Group in Great Britain; Shaul N. Eisenberg, who had organized much of China's industrial export business; and Albert Reichmann, creator of the world's largest property company, Olympia and York. These men all had extensive experience in the Communist sphere.[3] Hammer himself had been dealing with the Soviet Union, secretly and overtly, for seventy years, trafficking in everything from pencils and czarist art to petrochemicals, and he had learned the unwritten rules of doing business in a government-controlled economy. He had served as a "path" to the West for some of the most powerful Soviet leaders of the century, including Lenin, Stalin, Khrushchev, Brezhnev, and Gorbachev. Now, with the cold war drawing to a close, he wanted to use his connections to organize one last deal—the creation of a new aircraft industry. This would involve cooperation among the Soviet Union, the United States, and Israel. If it worked, Hammer and his partners could envision billion-dollar profits. Hammer had obtained President Gorbachev's personal sanction for the project in September 1989. Just days before he felt the pains in his chest at John Kluge's estate, he had presented the plan to President Bush in Washington, and with the help of Howard Baker, the former White House chief of staff, he had tried to persuade the president that the aircraft deal would speed the disarmament of the Soviet Union—while at the same time creating jobs for American workers. Hammer hoped that with another trip to Moscow, the deal could be brought to fruition.

Hammer's overriding concern in these last few months was protecting his reputation after his death. He had worked tirelessly for seven decades to present himself as a philanthropist, a patron of the arts, and a peace broker. His collection of international awards included the Soviet Union's Lenin Order of Friendship Among the Peoples, which no other American capitalist had been, or will ever be, awarded; the U.S. National Arts Medal; France's Legion of Honor; Italy's Grand Order of Merit; Sweden's Royal Order of the Polar Star; Austria's Knight Commander's Cross; Pakistan's Hilal-i-Quaid-Azam Peace Award; Israel's Leadership Award; Venezuela's Order of Andres Bellos; Mexico's National Recognition Award; Bulgaria's Jubilee Medal; and Belgium's Order of the Crown. No fewer than twenty-five universities had awarded him honorary degrees, and one school, the Armand Hammer United World College, was named in his honor. He had so successfully cultivated his relationship with Prince Charles of Great Britain that he had been considered as a godfather to one of Charles's sons. He even had himself nominated for the Nobel Peace Prize.

Hammer's posthumous reputation depended on the removal of blemishes from his record. To this end, he had his lawyers file Freedom of Information requests for access to all the U.S. government's investigations of him, investigations that extended over sixty years.[4] They could then attempt to expunge from them allegations filed by the FBI and other intelligence services pertaining to Hammer's long career in Soviet Russia as Lenin's chosen capitalist. After all, such reports, without access to Soviet files, remained unsubstantiated hearsay. The previous year, Hammer had succeeded in persuading President Bush to grant him a full pardon for the only crime he had ever been convicted of: an illegal contribution to Nixon's 1972 presidential campaign, which had been used in the Watergate cover-up. Now he exerted his power and authority to prevent damaging secrets about his life and work from surfacing posthumously in the inevitable legal battles over his estate.

The instrument Hammer had used to control his secrets was the Armand Hammer Living Trust. Under California law, a living trust provides one main advantage over a conventional estate: secrecy. Unlike an estate, a living trust is not open to probate or any other form of public scrutiny. No one except the trustee of the living trust could learn how much money Hammer had accumulated in his life or under what terms it would be dispersed to his relatives, mistresses, associates, and other interests.

AFTER LEAVING THE UCLA MEDICAL CENTER IN HIS MERCEDES limousine, Hammer stopped briefly at his sixteenth-floor office at Occidental. He removed a sheaf of papers from the safe in his desk, to which he alone had the key. He then had his chauffeur drive him to his home at 10431 Wyton Drive in the Holmby Hills section of Westwood, where he had resided ever since he moved to California in 1956.

Rosamaria Durazo, the doctor who had traveled with him to the bird shoot in Virginia, was waiting for him. She had been with him almost every day since his third wife, Frances, died. Hammer had met Durazo some six years earlier. She was then in her early thirties and very attractive. A Mexican citizen who attended UCLA on a medical fellowship, she came to Hammer's office seeking help with an immigration problem: she had been offered an appointment as an assistant professor of anesthesiology at the Jules Stein Eye Institute at UCLA, but the Immigration and Naturalization Service had not yet given her the requisite green card. Hammer told his executive assistant to place a call to the White House. He then told Durazo that the problem would be taken care of, and as she learned a few days later, it was. She was made acting chief, and a professor, of anesthesiology at the Jules Stein Institute.

In 1985, when an earthquake leveled the hospital in Mexico City where she had studied, Durazo appealed to Hammer for help again. He responded by airlifting a team of doctors and two tons of medical equipment to Mexico.[5] Durazo went along with Hammer on the relief flight, and then he took her with him on other trips. They went to China, Japan, and Russia. He enjoyed introducing her to heads of state as his "personal physician" (although after leaving the Jules Stein Institute, she was not licensed to practice medicine in the United States). By 1989, one Occidental employee remembers, she was "traveling everywhere with Dr. Hammer." This observation is borne out by Hammer's personal travel logs. Durazo even accompanied him to Washington, D.C., for President Bush's weeklong inauguration celebration.

Hammer had maintained the appearance of an intact marriage by continuing to live with Frances, but their relationship had become increasingly strained. The marriage had deteriorated to the point where, on October 10, 1989, Frances called her niece and heir, Joan Weiss, and told her she was considering divorcing Hammer. She also told Weiss that she had stored her financial papers in a closet that was concealed behind a bookcase in the guest room. Adding to the tensions that fall, Hammer had been pressing Frances to sign a document waiving her legal claims to the art collection that he had consigned to his museum. Finally, on November 15, she scribbled her signature on the document. Ten days later, Frances slipped and cracked her hip and was rushed to UCLA for emergency surgery. Although the hip was successfully repaired, postoperative complications developed. She had been sedated with the muscle relaxant Halcion after her general anesthesia, and it became difficult for her to fully expel fluid that collected in her lungs.

When Joan Weiss arrived at the hospital the day after the operation, Frances still seemed woozy from the sedation. She also seemed discombobulated by the presence of Durazo. Frances whispered to Weiss, "What is she doing here?" Weiss assumed Durazo had been sent by Hammer to assist in the patient's recuperation. The next day, Frances's condition worsened, and by the end of the month she was in intensive care.[6]

While his wife was in critical condition, Hammer left for Moscow with Durazo to finish his negotiations on the still-secret Elders of Zion deal. He met Gorbachev in the Kremlin on December 7—his fortieth meeting in the Kremlin since he had visited Lenin there in 1921—and was presented with a vase in appreciation of the services he had rendered the Soviet Union. They went directly from Russia to Morocco, where they vacationed for three days at a villa in Marrakech. Just after they returned, Frances, who had been in intensive care for two weeks, died of pneumonia. Hammer refused to permit a postmortem examination—which is ordinarily performed in deaths that follow surgery—and arranged a quiet funeral. Durazo began living in the Hammer home several days later.

After the first signs of cancer of the bone marrow were detected and conventional hormonal therapy proved ineffective, Durazo told Hammer that her family knew of a cancer-arresting herbal tea, and that January she arranged for him to get a supply of the *té negro* from Mexico. It gave him, he told his doctors, a whole new lease on life. In the first nine months of 1990, he had logged more than a quarter of a million miles in his private plane, the *Oxy One,* the interior of which was configured like a luxurious hotel suite. He and Durazo returned to Moscow, where he was treated with the pomp usually reserved for heads of state, and then proceeded to Beijing and Tokyo. In Paris and London, they went to art auctions. In Mexico City, they dined with the president of Mexico; in Washington, with the president of the United States. In Louisville, they attended the Kentucky Derby and in Baltimore, the Preakness Stakes. In a spa in Romania, they explored a "fountain of youth" therapy. In Maui, they spent a weekend on the beach with Hammer's grandchildren. In Los Angeles in May, he threw a gala party for his ninety-second birthday, with a troupe of cancan dancers in Gay Nineties costumes. In Tel Aviv, they celebrated Durazo's thirty-eighth birthday, and shortly afterward he proposed marriage.

Hammer had amended his living trust to provide Durazo with approximately $1 million. He had created similar funds in the living trust for three other women who had shared his life. As long as these women abided by the rules laid down by the living trust, they would receive monthly checks for the rest of their lives. He had hoped this arrangement would keep his relationships with the women secret.

But there was one contingency Hammer had not reckoned on. After the death of Frances, Joan Weiss and her husband, Robert, the executor of Frances's estate, went to the concealed closet that Frances had told Joan about and removed the financial records that Frances had stored there. The transactions these records describe date back to before Frances's marriage to Hammer, in 1956, and show the extent to which Hammer had relied on her inherited wealth in paying off his debts in the art business and buying control of Occidental Petroleum. After examining them, the Weisses were convinced that Hammer had systematically turned Frances's money into his own. In July 1990, Robert Weiss filed a suit against Hammer on behalf of the estate, charging that he had defrauded Frances of some $400 million in community property, including her rightful share of the art collection.

Hammer was at first confident he could beat the case. After all, as he told his lawyer, he had been sued over the past half century by dozens of claimants—partners, bankers, art dealers, cattle breeders, relatives, former employees, liquor authorities, the Internal Revenue Service, the Securities and Exchange Commission, and his own shareholders—and he had always prevailed.[7] With Occidental's resources at his disposal, he could exhaust an opponent. So he assumed that in time he would defeat or settle with Frances's niece and heir. But then, in October, he learned that he was about to die, and that changed everything. If the litigation continued after his death, it could dredge secrets out of the living trust. The disclosure that he had provided trust funds for four women whose relationships with him he had concealed from his wife could itself help persuade a jury that he had, as was alleged, deceived her when he persuaded her to sign away her rights to their community property. If that happened, his posthumous reputation would be damaged badly.

These new circumstances compelled Hammer to devise a new strategy. He decided to remove all traces of the four women and any potential embarrassments. On the evening of October 12, Hammer called his lawyer, Stafford Matthews, at home. It was the beginning of the weekend, but that did not matter to Hammer—even in the best of times he called his lawyers whenever he needed them. Matthews's firm—Mitchell, Silberberg and Knupp—had represented Hammer since 1955. Hammer insisted that Matthews begin drafting a new will for him. He then ordered him to remove from the living trust the arrangements for supporting the four women and to reduce the assets in the trust so it would be mainly an empty vessel. Hammer would find other ways to provide for his women friends and remaining family.

The next day, Hammer had his chauffeur and nurse, Nick Butcher, drive him to the Armand Hammer Museum. Hammer had at one time promised his entire collection—which included paintings by Rembrandt, Rubens, Fragonard, Goya, Gauguin, Renoir, Modigliani, Cézanne, Monet, and van Gogh—to the Los Angeles County Museum of Art. Then he had imposed conditions: he wanted the collection in a separate wing, he wanted it to have its own curator, and he wanted that curator chosen by, and under the control of, the Armand Hammer Foundation. He wanted, in effect, a private museum within a public museum. The museum refused to acquiesce to these conditions, and in 1988, Hammer withdrew his commitment to it. Instead, with funds from Occidental and real estate deals, he built his own institution. He selected the architect, approved the design, and supervised its construction. Now, although hard-hat workers were still adding finishing touches, it was scheduled to open on November 25 with a gala tribute to him and an exhibition of futurist paintings and stage sets by the Soviet artist Kazimir Malevich.

The museum's curator, Hilary Gibson, was waiting for Hammer when he arrived, as she was almost every Saturday. He had first met Gibson in 1974, a few months after his seventy-sixth birthday. She was then a thirty-two-year-old journalist called Martha Wade Kaufman. She came to his office to interview him about his celebrated art collection. Hammer, eight hours late for the appointment, joked that he collected "old masters and young mistresses" and flatteringly compared her to a nude in a painting he owned, but said little about art during the supposed interview. He took her phone number, and a few weeks later he made a proposition to her that would change her life. He wanted her to give up her career as a journalist and become his personal art adviser. She would travel with him, and although she was married and had two children, she would also be his lover. She accepted the arrangement, and she was put on the Occidental payroll as an art consultant.

During the next ten years, she traveled with Hammer all over the world, setting up exhibitions. While he met with government officials on these trips to negotiate oil deals, she met with museum curators to arrange showings of the Armand Hammer Collection. She was not only his mistress; she was, as she put it, "his confidante, consultant, and partner."[8] In 1976, he insisted that she seek neither alimony nor child support for her two daughters when she divorced her husband. He explained that he could not risk her husband's contesting her divorce, since his name might surface in the proceedings. Instead, he offered to provide her with the support she needed. And he did—through the payroll of Occidental Petroleum and the Armand Hammer Foundation.[9] He made it clear that this was in part a business arrangement. She understood, as she later noted in a lawsuit, that "in order to maintain her continued employment," she had to "submit to the sexual demands of Hammer," including demands "which were extremely humiliating." At one point, she related, he even forced her "to undergo surgical procedures to facilitate impregnation" by him—while he watched and directed.[10]

In the late 1980s, when Frances became suspicious of the younger woman's role as the foundation's art consultant, Hammer devised an incredible deception. He had Kaufman legally change her name to Hilary Gibson, and he had her change her appearance and voice so that neither Frances nor, supposedly, her fellow workers would recognize her. He asked her, she recalled later, "to wear wigs, glasses, make-up and attire which made her appear decades older." He then told Frances that he had fired Martha Kaufman and appointed Hilary Gibson as the new foundation consultant.[11] He made Gibson the director of planning for his personal monument—the Armand Hammer Museum of Art and Cultural Center.

After going over the invitation list for the opening, Hammer told Gibson, without showing any sign of emotion, that he might not be there. He then told her the reason. While she was still recovering from her surprise, he began explaining the "legal problem," as he called it. He had previously told her that he had provided an income for life for her in his living trust and from a Swiss account that contained $10 million. Now he told her that his lawyers had warned him that this arrangement could be revealed by the lawsuit filed by the estate of Frances Hammer. It was a dangerous situation, he said, telling her that if the Swiss account (which she later learned was called the Graziosa account) was exposed, he could "go to prison." He explained that he had to return the money in the account to his foundation. Instead of directly receiving money from Switzerland, she would get an ironclad contract from the tax-exempt Armand Hammer Foundation, which upon his death would receive some $18 million from Occidental as his severance pay. The foundation would give her $200,000 a year for the rest of her life, and she would nominally serve as a consultant. In addition, he said he would also provide for her daughters from other funds. He suggested she draft her own contract with the foundation, and he would sign it.

THAT SUNDAY, AS HE DID MOST SUNDAYS, HAMMER VISITED HIS thirty-five-year-old grandson, Michael—and saw his two-year-old great-grandson, Armand Hammer. Michael is the only son of Hammer's only son, Julian, who had been born to Hammer's first wife, Olga, in Moscow just before Armand and his family left the Soviet Union. Not long afterward, Hammer separated from Olga. Since he could never control Julian, he had decided to skip a generation and make Michael his successor. He had hired special tutors to help Michael through Columbia Business School, gave him an apprenticeship at Occidental, and made him vice president, corporate secretary, and a member of the board of directors. He also appointed him president of the Armand Hammer Foundation. He now told Michael that he did not have long to live. Michael would be the head of the family and take responsibility for his younger sister, Casey, and his father. Hammer explained that the funds in the living trust had to be cut to a bare minimum, but through Occidental and the foundation ample provision would be made for his family members. Not only would Michael continue to draw his salary of some $500,000 a year from Occidental, but he would be given a multimillion-dollar severance settlement if he ever decided to leave. Hammer was also transferring $1 million worth of his own stock in the company to Michael and providing him with the keys to safe-deposit boxes in banks in California and Europe that held other assets.[12]

Hammer met two days later with Casey Hammer, who had just turned thirty. She had been living in Hawaii but rushed to Los Angeles after Hammer's doctor called her to suggest that her grandfather might want her to donate blood if he needed a transfusion. When she was ushered into Hammer's bedroom by Rosamaria Durazo, Casey found her grandfather sitting up in bed in his red flannel pajamas. Next to him, with limp balloons attached to it, was the stuffed toy bear she had dropped off at the house the day before. She noted later in her diary that she had been startled by how old he suddenly looked. "He had a lot of sadness in his eyes and looked very alone." He spoke so quietly she had difficulty at times hearing him; then, with great deliberation, he began telling her about her inheritance. He explained that she would receive $1.5 million from him, free of taxes, as well as the deed to her house. He stressed that this would be "separate from the will so therefore nothing would get tied up."[13]

He made one request of her. He asked her to consent in writing to be buried in his mausoleum—the Armand Hammer family mausoleum at Westwood Memorial Park. He had already re-interred there the family members who had gone to Russia with him and helped him establish his business and art empires: his father, Julius; his mother, Rose; his half brother, Harry; and his younger brother, Victor. He wanted his family unified in death as they had not always been in life. Hammer had made provisions in his will for the crypt to be adorned with fresh flowers in perpetuity. He explained to Casey, "After I am gone, there will be three places remaining in the mausoleum." They were for her father, her brother, and her. "Casey, you are a Hammer by blood. We are the only ones left," he continued, as if issuing a fiat. "You will be buried with the Hammer dynasty, my parents, my brothers, my son, and my grandchildren. You are part of me." He instructed her to meet with Stafford Matthews the next morning and sign the mausoleum arrangement.

He then turned to the task of providing for Rosamaria Durazo. He decided that if she could not be paid through his living trust, she would be paid by the treasury of Occidental. On the evening of October 18, he had his second-in-command, Occidental's president and chief operating officer, Ray Irani, come to his house. Irani was also Hammer's designated successor at Occidental. Hammer explained that he wanted Durazo to be given a contract with the company.

Even though the request was unconventional, it couldn't be ignored. Hammer did not gladly brook dissent. In the past, he had fired his top executives as though they were errand boys—even when, as happened more than a dozen times, his doing so had resulted in wrongful-dismissal suits.

Apparently, Hammer was not entirely satisfied with Irani's response, and after Irani left, he called his personal assistant, Catherine Kosak, at home. This did not surprise her, since she had often received calls from him at odd hours. Time or place never constrained Hammer. Now she found him strangely disoriented, as if he were half-asleep, uncharacteristically slurring and repeating words. He told her that he wanted to dictate a contract to her that she was to deliver to Irani the next morning. The terms of the contract shocked her.

Durazo was to get $250,000 from Occidental upon signing and $200,000 a year for life. She was also to get medical insurance and other corporate benefits. Kosak knew that Hammer paid many of Durazo's expenses. That was his private business. But he was now putting her on the Occidental payroll for life when she did not work for Occidental. Kosak did not know what conceivable corporate purpose the contract could serve, but she carried out Hammer's request.

Kosak brought the contract to Irani the next day. To her surprise, he reached into his desk drawer and handed her an almost identical version. According to Kosak, he said, "Here's the real goddamn thing. Hammer put a gun to my head." He then added plaintively, "This thing is driving me up the wall." He told her to lock her copy in her safe.[14] She did not hear anything further about the status of the contract.

On Friday, October 19, Stafford Matthews delivered to Hammer the revised version of his living trust. It now provided for the maintenance of the mausoleum but little else. Gone from it were the separate trusts for the women who had shared his secret life and any mention of them or other "friends" of the trust. Matthews had also deleted, as Hammer had instructed, all the substantial bequeathals that might be tied up in litigation, including the trust fund for his son, Julian, and $1 million previously pledged to the Metropolitan Museum of Art in New York in return for agreeing to name its equestrian gallery after him. After carefully reading his new will and the codicils that changed the living trust, Hammer signed them.

He now had to explain to his son why he had been cut out of the living trust. His relationship with Julian had never been easy. Julian was born in Moscow in 1929. From the beginning, Hammer had wondered whether he was even the child's father. After separating from his wife, he saw little of Julian. Then, when he was twenty-four, Julian was arrested for shooting and killing a friend. Eventually, all the charges were dropped, and Hammer briefly put his son on Occidental's payroll. He used him from time to time for what he called James Bond stuff, such as having him conceal microphones in Hammer's office, in his home, and even in his cuff links so that he could surreptitiously record the conversations of business associates. Hammer found this secret taping system especially useful for recording sensitive events, such as the disbursement of bribes, to which he did not want even his confidential secretaries to be privy. But when Julian had further encounters with the police, Hammer made it clear to him that his real job was to stay out of the public eye and not embarrass his father. For this service, Hammer paid Julian a monthly retainer and bought him a house in Bel Air. But he insisted that if his son wanted to see him or even speak to him on the phone, he had to make an appointment with Hammer's secretary.

In 1988, when Hammer heard of a new DNA test to verify paternity, he had a sample of Julian's blood taken at UCLA Medical Center and secretly checked on Julian's genealogy. It turned out that he had not been defrauded by Olga in Moscow: Julian was his progeny. But the DNA match did not improve their relations.[15]

When Julian arrived at his father's house in October 1990, Hammer did not tell him about his medical condition or prognosis. He talked to him about taxes that had become "prohibitive." He explained that to avoid levies on his estate, he was going to provide for Julian outside its formal structure. He continued rapidly, as if outlining a business proposition, saying that Julian's mortgage and other debts would be paid off immediately after Hammer died and that Julian would then receive "a lifetime consulting contract" from Occidental Petroleum, which would give him an annual income of more than $100,000 and corporate health insurance. In return, he would be required only to act as nominal consultant on the acquisition of Occidental's video library.

Julian, who did not know about the lawsuit threatening the estate, was baffled by this change. Inheritance taxes had not been raised: why was he suddenly being cut out of his father's will? He knew how much his father enjoyed getting the edge in a deal, even when it concerned his own family, and he assumed his father's intention of putting him on Occidental's payroll was another of his dodges. But Julian's inheritance was at stake. He reminded his father that he had tried to give him a similar contract once before but that it had not been permitted by Occidental's legal department. He argued that if this happened again, he would be left without any income.

Hammer held up his hand peremptorily. He said that those previous problems had been "worked out" and that Julian's contract now would be "foolproof." Julian, quite shaken, excused himself and left.[16]

Hammer could not resolve another family problem so easily—that of his secret daughter, Victoria, whom he had been anonymously supporting for nearly thirty-five years. He had met Victoria's mother, Bettye Jane Murphy, in a café in Marathon, Florida, in 1953. He had gone to the Florida Keys that year in his seventy-eight-foot yacht with his captain, his Japanese chef, and his pilot. He had left his second wife, Angela, whom he had married in 1943, behind on their farm in New Jersey. Their marriage had become increasingly strained as she became hard of hearing and alcoholic.

Bettye was twenty-five years his junior, and she made Hammer laugh. He invited her to go with him to Cuba. They flew there in his private Beechcraft and stayed in the bridal suite of the El Presidente Hotel in Havana. When he finished his Florida vacation, Hammer brought Bettye back to New York and quietly set her up in an apartment. For several months, not even his brothers, Victor and Harry, who had been partners with him all his life, knew of her existence. When she traveled with him, he introduced her as his secretary, which was a perfect cover since one of his secretaries was in fact named Murphy. He also assigned her aliases that amused him. One night, he introduced her to guests at a party in Sag Harbor, Long Island, as the daughter of a U.S. senator. This turned out to be an unfortunate choice since that very day the senator's real daughter had made headlines by committing suicide in New York.

Hammer often promised Bettye that they would get married when he divorced Angela. But that was not to happen. Instead, he married Frances, a multimillionairess.

At the time of Hammer's marriage to Frances, Bettye was expecting his child. To keep this secret from his new wife, he moved Bettye to Mexico City and had her undergo a fake marriage there so that the child would not have Hammer's surname. When his daughter was born that May, he named her Victoria after his grandmother. Every month, Bettye received a check from him through a chain of lawyers. He insisted that Bettye not tell Victoria the identity of her benefactor. Meanwhile, he had gone into the oil business with Frances's money.[17]

In 1976, after Victoria learned his identity, Hammer began visiting her. He made her and her mother beneficiaries of his living trust. But now, faced with the lawsuit, he again had to conceal her. How would he look to a jury if it emerged that he had deceived Frances from the start? He would rely on his grandson, Michael, to take care of Victoria with cash after his death.

The fourth woman Hammer had provided for in his living trust was Barbara Newman. She was a registered nurse whom he met in 1984 at the UCLA Medical Center while he was recovering from a prostate operation. After leaving the hospital, he kept in touch with her, and when he was readmitted to UCLA—which was about twice a year—he had her attend him as his private nurse. Now there was no plausible way to put her on the payroll of Occidental or the foundation, and he had to expunge her from the living trust.

ON NOVEMBER 1, HAMMER MET WITH RABBI DANIEL LAPIN OF the Pacific Jewish Center to plan one final event: his belated bar mitzvah ceremony. He had denied his Jewish heritage for most of his life. When he had gone to Russia in the 1920s, he had identified himself as an atheist. When he had gone to Saudi Arabia and Libya in search of oil in the 1960s, he had given his religion as Unitarian. Even in Los Angeles in the 1980s, he had listed himself on hospital records as Protestant or WASP. But now, with only weeks left to live, he planned to return to Judaism in a dramatic way: by the initiation into manhood. This ceremony traditionally takes place when a boy turns thirteen, but Hammer had not had a traditional childhood.

His father, Dr. Julius Hammer, who had spent most of his youth in Russia and then worked his way through medical school in New York, had been one of Lenin's main supporters in the United States. He had helped organize the notorious left-wing faction of the Socialist Party, which became the Communist Party in 1919. When his first child was born in 1898, he named him Armand for the arm-and-hammer symbol of the proletarian revolution. When Armand was only seven years old, his father was placed under surveillance by the New York City police, suspected of manufacturing bombs for anarchists. When he was nine, his father went to Germany, where he met Lenin. For most of the next six years, Armand lived in Meriden, Connecticut, with a Socialist colleague of his father's. When he was thirteen, he was still separated from his family and was in no position to have a bar mitzvah.

But now he was. He had acquired two ancient Torah scrolls from Eastern Europe, and he would donate one to Rabbi Lapin's synagogue in Los Angeles and one to a synagogue in Israel. He would also raise $100,000 for the Pacific Jewish Center—by asking his guests to contribute $500 apiece. He would assume the Hebrew name Avraham ben Yehuda Maccabee (Abraham son of Judah Maccabee), since he did not know his own or his father's Hebrew name.

Hammer's bar mitzvah ceremony was scheduled for December 11, the first night of Hanukkah.

ON NOVEMBER 6, HAMMER MET WITH JEAN STONE, THE WIFE OF the novelist Irving Stone. For the past year, she had been helping him write what was to be the final volume—and version—of his life story. Autobiography was for Hammer a highly useful tool. He used it to sculpt events to his liking, cutting away things that detracted from his image and adding apocryphal material that enhanced it.

Nearly sixty years earlier, he had begun his autobiographical project by writing a 241-page memoir of his first sojourn in Russia, called *The Quest of the Romanoff Treasure*. This early "autobiography" was written for a practical purpose; on his return to the United States in 1932, he desperately needed an acceptable explanation for why he had remained in the Soviet Union for a decade. Since he had to hide the secret tasks that he had undertaken for the Soviets, he constructed a story about coming to Lenin's attention fortuitously and falling into a humanitarian role in the early Soviet Union. In preparing the volume, he invented incidents to serve his purpose. For example, Hammer wrote that in 1923, on his deathbed, Lenin spoke of him favorably:

"Lenin, in that dark valley, thought of me and sent me a message," he notes. " 'Tell young Hammer,' he gasped painfully, 'I have not forgotten him and wish him well. If he has difficulties tell him to be sure and let me know.' "[18] Hammer thus makes himself central to Lenin's dying thoughts (even though he had met Lenin only once) and provides a reason for the exceptional treatment he received from Soviet leaders. In fact, Lenin was in no position to issue such a deathbed message. The stroke he had suffered on March 9, 1923, had left him with nearly total aphasia. We now know that although the Politburo attempted to conceal the extent of the damage to Lenin's brain, he had lost the power of speech to the extent that he was only able to mouth a few words, such as "*vot-vot.*" He could not, even if he recalled Hammer, have sent him the coherent message that Hammer reports.[19]

Hammer similarly invented his own version of Lenin's funeral in January 1924—one in which he placed himself so close to the center of the event that he could see the faces of the new Soviet leaders. "The day of the funeral," he writes, "I saw Trotsky, then War Lord of the Red Army, standing in the little group on the Mausoleum gallery. As his legions roared salute I saw his face light up with pride."[20] Even if Hammer had attended the funeral, he could not have seen Trotsky there or in Moscow. The day of the funeral, Trotsky was in Tbilisi, in Soviet Georgia.[21] Hammer learned that he could fabricate such anecdotes with impunity since there was then little way of checking what had actually happened in the Soviet Union.

His second attempt at autobiography was made in 1951, for a more limited audience: J. Edgar Hoover. Although Hammer had not known it, Hoover had been tracking his career since 1921. Hoover was then a twenty-six-year-old assistant in the Justice Department, and Hammer was a twenty-three-year-old medical student embarking on a trip to Europe. Hoover had received a tip from an informant alleging that Hammer was a courier for the newly organized Communist International, or Comintern. Hoover's suspicions set into motion actions against Hammer by the FBI and several international intelligence agencies. For the next twenty years, Hammer, who had by then built up a substantial whiskey business, called United Distillers, found himself blocked by Hoover each time he sought a government contract or favor.

In early 1951, Hammer had decided to clear the air by offering Hoover a lengthy autobiographical memorandum on his activities in the Soviet Union in the 1920s, supplying an innocent explanation for charges that had been made linking him to espionage agents. In it, he describes himself as a dedicated capitalist who had disagreed with his father on politics and who had gone to Russia to collect debts owed to the family company. Some of the statements he volunteered are untrue, but he gambled, as he had done in his first autobiography, that they were also unverifiable without Soviet files. He was right. Hoover closed the security case against him, and the autobiographical sketch became the basis of the FBI summary report that would be furnished to five future presidents.

In 1974, Hammer hired the columnist Bob Considine to write an updated biography, entitled *The Remarkable Life of Dr. Armand Hammer*. Hammer had, after all, embarked on a new life in the oil business in the 1950s. He had managed in the 1960s to obtain a huge concession for Occidental in Libya by paying a multimillion-dollar bribe to a key official in the Libyan royal court. It was one of the few concessions in the Middle East not controlled by major international oil companies, and Hammer made a fortune that he then used to finance immense barter deals with the Soviet Union. He also used his Libyan oil to undermine the power of the established oil companies, and in doing so, he radically changed the rules of the international oil business. He now needed to rewrite the history of this Libyan oil concession to conceal the role of his bribe. He wanted to make it appear that his Libyan success had resulted from his enlightened altruism. He thus portrayed himself not merely as a businessman but as a humanitarian. He also wanted to show that he was patriotically serving the interests of the United States.

In *The Remarkable Life of Dr. Armand Hammer*, a new role was invented for him: that of the behind-the-scenes agent of U.S. presidents. He was said to be a strategic adviser to President Franklin D. Roosevelt during World War II, a consultant to President Harry S Truman on postwar relief, and the "roving emissary" of President John F. Kennedy. Hammer even credited himself with personally persuading President Herbert Hoover "to organize the American Relief Administration which saved 10 million Russians from starvation."[22] In fact, Hammer never met President Hoover and had nothing to do with the American Relief Administration, which was chartered while he was still a college student. He met FDR only once. He met President Truman once—for a group photo opportunity. His contact with JFK during his presidency was also fleeting. He visited the White House once as part of a large ceremonial gathering. He also had a brief telephone conversation with Kennedy on May 11, 1963, which he secretly recorded, and in which the president seemed totally unfamiliar with Hammer. Yet, as he had found in his earlier experience with fictive autobiography, he could take great license in fashioning grand political relationships for himself.

In a form of Gresham's law, in which debased currency replaces more valuable currency, Hammer's version of his past enjoyed considerable success. He had Occidental's public relations department dispatch copies of *The Remarkable Life of Dr. Armand Hammer* to journalists who wanted to write about him, and they used the book as background material. His assertions thus passed into the clip files and archives of credible publications and, through repetition, attained the status of quasi fact.

Eventually, life, as it often does, imitated artifice. As people came to believe the Hammer legend, they treated the man with deference and sought his favor. Heads of state arranged to see him when he landed in their countries in his private airliner. Finally, in 1981, he received the sort of presidential mission that he had, a half century earlier, only pretended to have: the chairmanship of the President's Cancer Panel.

By 1985, Hammer was ready for an autobiography that consolidated and brought up to date his achievements. To assist him in this endeavor, he retained Neil Lyndon, an accomplished and well-respected British journalist who had previously written a favorable story about him in the London *Sunday Telegraph.* He made clear to Lyndon that his job was not to investigate the events in the book but to make more lucid his version of them. He demonstrated no compunction about concealing the parts of his life that did not fit this version. For example, he told Lyndon that he would not make available to him any of his diaries and other records pertaining to his life in Russia prior to 1932. He instructed him to repeat verbatim the account of this crucial period he had rendered in *The Quest of the Romanoff Treasure.* In reconstructing events in his later life, Hammer would refine, stretch, and even fabricate happenings so that they more effectively made the points he wanted to advance. He would place himself at the center of great moments of history—such as summit meetings—even though Lyndon could find no independent verification of Hammer's accounts.[23] The mythical nature of this book again went largely unchallenged by reviewers.

Hammer attempted in 1989 to extend this kind of inventive self-portraiture to the popular medium of movies by commissioning Harold Gast to write a screenplay about his life. The script was based entirely on the two published autobiographies and repeated the stories of Hammer's business success and the global political importance the books established. Hammer made his own contributions in marginal notes, adding to the stilted dialogue lists of more accomplishments and indications of greater prestige.

When Communism was unraveling in 1990, Hammer decided he needed to add to his autobiography a new volume in which he could establish a role in ending the cold war. He had, after all, met personally with Gorbachev six times, and he had arranged emergency aid for the Chernobyl nuclear meltdown in 1986 and the earthquake in Armenia in 1988. He turned to Jean Stone for help with the writing of this portion of his life. As he explained to her, he would now chronicle his diplomatic interventions over the past decade. He also firmly believed that the discovery of a cure for cancer was imminent, and he wanted to credit himself with mobilizing the scientific and medical resources leading to it.

But in late 1990, it was clear that Hammer had come to the end. He was disoriented by constant blood transfusions and medication. He was also dispirited. Though he had reached the book's last chapter, he told Stone that he no longer wanted to work on it. Unlike his previous autobiographical works, this book could not be controlled completely.

ON NOVEMBER 12, HAMMER MET WITH HIS LAWYERS TO DISCUSS the $440-million lawsuit brought against him by his wife's estate. The lawyers brought to his bedroom videotapes of the deposition that the executor of the estate, Robert Weiss, had just given. It outlined the claim that Hammer had defrauded his wife of her share of their community property. The legal issue was whether or not Frances had abnegated this share. She had signed a document to that effect just ten days before her fatal accident, but her estate claimed that Hammer had tricked her into signing it.

His lawyers were showing him the tape because they wanted to avoid any surprise revelations in court. They had to know what Hammer and Frances's relationship had really been.

In his autobiography, Hammer had portrayed a blissful union that spanned a third of a century. In reality, he had betrayed Frances from the very beginning. When he initiated their courtship in 1955, she was a wealthy widow in her early fifties, and he was involved in the secret liaison with Bettye Murphy. Later, using Frances's money to build Occidental Petroleum into a major oil company, he deceived her by having affairs with still other women, women he put on the payroll of Occidental. During most of this period, Frances appeared to be unaware of any of this. She continued to travel with Hammer to meet heads of state until 1987, when, during a visit to Moscow, she slipped and fell and he left her on the floor of the Kremlin while he rushed to embrace Gorbachev.

What Hammer had not fully realized, at least not until seeing the videotaped deposition, was that Frances had been suspicious of him from the start and had kept copious records of all the money she lent him, as well as of other financial transactions. By 1988, she was so distrustful that she rewrote her will, cutting him out and leaving almost everything to her niece, Joan Weiss, her only surviving relative. She even left Weiss the house in which she had lived with Hammer since they were married. She had also begun considering, at the age of eighty-eight, getting a legal separation from him. All this animosity could weigh against him: a jury might not believe that Frances would have voluntarily renounced her claim to the fortune.

Although Hammer's lawyers had believed that he could dispel these doubts with his testimony, he knew that he would be dead well before the case came to trial. So it would be a battle between estates.[24]

After the lawyers left, Hammer asked that his sixty-three-year-old namesake nephew, Armand Hammer, fly immediately from Moscow to Los Angeles. Armasha, as he was called, was the son of Hammer's brother Victor. He had been left behind in Russia as a two-year-old when Victor had divorced the boy's Russian mother and returned to New York. For the next quarter of a century, the Hammer family had had no contact with Armasha. But after Hammer had renewed his contacts with the Soviets in the 1950s and used Occidental to trade commodities with Eastern Europe, Armasha was granted a visa to visit the United States. In a highly emotional meeting, the thirty-three-year-old Armasha was reunited with a family he had never known. For Hammer, this was a reminder of his hidden past in the Soviet Union, and when Armasha arrived in the third week of November 1990, Hammer asked him to undertake an important task to help keep that past hidden. He wanted Armasha to search through the files he kept in Moscow. He had provided some Soviet leaders with compensation that was not part of any official transactions, and he wanted Armasha to make sure that these relationships remained secret after his death.

ON NOVEMBER 25, HAMMER MADE HIS LAST PUBLIC APPEARANCE. He had been determined not to miss the opening-night ceremony for the Armand Hammer Museum. He tried to conceal his telltale weight loss by having his tailor fit him with a new tuxedo, but that hardly mattered, for he was barely conscious when, strapped into his wheelchair, he was carried into the museum.

The leading lights of Los Angeles society were assembled that night. Danielle Mitterrand, the wife of the president of France, was also there. Hammer had promised to donate $300,000 to Mme. Mitterrand's private foundation, and she was seated next to Hammer for the evening. Though still woozy from drugs and blood transfusions, he greeted the long parade of guests: executives from Occidental who were waiting to take over from him; art curators who had authenticated his collection of paintings for decades; politicians whom he had helped finance; diplomats from Israel, China, and the Soviet Union; doctors who could do little further for him; and lawyers ready to litigate his estate.

When he got home that night, he had a prolonged hallucination. He saw his dead mother in the room, and in front of his staff he carried on a rambling conversation with her, asking her over and over again where his missing father was. Nick Butcher, who now served as his night nurse, could not convince him that his mother was not really there. Twice earlier that year, Butcher had revived him with artificial respiration, but now he had been instructed not to attempt to save Hammer's life again.

ON DECEMBER 7, ROSAMARIA DURAZO BROUGHT TWO MEXICAN faith healers to the house. They floated Hammer on the surface of the swimming pool. Then, recreating an ancient Aztec ceremony, they danced around him for two days.[25]

On the morning of December 10, Durazo summoned Julian to the house. With a note of panic in her voice, she told him that his father was dying of incurable cancer. Julian was stunned. All his life, he had tried to make contact with his father—and had failed. Hammer had kept so much of his life from him, even when Julian was a child, that after six decades he still did not understand his father or what it was that drove him to seek his approval even in these last moments. His father did not seem to recognize him, and Julian whispered in his ear a stream of Russian curse words—words that in the distant past had provoked Hammer to react. This time he did not.[26]

That evening, only two people remained in the room with Hammer: Rosamaria Durazo and Nick Butcher. Durazo placed her stethoscope on Hammer's chest. There was no heartbeat. Butcher checked his watch. He recorded that Hammer had died at 7:22 P.M.

While Rosamaria Durazo was still collapsed in tears on the dead man's chest, Butcher telephoned Edmund Birch, the security chief at Occidental. Birch, who before joining Occidental in 1975 had worked for the FBI for twenty-five years, set in motion a carefully scripted scenario. Hammer's physician, Allen Metzger, rushed to the house to sign the death certificate, on which the cause of death was listed as cerebral arterial sclerosis. An ambulance was dispatched to take Hammer's body to the mortuary. The funeral director, Larry Davis, was instructed to embalm the body. Public relations officers drafted the press release. Locksmiths changed the locks on the doors to Occidental offices on the sixteenth and eighteenth floors, where sensitive documents were kept. Security men sped to Hammer's house to retrieve his papers. Michael Hammer and the rest of Hammer's family were notified.

About an hour later, Michael arrived at the house. He had just returned in his new Ferrari from a weekend balloon festival in Palm

Springs. He sorted through his grandfather's personal effects and gave Nick Butcher Hammer's gold Rolex watch, a tie clip, and a bottle of Dom Pérignon champagne.

Meanwhile, the Occidental security men loaded cartons of Hammer's papers into a van in the driveway. Before they could leave, they were blocked by Richard Cleary, the lawyer representing Frances Hammer's estate. He said that since Hammer's home had reverted to his wife's estate the moment Hammer died, they had no right to remove anything from the house without the estate's permission. He called in the Los Angeles police while the security men called Michael out to the driveway. The standoff continued until about 1:30 A.M. Finally, Stafford Matthews, Hammer's lawyer, arrived and worked out an agreement whereby all the cartons were returned to a locked room in the house, to which Michael retained the key. Cleary then had an all-night locksmith change the front-door locks, effectively evicting Michael, Rosamaria Durazo, and Nick Butcher.

The reports on the police radio about the confrontation in the street alerted the night editors at the *Los Angeles Times* to Hammer's death. His obituary, drawn from a clip file that spanned nearly seven decades, had already been prepared. At 6:00 A.M., they flashed out over their wire service the headline ARMAND HAMMER DIES; BILLIONAIRE, ART PATRON.

HAMMER WOULD NOT SEE HIS BAR MITZVAH CEREMONY. IT WOULD take place posthumously. He would not celebrate the Jewish heritage he had hidden in the past or see another life story constructed for the lavish tribute to himself he had so carefully prepared.

For more than a half century, and up until the week he died, Hammer had assiduously constructed the legend of his life. The tale of an American capitalist who made a fortune in Communist Russia and became a great humanitarian eventually came to be accepted as fact by the public, the press, and several presidents of the United States. What Hammer did not foresee was that after his death, the Soviet Union would come asunder and spew from its archives the secrets that would expose the truth.

PART ONE

WHAT REALLY HAPPENED IN RUSSIA

The Hammer family, ca. 1903. Armand's father, Julius, stands at the rear, between his wife, Rose, and his half brother, William. Young Armand is at left, standing next to his brothers Victor and Harry. His grandfather, Jacob Hammer, is seated on the bench.

CHAPTER ONE

THE
MATRIX

ON SEPTEMBER 18, 1920, JULIUS HAMMER ENTERED SING SING State Prison, in manacles and leg irons, as prisoner 71516. He stood naked while clerks examined his body for scars and other identifying marks. They found none. The prison's entry blotter describes him as "age 46, 5 foot 11 inches, 195 pounds, Hebrew religion."[1]

Julius Hammer was in fact an extraordinary man.

He was born in the Jewish ghetto of Odessa on October 3, 1874, to Jacob and Victoria Hammer. Jacob Hammer made his living as a merchant, moving back and forth between America and Russia. Julius spent most of his youth in Russia, and when he was sixteen, he immigrated to the United States with his family. His father had already become a naturalized U.S. citizen, which made Julius a U.S. citizen.

The Hammer family first lived in Branford, Connecticut, where Julius worked in a foundry, and in 1892 they moved to New York City's Lower East Side, where Julius found employment as a clerk in a drugstore. Like many other immigrants who came from czarist Russia in the 1890s, he was seeking a better life and the freedom America offered. As a teenager, he was quickly drawn to socialism. He assiduously read every pamphlet and polemical tract he could get his hands on. By the time he was eighteen, he had joined what was probably the most radical faction of the socialist movement, the Socialist Labor Party, whose slogan was "Down with the Political State, Up with the Industrial State." Most of its other members were like him: young, poor, and fiercely idealistic. The leader of this party was Daniel De Leon, a bearded Marxist who wore an opera cloak and advocated civil war.

Julius's social as well as political life revolved around the Socialist Labor Party, and he became the friend and close associate of a veteran revolutionary, Boris Reinstein, who was some ten years older than he was. Reinstein had been expelled first from Russia and then from Germany, Switzerland, and France for his radical activities. In France, he had served two years in prison for his involvement in a terrorist bombing. He was now a druggist in Buffalo, New York. Julius admired Reinstein and found they had much in common. They had both come from Jewish ghettos in the same area of southern Russia. They both spoke the same languages—Russian, Yiddish, German, and English. They had both immigrated to New York in the early 1890s, and they were both dedicated to the idea of total revolution.

Hammer met his wife-to-be, Rose Lipshitz, at a Socialist Labor Party picnic in 1897. Rose was a seamstress who was working as a waitress. She had arrived in New York from Russia about a year before Julius had. Buxom and outspoken, she immediately appealed to him. They were married later that year, and Julius adopted her four-year-old son from a previous marriage, Harry. Their first home was a small cold-water flat in a tenement on the north side of Cherry Street in lower Manhattan. Cherry Street at that time was strictly divided between Jewish and Irish immigrants: the Jews on the north side, the Irish on the south side.

Jewish socialists often met in the evening on the rooftops of Cherry Street to discuss politics in a multitude of eastern European languages. The burning issue was assimilation: should Jews remain within their own culture and seek a Judaic form of socialism, or should they seek a nonsectarian form? The Jewish radicals subscribed to the latter position. They passionately rejected ghettoization. In doing so, as the social critic Irving Howe points out, "The Jewish radicals . . . hoped to move from the yeshiva to modern culture, from *shtetl* to urban sophistication, from blessing the Sabbath wine to declaring the strategy of international revolution. They yearned to bleach away their past and become men without, or above, a country."[2] Julius Hammer, one of these radicals, was determined to accomplish this transformation.

On May 21, 1898, Julius's first son was born, and he proudly named him Armand Hammer. He told friends that he had named him after the symbol of the Socialist Labor Party (and decades later, Armand would use the arm-and-hammer insignia as the flag on his yacht).[3] A photograph of Armand taken a few months after his birth shows him to be a bright-eyed infant with a disproportionately large head and a bang across his brow. When he was about two and a half years old, he pulled a toy coffee grinder down from a shelf, puncturing his head and almost killing himself. His mother found Armand covered in blood and rushed him to the hospital. The wound left a permanent scar above his right temple.[4] Armand's earliest memory was this trauma. He also recalled the horse-drawn carts in the narrow streets surrounding his house and the strong stench of the neighborhood.

Now with a family to support, Julius enrolled in medical school at Columbia College of Physicians and Surgeons, which was then only a two-year program. To cut down on his expenses while at school, he moved his family to his father's home. In the 1900 census, Julius Hammer was listed as residing at Jacob Hammer's home on Lewis Street in Manhattan. In 1901, Rose gave him his second son, whom he named Victor after his mother, Victoria. When he graduated from medical school, Julius moved his family into a large new home in the Bronx, where many of his comrades in the Socialist Labor Party now lived. He opened his first medical practice there.

There was a synagogue next door, but Julius had long since forsaken the Jewish religion for the secular religion of radical socialism. Armand Hammer recalled that neither he nor any other members of his family ever attended services at the synagogue. Nor were there any seders or other Jewish observances at home: No religious feasts or festivals were ever celebrated in their house.[5]

Julius Hammer began investing in drugstores. He bought them by issuing the previous owners his personal promissory notes, the only form of credit available to him, with the understanding that these were to be repaid out of future profits. By 1903, he owned eight drugstores. But instead of using the money he took in from them to repay his outstanding loans, he used much of it to finance the Socialist Labor Party, which was then in danger of running out of funds. He also contributed to Reinstein's chapter in Buffalo. For him, politics would always take precedence over business. The problem was that his political expenditures soon exceeded his business resources. When his creditors did not get paid, they took him to court, and still not quite thirty, he was forced to declare personal bankruptcy. For the next six years, he managed to evade his creditors by transferring his assets, in name only, to his wife's relatives. To maintain the fiction that he had no assets, he and his family lived a life of subterfuge. Even his young sons learned to conceal family business from outsiders, especially when the Red Squad took an interest in Julius.

The New York City Police Department's Red Squad had been created in 1905 to counter a spate of anarchist bombings in Manhattan, but it soon got into the business of keeping left-wing socialists under surveillance. Because of Julius Hammer's political activities—and perhaps because of his association with Reinstein, who had been arrested several times in Buffalo for political agitation—the Red Squad placed his home under surveillance. At one point, it suspected that Julius Hammer might be involved in supplying the dynamite for bombs, and two plainclothes policemen were stationed round the clock outside his house, but no evidence was found to confirm the suspicion.

In the summer of 1907, Julius got an opportunity to leave the United States. Reinstein arranged for Hammer to accompany him to the Seventh Congress of the Second International in Stuttgart, Germany. They both went as delegates of the Socialist Labor Party. At the conference, Julius Hammer saw the man whose words and deeds he had been vicariously following for the past fifteen years—Lenin.

Lenin was then a thirty-seven-year-old political exile. He had a huge domed head, high cheekbones, and traces of fiery red hair at his temples. He had narrow, slanting eyes that were almost wolflike. His face was brought to a point by a reddish mustache and beard. Julius Hammer was introduced to him by Reinstein. It was a brief encounter, but one that would forever change his life and that of his family. By the time the Stuttgart conference ended, Julius Hammer had become part of the elite underground cadre that Lenin would depend on to change the world. This conspiratorial movement went a step beyond starry-eyed idealism and fiery rhetorical disputes about the nature of society. It sought to create the concrete means— networks of agents, sources of funds, secure communications, internal discipline—to bring about the desired world revolution. It was predicated on the Leninist principle that any means employed, no matter how much they diverged from Marxist ideology, were justified by the ends.

Julius Hammer returned to New York that October with a solid commitment to the socialist cause. He would help lay the groundwork for Lenin's revolutionary apparatus in America. This would entail meeting with Lenin's backers at socialist conferences in Europe and linking them to sources of support they needed in America. To finance the enterprise, he would have to rebuild his pharmaceutical business. Julius also moved to free himself from entanglements at home. He sent his three sons to live with colleagues in the Socialist Labor Party. Victor moved to Pleasantville, New York, to live with the family of Daniel De Leon, Julius's ideological mentor. Harry moved to Waterbury, Connecticut, to live with the family of Saul Wellington, a socialist firebrand who had become a rabbi. Armand moved to Meriden, Connecticut, to live with the family of George Rose, who had helped De Leon found the Socialist Labor Party in 1890. The Hammer family would remain separated for nearly five years.

Of the three Hammer children, Armand suffered the most from this exile from his parents. He had become in his early childhood so deeply attached to his father that he would at times refuse to speak to other family members when his father left on trips. Now nearly ten years old, he found himself suddenly transported to a small town in rural Connecticut, living with an unfamiliar family in a shabby working-class house on the wrong side of the railroad tracks. In the summers, he was sent to a camp that was organized for the children of socialists. "I *was* lonely," he recalled years later. When other children were having happy reunions with their parents, Hammer would go off by himself, "feeling very morose and neglected."[6]

Armand returned to his family in New York in 1914. He enrolled as a junior at Morris High School. On May 11, Daniel De Leon died suddenly, and Armand took off a day from school to hear his father eulogize him at a memorial service in Kessler's Theater in lower Manhattan. His father was now the principal financial angel of the Socialist Labor Party and the center of attention at the ceremony.

That summer, the great powers of Europe—Germany, Russia, France, Austria-Hungary, and Britain—went to war, and the Social-

ist Labor Party strongly campaigned against the United States' joining in Armand Hammer won his high school's gold medal for ora-
tory by making a pacifist speech, "The Last War of Mankind," in
which he inveighed against American parents' allowing their sons to
fight a foreign war.

Victor Hammer, who sat in the audience that day, was both impressed and surprised by this sudden flourish of rhetoric from his
older brother. Since he had returned from Connecticut, Armand had
tended to shy away from expressing himself. He would answer questions with either a simple yes or no, or he would just sit in brooding
silence. Now Victor realized he had an extraordinary way with words.

Julius Hammer was probably less surprised by Armand's speech. It
echoed the Socialist Labor Party's rhetoric on the war. He had always treated Armand as the favored child, and now he did something
else for him that he did not do for his other sons: he enrolled him in
the party. Armand listed himself as a student on the application,
which was approved by the party's executive committee.[8]

In 1915, Armand entered Columbia University. Julius was grooming
him to follow in his footsteps as a doctor. Armand desperately wanted
to emulate his father. "My dream of boyhood was to grow up to become my father's partner," he later wrote.[9] At Columbia, Armand
took part in a number of activities, including fencing and debating, but
his main focus was preparing to go to medical school.[10] Meanwhile,
Julius Hammer continued to expand his business, which was now
called Allied Drug and Chemical. It employed about eighty workers,
who supplied skin creams and herbal medicines to drugstores. The
Hammer family had two full-time servants and a chauffeur-driven car,
and during the summers they vacationed at an ocean-side resort in Bel-
mar, New Jersey. Julius could afford to send his sons to elite colleges
at a time when 90 percent of the American population did not finish
secondary school. While Armand was taking his examinations for
medical school, Harry was at Columbia College of Pharmacology,
preparing to work in the family business.

DESPITE HIS AFFLUENCE, JULIUS HAMMER NEVER LOST HIS COM-
mitment to Lenin. He chaired meetings of the Socialist Labor Party,
drafted planks for the party platforms, adjudicated disputes between

factions, served on committees, and raised funds. Bertram Wolfe, a member of the party who also attended these functions, described him as "a robust, stocky, swarthy man, always faultlessly dressed in a dark-blue or black suit. He wore . . . a dignified black Vandyke." He also was, as Wolfe learned, "the most discreet and able of Lenin's 'men of confidence.' "[11]

In November 1917, Lenin seized power in Russia. He declared a "war on wars," taking Russia out of the Great War, and plotted a world revolution. With Lenin's sudden success, Julius Hammer took on an added responsibility: establishing a Bolshevik apparatus in the United States. Lenin had already sent to New York one of the most trusted agents in his inner circle, Ludwig Christian Alexander Karlovich Martens. A wiry-thin, energetic man with blond hair and a mustache, Martens spoke such perfect German, French, and English that he could have passed as being any one of those nationalities—and on occasion, he did. Indeed, he was often assumed to be a German businessman. But he was a Russian revolutionary.

Martens was born in the village of Bachmut in southern Russia in 1875, and while still a youth he had joined Lenin's revolutionaries in Saint Petersburg. At the age of twenty-one, he was thrown into prison. Three years later, he was deported by the czar to Germany, where, since he was thought to be of German origin, he was dragooned into the German army. In 1905, he fled to Switzerland, where he became one of Lenin's aides and supervised the smuggling of explosives and pamphlets to the underground in Russia. He then went to Britain, where he set up a clandestine machine-gun-manufacturing facility for Lenin. After he came to the attention of British intelligence in 1914, he registered as a German alien and moved on again, to America. In New York, he took a job as an engineer with an import-export firm while developing Lenin's cadre in America.

On January 2, 1919, Lenin named Martens his ambassador to the United States. This was a bold move on Lenin's part, since the U.S. government still recognized the prerevolutionary Russian government, which occupied the official Russian embassy in Washington, D.C. Ignoring the vigorous objections of the Americans, Martens set up an unofficial embassy in a shabby office at 110 West Fortieth Street in New York City. It was called the Russian Soviet Government Bureau.[12] Its most urgent mission was to break the Western economic blockade imposed on Russia.

Julius Hammer was given the unenviable job of generating support for the Russian Soviet Bureau. He became its financial adviser, administrative head, and "commercial attaché." Since Russian funds in bank accounts in the United States had been frozen by the federal government, Soviet couriers had been smuggling diamonds to New York to finance the operation. Julius Hammer arranged to sell this contraband to various jewelers, and after laundering the proceeds through Allied Drug, he paid the mounting debts of the Russian Soviet Bureau. He also recruited disciplined personnel. He selected Gregory Weinstein, a passionate advocate of Lenin and later an editor of the Socialist newspaper *Novy Mir* (*New World*), as "chief of chancellory," and Abraham A. Heller, a wealthy New York businessman who had been his partner in Allied Drug, as the head of the "commercial department." By March 1919, the Russian Soviet Bureau had thirty-nine employees, almost all of whom were dedicated Leninists.

At its most public level, the Russian Soviet Bureau operated as a sort of glorified Bolshevik chamber of commerce. Hammer and Heller traveled to Washington, Detroit, and San Francisco to see executives of American companies—such as Ford Motor—that made products that could be exported to Soviet Russia. They then tried to convince them that Russia would be a lucrative market, hoping that pressure would be put on the U.S. government to end the isolation of the Soviet regime. While these were entirely legal activities, the Russian Soviet Bureau had other agendas that involved Julius Hammer.

One of these missions was to create an American Bolshevik party. At this time, the majority of American socialists were anti-Bolshevik and took the position that national considerations should take precedence over international considerations. But a minority left-wing faction, of which Julius Hammer was a financial angel, took the opposite view. Hammer's faction, with the secret support of Martens, made more and more radical demands on the majority, calling, for example, for the creation of workmen's councils that would serve as instruments for overthrowing the government, expropriating banks, and establishing a proletarian dictatorship. Benjamin Gitlow, who worked with Julius Hammer on this program (and later was a Communist Party candidate for vice president of the United States), wrote in his auto-biography, "To transform the Socialist Party into a Bolshevik party, we proposed the elimination of the reform planks in its platform, the building of revolutionary industrial unions, . . . and the election of delegates to an International Conference to be held in Moscow, called by the Communist Party of Russia." He added, in retrospect, "Only lunatics or hopeless romantics could even consider such a program."[13]

These machinations, which intensified throughout the spring and summer of 1919, culminated in—as no doubt they were intended to—the expulsion of the left-wing faction, making it possible to achieve Lenin's objective of creating a Bolshevik party. On August 31, the expelled faction transformed itself into the Communist Labor Party. Julius Hammer held party card 1. Gitlow later wrote that Julius Hammer "not only paid the rent [for the party's national headquarters] but later bought the house and turned it over to our party."[14] The Communist Labor Party, joining another extremist faction, then became the Communist Party of the United States—and joined the Communist International (the Comintern).

Julius Hammer was also heavily involved at this time in a clandestine mission to provide Lenin's regime with equipment and spare parts for which the U.S. government refused to issue export licenses. Hammer used Allied Drug as a conduit. He also set up, with the help of Martens and Heller, other corporate fronts to camouflage the exports. The loophole he found was the Baltic port of Riga in Latvia, which was not subject to the Allied blockade of Russia. The goods destined for Soviet Russia were purchased in the name of the corporate fronts and transferred to Allied Drug with falsified export documents certifying that they were destined for use in Latvia. They were then shipped to Riga, where they were reshipped by rail into Russia.

By the summer of 1919, such intrigues left Julius Hammer with little time for his medical practice, which he had maintained along with his pharmaceutical business. He needed help with his patients. Armand, who was now a twenty-one-year-old second-year medical student at Columbia College of Physicians and Surgeons, took off afternoons from classes to work at his father's clinic, on the ground floor of the family home. When his father was occupied elsewhere, he treated patients with routine ailments himself, although he was not yet legally permitted to practice medicine.

That same summer, the roof fell in on Julius Hammer. First, a crusading anti-Red contingent of the New York state legislature, called the Lusk Committee, had the police raid the West Fortieth Street headquarters of the Russian Soviet Bureau, seize its documents, and arrest most of its personnel. Although Martens himself escaped the raid, he was forced to go underground. For a while, Martens hid out in the Hammer home.

Then, on August 12, police told Julius Hammer that he was about to be charged with manslaughter. They claimed that a woman had died after undergoing an abortion at the clinic at Hammer's house. The dead woman was Marie Oganesoff, the thirty-three-year-old wife of a Russian diplomat who had come to America for the czarist regime. According to the testimony of her chauffeur, she had gone to the Hammer house for the abortion on July 5 and collapsed when she returned home later that day. No nurse had been present during the medical procedure, and there were no witnesses to it.

When questioned by prosecutors, Julius Hammer did not deny that an abortion had been performed, but he claimed that it was medically justified, and that he, as her doctor, had the right to make such a decision. Nevertheless, he was indicted.

The trial—which was interrupted by the charge that William Cope, a public relations man retained by Julius Hammer, had tried to bribe a juror—dragged on for the better part of a year. On June 26, 1920, the jury found Julius Hammer guilty of first-degree manslaughter. The judge then pronounced his sentence: three and one half to twelve years of hard labor at Sing Sing State Prison.

Six months later, Martens and most of his associates were deported to Russia. In Moscow, Lenin appointed Martens to the Supreme Council on the National Economy, and his Russian Soviet Bureau was reorganized as a unit of the Commissariat of Foreign Trade. Though Martens was now operating from Moscow, he was still charged with the mission of opening a path to American business. He again turned his attention to Allied Drug, which in the chaos of the past year had been left with unpaid-for Russia-bound equipment stacked up in warehouses in New York and Riga. It had also incurred enormous debts. Martens had the idea of assigning a concession in Russia to Allied Drug, which would help the company out of its financial difficulties. Such a concession might then lure other corporations to Russia. In

March 1921, Martens sent a letter to Allied Drug through the Soviet mission in Revel (now Tallinn), Estonia, inviting it to send a representative to Moscow.[15]

Martens's offer put Julius Hammer in a quandary. Though he had at least three more years to serve at Sing Sing, he did not want to miss the opportunity to get a potentially valuable concession that might revive the flagging fortunes of Allied Drug, whose ownership he had transferred to his two eldest sons, Harry and Armand. Harry Hammer was trying to save the pharmaceutical part of the business, and he could not leave New York. That left Armand, who was just completing his medical education. Julius fully realized, as he later noted in a letter, that Armand had no "business experience."[16] Nor had Armand any experience in foreign travel. He had never gone more than one hundred miles from New York City. Moreover, he did not speak a word of Russian. Yet, as everyone in the Hammer family had come to realize, he was an exceptionally eager and resourceful young man. Julius had always considered Armand his successor in his professional life. He now called on his son to complete the concession deal for him in Moscow.

: : OFFICES : :
2413 THIRD AVENUE
: TELEPHONE :
MELROSE 8382-8383

LABORATORIES
C-397 MARKET STREET
NEWARK, N. J.
A-2356 THIRD AVENUE
B-2413 THIRD AVENUE

NEW YORK Apr. 18, 1921.

Department of State Passport Agency,
  Room 445 Custom House,
   New York City.

Gentlemen:-

   We have arranged for our Mr. Armand Hammer to go to
Europe and attend to some of our business. We hold an export
and import permit, and we would like him to buy in England,
France and other countries perfumes, wines and other articles
which are used in our business and which we think could be
purchased easily in Europe.

   We have therefore arranged that he take care of our
interest and in our behalf while in Europe of all the necessary purchases to be made by us and that he attend to it during his stay in Europe, and would therefore appreciate if you
would grant him a passport so as to enable him to take the
trip.

       Respectfully yours,

     ALLIED DRUG & CHEMICAL CORPORATION,

HK/G   By *Harry J. Hammer*.
            President.

*The letter from the family firm that was attached to
Hammer's application for his passport.*

CHAPTER TWO

THE JOURNEY EAST

ON APRIL 16, 1921, A COLD AND RAINY DAY IN NEW YORK, Armand Hammer arrived at the passport office on Varick Street. He noted on his application that he was five foot seven inches tall with gray eyes, a straight nose, an oval face, brown hair, and a dark complexion. He noted that he resided at the Ansonia Hotel, and he provided a photograph of himself impeccably dressed in a white shirt, a tie, and a tweed jacket, with his hair parted in the center and swept back.

Passports then were given at the discretion of the State Department, which required that an applicant divulge his full itinerary and purpose in traveling abroad. Hammer listed five countries he intended to visit—England, France, Holland, Norway, and Sweden—and his departure date as June 1. He stated that the purpose of his trip was "commercial and pleasure." In support of this purpose, he attached a letter written on the stationery of the Allied Drug and Chemical Company, saying that "Armand Hammer is going on business to Europe." It further explained that Hammer was being sent to purchase perfumes, wines, and other goods in France and England that the company needed to conduct its business. The letter was signed by Hammer's older brother, Harry Hammer, the company's vice president.

What was not reflected in the application was the incredible series of traumas that this young man had experienced during the past year. A young woman had died from an abortion performed in his house. His father had been sent to prison. His father's company had lost almost all its business. His family's house had been sold, forcing his mother to move to a hotel. The radical political party his father had helped found was outlawed. The world he had lived in since he was a child had suddenly disappeared. He had planned to take up a promising internship at New York's prestigious Bellevue Hospital after his graduation from medical school in June, but now even that was in doubt.

Despite what Hammer had written on his application, he did not reside at the Ansonia Hotel, where his mother had moved upon Julius's imprisonment. He lived in a one-bedroom carriage house in Greenwich Village that his father had used for his more private political meetings before he was imprisoned. Hammer had also misrepresented his purpose for applying for a passport: Allied Drug was not in the business of importing wines or perfumes, and he was not traveling to Europe to buy these or any other products for the company. Nor was his true destination any of the countries he had listed on his itinerary. He was traveling to a country still in the throes of a social revolution, a country that the United States neither recognized nor encouraged its citizens to visit: Soviet Russia.

After leaving the passport office, Hammer made the train trip from Grand Central Terminal to Ossining, New York, where Sing Sing Prison is located. The prison is a fortresslike stone building with massive steel doors on a treeless hill high above the Hudson River. In it, in a damp limestone cell with iron bars on the windows, his beloved father, who had been a model for him all his life, was incarcerated.

Armand Hammer knew that his father was not guilty. He would keep this knowledge a secret for three decades. Then, afraid that he was dying, he explained to his longtime mistress that it was he, not his father, who had performed the illegal abortion in 1919. He was then only a first-year medical student, unlicensed to practice medicine, and would certainly have gone to prison if his father had not stepped in to take the blame. Ordinarily, doctors in New York State were permitted leeway in performing such abortions and were rarely prosecuted. Not only was Julius Hammer put on trial, but the judge threw the book at him.[1]

Years later, Hammer attributed his father's imprisonment to a political conspiracy, explaining in an interview, "When my father was sentenced, . . . he was a member of the Socialist Labor Party and he had incurred the wrath of the local Tammany Hall politicians, who were out to get him." At the time, Hammer believed "my world had come to an end."[2] When his father arrived in the visitors' room that spring day in 1921, he was wearing the standard prison uniform: a pair of loose-fitting gray pants, a gray jacket with metal buttons, and heavy, crude shoes. He was followed, like all prisoners, by a "keeper," who had a long metal-tipped stick in his hand. Julius did not complain, but Hammer knew from the letters his father had written to his mother that he was sleeping in a cell only seven feet long and three feet wide. His father needed his help, and no matter how much he wanted to take up his internship, Hammer could not refuse.

Julius Hammer spoke little about prison life that day. He had more important information to impart to his son, about the covert side of Allied Drug and the arrangements that were to be made with Martens in Moscow.

Since the Supreme Council on the Economy, of which Martens was a member, wanted to award concessions to American capitalists, it was important to Martens that Allied Drug appear to be a conventional American capitalist enterprise. While Julius Hammer had managed to keep secret from U.S. authorities his company's activity on behalf of Soviet Russia, he could not do the same for his personal service to the Bolshevik cause. He had openly worked for Martens in New York. He had provided bail to free Gitlow and other high-ranking radicals who were arrested in police raids. He had paid for the Communist Party headquarters in New York. During his trial, newspapers had gone to great lengths to call attention to his activities in behalf of Lenin. Yet, while he could not separate his persona from radical politics, his son had no such taint.

Armand had been interested in his father's politics, but he was not identified with that world. Julius had kept Armand's enrollment in the Socialist Labor Party a private matter (or believed he had, not realizing that the party's records had been intercepted by U.S. Army intelligence in 1919). Even his son's contacts with the Russian Soviet Bureau could be easily explained in terms of his medical interest in combating famine and pestilence in Russia. From this point on, however, Armand would have to play his part well. He could not reveal to the outside world any political commitments of his own. He would have to suppress, if not forget, everything he'd been exposed to while growing up in the homes of active socialists. He was going to Russia as the American capitalist that Martens now needed.

Hammer met, on his father's instructions, with Charles Recht, whose law office was located at 110 West Fortieth Street, in the same suite of offices that the Russian Soviet Bureau had used. Recht, despite his avuncular manner, was a tough, deadly serious lawyer who, in the anti-Bolshevik atmosphere of the 1920s, had one of the least popular clients in the United States: Lenin. He represented the interests of Soviet Russia in the United States, and he assured Armand Hammer that the Soviets would provide him with the documentation he needed to go to Moscow. Recht then handed him a package that he was to deliver to Martens, who would be his Soviet connection.

The parcel Recht gave Hammer contained a film that symbolized the transfer of Martens's mission from New York to Moscow. It had been shot from the pier in New York from which Martens and other Communist deportees had boarded the S.S. *Stockholm.* It showed Martens on the deck waving to his American supporters as the ship slowly pulled away. Whatever interest the film may have had to Martens, Hammer hardly needed it to introduce himself. He already knew Martens well, of course. After Julius Hammer was jailed, Martens had been a surrogate father to Armand.

On July 5, Hammer boarded the S.S. *Aquitania* in New York for the first leg of the journey. He had with him a suitcase of clothes, his travel papers, and the film that showed Martens being deported. It was his first trip abroad and his first time on a ship. Up to this point in his life, he had had little social experience with anyone beyond his family circle and his father's cadre of close political associates. Hammer was a reserved and insular young man. He had spent his time studying for college and medical school so that he might follow in his father's footsteps. He had few friends and stayed very much to himself at medical school, establishing an isolation made that much deeper when his father was tried for manslaughter and pilloried in the newspapers for his political activities. On board the ship to Europe, Hammer remained isolated, spending his time studying Russian. Each day, he tried to learn one hundred new Russian words. He even made a point of eating alone so as to avoid casual conversations with other passengers.³ The last thing he wanted was any prying questions about his father or his plans to travel to Russia.

Hammer's fears of the outside world were unexpectedly heightened when he arrived in the port of Southampton, England, on July 13. Just as he prepared to disembark with the other passengers, he felt a tap on his arm. Turning around, he saw a well-dressed stranger with a cane, a man who identified himself as a representative of Scotland Yard. The man pulled him aside and informed him that he would not be allowed to land in Britain until he answered questions about his planned activities. "I was absolutely flabbergasted. . . . I was completely dazed," he recalled later. Interrogated about his travel plans, he initially claimed he was en route to France, Belgium, and Germany. The officer was not satisfied and asked pointedly about Russia. When Hammer acknowledged that he might travel there to help with the famine relief, the officer ordered him to remain in his cabin "until further notice." Two days later, he was released from detention and allowed to proceed to London. "Instead of becoming disheartened by my experiences," he wrote, ". . . I was now more determined than ever to visit Russia, and hurriedly made my preparations to leave for Berlin." At the time, Hammer attributed his unpleasant encounter with Scotland Yard to little more than the "neurosis" of "European post-war officialdom."⁴ What he did not realize then was that he had come to the attention of a tenacious lawyer at the U.S. Department of Justice: J. Edgar Hoover.

HOOVER HAD FIRST ENCOUNTERED THE COMMUNIST CONSPIRACY that would fascinate him for the rest of his life while he was attending George Washington Law School. To help pay his tuition in 1917, he had taken a part-time job as an indexer at the Library of Congress, where he was assigned the task of tracking the members of the international socialist movement. He soon became an expert in this new field and did his wartime service in the Alien Enemy Division of the Department of Justice, where he began building files on the more prominent radicals. Army intelligence had kept many political and labor leaders under wartime postal and physical surveillance, which provided Hoover with a wealth of data for his dossiers. In 1919, when he was only twenty-four, he had already become the department's resident expert on subversives. That same year, in the midst of a Red scare greatly excited by leaked reports of radical bomb threats, Attorney General Mitchell Palmer launched a nationwide crackdown on radicals—the Palmer raids. To dig up targets, he appointed Hoover head of the department's newly formed Radical Division, which, at Hoover's suggestion, was more broadly renamed the General Intelligence Division. Hoover, who had personally prepared the deportation case against Ludwig Martens, focused on the activities of the Russian Soviet Bureau—an easy target since it was the acknowledged agency of an unpopular foreign power. Army surveillance showed that the bureau channeled funds to Soviet agents, left-wing labor organizers, propagandist institutions, and the left-wing faction of the Socialist Labor Party, which was to emerge as the Communist Party of the United States. Hoover considered the Russian Soviet Bureau the cockpit of Lenin's underground in America.

Even after the Russian Soviet Bureau was closed and Martens was deported, intercepts of messages from Moscow showed that Martens was still engaged in arranging trade with U.S. companies. The government did not encourage such traffic even though for most goods the legal prohibition on exports to Soviet Russia was lifted in 1921. In February 1921, Martens attempted to charter two ships to carry U.S. grain to Russia and a third to carry Russian asbestos to the United States. Although these particular charters were canceled, Martens would presumably make other efforts to exchange goods with firms in the United States.

By this time, Hoover had managed to establish a number of informers for his General Intelligence Division who kept him abreast of the movements of Martens's key operatives. One of them was William Edward Cope, a former journalist and the public relations man who had been employed to help Julius Hammer in his manslaughter trial and who had been caught trying to bribe a juror. Soon after the bribery case was dropped, Cope entered into his relationship with Hoover.

On June 11, 1921, Cope reported that Martens had remained, even after his deportation, a secret owner of Hammer's company, Allied Drug. Martens had, according to Cope, "concealed" a 50 percent interest in it. Cope further advised that Hammer's son Armand, who was still a medical student, planned to go to Russia that July. His purpose, according to Cope, was "to carry some messages for Martens." Hoover now became keenly interested in the movements of the younger Hammer. He obtained from the State Department his passport file, which confirmed that he was scheduled to depart for Europe.

Meanwhile, Hoover found that another former "notorious Bolshevik" had been listed in corporate records in Delaware as a part owner of Julius Hammer's Allied Drug: Abraham Heller. U.S. Army surveillance reports further showed that Heller had worked with Julius Hammer in attempting to recruit American businessmen for the Russian Soviet Bureau. Heller, according to State Department intelligence, had recently been briefly arrested in Estonia while trying to get into Russia without a valid passport. He was released and had crossed the Russian border on June 2. So two principals of Allied Drug—Hammer and Heller—were heading for Moscow. The General Intelligence Division also learned that David Dubrowsky, who had been with the Russian Soviet Bureau in New York, was traveling abroad as an Allied Drug employee and had delivered medical instruments to Russia. Clearly, something was happening. But by the time Hoover's agents had tracked down the ship Hammer had bought a ticket on—the S.S. *Aquitania*—it had already departed for England.

Hoover alerted the U.S. Embassy in London to Hammer's scheduled arrival there. Two years earlier, in what became known euphemistically as a special relationship, Great Britain had secretly agreed to exchange counterintelligence reports with the United States and in 1920 had set up a "clearinghouse" in London to keep records on all suspected Communist agents. This was a particularly important resource for Hoover, since MI-5, the British Security Service, had already planted a mole on the staff of the Soviet trade mission in London, which maintained communications with Martens's Russian Soviet Bureau in New York.[5] MI-5 informed Hoover that Julius Hammer was known to have been "a close associate of Trotsky and later of Martens." It also reported that in 1916, Armand Hammer had enrolled in the Socialist Labor Party (which MI-5 kept under surveillance). Hoover's tip that the younger Hammer was carrying material for Martens led MI-5 to meet Hammer's ship.

MI-5 detained and questioned Hammer and searched his baggage. On July 15, Hoover was advised that the baggage contained a sixteen-millimeter film of Martens's departure from New York and a letter to Martens. After examining these items, Hoover noted: "The propaganda film . . . contains nothing of especial interest." The letter did reveal, however, that the film had been consigned to Hammer by the Soviet government's lawyer, Charles Recht, who, as far as Hoover was concerned, was acting as a stand-in for Martens in running Soviet operations in the United States.

Hoover next received a report that Hammer was in Berlin on July 20. He had registered at the Adlon Hotel, which was conveniently located near the new Soviet trade mission, and had sent a cable to Moscow, saying that he was traveling at the behest of Recht. Ten days later, the Soviet Commissariat of Foreign Affairs cabled Hammer's visa to its mission in Berlin. Copies of these cables reached Hoover. But on July 31, Hammer checked out of his hotel in Berlin and vanished from Hoover's screen for the next three months.

GETTING INTO RUSSIA WAS NO EASY TASK IN THE SUMMER OF 1921. The country had been torn apart and plunged into near ruin by the civil war that followed the Bolshevik revolution in 1917. By 1919, the anti-Bolshevik armies occupied well over 90 percent of what had been Russia. The Ukraine, Poland, Georgia, Finland, Lithuania, Estonia, and Latvia, all once part of the Russian Empire, had declared themselves independent states. Meanwhile, there was massive foreign intervention: the Czechoslovak Legion seized the Trans-Siberian Railroad; British troops took over the oil fields of the Black and Caspian Seas and the Arctic ports; the Japanese held large parts of Siberia. All Soviet ports were blockaded by foreign navies. In the area they still controlled—mainly the territory between Moscow and Petrograd (which until 1914 had been known as Saint Petersburg)—the Bolsheviks, under the banner of War Communism, abolished money, banks, and savings and disrupted much of what remained of the economy. Winston Churchill, then the British secretary of state for war, noted that Russia "is rapidly being reduced by Bolsheviks to an animal form of Barbarism."

By the summer of 1921, the Red Army had recaptured most of the lost Russian territory, and the foreign interventions had ended, but Russian industry, communications, and agriculture remained in shambles, and a drought left thirty million Russians in danger of starvation. Even war-hardened Bolshevik leaders were begging the West for food to avert the impending famine.

Latvia was one of the few countries that maintained even irregular rail communications with Russia. In August 1921, Riga, the Latvian capital, became the site of the first serious negotiations for famine relief between the U.S. and Soviet governments. The American Relief Administration, headed by Secretary of Commerce Herbert Hoover, offered massive quantities of food if the Bolsheviks would guarantee that they would distribute it fairly.

Hammer arrived in Riga from Germany on August 16, 1921. The overnight trip across the Baltic Sea on a steamer, which he described as a "hell-bound crate," had left him nauseated and exhausted. He was met in Riga by Boris Mishell, a forty-year-old Russian-born yarn salesman from New York whom his father had hired to assist him in Russia.

Mishell was taken aback by Hammer's pallid face and shaky condition. For his part, Hammer found Mishell "a very robust fellow with plenty of energy and a huge laugh." He watched with great interest as Mishell bribed Latvian customs officials to clear Hammer's baggage. After nearly a month of solitary travel, Hammer enjoyed having a companion, especially one who also worked for him. Mishell knew about things that Hammer had never concerned himself with: food, wine, clothes, and women. He also spoke fluent Russian and could interpret for Hammer. Although Mishell had been unable to book rooms for them in any of the better hotels in Riga—they were filled with American and British reporters trying to get Russian visas so they could cover the mass starvation, and with international relief workers awaiting Russian visas so they could organize the famine relief—he found a run-down hotel, the Rome, where they spent the night.

Mishell spent the next day desperately trying to get a shipment of surgical instruments out of the Riga customs warehouse. It had been sent from the United States by Julius Hammer so that his son could present a gift to the Soviet government; but despite the gratuities he distributed to Latvian clerks, Mishell was unable to retrieve it in time to catch the night train, which Hammer boarded for Moscow.[6]

The train was extremely primitive, with wooden benches, and after dark the only lighting was from the candles Mishell had bought for

Hammer for the three-day trip. Hammer was afraid to eat most of the food that was sold at the stations the train stopped at, and he was unable to sleep; so he was sick by the time the train reached the Russian border, but he kept his mind focused on his purpose. This was not some youthful adventure; it was a mission, a mission he was performing for his father.

Moscow itself, which since 1917 had been caught in a nonstop cycle of war, revolution, counterrevolution, and civil war, was grim. *The New York Times*'s correspondent, Walter Duranty, who arrived in Moscow that same month, reported leaving the station:

> The street was full of holes where water-mains had burst or where there had been digging in the attempt to clear choked drains. For two and one half years at least there was no running water in Moscow. . . . And no steam heat, in a climate where thirty below zero occurs almost every winter.[7]

On his arrival, Hammer was given a book of food coupons (since currency had been abolished) by a Communist official and then escorted to his hotel, the Savoy. "Never in my life have I seen a hotel less worthy of the name Savoy," he later recalled. His small room was "filthy," with a mattress that had no sheets or blankets. "There was not only dirt, but rats and mice and smaller vermin," he wrote. It was unlike anything he'd ever experienced. Its only advantage was its proximity to the Commissariat of Foreign Affairs, where he had pressing business.[8]

Hammer's contact there was Gregory Weinstein, a former associate of his father's at the Russian Soviet Bureau, who, after being deported to Russia in Martens's entourage, was now in charge of the American Division of the Commissariat of Foreign Affairs. As such, he was involved with the Soviet strategy for breaking the unofficial U.S. boycott, and Hammer was to play a role in that strategy.

Hammer met Weinstein the day after his arrival to discuss the surgical instruments that were now on their way to Moscow with Mishell. Weinstein had already made arrangements for Hammer to present them to Nikolay Aleksandrovich Semashko, Russia's commissar of public health. Semashko, who had been commended by Lenin for his "energetic suppression" of peasant farmers and the confiscation of grain, was now, ironically, in charge of famine relief.

Even though the instruments were a gift from Julius Hammer, Armand—in what may have been his first gesture of self-promotion and self-assertion—insisted on taking credit for donating them. He persuaded Weinstein that since he would be representing Allied Drug in Moscow, it made sense for him, not his father, to have this credit. Years later, the deception would provide him with a philanthropic rationale for this first mission to Moscow.

With a growing sense of confidence in, and understanding of, his role as a stand-in for his father, Hammer proceeded to the next order of business. Martens had arranged for him to inspect asbestos mines and other potential mineral concessions. On September 5, Hammer boarded a private train that had been commandeered by the Supreme Council on the Economy for the monthlong rail trip through the Urals to Ekaterinburg (later, Sverdlovsk) to look at the mines. It was luxuriously outfitted by Russian standards, having both soldiers to protect the elite company and an American jazz band to entertain it. Hammer was impressed by the VIP treatment, which added to his sense of worth. He was now being dealt with not as some naïve medical student but as a valued participant in an enterprise of political and economic importance.

Accompanying Hammer on the trip were two men he knew well from New York: Ludwig Martens and Abraham Heller. Heller was already arranging to set up a business in New York, called International Publishers, which would acquire American technical manuals for the Soviets. Though he had been a regular visitor to the Hammer household in New York, he had previously paid little attention to Armand. There was also a twenty-five-year-old American woman in the party, Lucy Branham, who represented the Woman's Committee for the Recognition of Russia. She accompanied Hammer on a number of side trips to Russian villages, and a photograph of them together shows him towering over her and beaming a broad smile.

On one of these excursions, a visit to a factory in the town of Kasli, Hammer was able to demonstrate his ingenuity. Heller, who went along, noted in his diary:

Our machine was an old Stevens car without a top. . . . The distance to the factory was about 130 versts [86 miles]. . . . About 20 versts out something went wrong with the motor. The chauffeur refused to go further. . . . We decided to look into the cause of the trouble. This was soon discovered by our enterprising doctor, who thereupon took the wheel, to the great disgust of the chauffeur, and started off at a good pace.[9]

Hammer, as Heller was now able to see, was becoming a man of action. Martens also became increasingly impressed with him.[10] Armand was no longer merely his friend's son; he was his colleague.

As the train went through the famine-ravaged areas of Russia, Hammer saw shocking scenes of human suffering and desolation. People were starving. Martens suggested that a foreign company willing to supply Russia with grain to alleviate the suffering could be guaranteed a profit: the company would be awarded a rich mineral concession. Hammer, who at this point still had more imagination than business experience, quickly seized on Martens's idea. He now wanted to see possible mineral concessions.

On September 18, the train and entourage arrived in Ekaterinburg, a shattered city at the eastern extreme of European Russia. Its history encapsulates the rise and fall of the czar's empire. Founded by Peter the Great at the beginning of the eighteenth century and named after Empress Catherine, it rapidly became one of the richest mining centers in the world. It was also the city to which Nicholas II, the last czar of Russia, and his family were exiled—and where they were brutally murdered by the Bolsheviks.

Martens took Hammer and Heller from Ekaterinburg to nearby Alapayevsk to see an abandoned asbestos mine. It was a huge open pit about one thousand feet in diameter. The inside had been cut into a series of terraces that, like some giant's staircase, descended for a hundred feet. The bottom of the pit, which contained the vein of asbestos, was covered with debris. Martens told Hammer that the mine could easily be brought back into operation by clearing away the debris. The asbestos could then be dug out with explosives, carted to the surface, put on a train at a nearby siding, shipped to western Europe by rail, and sold at a high price. He offered to arrange to have the asbestos concession awarded to Allied Drug if Hammer would help get American wheat to Russia.

The wheat plan proposed by Martens sounded lucrative: the Hammers would charter ships that would be loaded with Russian caviar,

furs, and other exports that could be sold in the West, and the proceeds from the sale of these exports would be used to purchase American wheat, which would then be sent back to Russia. For allowing
their corporation to be used for this purpose, the Hammers would receive 5 percent of the value of the wheat. For Hammer, these deals
were more than a business opportunity; they were his chance to fulfill his father's wishes. Without gathering any significant information
about the mining or export operation, Hammer quickly agreed to the
arrangement. He telegraphed his brother Harry in New York, who
took care of the more prosaic needs of the business, requesting that
he find ships.

BY THE TIME THE SPECIAL TRAIN HAD REACHED THE URALS, LENIN
had been told about the role proposed for Hammer. It was a small
part, but one that was vital for Lenin's grand design. Lenin had already achieved what had seemed impossible a mere four years earlier.
Indeed, in the spring of 1917, Lenin was merely the pen name of
Vladimir Ilich Ulyanov, a balding forty-seven-year-old exile living in
a shabby two-room flat next to a sausage factory in Zurich. He
barely supported himself and his wife by editing a tiny socialist journal called *Iskra* (*The Spark*). More than a decade earlier, he had decided that the revolutionary movement in Russia would be best
served by a small, well-disciplined group operating from abroad, beyond the reach of the czar's secret police. He therefore reorganized
the Russian Social Democratic Labor Party as a conspiratorial organization dedicated to overthrowing the existing order.

   Lenin was caught by surprise when the government was actually
overthrown by radicals inside Russia, but he was soon to be thrust
into the center of the rapidly unfolding events. The German general
staff offered him a deal that he could not refuse. The Germans were
fighting a two-front war—Russia in the east; France and Britain and
their allies in the west—and were desperate to get Russia to quit. The
German generals proposed inserting Lenin and his radical followers
back into Russia like a virus to subvert the war effort. General Erich
Ludendorff, the mastermind of the operation, wrote that "the enterprise was justified from a military point of view. We had to bring
Russia down."[11] The German foreign minister approved the plan,

noting that "it is in our interest that the influence of the radical wing of the revolutionaries should prevail in Russia."[12] Lenin and some two dozen of his followers were thus transported in a sealed car on a German train from Switzerland to Russia.

On April 16, 1917, after having been away from Russia for seventeen years, Lenin stepped off the train in what had been the czar's capital of Saint Petersburg. He was quickly surrounded by a tumultuous crowd of supporters. He told them that the long-awaited proletarian revolution had begun—and that his Bolsheviks represented that revolution. At the time, his party had only a small minority of the delegates in the provisional parliament, but by November he had managed to maneuver enough of his supporters into key positions in the security forces to seize power in the name of the proletariat. One hundred fifteen days later, he altered the balance of military power in Europe by unilaterally ending Russia's war with Germany.

Lenin's problem was managing the nation he had taken over. "We cannot run the economy," he admitted. And he was right. By 1920, industrial production in Russia had fallen to about one fifth the level it was in 1913. In addition, the effort to take over private farms resulted in bloody and continual peasant wars—some ten million people were killed in all—and the near total collapse of the agricultural system.[13] Without vital spare parts from abroad, Soviet oil fields could not continue to supply fuel for tractors and trucks, and Soviet trains could not transport the food that was harvested. The only way to keep people from starving was to obtain from abroad the spare parts, fuel, trucks, and other items that were desperately needed. But the foreign governments that were in a position to provide such aid viewed the Communist regime as their implacable enemy.

Lenin needed to change the West's perception of what was happening in Soviet Russia. While conventional politicians might have doubted the possibility of achieving such a thing, Lenin did not. He had spent most of his life at the epicenter of an international conspiracy that was predicated on the idea that an entire world order—capitalism—could be subverted and overthrown. As early as 1902, in his essay *What Is to Be Done?,* he had outlined the strategy by which a small cadre of professional conspirators would bring about world revolution for the masses. Its success would proceed from secrecy, discipline, and deception. The real would be hidden, the false displayed. Opponents would be confused, diverted, and ultimately misled into collaborating in their own destruction. The tactics had worked. Now Lenin had to apply the same conspiratorial principles to statecraft. He had to do and say whatever was necessary to advance the image of a nonthreatening and potentially profitable Soviet Russia—even when such measures deviated from, or contradicted, Marxist ideology. The end still justified the means where the survival of the revolution was at stake.

Concessions, in which foreign capitalists would receive exclusive access to Russian minerals, were a part of this strategy. Lenin explained to his economic commissar, Simon Liberman, that concessions were the "bait" that would help to overcome the political hostility of businessmen.[14] He assumed that U.S., British, and German capitalists would vie with one another for the concessions, and to get better terms they would pressure their respective governments to lift restrictions against trading with the Soviet Union. Lenin had even discussed the idea of turning over the port of Vladivostok and the Soviet Far Eastern provinces to American capitalists so as to turn the U.S. government against Japan.) He had little problem persuading his colleagues that the capitalists' presumed greed could be used to Soviet advantage. When one of them asked him where the Soviet state would obtain the rope with which to hang the capitalist nations—since rope, like every other commodity, was in short supply—he answered, "They'll supply us with it."[15]

In March 1921, Lenin proclaimed a New Economic Policy, or NEP. War communism, in which all profits had been banned, would be replaced by a mixed system of public and private ownership. Money, which had been theoretically abolished in 1918, would be reintroduced, and private property, free markets, and capitalist enterprise would be permitted. The NEP, which would be amenable to foreign investment, was scheduled to go into effect in August, and in order to begin the competition for concessions Lenin needed a capitalist—preferably one who was controllable—who would obtain the first concession in the new era.

After several false starts that spring, Martens finally came up with an appealing candidate: Armand Hammer. On October 13, Lenin was briefed on Hammer by Julius Hammer's old comrade-in-arms, Boris Reinstein, who was now a gaunt, twisted man of fifty-seven. When the revolution came in 1917, Reinstein had rushed back to Russia to join Lenin, and he became the American representative to the Comintern, which was set up by Lenin in 1919 to coordinate an international conspiracy that had few, if any, parallels in modern history. The headquarters of the Comintern was in Moscow, and its funds were supplied by the Kremlin. Its tactic was subversion: it assigned agents the task of infiltrating and taking over labor unions, student organizations, granges, political parties, and governments. Although it probably did not have more than a thousand active members in 1921, they had burrowed into revolutionary movements in twenty countries. They used all the equipment of espionage: aliases, false documentation, laundered money, codebooks, safe houses, and clandestine couriers. The Comintern operated under the supervision of the Kremlin, but it maintained the fiction that it was an independent political organization.

Reinstein, who had helped found this unique organization in Moscow, had dual positions. He was the secretary of the Profintern, which coordinated efforts to penetrate the labor movement around the world. And in the Soviet government, he headed the American propaganda section of the Commissariat of Foreign Affairs. He had also become one of Lenin's chief Americanologists. The plan to recruit American capital and technology in the form of concessions came under his purview, and he told Lenin that Julius Hammer was a "sincere and selfless Marxist"—one whom he credited with playing a leading role in initiating "the Communist movement" in the United States. Reinstein reported that Julius had been falsely imprisoned by the American government because of his activities on behalf of the Russian Soviet Bureau, but that from behind bars he had continued to support the cause. He further explained that Julius had sent his son Armand to Moscow as his proxy with a present of a complete set of surgical instruments for the People's Commissariat of Health.[16]

Lenin was impressed. He telegraphed Martens in the Urals to find out whether Hammer could "be persuaded" to finance other business activities.[17] He was worried that Hammer might not live up to his promise to deliver grain, but both Martens and Reinstein assured him that Hammer was earnest about it. Since Lenin could not break the impasse in the negotiations on concessions with the Europeans— "the British and the French want to plunder us," he wrote that same day[18]—he decided to spur the competition between the "blind pawns" by conspicuously granting the first concession to an American. On October 19, he ordered Martens to draft a contract for Hammer. "Let it be a *concession,* even if a fictitious one," he wrote, suggesting that a fake mining concession, like the deceptive Potemkin villages that were supposedly erected to impress Catherine the Great, would serve an important purpose. "What we want to show and have in print . . . is that the Americans *have gone in* for *concessions,*" he continued. "This is important politically."[19]

Martens had already drafted a contract for Hammer for a concession in the asbestos mines outside the town of Alapayevsk. To add to the credibility of the deal, Lenin agreed to meet personally with the young American concessionaire-to-be.

THE CITY OF MOSCOW WAS BUILT ON SEVEN HILLS, ON ONE OF which, surrounded by a great wall constructed by the czars, is the Kremlin. Hammer received his summons to the Kremlin the day he returned from the Urals expedition. At 9:00 A.M. on October 22, 1921, he was met at the fortresslike Trotsky Gate of the walled city within a city by Boris Reinstein. Just as Reinstein had taken Julius Hammer to Lenin fourteen years before, he now took Julius's son to Lenin. After Hammer had exchanged his passport for a pink pass at the guardhouse, Reinstein escorted him across a stone bridge that had once spanned a moat. Inside the walls, Hammer was awestruck by the profusion of medieval palaces with multicolored towers from which the czars had governed before they had moved their capital to Saint Petersburg in the eighteenth century. He passed through an impressive square lined with cannons that had been seized from Napoleon's retreating army, and then he entered a relatively modern building, which had previously been the High Court of Moscow. Lenin's operational headquarters was on the second floor. After again having their passes checked by guards, Hammer and Reinstein proceeded to the outer office, in which a staff of female aides sat at rolltop desks, busily typing. At noon, they were ushered by a secretary through the double doors that led to the inner sanctum of the world revolution: Lenin's office.

Lenin rose to meet his visitors. "He was smaller than I had expected," Hammer wrote later, "a stocky little man about five foot three with a large domed-shaped head." (Hammer himself was five foot seven.) Hammer was fascinated by the densely cluttered room filled with "books, magazines and newspapers in a half a dozen languages. . . . On shelves, on chairs, piled up in heaps on the desk itself." The only uncluttered part of the desk he could make out was reserved for a battery of telephones.

According to Hammer, Lenin's eyes welled up with tears as he spoke of the dire economic conditions in Russia and the failure of Communism. "Russia today is like your country was during the pioneer stage," Lenin said, making Communism sound like a phase that had already ended. "We need the knowledge and spirit that has made America what she is today." He then came to the point: "What we really need is American capital and technical aid." He then asked Hammer's help. "Someone must break the ice." He further suggested, "Why don't you take an asbestos concession yourself?"[20] Hammer accepted. He was not only flattered by the attention of a world leader, but he was, as he confided years later to his tape-recorded diary, "captivated" by the force of Lenin's personality. "If Lenin had told [me] to jump out that window," Hammer reflected, "[I] probably would have done it." He was now Lenin's man.[21] The meeting ended at 1:30 P.M., when Lenin left to observe the demonstration of a newly designed electric plow.

Lenin did not object to Hammer's making public the innocuous part of their discussion concerning the concession, which he suggested should be "well publicized" abroad. But not all the elements of it were innocuous. He had put Hammer's concession under control of the Special Concessions Committee, a newly created unit co-chaired, and run, by Feliks Edmundovich Dzerzhinski, the head of the secret police. Dzerzhinski, the son of a wealthy Polish aristocrat, had contemplated becoming a Catholic priest but became a revolutionary instead and spent nearly ten years in czarist prisons. In December 1917, he was appointed by Lenin to be the first head of the Extraordinary Commission for Combating Counterrevolution and Sabotage—the Cheka, as it became known by its Russian initials. The Cheka had the power to investigate, detain, try, sentence, and execute virtually anyone in Russia.

In the spring of 1921, Dzerzhinski had organized one of the most elaborate deceptions in modern history—the so-called Trust Operation. It involved Cheka-controlled agents masquerading as anti-Communists in order to convince Western intelligence agents that the fictional group they represented, known as the Trust, was actually a powerful anti-Communist organization in Russia. The double agents achieved this effect by passing on (and selling) to Western intelligence agents reports that were secretly authored by Dzerzhinski's people. The message planted in these reports was that the recently introduced NEP reforms signaled the abandonment of communism, and all that kept the Bolsheviks in power was Russian antipathy for foreign subversion. The point of the exercise was to convince Western governments that they could achieve their objective of overthrowing the Communists by giving up their blockade and intervention.

Such a complex deception required up-to-the-minute intelligence from abroad. The immediate problem in 1921 was not recruiting spies outside Russia—the Communist International had provided a large pool of dedicated believers—but communicating with them and paying them. Since Russia did not yet have diplomatic embassies abroad to serve these functions, Dzerzhinski used Soviet-controlled commercial enterprises as cover. He had already established secret bases for his agents in Europe: the All-Russian Cooperative Society in London, known as Arcos, and the Soviet trade mission in Berlin. But in the United States, where J. Edgar Hoover had closed down the Russian Soviet Bureau, Dzerzhinski had to move with more discretion. In this regard, Hammer's privately owned Allied Drug and Chemical Company had considerable interest. Its mining concession, which according to Lenin's instructions would be well publicized, would provide the New York–based company with a plausible reason for transferring money to Moscow. Moreover, Moscow would have the necessary measure of control over the venture with Allied Drug. The company would be reorganized so that while it continued to appear to be an American-run business, its board of directors would be made up of Soviet appointees whose votes would equal those of all the non-Soviet-appointed directors.

Up to this point, Hammer had been acting merely as a dutiful son carrying out a business venture for his imprisoned father. But now his role had become more serious. By accepting the concession, he had also agreed to cede control of Allied Drug to the Soviets. As he reorganized the company to this end, he found himself dealing with the Cheka, which had supervisory responsibility for his entire operation.

Dzerzhinski had assigned Lev Mironov, a rising counterintelligence officer in the Cheka, to coordinate and oversee the new concession.

Mironov also had the responsibility, according to the testimony of a defector who served with him in the Cheka in 1921, to exploit the concessionaires for espionage purposes. Shortly after his meeting with Lenin, Hammer was told that his family firm would do more than operate an asbestos mine in the Urals. It would also act as a financial conduit for Soviet activities in the United States at a time when funding such activities was illegal.

The plan called for Allied Drug to set up a banking operation in New York City that would have the exclusive franchise for sending money orders to Russia. Any immigrant in America wanting to send money to relatives in Russia would have to use this bank. The Russian relatives would then receive a supposedly equivalent sum of Soviet rubles from the National Bank in Moscow, but this money actually had little value. As Boris Reinstein explained in a report to his superiors in the Kremlin, "This [scheme] will be a stream of gold to Russia . . . to help us in our financial operations abroad."[22]

Hammer made the necessary arrangements with Aron Lvovic Scheinman, the Soviet official in charge of foreign trade at the National Bank of the Soviet Republic, who opened in Hammer's name account 1. It was the first account ever given to a foreigner.

While this scheme was being organized, Hammer was given $75,000 to secretly take back with him to New York. This money, which would be the equivalent of nearly $600,000 today, was to be distributed there to underground agents of the Comintern. Hammer thus demonstrated that he and his father were "convinced Communists and sincere comrades," as Reinstein wrote in his report.[23]

WHILE HAMMER MET WITH COMINTERN AND CHEKA OFFICIALS, the job of working out the details of the concession contract fell to Boris Mishell. Mishell was amazed by Hammer's newfound confidence. Only a few months earlier in Riga, he had seen a shy, unsure, and quivering Hammer board the train to Russia. He now saw a man who bragged about his contacts with the Cheka and demanded special privileges. While Mishell had not been impressed with the profit potential of the dormant asbestos mine, he was impressed with the extraordinary cooperation Hammer was getting from the Soviet government. As part of the contract, the Soviets agreed to supply not only offices, communications facilities, and warehouses but also armed troops.

Less than a week after the meeting with Lenin, the final version of the concession contract was ready for signing. A ceremony took place on October 28 in the Commissariat of Foreign Affairs. Mishell signed the contract, as did Hammer on behalf of Allied Drug. Two key architects of Lenin's NEP—Maksim Litvinov, the deputy commissar for foreign affairs, and Pyotr Alekseyevich Bogdanov, the chairman of Russia's Supreme Council on the Economy, signed on behalf of the Soviet government.

These top officials were celebrating more than the reactivation of an asbestos mine. Indeed, if asbestos extraction had been the objective, they hardly needed the services of two inexperienced Americans. But the asbestos deal was just the beginning of a concerted effort to establish a corporate vehicle in New York that could be used to open up trade and other activities in the United States. "The beginning is extremely important," Lenin wrote Hammer.[24] He also sent him a photograph of himself. It was inscribed to "Comrade Armand Hammer" —an appellation that Lenin almost always used for a fellow Communist and one that he applied to no other Western businessman.

On November 3, with great fanfare, a spokesman for the Soviet press officially announced the granting of the concession, and Armand Hammer's name flashed across the news wires for the first time. That very evening, Hammer, carrying with him Lenin's greeting to his father and other "comrades now in American jails," left Moscow for Riga to arrange for the first shipment of Russian exports to the United States.

Armand Hammer had begun his voyage on the S.S. *Aquitania* as a shy, isolated youth with his own burden of secrets—his involvement in the crime his father was imprisoned for and knowledge of the clandestine business his father had carried on with the Soviet regime. Now he had gained a great deal of experience in the way the world worked— at least the world of conspiracy—and he had begun to emerge from his father's long shadow. But Hammer also departed Russia with a new burden of secrets—his commitment to using his family's company to help finance Soviet espionage in America. He had crossed a line into a land of intrigue, from which there was no return.

Armand Hammer returned to New York from his second trip to Moscow on the S.S. Majestic *in the spring of 1922. Less than a month before, Lenin had written Stalin that he was secretly designating Hammer a "path" to American business.*

CHAPTER THREE

LENIN'S PATH

ON DECEMBER 4, 1921, ARMAND HAMMER RETURNED TO NEW York as the public face of his family's business. He dressed in noticeably better-cut suits, had grown a rakish mustache, and wore a diamond pin in his tie. And as if dress made the man, he behaved more confidently. He sought out journalists to brief them about his meeting with Lenin, a meeting he expanded with a bit of self-aggrandizing hyperbole.

Instead of joining the staff of Bellevue Hospital as he had been planning to do before he left for Moscow, he now plunged headfirst into the intrigue surrounding Russian trade. He not only had the opportunity to redeem the enterprise begun by his father before he was taken off to prison, but he also had a personal mandate from Lenin. Although he may not have had the ideological commitment his father did to communism, he had managed to achieve something unique for himself. He was the first American concessionaire in Russia. He took care not to identify himself with his father's politics or be associated with Communist causes. Instead, he made every effort to represent himself as a full-fledged capitalist dedicated to making money by opening up a Russian channel to American business.

Hammer proceeded with extreme caution in delivering money to Communist leaders in the United States. Even though the U.S. government now allowed most goods to be shipped to Russia, the government in Moscow was still considered an outlaw regime. Its instrument, the Comintern, was seen as actively sponsoring a program of subversion, and the U.S. Communist Party, which Julius Hammer and his associates had helped found, was still banned.

Hammer's most urgent problem was financing the delivery of wheat and other American products to Moscow. He also had to set up the bank catering to Russian émigrés that Boris Reinstein had outlined. To accomplish all this, he somehow had to raise money from American businessmen. On December 15, Hammer invited potential American backers of the bank to a private dinner at New York's swank Commodore Hotel. The surroundings provided an aura of prosperity that Hammer did not actually possess. He chose businessmen who could profit enormously from the opening up of Russian trade—such men as Sidney Klein, whose United States Food Products Corporation, a $100-million concern, was looking for new markets for its grain and other commodities; Julius Roten, whose Sonneborn and Sons was America's largest importer of oil; and Alan Hanson, whose giant Equity Steamship Company could benefit from shipping commodities. He also brought with him Jacob Schapiro, an extremely shrewd thirty-one-year-old lawyer, accountant, and moneylender who had already provided Hammer with some of the funds he needed.

Hammer insisted on secrecy at the outset. Even at the age of twenty-three, he had a flair for imparting drama to things. He passed Lenin's letter to him around the table. Although it merely stated that "you have my best wishes for the success of your first concession as it is of the utmost importance for the trade relations between our Republic and the United States," he told the assembled businessmen that Lenin had made clear to him in their private meeting that he recognized that communism was unworkable. The New Economic Policy, which Lenin had proclaimed in August with great fanfare, was only the first step in moving Russia back to a more conventional economy. Although Lenin could not yet state it publicly, Hammer continued, he wanted American capitalists to come to Russia and help run the Soviet economy. With a calculated measure of exaggeration, Hammer then told his audience of the "huge concessions" he had obtained and how his contract provided that they would be protected by Soviet troops. When one of the businessmen questioned him about the stability of the Soviet government, he replied, without missing a beat, that it was "stable enough to keep order."[1]

Hammer insisted that he had the necessary clout with Lenin, as his letter and concession demonstrated, to ensure that businesses he supported would get favorable treatment. "I thought I could use my connections and knowledge of the Russian market," he later reflected.[2] His final pitch to these businessmen was straightforward: if they put capital into the bank he was forming, he would see that they had an inside track in getting the products they wanted in and out of Russia.

The proposition intrigued a number of the participants so much that they held private meetings with Hammer over the course of the next week. Jacob Schapiro was especially interested in the franchise for the private bank that Moscow had offered Hammer. He instantly moved to get control of a defunct New York bank that had been owned by Portuguese businessmen and could serve as their "American bank." He succeeded, and on December 25, Hammer sent a telegram to Aron Scheinman in Moscow more or less summarizing the deal:

AN AMERICAN BANK CORPORATION WISHES TO OPEN AGENCIES IN MOSCOW, AND THEN KIEV, ODESSA AND MINSK, TO CARRY OUT AMERICAN MONEY TRANSFERS UNDER CONDITIONS TO BE APPROVED BY THE SOVIET GOVERNMENT. THE AMERICAN BANK WISHES TO OBTAIN THE CONCESSION FOR 6 MONTHS FOR TRANSFERS OF UP TO $100 APIECE. ALL SUCH AMERICAN TRANSFERS MUST BE CONTROLLED BY THIS BANK. THE AMERICAN BANK AGREES TO DEPOSIT $50,000 [WHICH WOULD BE] AT THE DISPOSAL OF THE RUSSIAN STATE BANK.[3]

The cable went on to explain that these dollar funds would be available to the Soviet National Bank "in any country." Meanwhile, the Russian citizens who were sent the money by their American benefactors would be paid in rubles at the discretion of Soviet authorities—if at all.[4] Copies of the cable went to Martens, Reinstein, and Lenin.

There were still details to be worked out in this scheme, such as other activities that Hammer's bank would engage in, but at the very minimum, as Hammer noted, "a source of American currency is created in this way." Finding a source of hard currency was no minor matter in Russia in 1921. Three months earlier, Lenin had advised Trotsky that "the wail about the lack of money is general. . . . We could very well blow up."[5] Now Hammer was promising to get money from Russian émigrés in America. Scheinman quickly approved the "concession" for this well-connected American bank.

The Cheka-controlled Special Concessions Committee also furnished Hammer with an extraordinary four-story headquarters at Kuznetsky Most 4 in downtown Moscow. The building had formerly housed the Fabergé workshops. The French jeweler Peter Carl Fabergé had established the workshops in the late nineteenth century, and they had produced an enormous array of jewels, toys, miniature boats, and jeweled enamel Easter eggs for the courts of czars Alexander III and Nicholas II. Then, during the revolution, they fell into Soviet hands. They were now being leased to Hammer's company for a token rent of twelve dollars a month.[6] A photograph of the headquarters shows nineteen Russian employees crammed around wooden desks, sorting through stacks of paperwork under a portrait of Lenin.

In New York, meanwhile, Harry Hammer was preparing the corporate structure for the new businesses. Harry's involvement in Allied Drug went back to 1915, when it was called Good Laboratories and its main business was selling saline laxatives, body lubricants, and skin creams to pharmacies in New York. By 1919, when he became vice president of the company, it was on the verge of bankruptcy, and his father, who still had his lucrative medical practice and was working with Martens, was able to buy out the 50 percent interest of his partner, Charles Fingerhood, for only $1,500 (which put a maximum value of $3,000 on the whole company). The company's subsequent involvement with Martens led Fingerhood to sue Harry and Julius Hammer for fraud on the grounds that money had been diverted for Soviet activities.

Whatever else the involvement with Martens accomplished, it did not alleviate the company's financial problems. By the time Harry Hammer received word that the Russian deal was working out, he had already liquidated Allied Drug. But since the concession contract had been signed in its name, he somehow had to resurrect the company. So in December in Delaware, he incorporated the Ural-

American Refining and Trading Company as a vehicle for the asbestos concession. But Armand, who had just returned from Russia,
objected to the name. It did not project the right image. He wanted
a name that sounded like Allied Drug (since the concession to the
nonexistent Allied Drug had already been announced) and did not
sound Russian or even foreign. So he incorporated another company, called the Allied American Corporation, which effectively replaced Allied Drug (although part of this new corporate entity, the
pharmaceuticals-distribution arm in the Bronx, continued to use the
name Allied Drug and Chemical). Hammer was corporate secretary;
his brother Harry was vice president and treasurer. In early January
1922, Allied American moved its import-export business to an expensive suite of offices at 165 Broadway, a location that would become the focus of espionage investigations for the next two decades.

J. EDGAR HOOVER PICKED UP HAMMER'S TRAIL AGAIN ON
November 4, 1921, after the Associated Press announced the Soviet
concession. Some initial confusion about the corporate sponsor—the
Associated Press mistakenly reported that it was the Allied Chemical
and Dye Corporation instead of Allied Drug—was soon resolved.
Hoover already had substantial intelligence that Allied Drug was
controlled and run by Martens from Moscow. He now labeled the
key dossier in the investigation "Armand Hammer: Allied Drug &
Chemical Corporation; Bolshevik Activities." The dossier grew
rapidly as federal agents received reports that Hammer, on his return
from Russia, "was carrying messages" from Ludwig Martens. They
also learned that Hammer was a "frequent visitor" to the offices of
the Society for Technical Aid to Soviet Russia at 110 West Fortieth
Street, which they believed represented Soviet intelligence interests in
New York and identified as "the headquarters of the Soviet outfit."
On Hoover's instructions, agents began questioning sources there
and elsewhere.

It turned out that one of Hammer's activities at 110 West Fortieth
Street was setting up an organization called the American Medical
Society for Aid of Soviet Russia to collect money for a medical facil-
ity in Moscow. Donations were to be piped through the bank he and
Jacob Schapiro were creating in New York. His associate in this ven-

ture was none other than David Dubrowsky, the former employee of both Allied Drug and the Russian Soviet Bureau who had preceded Hammer to Moscow. Dubrowsky had now been appointed head of the Soviet Russia Red Cross and was assumed by the State Department to be an employee of the Soviet government. The entire project appeared to be a cover for getting funds to the Soviets, as Dubrowsky himself later confirmed it was.[7]

Meanwhile, George J. Starr, Hoover's agent in New York, had received important information from London about the concession that had been so publicly awarded to Hammer: although it had been announced that Hammer's company had agreed to deposit $50,000 in gold with the Soviet National Bank, it had not yet delivered the money. Starr's report, which Hoover received on November 29, 1921, raised serious questions about the provenance of Hammer's financing. A check of Hammer's account at the Gotham National Bank showed that he had less than $100 when he left for Russia. His company was hardly in any better financial shape. This discrepancy raised the intriguing question: where would Hammer get $50,000 to pay a Moscow bank?

Hoover turned to the State Department, which had already put the Hammer brothers on its refusal list (so that they could not renew their passports). At that time, the State Department had primary responsibility for foreign intelligence.

The State Department's special agent in New York was W. B. Bannerman. In early December, he visited the offices of Allied Drug and Chemical, which were then still located at 2413 Third Avenue in the South Bronx. He found a hole-in-the-wall company with about thirty-five employees. The company's main business was manufacturing and selling "skin foods," as he called cosmetics. In questioning the employees, Bannerman established that Julius Hammer had put all the shares of the company in the names of his sons Armand and Harry the previous year but that they took "no active part in the management" of the company. The brothers usually did not even come to the offices. He learned that Allied Drug had been put in the hands of Henry Kuntz, a convicted felon and disbarred lawyer who so mismanaged it that it had gone bankrupt in all but name the previous May. Since then, management had been turned over to Alfred Van Horn, an experienced pharmaceutical executive, but the company was at best only marginally profitable. Indeed, Bannerman was told that Armand Hammer had never paid $50,000 to the Russians—at least, not out of corporate funds.

Hoover later received a clearer picture of Hammer's role from a source apparently well located in the Comintern hierarchy. In a report Hoover received in 1924, this mole, identified only by the code name Finger, said that Hammer had been given $75,000 in Moscow to pay underground Comintern agents in the United States. If Finger's information was accurate, it suggested that Hammer was an integral part of the apparatus through which the Kremlin intended to distribute money in the United States. But Hoover decided not to move against this "rotten bunch," as he noted in Hammer's file years later. In counterespionage work, it is often more profitable not to arrest a detected courier, especially if it is assumed that the known courier will be replaced by an unknown one. The State Department thus agreed to renew Hammer's passport, explaining in his file that doing so would provide opportunities to surreptitiously inspect the mail he was carrying. Hammer had become a watched man.

IN JANUARY 1922, HAMMER BOARDED A TRAIN FOR DETROIT. Again following in his father's footsteps, he was going to meet top executives of the Ford Motor Company.

Henry Ford was not only America's richest capitalist; he was also its most prominent anti-Semite. He had given wide vent to the conspiracy theory that "international Jews" were behind Lenin and the Bolshevik revolution and were attempting to profit from it. He had acquired and published as proof of this cabal the so-called *Protocols of the Elders of Zion,* a faked document originally circulated in czarist Russia, and a book entitled *The International Jew,* which blamed Jews for the world's troubles throughout history. But despite these views, Ford was more than willing to do business privately with Jewish financiers representing the Bolshevik government in Moscow.

Ford had demonstrated his pragmatic side in February 1919, when he was approached by Julius Hammer and Abraham Heller on behalf of the Russian Soviet Bureau. He had put immense resources into developing the Fordson, a horseless tractor that he was convinced would revolutionize agriculture in the way that the horseless car had revolutionized transportation. Russia provided a tempting test market for the Fordson, since most of the country's draft horses had been slaughtered during the civil war. So Ford had arranged for the representatives of the Russian Soviet Bureau to meet with Ernest Liebold, his personal secretary and factotum. He could count on Liebold to make sure the negotiations remained discreet. At that time, and up until 1921, the United States still maintained an embargo on shipping motor vehicles to the Soviet Union.

Liebold, who had been Ford's point man in publicizing the Elders of Zion plot, traveled to New York incognito, where he received messages from Ford in code. Ford clearly wanted an opening into Russia, but he also wanted a fig leaf for cover in case it came out that his products were being sent there. Julius Hammer and Abraham Heller had proposed that Ford's contract be placed with the Communist People's Industrial Trading Corporation, which was an arm of the Russian Soviet Bureau. But Liebold worked out a deal whereby Ford would sign a contract with a nominally private company in Petrograd called Ivan Stacheef and Company. In fact, Stacheef was merely a convenient front for the Russian Commissariat of Foreign Trade. Once Ford had entered into a two-year contract with the fictional company in March 1919, the actual business was then conducted with the Communist People's Industrial Trading Corporation in New York.[8]

At about this time Ford brought in Jacob Schapiro—the man who two years later would help Hammer orchestrate the bank for Soviet remittances—to reorganize the procedures of his international auditing department. Although Schapiro was a qualified accountant and lawyer, he seemed to be a curious choice, since Ford's policy excluded the hiring of Jews. But Henry Ford openly referred to Schapiro as "my kike," and gave him responsibility for auditing the secret exports to Russia.[9]

Schapiro, after leaving Ford in 1921, became involved in organizing Allied American. He was its lawyer, accountant, banker, and designated representative in New York, and he used his connections at Ford to make sure Armand Hammer was well received.

Although Hammer was by then more accustomed to conducting business at high levels, he was uneasy about the prospect of meeting Henry Ford, especially in light of Ford's reputation as an anti-Semite. Hammer was met at the railroad station in Detroit by one of Ford's executives and driven to Ford's newspaper office in Dearborn. After being interviewed there about his views on Russia, he was introduced to Ford.

Hammer found Ford to be down-to-earth in both his dress and his manner. He had finally perfected his Fordson tractor, and he took his visitor on a tour of the model farm he had built to demonstrate the effectiveness of mechanized farming. According to Hammer's account of the conversation, Ford asked him how many tractors they wanted.

"Millions," Hammer replied, using the pitchman's excess that was becoming natural to him.[10]

Hammer wanted Ford to replace the expired Ivan Stacheef contract—through which only 238 Ford vehicles had been delivered to Russia—with an Allied American contract. The U.S. embargo against direct trade had been ended, and there was no further need to operate by means of a cover. As part of Hammer's concession arrangement, Allied American had been named the exclusive "purchasing agent" for Ford-type vehicles, and so within two weeks of Hammer's visit to Dearborn, Ford appointed Allied American as its agent in Soviet Russia. He also agreed, in what was to become the first of a number of technology transfers by Ford, to train a group of Soviet automotive engineers in his Dearborn factory and send to Russia manuals, blueprints, and other technical data so equipment could be serviced there. Hammer sent Boris Mishell to Detroit to work out the delivery details.

Jacob Schapiro worked out the complex credit and financing arrangements. Once the contract with Ford was in place, Schapiro went to other companies that made attachments for the Fordson tractors and negotiated Allied American's representation of their products in Russia. Since Allied American had what amounted to a temporary monopoly on the U.S. end of Russia's foreign trade, he was able to exact a high "commission." For example, the Moline Plow Company agreed to pay Allied American one third of the sales price of the products it exported to Russia. By the end of 1923, similar deals were struck with thirty other U.S. companies.

To pay for these imports, the Soviets agreed to sell Russian furs, which were then heavily in demand, and other exportable items to U.S. companies, with Allied American acting as their sales office in

New York. Allied American would also get a commission on these sales.

This arrangement was not as profitable for the Hammers as it appeared. They had to return half the profit from the sale of the furs directly to the Soviet Commissariat of Foreign Trade and send another large part of the commissions they received to the Midland Bank in London for deposit in a special joint account, which, as British intelligence later determined, was under the control of Soviet intelligence.[11]

Armand Hammer was now deeply obligated to powerful men. On March 15, 1922, he sailed on the S.S. *Majestic* to London, where his firm had just opened an office on Moorgate Street, next to the complex called Soviet House, which housed both the Soviet trade delegation and Arcos, the Soviet import-export organization in Britain. Arcos was later described by Julius Hammer's former colleague Benjamin Gitlow as the principal conduit in 1922 for Soviet clandestine funds "destined for" the United States and Canada.[12] It was an organization that Hammer would do considerable business with and would cause him grave problems in the future. That March, he signed the documents necessary for opening the Midland Bank account and processing the money transfers, and he arranged for Arcos to act as a link in this chain. He then proceeded to Berlin.

IN THE SPRING OF 1922, BERLIN WAS IN TUMULT. IMPERIAL Germany had been dismantled three years earlier, and in its place was a weak and fragile republic buffeted by plots to seize power. The Treaty of Versailles had imposed on Germany onerous terms for reparations that the republic could not meet. The treaty had also demilitarized what remained of the country. The powerful German general staff was done away with, and the "army of peace" was prohibited from having any weaponry for offensive war—such as planes, artillery, ships, or chemical weapons. Its officer corps was limited to a maximum of four thousand men.

The general staff, which had served as the cockpit of power in Germany for more than a century, could not accept such a humiliating fate. Soon after the Versailles treaty was signed, General Hans von Seeckt, the chief of the general staff, placed his top officers in the "logistics command" of the Department of Defense, where they continued to operate as a hidden state within a state, the Black Reichswehr. Under the leadership of Seeckt, this covert general staff moved to counter the "poison" of the Treaty of Versailles by secretly rebuilding the army.

Since Soviet Russia was also a pariah state and not a party to the Versailles treaty, it was a natural ally for Germany. So in April 1922, Germany signed a nonaggression pact with the Soviets, the Treaty of Rapallo, which veiled a secret military arrangement through which, as Sir John Wheeler-Bennett notes in his study of the German general staff, "it would be possible to instruct German officers and men in those branches of military training and armament prohibited to Germany [and] to establish in Russia factories for aircraft and other type of military material for delivery to Germany."[13]

The deal was straightforward: the German general staff would secretly ship to Russia the materials, tools, and personnel with which it could manufacture everything from bombers to poison gas. These resources would then be used to secretly rearm and train the German army and air force. In return for permitting this evasion of the Versailles treaty, Russia would get from Germany the machine tools and other technology it needed to modernize the Red Army. Through this marriage of convenience, the Soviet Union built a large part of the German war machine that two decades later would overrun much of Russia.

The arrangement, code-named Operation Kama, required a high degree of cooperation between Soviet and German intelligence. Sondergruppe R, a secret unit of the German general staff created for the purpose of carrying out the technology transfer to Russia, formed a liaison with a unit of the Soviet military intelligence in Berlin to disguise the shipments. The main front for smuggling material and technicians from Germany into Russia was the Company for the Promotion of Industrial Enterprises, known by its German initials, GEFU. With inconspicuous offices in Berlin and Moscow staffed by officers of Sondergruppe R masquerading as executives, and with the considerable capital of 75 million marks (supplied by the German general staff), GEFU represented itself as a private corporation engaged in investing in Russia.

Soviet intelligence needed its own corporate fronts to cloak its dealings with GEFU and to use for acquiring from other companies in Europe the components for the clandestine rearmament. For this purpose, the Soviets evidently decided to widen the role of Allied American, which had the advantage of appearing to be an American-owned import-export company. Boris Reinstein had sent a note to Hammer in New York about this new development in Germany.[14]

When Hammer arrived in Berlin, his Soviet associates had already opened an office for him, staffed with German-speaking Russians. The office was on Lindenstrasse, two doors down from Westorg, the Soviet trade organization that most of Hammer's transactions would be processed through and that also served as the principal base for Soviet intelligence in western Europe. Westorg was then involved in buying from European companies the components necessary for building an air force in Russia, and Allied American's Berlin subsidiary had the task of arranging "joint ventures" with German firms.

Hammer was not inhibited by the armament prohibitions of the Versailles treaty. They presented an opportunity, and he did not hesitate to sign a joint-venture deal with the German firm of Soblatnik, which had already supplied a number of planes to Westorg. Soblatnik had been a major supplier of airplanes for the German army during World War I and was now developing new bombers under the guise of building civilian aircraft. Since it was illegal to test military technology in Germany, the equipment was transferred to Russia. The project, as outlined by Hammer, included "reconstruction of the airplane plants existing in Russia in order to assemble airplanes in the shortest time" and "the organization of an aviation school" to train pilots. It also called for sending to Russia the machine tools to produce airplane engines. The Soviet government would secretly participate in the joint venture and share the cost of the transfer, which was estimated to be 100 million marks (about $10 million).[15]

Hammer was more deeply involved in this scheme than any other businessman. He was flown to Moscow in a Soblatnik plane, and on April 11, along with Boris Reinstein and Heinz Zigert, the former inspector general of the Luftwaffe, he went to meet the man in charge of the Soviet side of the secret rearmament plan, Air Marshal Arkady Rozengoltz, then one of Lenin's most trusted aides. Rozengoltz had offices in both the Commissariat for Military Affairs and the Commissariat of Finance. According to notes of the meeting now in Russian archives, Soblatnik was ready to deliver the parts for fifteen planes immediately and would be able to produce several hundred aircraft in short order. The proposed site for Russian production of aircraft engines was the town of Fila, outside Moscow, where another German company, Junkers Aircraft, was already building a large aviation complex. Air Marshal Rozengoltz approved the plan.[16]

Almost overnight, Allied American had mushroomed into a multinational company with scores of employees. Aside from those in Moscow, New York, London, and Berlin, it had bustling offices in Riga, Kiev, and Petrograd.

THE ASBESTOS MINE IN THE URALS HAD NOT YET GONE INTO PRO- duction. Labor problems and a shortage of equipment had delayed its opening, and Hammer was having no better luck with his much-publicized offer of American wheat. The first shipment was only four thousand tons, a quarter of what he had promised the previous September to deliver. That was all he could afford to buy with the proceeds of the sale of Russian goods that had been sent to the United States in December. A further problem was that the Russian caviar contained chemical preservatives that were prohibited in the United States, and so the shipment had to be diverted to Canada, at a huge loss. Moreover, much of the rest of the goods turned out to be shoddy and brought a far lower price than had been expected. The whole enterprise proved so disappointing that later in 1922, Hammer's wheat contract was canceled by the Soviet government.

This shortfall did not discourage Lenin. He blamed it on a "blunder" by the Commissariat of Foreign Trade and insisted that "we must pay greater attention to the whole business."[17] He had stressed from the outset that the importance of Hammer's concession was largely symbolic—which meant, as he had suggested, it could even be "fictitious." If nothing else, the wheat deal had generated publicity and provided a useful (if untrue) humanitarian reason why Allied American had been granted exclusive trade monopolies in Russia.

Lenin had received from Hammer on his return to Russia a gift: a curious bronze sculpture of a monkey perched on a volume of Darwin's *On the Origin of Species*. The monkey is inspecting a human skull. The whimsy this expressed about the bourgeois theory of evolution—as opposed to Marx's dialectical theory of history—evidently amused Lenin, since he kept the bronze on his cluttered desk. Hammer also sent a letter signed by his father's Communist friends who were in prison in America. In his letter thanking Hammer for these items, Lenin again referred to him as Comrade Hammer. Hammer had, it appeared, carried out his missions in America and Germany.

While he was waiting for a further report on Hammer, Lenin instructed his secretaries to "make note of *Armand* Hammer and *in every way help* him on my behalf if he applies." Lenin also ordered Grigory Y. Zinoviev, the head of the Petrograd Soviet, to provide "Comrade Hammer" with special care and "issue orders at once to see that there is no red tape." He added that "reliable comrades," which usually referred euphemistically to Cheka, "should personally keep an eye on the progress and speed of all operations for this concession. This is of the utmost importance."[18] The man chosen to make the full assessment on Hammer was Boris Reinstein.

Reinstein's four-page report to Lenin showed that Hammer had already been deeply compromised by his secret activities over the previous nine months. The report began by warning Lenin that "this memorandum cannot fall into unreliable hands" because "if this copy falls into the hands of the American government it can have a fatal effect on the position of Comrade [Julius] Hammer which is already very difficult." He explained that Julius Hammer's activities in support of the Communist cause spanned more than a quarter of a century, and that on the recommendation of Ludwig Martens a contract had been concluded with the Hammers' company, Allied American, through which "our goods are sold in New York under its control." The "remaining profits from the sale [are remitted] to the Soviet government." Reinstein reported that although the wheat shipments had been delayed by unforeseen problems, the collaboration had achieved a number of successes.

Reinstein viewed Hammer's contract for asbestos mining as, if nothing else, an important enticement to get other foreigners to take concessions on favorable terms. He noted that "its conditions are sufficiently beneficial for us to wish that all future foreign concessions emulate it." In addition, he added, Hammer had purchased for the asbestos mine modern German mining equipment that Russia needed. Allied American had also received from Ford the "exclusive agency" to sell its cars, trucks, and tractors in Russia. And it was making similar arrangements with other American manufacturers. In Berlin, "Allied American entered into an agreement with the German firm Zatlantik," which was an offshoot of the Soblatnik venture. Its mission was, in collaboration with the Soviet air command, "the development here of an airplane business for civil and military purposes (including engines)."

Finally, Reinstein noted that Hammer had undertaken to help the Soviets acquire radio telephone technology from "the already developed organization of it in America." Hammer suggested that he could buy key pieces of this new technology in the United States, and he offered "to get, with the help of his father, at least part of the money necessary to solve this problem," which, Reinstein added, "is extremely important to us."

From the Soviet perspective, Hammer had opened up a route through which funds and technology were flowing into the Soviet Union and could be expanded in the future. Reinstein concluded that "it is clear from all the aforesaid that in the persons of Comrades Hammer and their Allied American Corporation we have a connection which is very valuable for us."[19]

Lenin evidently accepted this assessment. On May 24, he forwarded Reinstein's report to Joseph Stalin, the general secretary of the Central Committee of the Communist Party. In an accompanying message, he noted:

> On the strength of this information from Comrade Reinstein, I am giving both Armand *Hammer* and B. *Mishell* a special recommendation on my own behalf and request all [Politburo] members to give these persons and their enterprise *particular* support. This is a small path leading to the American "business" world, and this path should be made use of *in every way.*[20]

Lenin underlined the words *in every way,* and he called attention to how important he deemed the exploitation of this "path" by marking the letter to Stalin "Urgent" and "Secret." He also ordered Stalin to circulate his note to Zinoviev and all other members of the Politburo. It was Lenin's last message to Stalin before the stroke that incapacitated him for the next several months.

Stalin took the requisite steps to fulfill the plan to solidify the connection with Hammer. He instructed the organs, as the Cheka and other Soviet security services were referred to by the leadership, to investigate and report on his activities in Russia. Then, on June 2, at Stalin's behest, the full Politburo met and approved the plan to use Hammer as the Soviet-controlled "path" to the American business world. That same day, Hammer left Moscow. After brief stops in Berlin and Paris, he boarded the S.S. *Majestic.* When the ship arrived in New York on June 13, he scheduled an interview with *The New York Times* and announced with great fanfare the opening of his asbestos mine.[21]

The FBI noted Hammer's return to the United States, but not knowing about the arrangements that had been made in Moscow, it described him merely as a suspected Soviet courier.

Hammer brought back from Russia much more than the FBI suspected. He returned with an invaluable education. As Lenin's chosen first capitalist, he had learned a mode of business very different from that taught in the West. It was not based on the concepts of competition advocated by Adam Smith, according to which only the most efficient producer survives, nor was it even based on a free market. It was based on the Leninist concept that economic rewards proceed from the state. Rather than exposing businessmen to withering only-the-fittest-shall-survive competition, the state protects its concessionaires. The chief skill, therefore, is getting a concession from the government—and holding on to it.

HAMMER HAD JUST TURNED TWENTY-FOUR WHEN HE RETURNED to New York. He had missed celebrating his birthday with his family for the second year in a row, and he made plans to hold a belated party for himself at the Ansonia Hotel. But his business was setting too frenetic a pace. After he went to Sing Sing to see his father that June, he received an urgent telegram from Boris Mishell, telling him of serious problems at the asbestos mine. Another message from his office in Berlin advised him that he was needed there. He booked passage on the S.S. *Homeric,* which was scheduled to depart for London on July 1. This time, he had company on the voyage: his brothers, Harry and Victor.

Harry had always been the staid and dependable member of the family. When Armand was a young boy in the Bronx, Harry had used his pugilist's skills to defend him from bullies, and now he was to try to relieve the pressure on Armand by managing the London part of the business. This involved shuffling money back and forth among secret accounts controlled by the Soviets.

Victor was less serious than Harry and more lighthearted. He had always liked to dance, sing, and amuse people. When he was five years old, he had performed "Mary Had a Little Lamb" in different dialects as a vaudeville act. Victor had attended Colgate and Princeton but did not graduate. He had planned to study acting, but Armand persuaded him to go to Moscow instead and work for him as his personal assistant. Hammer had even enrolled him in a course in shorthand so he could take dictation. Victor agreed to go on condition that he could also study theater in Moscow.

The fraternal reunion aboard the S.S. *Homeric* in the summer of 1922 ended when the brothers reached England. Harry and Victor remained in London. Armand, appearing increasingly nervous and distracted, immediately boarded the night train for Berlin. From Berlin, Hammer went to Hamburg, where he met with German engineers, and then to Riga, where he dealt with customs officials who were delaying the shipment of imports he had contracted for, and then to Baku and Grozny to look into the possibility of an oil concession. He was debilitated by this constant travel, much of it on unsanitary trains.[22]

That October, there was another crisis. The workers at Hammer's asbestos concession, infuriated by the poor conditions in the mine, refused to work. Hammer visited the mine, but this only seemed to exacerbate the situation. Leo Wolff, the manager of the concession, carried a revolver to protect himself from angry employees. He told Hammer that his workers were so short of food rations that they were on the verge of rioting. Hammer also ascertained that vital machinery, spare parts, and food supplies for the mine that he had shipped months earlier had still not arrived. Dismayed and horrified, he called for the assistance of the Cheka, and by December the strike was suppressed and the other problems were temporarily alleviated.[23]

Hammer was enormously impressed by the cold-blooded efficiency of the Cheka and of its chief, Feliks Dzerzhinski. He later wrote approvingly about Dzerzhinski's personal intervention in railroad delays that same year. In considerable detail, he described an incident in which Dzerzhinski was on an inspection tour of the railroad in the

Urals and cabled the local administrative center at Omsk to dispatch a train to pick him up. When the train did not arrive promptly, he went to the center with a detachment of Cheka troops and ordered the chief administrator and his assistant to step forward. They did, and were both taken to a courtyard and shot as a "lesson." Hammer saw the "lesson" as evidence that the end justifies the means. He pointed out that after the two lax officials were summarily executed, the trains ran more efficiently.[24]

Hammer told a story about his own effort to resolve a transportation problem that is eerily similar to the one he told about Dzerzhinski. In this account, Hammer finds that several railroad cars carrying food supplies for his mine workers have been delayed at a siding by a station commandant who wants a bribe to release them. Instead of complying with this request, Hammer cables for assistance to the authorities in the nearby city of Sverdlovsk. He has with him a passport signed by a top Cheka official that works "like pressing a magic button." The Cheka acts within hours to release the train to Hammer, and "the station commandant was recalled at once to Sverdlovsk and after a brief inquiry was shot."[25]

Hammer may have exaggerated for dramatic effect his role in the execution of this official, but even so it is a telling exaggeration. Hammer no longer saw himself as the powerless and isolated young man kept cowering on a ship by a British official. Now he depicted himself as someone with awesome connections, someone to be feared rather than trifled with, and someone who, like Dzerzhinski himself, could destroy a petty official who abused him. It is a story he would tell over and over again, with slight variations, throughout his career.

When Hammer returned to Moscow later that December, he moved into the apartment of Boris Mishell. He told Mishell that the Russian winter was getting him down and that he needed companionship. Mishell's nineteen-year-old son, Joseph, was also living in the apartment. Hammer seemed to enjoy Joseph's company and, on one occasion soon after they met, took him to a Russian bath located near the Kremlin. Hammer called over a three-hundred-pound masseur to give Joseph a massage, and when Joseph, who did not speak Russian, asked Hammer to have the masseur ease up on the pounding, Hammer instead used the Russian word for *harder*. As Joseph's pain increased, Hammer laughed uproariously. It was the first and only time Joseph had seen Hammer laugh like that.

Hammer became increasingly tense and troubled that December, spending more and more time alone in his room. Then one day just before Christmas, he failed to emerge at all. At first, Boris Mishell assumed that his guest was suffering from a stomach illness, which was common in Moscow then. But as Hammer grew more remote and refused even to speak, Mishell feared he might be suffering from a nervous breakdown. In a panic, he called Victor Hammer, who had arrived in the city and just been accepted as a student at the Moscow Art Academic Theater. Victor rushed over and found that his brother suddenly seemed to have grown older and sadder. He tried with all his charm to cheer him up, but it did no good. For nearly a week, Hammer just gazed out the window at the heavy snowfall that was enveloping Moscow. He refused to see a doctor. Victor urgently wrote their father, as did Mishell.[26] A week went by, and then Hammer seemed to recover his composure. He said he had to make a business trip to Germany, and as if nothing had happened, he left for Berlin the next day.[27]

Armand Hammer was obviously under great pressure. His entire life had changed. Less than two years earlier, he had been a shy and withdrawn medical student. Now, he headed a company that had over one hundred employees in five countries. He had met and done business with two of the most powerful men in the world: Lenin and Ford. He had been taken on as a protégé by Boris Reinstein in the Comintern and had dealt with many of the top leaders of the Soviet Union. He had also undertaken obligations that he had not confided to anyone outside Russia except his father, obligations to facilitate the secret business of the Soviet regime. However he reckoned the consequences of this involvement, there was no escaping his obligations to the Kremlin. Nothing in his life had fully prepared him to carry out such immense and dark commitments.

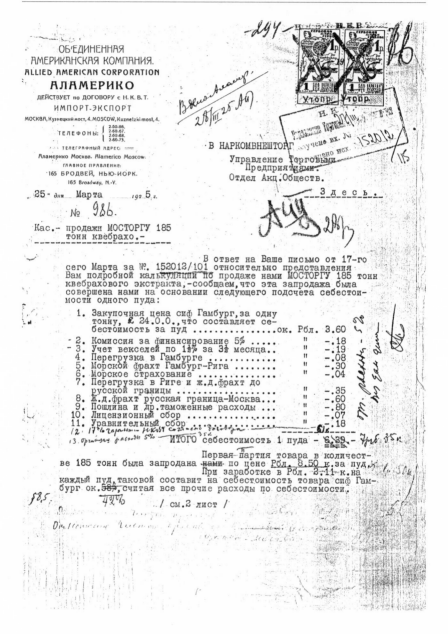

ОБ'ЕДИНЕННАЯ
АМЕРИКАНСКАЯ КОМПАНИЯ.
ALLIED AMERICAN CORPORATION
АЛАМЕРИКО
ДЕЙСТВУЕТ по ДОГОВОРУ с Н.К.В.Т.
ИМПОРТ-ЭКСПОРТ
МОСКВА, Кузнецкий мост, 4. MOSCOW, Kuznetzki most, 4.

ТЕЛЕФОНЫ: { 2-60-66.
2-60-67.
2-60-68.
2-60-73.

ТЕЛЕГРАФНЫЙ АДРЕС:
Аламерико Москва. Alamerico Moscow.
ГЛАВНОЕ ПРАВЛЕНИЕ:
165 БРОДВЕЙ, НЬЮ-ИОРК.
165 Broadway, N.-Y.

"25" дня Марта 192 5 г.

№ 986.

Кас.- продажи МОСТОРГУ 185
тонн квебрахо.-
_____

В НАРКОМВНЕШТОРГ
Управление Торговыми
Предприятиями
Отдел Акц.Обществ.

З д е с ь.

В ответ на Ваше письмо от 17-го
сего Марта за №. 152013/101 относительно представления
Вам подробной калькуляции по продаже нами МОСТОРГУ 185 тонн
квебрахового экстракта,-сообщаем,что эта запродажа была
совершена нами на основании следующего подсчета себестоимости одного пуда:

1. Закупочная цена сиф Гамбург,за одну
тонну, £ 24.0.0.,что составляет себестоимость за пуд ....ок. Рбл. 3.60

- 2. Комиссия за финансирование 5% ..... " -.18
- 3. Учет векселей по 11% за 3½ месяца.. " -.19
4. Перегрузка в Гамбурге .... " -.08
5. Морской фрахт Гамбург-Рига .... " -.30
6. Морское страхование .... " -.04
7. Перегрузка в Риге и ж.д.фрахт до
русской границы .... " -.35
8. Ж.д.фрахт русская граница-Москва... " -.60
9. Пошлина и др.таможенные расходы ... " -.80
10. Лицензионный сбор .... " -.07
11. Уравнительный сбор .... " -.18
_____
ИТОГО себестоимость 1 пуда - 7руб.35к.

Первая партия товара в количест-
ве 185 тонн была запродана нами по цене Рбл. 8.50 к.за пуд.
При заработке в Рбл. 2.11.к.на
каждый пуд,таковой составит на себестоимость товара сиф Гамбург ок.58%,считая все прочие расходы по себестоимости.

/ см.2 лист /

_In the 1920s, an import-export business, the Allied American Corporation,
was set up by the Hammers as a conduit between the Soviet Union
and the United States._

CHAPTER FOUR

THE PRODIGAL FATHER'S RETURN

THE LETTERS THAT JULIUS HAMMER RECEIVED FROM HIS SON VICtor and Boris Mishell in December 1922 were worrying. Julius realized, from the symptoms they described, that Armand had probably suffered a nervous breakdown.[1] Although he seemed to be recovering, he was in need of his father's help. Julius had to get out of Sing Sing.

Julius Hammer still had a minimum of nearly one year to serve on his sentence, but he devised a brazen strategy to expedite an early release. Using all his influence and connections, he made the case that his return to Moscow was necessary to maintain the sales of American-made products overseas and that his release was therefore in the national interest. He wrote in a letter to his parole board that Allied American was the authorized dealer for Ford Motor and other companies in Russia and that in his absence the responsibility for this business had fallen on his son Armand, who "was not equal to the concession, being only 24 years of age and a student all his life." He also cited Armand's breakdown. He added that unless he took over the business from his inexperienced son, it would collapse, and if that happened, other American exporters who used the services of Allied American would be in "jeopardy." He wrote a similar appeal to the U.S. Bureau of Foreign and Domestic Commerce, which was responsible for promoting American business abroad, noting that his company's activity in Russia "is bound to be of considerable benefit to the business interests of this country and the employment of large numbers of American workmen."[2] The strategy worked. He was released from prison on April 5, 1923, and given permission to go to Russia.

Julius's wife, Rose, had kept the rooms at the Ansonia Hotel on New York's Upper West Side during his confinement. While she packed up their belongings for the move to Moscow, Julius Hammer went to Detroit to see Henry Ford.

Again, Ford did not let his fervently espoused anti-Communism interfere with business. Even though Julius Hammer had been one of the founders of the Communist Party in the United States and was just out of prison, Ford had no compunction about meeting with him or allowing him and his sons to act as Ford's representatives in the Soviet Union. He had even granted Allied American six months' credit on vehicles delivered to Russia.

Julius Hammer now proposed to Ford that rather than export Fordson tractors he produce them in Russia with local labor. Julius Hammer stressed "the growing stability of the present Russian regime" and his own connections to it. He told Ford he was going to Moscow and offered to help set up such a plant.

Ford was evidently interested in the idea. He mentioned that his company was "developing plans" for the construction of factories in every country in which it planned to sell tractors, and Russia was an obvious candidate for such a factory.[3]

Julius and Rose Hammer left for Russia, by way of France, Germany, and Latvia, in mid-April. They arrived in Moscow in time for the Bolshevik celebration of May Day.

RUSSIA, IN THE SPRING OF 1923, WAS EMERGING FROM—OR AT least seeing a ray of light at the end of—a bleak tunnel. The devastating famine, which Armand Hammer had witnessed nearly two years earlier on his trip to the Urals, had been followed by a bountiful harvest. For the first time in years, there was no rationing of bread or meat. Foreign goods were again appearing in stores. In just two years, Lenin's New Economic Policy had dramatically revitalized commerce. By 1923, over four fifths of all retail trade was in private hands. Entrepreneurs and speculators, known as NEP men, made and spent fortunes with ease.

Julius Hammer did not discover the utopia that Lenin had promised, but he was optimistic. "I found Russia to exceed all my expectations," he wrote to Henry Ford in June. "Reconstruction is going ahead at a more rapid rate than in any other country I visited in Europe, such as Germany, France, Poland, and the Baltic States." He added, "Living is most interesting here with Arts maintaining their excellent standards." He was, along with his family, living in considerable comfort. Deemed a Communist "martyr" by Lenin because of his American ordeal, Julius Hammer had been provided with a palatial thirty-room mansion in the heart of Moscow known as Brown House. It had been built in czarist times by a textile millionaire and was leased to the Hammers for a nominal sum.

A 1924 photograph shows Armand entertaining four members of the American Relief Administration with drinks and cigars in a dark, baroque room. The walls are cluttered with rifles and escutcheons, and the table is draped with an oversize cloth. The Hammers soon made Brown House an oasis of luxury in an otherwise drab city. It was described a few years later by a guest, Eugene Lyons:

> The house was excessively ornate within, and without, its doors reinforced with elaborate grillwork, its stone facade tortured with sculptured decoration, and its broad inner stairway of gleaming marble spiraling magically to the upper story. The place was filled with rococo statuary and paintings and reindeer heads looked down in astonishment from the vestibule wall. The generous proportions of all the rooms, especially the immense high-ceiling ballroom, represented heady freedom.[4]

Armand had his own apartment there, and back among his family he was restored to health. His brother Victor, now twenty-two, also lived in Brown House while he continued his acting studies. Despite the brothers' very different approaches to life, "Armand doted on him," a Moscow friend of Victor's recalled many years later. "Armand would light up whenever he was in Victor's presence." Only the oldest son, Harry, who was now supervising Allied American's operations in London and New York, remained apart from the family. Rose Hammer ran the household with the help of eight servants and two chauffeurs.

The Hammer family also had its own Russian teacher, Luba Elianoff, an attractive eighteen-year-old student who spoke fluent English, Russian, and Hebrew. She had befriended Victor at his acting school, and she came to Brown House two or three times a week in 1923 to tutor Armand, who still had only a rudimentary grasp of Russian. He often dined while she coached him, and she was struck by his crude table manners, especially his practice of using his hands rather than silverware. She found him to be an extraordinarily closed person. His deep-set eyes were always wary, and his facial expressions were both controlled and controlling. He would end a discussion by simply sealing his lips. His steely mien was so in contrast to Victor's cherubic openness that she wondered how two brothers only three years apart in age could have developed so differently.[5]

Julius Hammer began entertaining on a grand scale in Brown House in the summer of 1923. That August 4, he hosted a lunch there for the U.S. congressional delegation to Russia, which included Senator William H. King of Utah, Senator Edwin F. Ladd of North Dakota, and Representative James A. Frear of Wisconsin. They had come to Moscow to consider renewing economic relations with the Soviet regime, and Julius Hammer arranged for a dozen important Soviet officials to be at his house, including the president of the Soviet Commercial Bank and the head of the short-lived Moscow stock exchange. They had a sumptuous meal that lasted nearly three hours. A photograph taken in his garden that afternoon shows Julius Hammer in the center of the group, with Armand standing off to one side in the back row. The American delegates were impressed by Julius Hammer's hospitality—and favorably reported on the trip to Congress.

Brown House soon became an unofficial embassy for visiting U.S. congressmen, businessmen, foreign diplomats, and other VIPs. Over the next five years, its visitors included H. G. Wells, John Dewey, Douglas Fairbanks, Mary Pickford, Gene Tunney, and Will Rogers. Armand Hammer made a point of inviting prominent people—even if they were complete strangers. For example, when the artist Al Hirschfeld visited Moscow, he heard from friends about the Hammers' hospitality and, after looking up the phone number of Brown House, called it. Armand Hammer answered the phone and, though he did not know Hirschfeld, invited him over. "We're having a party and you probably know some of the people," he said. Hammer then sent a car for him. When Hirschfeld arrived, he found that the guests included *New York Times* correspondent Walter Duranty, the Russian-born American journalist Eugene Lyons, and a Russian opera singer.[6]

The only foreigners conspicuously absent from these dinners were Julius Hammer's old comrades in the U.S. Communist Party who came to Moscow to attend party congresses. When Benjamin Gitlow and others in the American delegation called on Hammer, they found him cold and abrupt. Only a few years before in New York, Julius had bailed Gitlow out of prison, and later they were fellow inmates in Sing Sing. Why was Julius being so distant now? Jay Lovestone, another member of the Communist delegation, later supplied a possible explanation. The Soviets did not want raids on the Communist Party apparatus in Western countries to expose their espionage operations. A fire wall was needed between Soviet intelligence operatives and national Communist Party officials. From hints that Julius Hammer had previously given him, Lovestone strongly suspected that Hammer was involved with the OGPU, the secret police organization that succeeded the Cheka, although Lovestone did not know in what capacity he served. He therefore did not take personally Julius Hammer's sudden coldness to his former comrades. He assumed it was part of the Soviet effort to build its fire wall.[7]

JULIUS HAMMER WASTED NO TIME ESTABLISHING HIMSELF AS THE head of Allied American. Up until his return from prison, Boris Mishell had served as the company's Russian-speaking general manager. Mishell had shown himself to be a competent and likable businessman, and he had offered Armand help and companionship during the time of his illness. Still, Mishell did not share Julius Hammer's Communist convictions,[8] and Julius knew that his Soviet colleagues were concerned about Mishell's knowledge of Allied American's rapidly expanding activities.[9] So Julius discharged him, telling him to return to the United States by the end of the year.

Julius Hammer also arranged that summer to dispose of what remained of Allied Drug's pharmaceutical business. Four years earlier, it had served as a useful veil for concealing, or at least distracting from, the company's embargo-running business with Soviet Russia. But now, with the blockade ended and Western nations scrambling to sign commercial accords with Russia, there was no reason not to emphasize the trading connections his company had with eastern Europe. So he sold the drug-distribution arm, which was only marginally profitable in any case, to Alfred Van Horn, the executive who had been running it since mid-1921.

The major problem Julius Hammer confronted was the highly publicized asbestos concession that Lenin had awarded to Allied Drug. His son had no experience in mining and had assumed it to be a boon. Lenin had of course stressed its political, not its economic, significance—and he turned out to be right. When Julius Hammer arrived in Alapayevsk in July to see the mine, he realized that the concession was a financial disaster. With its high production costs, the mine lost money on every pound of asbestos it produced. It was covered with thousands of tons of debris that had been excavated in czarist times. Although this "garbage" contained no recoverable asbestos, it had to be removed by workers before they could reach the asbestos ore. In practice, some fifty tons of garbage had to be mined for every ton of asbestos.

Moreover, the conditions under which the miners worked were horrendous even by Russia's low standards, and there were frequent work stoppages. The underground tunnels did not have even rudimentary air shafts. Also, there were no trucks, or even horses, to cart the rocks to the railroad sidings. The carting had to be done by the workers. Armand had used the harshest methods available to get the mine working, but it still failed to meet the production quota specified in the contract and was losing $20,000 a month. Aside from these losses, the company was liable for local taxes that were based on the annual tonnage extracted, not on profits.

Julius Hammer could not simply close the mine. The five-year contract Armand had hastily signed obligated their company to make costly improvements, and Allied American had already ordered $164,000 worth of mining equipment on credit in Germany. The debt was to be paid by asbestos exports, but in fact the European asbestos market was glutted. Indeed, by 1923 the price of asbestos had fallen so low that it was not worth transporting the stuff to foreign markets.[10]

Julius Hammer realized that it was only a matter of months before the asbestos mine bankrupted Allied American—and the Hammer

family. But he was not without leverage. The Soviets, who were offering concessions to hundreds of other foreign corporations, clearly
had an interest in preventing the collapse of this model venture.
Lenin, moreover, had associated his own name with it by meeting
with Armand.

Although Lenin had suffered a third stroke and was gravely ill,
Julius Hammer still had influence with Ludwig Martens and Boris
Reinstein, who now had powerful positions in the international labor
agency, the so-called Profintern. He petitioned them and other Soviet
officials for relief.[11] After a flurry of correspondence, the Soviets relented and amended Allied American's contract so that the Hammers
could first stem their hemorrhaging losses on asbestos and then slip out
of the concession without attracting any foreign notice. Their mounting debt would be partially transferred to a face-saving import-export
contract with the government's Foreign Trade Monopoly Department.

Under this new arrangement, Allied American would temporarily
remain the channel through which American companies would send
vehicles, agricultural machinery, and other industrial equipment to the
Soviet Union, but all the actual money and paperwork would be handled by Soviet officials. Government agencies would pay for the imported goods with proceeds from the export of Russian goods. Allied
American would get a fixed percentage of the profits. The Soviets
wasted no time in portraying this concession—as they had the asbestos
concession—as a prime example of how foreign companies could now
freely operate in the Soviet Union. A story in *The New York Times* in
July 1923 concluded that "the real importance of this contract to
American business men is that it forms a precedent for the independent
activity of Americans in Russia without interference or control on the
part of the Soviet organization."[12] In fact, the contract contained
clauses that placed Allied American firmly under the control of its
Soviet-appointed directors. All the company's decisions were subject to
approval by the Soviet Commissariat of Foreign Trade.[13]

ON JANUARY 21, 1924, LENIN DIED OF A MASSIVE STROKE AT THE
age of fifty-three. While his revolutionary disciples—Trotsky, Zinoviev, and Lev Borisovich Kamenev—vied for ideological supremacy
in the new collective leadership, real power had already begun to

gravitate to the hands of Joseph Stalin, the general secretary of the Central Committee of the Communist Party. Iosif Vissarionovich Dzhugashvili, the son of a Georgian shoemaker, had adopted the alias Stalin (which means "steel") some years after becoming a Marxist revolutionary. While Lenin had debated the intellectual basis of the revolution in Switzerland, Stalin robbed banks in Georgia and Russia to fund it. As party secretary, his focus and attention to detail were such that even before Lenin had his third stroke, Stalin had gained control of the Politburo and had placed his supporters in the key bureaus, or organs, that ran the machinery of the Soviet state and its intelligence services abroad. By June 1924, he moved to take full control of the Comintern even though, in theory, it was an international organization. Under Lenin, the Comintern had been cast as a vanguard of visionaries, drawn from dozens of nations, with a common goal: assisting the coming socialist revolution. Stalin indulged no such illusions. Under his regime, it was to be nothing more than a Soviet instrument.[14] Its members in the United States, Great Britain, Germany, France, and other countries would operate under the tight control of Soviet intelligence officers and be assigned such nonvisionary missions as organizing front groups, recruiting espionage agents and agents of influence, and providing material support for clandestine Soviet activities.

This changing of the guard in the Kremlin had serious implications for the Hammer family enterprise. The Cheka, which began as Lenin's committee for ferreting out counterrevolutionary enemies, had already been transformed into the ruthlessly efficient OGPU, the precursor of the modern KGB. It rapidly became a full-service espionage organization under the direction of the foreign intelligence chief, Meier Abramovich Trilisser, who also controlled the agents of the Comintern through its Verification Committee, which he conveniently headed. To professionalize his foreign intelligence gathering, Trilisser needed overseas bases that could provide his Russian agents with plausible cover for their activities. In countries where the Soviet Union had a diplomatically recognized embassy, such as France, this was no problem. The diplomatic mission could serve as a base and provide his agents with diplomatic accreditation. In countries where the Soviet Union had established quasi-official trade missions, such as Westorg in Germany and Arcos in Britain, these could provide temporary beachheads, at least until diplomatic recognition was achieved, and furnish his agents positions as trade officials. In the United States, however, the Soviet Union had neither an embassy nor a trade mission. Its attempt at establishing the Russian Soviet Bureau had failed during the 1919–1920 Red scare. Instead, it had consigned most of its commercial activities in the United States to Julius Hammer's Allied Drug. Now, with Hammer so publicly identified with the U.S. Communist Party and presumably still a target of an FBI investigation, his company could hardly be considered a secure foundation for building a Soviet intelligence base in the United States. Trilisser needed a safer vessel, a Soviet trade organization like the ones in London and Berlin.[15]

The Soviet commissariat of foreign trade was well disposed to ending the Hammers' U.S. franchise. From the beginning, officials there had misgivings about granting the Hammers such an exclusive agency. They described the Hammers' arrangements with Ford as "deleterious" and "damaging" to Soviet interests.[16] The commissariat inspectors who reviewed the Hammers' books found that they had been making "excessive profits," deducting large amounts for personal expenses, giving arbitrary discounts, and siphoning off money to "third persons."[17] They also saw that large sums of money were being suspiciously "lent" back and forth between accounts in New York controlled by the Hammer family.[18] They concluded, moreover, that a Soviet-owned trading company like Westorg could buy products from American manufacturers at lower prices. So in early 1924, the commissariat notified Julius Hammer that it would be terminating his concession.

This was a terrible blow. In 1923, Allied American had exported 624 Ford tractors and other vehicles to Russia. The tractors, along with plow attachments and spare parts, brought in revenues of $1.2 million. To pay Ford, the Russians had delivered goods of equal value, mostly fur pelts, to New York. But the commissions Hammer had received had either been paid out as expenses, returned as rebates to American manufacturers, or kicked back to Soviet-controlled organizations. The two deals Armand initiated while Julius was in prison, the showcase asbestos mine and the "humanitarian" wheat deal, had resulted in big losses. Julius had also transferred large sums to Berlin and Riga to finance the secret military aircraft project. And his son had borrowed heavily. According to his reckoning, if the Soviets pulled the plug on his concession, Julius stood to lose some $455,000, which would "totally bankrupt" him, his company, and his family. He had been personally bankrupt before, and his company had teetered on the edge of bankruptcy when he went to prison, but this time the bankruptcy that would inevitably result from the termination of his concession would do irreparable damage. Julius wrote to the Soviet official investigating his accounts that it "would deprive us of the opportunity to recover our investment," discredit the Hammer "name," and severely "damage the interests of the Soviet Union." He added bitterly, "We do not deserve such an approach since our capital of $455,000 went to cover losses connected with our operations for the USSR."[19]

Julius Hammer still had connections in the Kremlin. He turned for help to his old friend Boris Reinstein. Allied American had been Reinstein's project. Reinstein had taken Armand in hand in 1921 and recommended him to Lenin. He had backed Ludwig Martens's plan to give Armand the asbestos concession and the wheat exchange, both of which proved far more costly than anticipated. He had approved the diversions of money for such covert operations as the German aviation deal. Indeed, he had reported on them to Lenin and Stalin. So he knew that funds that appeared to be missing from the accounts of Allied American had not gone into the Hammers' pockets.

Reinstein sat in on the meetings of the Liquidation Committee that was charged with deciding the fate of Allied American. He recognized that Allied American no longer served the purpose it did in 1921 and that it would have to be replaced by the sort of government-owned organization that Trilisser needed in New York. But he argued that it would be better to preserve the illusion that the Hammers' concessions had succeeded. Why should the outside world know that projects that Lenin had attached his personal prestige to had gone bankrupt? The Hammers, moreover, were needed for other tasks. He thus helped broker the following compromise. The Hammers would immediately turn over their American operations to the designated successor organization, but their Moscow subsidiary, Alamerico (the contraction in Russian for Allied American), would continue to make import-export deals, selling what amounted to licenses for entry to the Soviet market. Over a limited period, Soviet authorities would even allow the Hammers to collect excessive fees, at least until the previous losses incurred on behalf of Soviet interests were repaid. The exact amount would be agreed upon by the Liquidation Committee. During this process, the Hammer firm would also be allowed to deal with Ford, though its transactions would be carefully controlled. Then Alamerico would quietly fade away.[20]

Julius Hammer accepted the decision. He had little choice in the matter. He insisted, as he later wrote, that the transition be handled quietly so that it "would not be used to create a lot of noise in the foreign press."[21]

In New York on May 27, 1924, sign painters changed the name on the door of suite 1707 at 165 Broadway from Allied American to Amtorg Trading Corporation. On paper, this company had been created by merging two Soviet shell companies in New York. In fact, it had, as if by magic, assumed the lease, the bank lines of credit, the employees, and the contracts of Allied American, including its import-export contract with the Soviet Commissariat of Foreign Trade. The new Russian-born chairman, Isaac Hoorgin, immediately informed Ford Motor that Amtorg would be handling its business with Russia. After this reorganization, Hammer continued to use Allied American as a corporate vehicle, but most of his remaining import-export business was done under the auspices of a newly incorporated Russian company, Alamerico, which had offices on Borodinsky Pereulok in central Moscow.

In Moscow, Julius Hammer went to Trotsky, who was still part of the ruling triumvirate. He had first known him as Lev Davidovich Bronstein when he had worked in New York City on the Socialist weekly *Novy Mir*. In January 1917, Trotsky had relentlessly pushed the left-wing faction to gain control of the entire Socialist Party, and Julius Hammer had faithfully followed his instructions, which resulted in Hammer's faction being expelled and then forming the Communist Party. Trotsky returned to Russia, where he engineered the coup in November 1917 that put Lenin in power. In 1924, he was still commissar for war—and one of the most powerful figures in the Soviet Union.

Julius Hammer now told Trotsky of the personal relationship he had with Henry Ford. He suggested that since he could represent himself as an American capitalist, he was in a better position than Amtorg to develop this potentially important alliance. To this end,

Julius Hammer asked Trotsky to authorize his continued contacts with Ford and to invite Ford's son to Moscow so he could be induced to build a tractor factory in Russia.

Trotsky approved this scheme. He told Julius Hammer that his son Armand could serve as the contact with Ford. He then wrote an "absolutely confidential" memorandum to Isaac Hoorgin's superior in the Commissariat of Foreign Trade, setting out the logic of continuing to use Armand Hammer to cultivate Ford:

> An American citizen, who makes deals in Russia, arrived in New York. This citizen, Hammer, is acquainted with Ford. He has the opportunity, speaking with Ford, to refer to his own experiences in the Soviet Union. Hoorgin should take hold of Hammer and use him as a scout and business propagandist since obviously every potential concessionaire would more readily believe an American-concessionaire capitalist—Hammer—than a Soviet official—Hoorgin.[22]

Shortly after Trotsky's secret dictate on Hammer, Isaac Hoorgin's body was found weighted down with chains in Lake George in upstate New York.[23] The game plan was now clearly established. Although Amtorg would be OGPU's principal base for Soviet espionage in the United States—and would remain so until the Soviet Union opened an embassy in Washington, D.C., in 1933—it was to work with Ford through Hammer.

While the Hammers succeeded in maneuvering to keep their company from forced insolvency, Armand assumed new and demanding responsibilities in Europe.

CHAPTER FIVE

THE LAUNDERER

THROUGHOUT MOST OF 1924 AND 1925, ARMAND HAMMER traveled across central Europe, tending to the secret side of what remained of the family business. If he could call any place a real residence, it was the Kaiserhof in Berlin, a hotel conveniently located near the Ostbahnhof, the main railroad station. He checked in and out of this bleak building almost weekly during this period.

Berlin was one of the main crossroads of commerce and intrigue in Europe. With its uninhibited cabarets, cosmopolitan restaurants, Expressionist art, and experimental films, it was also one of the most exciting cities in the world. But Armand Hammer's business required discretion, and many of those he dealt with in Berlin preferred not to call attention to their Soviet connection by being seen in public with him. Hammer had also to be careful to avoid contacts with any strangers that might, justifiably or not, arouse the suspicion of Soviet intelligence, which oversaw his business operations abroad. Thus, he kept to himself for much of the time. He would sometimes spend entire evenings sitting alone in coffeehouses. At times, this self-inflicted isolation put him in a "black mood," as he described it years later. When he was afraid that he would "go crazy" from the isolation, he would rent an entire nightclub just for himself and would pay the musicians to play his favorite songs while he bought magnums of

```
Have Hammer authorize New York office pay money sent Manley now

dead to Brodsky stop        Ruthenberg  15/XI




    Уполномочил ли(разрешил) Хаммер Нью-Йоркской конторе
выплачивать деньги посланные Манлею,теперь умершему Бродско-
му.Рутенберг.
```

The text of a Comintern telegram asking that Hammer arrange a clandes-
tine money transfer to a representative of the Communist Party in New
York, September 15, 1924. The telegram itself is now in the Comintern
Party Archives in Moscow.

champagne for the bar girls who danced with him. It was his way of "decompressing," he explained.[1]

From Berlin, Hammer traveled to Hamburg, Riga, Tallinn, Paris, and London. He slept on coaches on trans-European expresses, on ferries, in Baltic pensions, and at a bed-and-breakfast rooming house at 1 Duchess Street in London. He rarely stayed in any city, except Berlin, for more than two days in a row. He traveled to the Baltic states so often he acquired an Estonian passport.[2] This peripatetic existence was in keeping with the state of flux he had experienced most of his life. As a child, he had been moved first to his grandfather's house in lower Manhattan, then to his father's home in the Bronx, and then for five years to the home of a family in Connecticut. When his father went to prison, he moved into a rented apartment at 183 West Fourth Street in Greenwich Village. This was the only place that he could call his own home. It had a small bedroom, where he kept his medical-school books, a microscope, his stamp collection, and other treasured possessions, and it had a two-story-high living room with a grand piano, a balcony, and a skylight. But this home was now far away—in another world.

Hammer made his rounds, acting as a courier, a go-between, a negotiator, a salesman, a letter writer—providing whatever services his father needed. He was his father's facilitator, his representative, and his eyes. Much of Hammer's activity involved transferring money through surreptitious routes to Soviet agents in the United States. He would receive instructions from his father specifying the amount of money he was to pick up from a "friend," usually in Germany or the Baltic countries, and to whom it should be paid. After receiving this sum in cash, he would telegraph his New York office, instructing it to pay a similar sum to the designated party. Since these payments would be disguised as commercial payments for some notional commodity or services received by Allied American, they could not be traced to the Soviet Union. He would then deposit the cash he had collected in Allied American's bank account in London, where, through accounting legerdemain, it would be made to appear as the proceeds of various legitimate business commissions or commodity profits.

The precise workings of this money laundering were reflected in letters and telegrams to Comintern agents that were copiously recorded and filed in Moscow. Consider, for example, Julius Hammer's December 4, 1925, letter to Armand:

> I hope when this letter gets to Berlin, you will be there to receive it.
>
> A relative of Mr. Moness, the pharmacist from New York, visited me and told me that $6,400 should be received from their friend in Berlin. He is asking us to receive this money and send a telegram to our New York office so that this money would be given to Mr. Moness.
>
> Arrange this please. Expenses for the telegrams can be taken from that sum.
>
> Your loving father,
J. Hammer[3]

In New York, Harry Hammer, who had an office in Amtorg's suite at 165 Broadway, wrote a check from Allied American to Jacob Moness for $5,000—which was the balance due after the "telegram expense," or laundering fee, was deducted. Jacob Schapiro, who was both accountant and lawyer for Allied American, then further disguised this transaction on the corporate ledger, as he had done with previous payments to Moness, by making it appear as a business credit that Allied American had extended to Moness's company. So even if the item was investigated, it would appear to be nothing more than an unpaid debt that had proceeded from a commercial transaction.

The reason such lengths had to be taken to conceal the source of these funds was that Moness was not merely "the pharmacist from New York," as Julius Hammer had described him, or even the proprietor of an herbal-remedies business, as he appeared in Allied American's books. Born Jacob Monessowitz in Janowo, Russia, in 1885, he had become by 1923 one of the principal conduits through which the OGPU funded its agents in the United States and Britain.

Hammer was also a major launderer of money supplied to the Communist Party of the United States by the Comintern and by the labor agency known as the Profintern, which with the help of Boris Reinstein disbursed funds to Communist-run labor unions around the world. Coded communications in the Comintern archive between Moscow and Charles Ruthenberg, the national secretary of the

American Communist Party, illustrate the extent to which Armand and his father had become crucial parts of the Soviets' clandestine organization.[4] They had been, up until 1925, acting as conduits for funds for Ruthenberg and other Communist Party officials in New York, even though this activity was illegal and dangerous. The strain of carrying out these transactions became particularly evident in the spring and summer of 1925, when Allied American and its Russian subsidiary, Alamerico, were in crises. The OGPU, which was closely monitoring the situation, reported in September that Allied American's "financial situation . . . is still extremely tense," noting that its New York department was $29,819 in debt and that it had "no spare funds abroad."[5] During this period, the Communist Party desperately needed funds that Moscow had advanced to Allied American to keep the party newspaper, the *Daily Worker,* from going out of business. Since the Hammers—the cables often make no distinction between Armand and his father—had failed to deliver $7,000 of this money by the first week of June 1925, Ruthenberg urgently requested Moscow "to compel Hammer to pay this [sum] immediately."[6] When the Hammers had not come through with the money by July and owed even more, Ruthenberg, infuriated, dispatched another cable: "Hammer of Allied Trading Corporation now holding $16,000 of Party and Trade Union Education League money received from Comintern and Profintern." He urged that Hammer "be summoned before Comintern Secretariat" and disciplined.[7] Although $16,000 was a large sum of money in 1925 (roughly equivalent to $128,000 today), the Hammers were allowed to continue the laundering operation, and soon after this crisis the deliveries of cash became more routine. "We send you today through Berlin—Julius Hammer—the following sums" and then a list of what they were to be used for, is a typical message sent in code by Moscow to Ruthenberg.[8] For his part, Ruthenberg responded as if he were dealing with a banking service, making such requests as "Have Hammer authorize New York office pay money . . . to Brodsky," in reference to Joseph Brodsky, the party's attorney.[9]

The laundering activity provided Armand Hammer with valuable experience that would serve him long after Ruthenberg died in 1927.

· · ·

INTERNATIONAL ESPIONAGE REQUIRES MORE THAN AGENTS WHO steal government secrets and couriers who deliver them. They are merely cogs in a machine that must be kept running smoothly over extended periods of time. The vital lubricant is money—in particular, secret funds that can be drawn on without arousing suspicion. As they expanded their covert activities abroad in the late 1920s, the Soviets required a pipeline through which such money could be moved across borders without attracting suspicion. Allied American, which could claim to be an American company representing American businesses abroad, was well suited for this purpose. Its owners, the Hammers, had already cooperated in covertly disbursing Soviet funds through their subsidiaries in New York, Berlin, and London. The complex mechanism through which the Soviets arranged to get money into the pipeline at the Moscow end provided Hammer with a useful education in the malleability of international banking. The system worked as follows:

First, Soviet government trading organizations (Gostorgs) issued Hammer a "bill of exchange" with which to purchase a specified commodity abroad. The bill of exchange served as a government-backed guarantee that when the goods arrived, the Gostorg would pay the agreed-upon price.

Next, Hammer went to the Moscow branch of Lloyds Bank of London and offered the bill of exchange as collateral for a loan. Since it was guaranteed by the Soviet government, Lloyds Bank accepted it and through its London office lent Hammer's company the money it needed to buy the commodity in U.S. dollars, Swedish kroner, or British pounds.

Hammer then used some of this money to buy a portion of the commodity and diverted the balance to a "reserve account" in New York. This account was used, presumably at the direction of Soviet intelligence, to pay for various underground activities.

This chain of transactions of course left Hammer's business with a deficit, since less of the commodity than had been ordered was delivered to the Gostorg, and therefore only part of the money specified in the original bill of exchange was transferred to Lloyds Bank. The Soviets made up the shortfall by issuing Hammer another bill of exchange with which to buy another commodity.

Hammer's operation involved such huge sums of money that it was closely supervised by Genrikh Yagoda, who then headed the OGPU's powerful Economic Directorate. Yagoda, known for his ruthlessness, thoroughness, and close connections to Stalin, was then deputy chairman of the OGPU and would later head the entire Soviet intelligence apparatus. One of the concerns he addressed in the summer of 1925 was the possibility that the Hammer enterprise's borrowing might spiral out of control. In a "top secret" memorandum referring to the dissolution of Allied American, he explained that "since export-preparation operations are being passed to our state organs," the Hammers would receive no new contracts to purchase commodities for government organizations. So they would have no new "bills of exchange" with which to borrow new funds to pay existing loans and interest. According to "precise information," as Yagoda put it, the company owed banks abroad $1,719,798 at the official rate of exchange. Many of these debts were in foreign currencies—including £74,381, 8,115 Swiss francs, and 202,189 Swedish kroner. Yagoda further pointed out that the company did not itself have the funds abroad to meet these obligations, and unless Moscow intervened, it would result in the "undoubted financial insolvency of Hammer."[10]

In 1925, $1.7 million was a huge sum—the equivalent of approximately $13.6 million today—but the Hammers were not diverting this money for themselves. They could hardly take such a massive amount under the watchful eyes of the Economic Directorate, which as Yagoda's report shows, was tracking each kopeck going into and coming out of the Hammers' bank accounts. The report duly recorded the true amount spent on purchasing commodities, the inflated amount in the bills of exchange the Hammers borrowed against, and the step-by-step "combination" of banking transactions through which the excess was converted to hard currencies in London. In any case, the OGPU could not have missed the disbursements to the U.S. Communist Party, clandestine agents like Moness, or clandestine Soviet projects, such as the sub-rosa collaboration with Germany on rearmament, since all these activities came under its direct purview. Moreover, the financing of these intelligence operations was presumably authorized at the highest level. Thus, funds had to be juggled around in Moscow to pay off Lloyds and the other foreign banks.

Armand Hammer came under increasing pressure in the fall of 1925 to clean up the ledgers of Alamerico before the end of the year, when the company would be put out of business. The clock was running, Yagoda and his officers in the Economic Directorate were breathing down his neck, and the company's books were an accounting nightmare reflecting years of fictional entries and other legerdemain used to hide the money laundering. On top of all this, Hammer had to deal with the collapse of the Harju Bank in Estonia.

HAMMER HAD COME ACROSS THE HARJU BANK IN FEBRUARY 1924. It was then the fourth largest bank in the Republic of Estonia. Located in the port city of Tallinn, which, along with the port of Riga in Latvia, had served as a back door to Soviet Russia during the Allied blockade (1918–1922), the bank had profited handsomely from surreptitious Russian trade, and it had even put the Estonian ambassador to Moscow on its board of directors. But with the official reopening of Soviet ports to foreign trade, the boom fizzled, and to make matters worse, the bank lost huge sums of money in failed speculations and embezzlements. Under pressure from Estonian banking authorities, the owners put the Harju up for sale in January 1924. Within weeks, Hammer had arrived in Tallinn and approached the owners. Without any prolonged negotiations, he offered them their asking price of $250,000, of which one third would be paid immediately and the balance within a year. They accepted his terms, and after draining most of the remaining cash out of the bank by issuing themselves a dividend, they transferred control, in the form of 51 percent of the shares of Harju, to Hammer's company.

Although there was almost no capital left in the bank, Hammer had his own expedient means of improving Harju's balance sheet—bills of exchange. Just as he had done in London, he could deposit these pieces of paper, representing orders from Soviet Gostorgs to buy commodities, with the Harju Bank. Even though the Soviet agencies were not obliged to pay any money whatsoever to Harju until commodities were delivered, the bills of exchange created an instant asset on the bank's balance sheet. For example, if Hammer obtained a $10-million certificate of exchange from a Soviet Gostorg with which to buy butter and deposited it with the Harju Bank, the bank's assets would increase accordingly. And the bank could borrow on these new assets from the network of foreign-correspondent banks with which it was associated. So as long as his Soviet collaborators continued to supply him with credible-looking bills of exchange and other banks did not look too closely at Harju's books, Hammer could use the bank to generate new funds for the money laundry.

Hammer had acted with incredible speed and decisiveness in acquiring this bank. He did not act alone, however. As Soviet documents show, the plan was approved at every stage by Soviet authorities, and the purpose of the deal was to give the Soviet Union control over a bank in an independent country that would appear to be owned by American capitalists. The money used to purchase the bank came directly from the "reserve fund" in New York that was used to finance covert projects.[11]

That spring, Hammer transferred another $45,000 from New York to the Harju Bank and deposited with it a number of bills of exchange from Soviet Gostorgs. But before he could begin large-scale operations, serious leaks about his Soviet connections began to appear in the local press in Tallinn. He was described as "a great friend of Trotsky," and his company was reported to be a front for the Soviet government in the purchase of the bank. These stories came at an inopportune time. Throughout 1924, Estonian officials had been accusing Moscow of interfering in the independent country's internal affairs—a Soviet-backed putsch was actually attempted in December 1924—and anti-Soviet feelings were running at a fever pitch. The swirl of stories about Hammer's role as a cloak for Moscow became so persistent by mid-May that the U.S. Embassy in Riga, which was the main American listening post for the Baltic states, cabled Washington that the rumors might be realistic: "All informed people in Revel [Tallinn] believe that there is something far deeper than the ostensible butter shipments which the [Harju] bank proposes to finance." The suspicion was that "Moscow authorities might have advanced all or part of the money to purchase the bank to obtain a means of transferring funds abroad surreptitiously."[12]

Hammer knew that he had to discredit the reports that his company was controlled by the Soviets. He had learned three years earlier, when he announced his first Russian concession, that government officials, as well as journalists, were most easily satisfied by the most cynical explanation for commerce with the Communists: money. When he described himself as a capitalist who was doing business in Russia for profit, not for politics, he found a receptive

American audience—especially in the Department of Commerce, which was then encouraging other U.S. businessmen to seek out markets for exports in eastern Europe. So now he claimed that he had bought the Harju Bank as a business venture because he planned to move his export base from Latvia to Estonia. He took particular pains to brief the U.S. commercial attaché in Estonia, telling him that his company, Allied American, was American owned, American directed, and in the business of selling American products in Russia. Moreover, he protested that the allegation that his company had used Soviet funds for the acquisition of the Harju Bank was a libel being spread by a rival bank in Tallinn that feared having an American competitor in the banking business.

Although Hammer's version of the deal succeeded in persuading the U.S. Embassy to intercede in his behalf with Estonian banking authorities, his efforts to protect the bank were of little avail. The Estonian government, which evidently had its own intelligence sources, was not about to let a reputed Soviet front gain a foothold in its financial establishment, especially not in the midst of an escalating war of nerves with Moscow. In May 1925, the government ordered the Harju Bank, which had ceased to pay its bills, closed. By this time, Hammer had invested over $150,000 of Soviet funds in the bankrupt bank (including the down payment he had made to purchase it). Even with the help of a well-connected Tallinn lawyer, the money was almost all lost.

Hammer returned to Moscow in December 1925 for the legal burial of Allied American. It was imperative that the company's failure be kept secret. Confidence in the bills of exchange used as collateral in foreign banks would be undermined if it became known outside the Kremlin that Allied American was insolvent. And if the banks demanded payment, the entire debt-kiting scheme would fly apart. Hammer, along with his father, sternly warned Soviet authorities that any leak abroad about the liquidation of the company "will cause a panic among our holders of bills." They pointed out that such a panic, aside from ending their operation, would "reflect badly" on the credit of Soviet institutions (which, after all, had originally issued the bills of exchange).[13]

The real problem the Kremlin had was not sparing the Hammers the embarrassment of a bankruptcy but preserving their usefulness for laundering money for Soviet state organs. Even though their foreign trade concession had lapsed—and their Estonian bank had gone bankrupt—their subsidiaries in Berlin and London continued to funnel money to Comintern agents and shield the program to build German aircraft in Russia. Soviet intelligence had no reason to throw out the baby with the bathwater, but awarding the Hammers a new concession that could mask these activities was no longer an easy proposition. For one thing, the NEP had all but ended. With the opening of foreign markets to Soviet exports of raw materials and wheat, Stalin no longer needed foreign concessionaires to provide capital or technology. He could—and did—buy what he needed to modernize Russia. At the end of 1925, the Soviet Union was in the process of nationalizing existing foreign concessions, not awarding new ones. Moreover, most of the existing concessions had been given to foreign companies that had the ability to market Soviet raw materials—such as wood, emeralds, and iron ore—in the West. But now Soviet trade organizations, such as Amtorg in the United States, Arcos in Britain, and Westorg in Germany, had taken over this role. So if the Hammers were to be given a new concession, it could not be one to market Soviet raw materials abroad. The proposed solution was to give the Hammers a manufacturing operation in Russia that could sell some of its finished product overseas (and thereby allow the Hammers to transfer the money abroad needed for other purposes). The enterprise suggested was pencil manufacturing.

SOVIET BUREAUCRATS WERE UNDERSTANDABLY CONFUSED BY THE proposal to give the Hammers a franchise to manufacture pencils in Moscow. There was a flurry of memorandums pointing out why it made little economic sense. The Hammers had no familiarity with pencil making, no equipment, no foreign connections with pencil distributors, and no manufacturing experience in Russia. Their previous Soviet ventures—the asbestos mine, the wheat exchange, the import-export franchise, and the Harju Bank—had all got into trouble, and their ability to raise money or get credit from Western banks was now problematic. One official, questioning the Hammers' qualifications, pointed out that it would be clearly more advantageous to negotiate a joint-venture agreement with an established British,

German, or American pencil-manufacturing concern that had the necessary equipment, experience, and marketing skills.[14]

Others might be able to make pencils more efficiently than Armand Hammer, but political considerations outweighed economic ones. Soviet intelligence needed Hammer to distribute funds to its operatives. That it was willing to override objections and peremptorily award the Hammers the pencil-making concession demonstrated the value of the Hammers' laundry.

In January 1926, out of the debris of Allied American rose phoenixlike a new corporate vehicle: the American Industrial Concession. Its main asset was a ten-year agreement with the Soviet government to manufacture pencils in Russia. Its offices, personnel, and branches in Berlin and London were, for the most part, the same as its corporate predecessor's. It was owned by A. Hammer and Company, which had been incorporated in New York. The company's shares, like the shares in Allied Drug and Allied American, were owned equally by Armand and Harry Hammer.

CHAPTER SIX

THE PENCIL MAKER

"RUSSIA IS ROMANCE," ARMAND HAMMER WROTE IN THE EARLY thirties.[1] But during his first four years in Russia, he had little opportunity to indulge in romance of the personal kind. At twenty-seven, he was not an unpleasant-looking man. He stood tall. He had a dark brow, a large jaw, and an intriguing smile. He was well groomed and wore expensive three-piece suits. He moved with visible energy. Yet there was a hardness in his face that made him seem far older than his years.[2]

Armand invited no friends to his birthday dinner at Brown House in May 1925, except for his Russian teacher, Luba Elianoff, who was by then a member of the household. But when Victor arrived that evening, he brought with him a surprise—Vavara Sumski, a stunningly beautiful twenty-two-year-old theater student who earned her living singing Gypsy songs at a Moscow cabaret. He called her, with a beaming smile, his fiancée. Hammer paid little heed to Victor's announcement that night—he rarely took his brother's enthusiasms seriously—but three weeks later Victor and Vava were married.

Hammer seemed taken aback by this. He did not even attend the ceremony. And after Victor departed on his honeymoon, Hammer decided to go on a vacation in the resort town of Yalta in the Crimea. It was his first real vacation since before he entered medical

Armand Hammer, at right, with his first wife, Olga, and his brother Harry.

school. On his first night there, in a nightclub, he met Olga Vadina. She was onstage singing Gypsy ballads.

Olga was a young, delicately beautiful blonde with a sensuous voice. Hammer recalled later that he felt as if he had been struck by a bolt of lightning. "She knocked me out." Afterward, he went backstage and invited Olga to have dinner with him. At the restaurant, he learned that she was of German and Polish ancestry and also used the name von Root. By the time dinner was finished, she showed herself to be open to his interest in her but acknowledged that she was married. Her husband was her manager, and it was evidently not a happy arrangement.[3]

Hammer explained many years later that he wanted to help Olga escape her unhappy situation and that his feelings proceeded in part from a previous failure. He had once been infatuated with a young Irish American divorcée named Marjorie. She had tuberculosis, and he wanted to provide her with medical treatment, but she died before he could do so. Having lost Marjorie, he was determined to rescue Olga.[4] Within days of their meeting, he asked her to divorce her Russian manager and leave with him for Moscow. A divorce in Russia required only a declaration by the woman, and Olga accepted his offer.

Armand and Olga began living together in Brown House, where Victor and Vava were also ensconced. The similarities between the two women were striking. Both were in their early twenties; both were divorcées; both were sexy cabaret singers. It was almost as if Hammer had been trying to trump his brother's success—or at least match it.[5]

Initially, Hammer treated Olga like a trophy he had been awarded by fate. When they went to embassy receptions, he introduced her as the Baroness von Root. He made her the center of attention at dinners at Brown House, gathering his guests in the salon to listen to her sing Gypsy songs. He neglected his business and spent hours accompanying Olga around Moscow in a car, visiting her favorite shops and dressmakers. He insisted on selecting her wardrobe and had a furrier make her a hooded sable coat. He bought her two dogs, a blue-gray chow and a white poodle, that they took for walks around Red Square. When she suggested in January 1926 that they needed a separate residence, he rented a house surrounded by a high wall and a garden only a few blocks from Brown House. He called it their "love nest." But that spring, the relationship began showing signs of strain. Hammer resumed his business trips abroad, leaving Olga behind for weeks at a time. During these interludes, Olga made the rounds of Moscow's nightclubs, often escorted by a piano player whom she had known before she met Hammer. She enjoyed drinking and staying out all night, and she did not seem at all inhibited by the gossip her outings provoked.

Olga's brother-in-law had been arrested for bribery that spring. He was working for a Gostorg that imported goods from abroad, and when the police searched his house, they turned up large sums of foreign currency, the source of which he could not explain. For a while, it appeared that Olga might be involved, and Hammer worried that he might be drawn into the affair. He moved back into Brown House, alone.[6]

In the winter of 1927, Victor announced that he was about to be a father—Vava was pregnant. Armand now decided that he too wanted a child. Though Olga had caused him embarrassment, she was still the only woman in his life, and he approached her with a straightforward proposition. He would marry her if she bore him a child. This was not immediately possible, however. Years earlier, she had had her fallopian tubes blocked. Hammer insisted that the operation could be undone, and she agreed to see a specialist in Switzerland and then other specialists in Germany.

While Olga was traveling from surgeon to surgeon that July, Vava gave birth to a son in Moscow. Armand asked Victor to name the boy after him, and although in eastern European Jewish families children are not ordinarily named after a living relative, he agreed. Victor named the boy Armand Victorevich Hammer. Now there were two Armand Hammers in Russia.[7]

Armand had put Victor to work in his pencil factory, not as an executive but as a manual worker. Victor's Russian friends were shocked to find that the young man they knew as an actor and entertainer was working at a wood-shaving lathe from 8:00 A.M. to 8:00 P.M. six days a week. Armand explained that he needed someone to set the pace for the other workers; if his brother could produce, for example, one thousand pencils a day, the other workers could be expected to do the same. The long and fatiguing work shift played havoc with Victor's life, however, and his wife took a lover. When his mother found out about this, she insisted, with Armand's encouragement, that Victor and Vava separate. Vava moved out of Brown House, taking little Armand, then a year old, with her. The senior Armand insisted that Victor return to New York. Victor would not see his son again—his only child—for three decades.

While this drama was unfolding, Olga succeeded in getting pregnant. Although Armand suspected that he was not the father of the child—a suspicion he retained for nearly sixty years—he went through with his promise to marry her. On May 7, 1929, Olga gave birth to Julian Armand Hammer. Hammer now had the heir he had wanted.[8]

HAMMER'S PENCIL BUSINESS WAS A UNIQUE ENTERPRISE IN STALIN'S Soviet state: it was the only foreign-owned manufacturer of products for the domestic and foreign markets. In the previous import-export deals, Hammer's government concession involved an exclusive franchise for a product. Hammer simply had to buy or sell it abroad and deduct a percentage of the price as his share. This concession was different. He had to manufacture a product from scratch. Although pencils are relatively simple devices—graphite embedded in wood—mass-producing them required machinery and experienced labor that Communist Russia did not possess in 1925. Acquiring the machinery was no minor undertaking. Germany had supplied Russia with military technology, but it carefully guarded its near monopoly on pencil technology. Most of its pencil making was done in and around the medieval city of Nuremberg, which had local laws prohibiting foreign businesses from hiring workers who possessed trade secrets.

Hammer realized that he could get around these restrictions by using the corporate fronts he had set up in Berlin years earlier for shipping German aviation components to Russia. He also still had bank lines of credit guaranteed by Soviet trade organizations. So he bought precision tools and other equipment on the pretext that they were part of the ongoing clandestine German-Soviet rearmament effort. Getting German engineering personnel who could reconfigure the machinery to make pencils required a more sensitive operation, but with the help of the Soviet Embassy in Berlin he succeeded in both recruiting the German engineers and arranging false travel documents for them. In late 1925, they departed Nuremberg one by one for what their documents represented as a "holiday" in Finland. They then proceeded to Moscow.

Hammer's brain drain was successful. He settled the German workers in an abandoned soap-making complex on the outskirts of Moscow, which he described as "a regular little city." It had steam-heated cottages, a commissary, a clubhouse, a school, and a medical center. The Germans had no problem assembling a pencil-manufacturing factory from the equipment. Nor was Russian labor a problem, since the state labor exchange provided some four hundred Russian workers, who were paid a low piece-work rate for each gross of pencils they turned out. As for raw materials, the Soviet government had given Hammer temporary access to its scarce reserve of foreign currencies and permitted him to exchange rubles for them at an artificially low rate. He used this hard currency to import the wood and graphite he needed. By May 1926, five months after receiving the assignment, the A. Hammer–American Industrial Concession was in full production.

It was an extraordinary accomplishment. Though Hammer had not yet turned twenty-eight and was operating in a Communist country, he had created an industrial enterprise that in the best capitalist tradition exploited government-granted privileges. He had demonstrated that he could manage a complex and large-scale business.

Hammer had no problem selling the pencils, since Soviet state agencies needed an almost unlimited supply of writing implements for their bureaucrats. A single government agency representing cooperatives, Centrosuyus, took 45 percent of the factory's total production, and Yagoda's dreaded OGPU was also a major customer.[9] Hammer claimed, with his characteristic hyperbole, that he was manufacturing 180 million pencils a year by 1928. Actually, according to his audited records, he produced only one quarter of that number. Still, his factory was the largest pencil maker in Russia, and he was, at least briefly, the country's undisputed pencil king.

The pencil-making factory, which quickly added pens and other writing instruments to its line, appeared to be Hammer's first clear-cut business success. If quantity was a measure of success, he had proved doubting Soviet bureaucrats wrong. His abandoned soap factory was a going concern with a permanent market for its products.

*Armand Hammer (at right) with his mother, Rose,
and his older brother, Harry.*

In 1921, the building that had formerly housed the Fabergé workshops became the headquarters of the Hammer family business in Moscow. A portrait of Lenin, who had given his imprimatur to the enterprise, hung over the workers at their desks.

A pencil-manufacturing business based in Moscow was created in 1926, when Hammer's previous business failed. The Soviets shored up the Hammer enterprises because they were useful for laundering money to the Comintern.

HIGH GRADE PENCIL MANUFACTURERS

Telephone:
HOLBORN
7001-2-3

Telegrams:
OMNYGRAPH, HOLB
LONDON

HAMMER HOUSE

246, HIGH HOLBORN

LONDON, W.C.1

A · HAMMER LTD

Hammer met his first wife, Olga, in a nightclub in Yalta in 1925.
Their son, Julian, was born four years later.

*Armand Hammer, at right, with his wife, Olga, and his father, Julius,
in the early 1930s. Hammer had returned to the United States from the Soviet Union
in 1931 to set up a business selling the so-called Romanoff Treasure.*

Armand Hammer, left, with his two brothers, Victor and Harry, in the early 1940s.

August 13, 1957

THE DIRECTOR:

b7c

Attached is the summary which you wanted on Dr. Armand Hammer.

You may recall that the night we had the dinner for George Murphy back in 1951, Fulton Lewis brought Victor Hammer and his wife to our home. They had been spending the weekend with Fulton. Fulton and Victor are great friends. Fulton is also friendly disposed to Armand.

Respectfully,

L. B. NICHOLS

Enclosure
LBN:jmr
(2)

It looks to me as if these Hammers are no good.

RECORDED - 34 61-280-190

21 AUG 21 1957

EX-132

SENT DIRECTOR
8/13/57

J. Edgar Hoover became interested in the Hammers in 1921 and tracked their movements for decades. In the late 1950s he made a typical annotation on an internal FBI memo: "It looks to me as if these Hammers are no good."

The Hammer family in the late 1950s. Armand is holding Buttons, his sister-in-law's poodle. Next to him is his third wife, Frances. The others are, from left, his mother, Rose; Ireene Wicker Hammer (Victor's wife); and his brothers, Harry and Victor.

Armand with his son, Julian, and his grandson, Michael, in the late 1950s.

Hammer's mistress, Bettye Jane Murphy, and their daughter, Victoria.

But in the wider scope of the Hammer family business, the immense number of pencils manufactured did not translate into success. The problem was not in the quantity of pencils but in the value of the rubles Hammer received for them. Since these rubles were not convertible to foreign currency, they allowed him (and Olga) to live lavishly in Moscow, but they did little to reduce the huge debt in London that his family business had amassed in previous years through the operations of their New York, Berlin, and London subsidiaries.

According to Hammer's own reckoning, this debt amounted to £170,000 (the equivalent of about $1.7 million today) by the end of 1927. To service and repay the debt, Soviet authorities allowed Hammer to export about one fifth of his total pencil production to foreign markets, and he opened offices in Britain, China, and Persia. But the hard currency thus generated was not entirely his to dispose of. Most of it was tightly controlled by Arcos, the Soviet trade agency in London. Part of the money in the Arcos account was used to buy raw materials, such as cedar and graphite, for the pencil factory; part was paid to individuals and causes abroad involved with Soviet intelligence, which was a continuation of the money-laundering commitment; and the balance was used to reduce the Hammers' bank debts.

It became clear by the end of 1927 that the company needed a massive infusion of hard currency if it was to avoid bankruptcy. That December, Julius Hammer traveled to New York to raise $500,000. He went to American banks with a deal he hoped they would accept. He would sell them $500,000 worth of bonds issued by the pencil factory that would be guaranteed by Tsentrosoiuz, the Soviet government agency responsible for buying goods abroad for Russian cooperatives. Jacob Schapiro, who had worked out the details of other financing schemes for the Hammers, attempted to persuade the banks that this would be a safe investment, but none of them was willing to make such a commitment.[10]

The result was that when the Soviet government reclaimed the Hammers' pencil factory in October 1929, the Hammers still had a debt of £99,000 (about $500,000) outstanding in London. Armand made his desperate position clear to the Soviet authorities: if he was not able to continue his pencil exports, he would be unable to cover his foreign loans, and he, and his family, would be bankrupted.[11]

The Kremlin again decided against letting the Hammers go bankrupt. Armand Hammer had been Soviet Russia's first and last recipient of a concession, and as internal memorandums argued, his financial plight proceeded from activities and payments (including clandestine ones) made on behalf of the Kremlin. Such expenses, even if poorly documented, had been part of a larger mission: opening up alternative channels for trade. So the issue became not whether, but how, to bail him out of his immense debts.

By 1929, all the other foreign concessions had been nationalized, and Stalin was unwilling to continue to make Hammer the sole exception to his policy. Indeed, the Politburo had already decreed that his American Industrial Concession was to be Sovietized. But as compensation, Hammer would receive the equivalent of $500,000 in bonds payable in foreign exchange, which would pay off his London debts. In addition, the Soviet entity taking over his concession agreed to assume all its internal debt, but not all its foreign debt. This settlement, which was approved by Stalin, left Hammer with virtually no profit to show for the nearly ten years he had served as Lenin's "path" to American business. On the contrary, as he complained with some justification, he had lost a good part of his family's capital in Russia.

While Hammer would not leave Russia with any great fortune, he would take with him something that would prove in time to be more valuable. He had learned the rules for operating in a state economy controlled by ideological autocrats and run by pragmatic bureaucrats.

Rule 1. Always go directly to the top of the hierarchy. The value of having the highest-level imprimatur had been amply demonstrated to him by what he had gained from his single meeting with Lenin. Even though that encounter was essentially perfunctory, it provided him—as Lenin meant it to do—with credentials that impressed and intimidated others much lower down on the hierarchy. Such intimidation worked especially well in an authoritarian state where power was arbitrarily exercised, since it left those at a lower level of the bureaucracy constantly uncertain.

Rule 2. Collaboration is an essential part of the process. Unlike more traditional capitalism, in which success proceeds from making the cheapest or the best product, in Leninist capitalism success comes from collaborating with the key bureaucrat. Hammer had found that two high officials in the Cheka—Mironov and Yagoda—had the power to make his concession work or fail. They wanted him to perform services that were not directly related to his concession: supplying laundered funds to their agents abroad. By collaborating with them, he managed to thrive even when his businesses were losing money. Collaboration was the price of survival—and he came to realize that it could take many forms: supplying information, organizing transfers of technology, or delivering bribes.

Rule 3. Ambiguity is a virtue and clarity a vice. Whereas enterprises in traditional capitalism tend to have external measures of success, such as bottom-line profits, that tend to be unambiguous, their counterparts in Leninist capitalism have internal measures of success, such as convergence with government policy, that tend to be infinitely redefinable. The muddier the waters, therefore, the easier it is to operate. When Hammer had been forced by circumstances to mingle his import-export business with his money-laundering activities, he found this worked to his advantage. Bureaucrats were unable to decide which measure to judge him by.

Rule 4. Expediency should be disguised by sentiment but should not be tempered by it. Since the distribution of benefits in Leninist capitalism had to be explained in terms of a public, rather than a private, goal, it was necessary to pay lip service to some idealistic purpose. But it was also necessary to exploit that benefit expeditiously. Hammer found, for example, that his altruistic efforts to provide famine relief gave an acceptable explanation of why he was awarded the asbestos concession. At the same time, he found that no one objected to his calling in Cheka troops to suppress striking workers at the mine; on the contrary, the means justified the end.

Rule 5. The image of success must be maintained—whatever the reality. The Soviet government intervened in Hammer's behalf over and over again, even though he was unable to pay his debts, because it had an interest in maintaining the illusion that concessions were profitable. When he returned to America—and the folds of traditional capitalism—he could also count on its taking steps to preserve for the outside world the illusion that he had made a fortune.

IN AUGUST 1929, ARMAND HAMMER DECIDED IT WAS TIME TO leave Russia. He had already taken the precaution of sending his wife, Olga, and three-month-old son, Julian, out of the country on a "vacation," from which they would never return. He was concerned that the Soviet authorities might not let him travel until his company's debts were paid, so he slipped across the Finnish border in a horse-drawn carriage, leaving his father behind in Moscow to work out the remaining details of the financial settlement.

On August 21, he joined his family at the Eden Hotel in Berlin. The next day, he paid a visit to the U.S. Embassy, where he registered his son as an American citizen and applied for a new passport for himself. In those days, the State Department required an applicant residing abroad to provide information about his tax status. Hammer declared on his application that he had not earned enough in the previous year to file a tax return. He also stated that he planned to move, with his family, to the United States.[12]

But he had considerable trepidation about the reception that awaited him in the United States. In 1921, as he began his journey to Russia, he had a terrifying nightmare. He dreamed that he was crossing a trackless steppe on a horse-drawn sled. Suddenly, he was aware of a pack of wolves hotly pursuing him. As the wolves drew closer, he saw that they had human faces. The nightmare was repeated many times, in slightly different versions, during his eight years in Russia.[13] Now he wondered whether his fears would continue. How much had the FBI found out about his service to Soviet intelligence? Had the money trail been uncovered?

In Berlin, Hammer sought the advice of a top Comintern official named Zigmas Aleksa, who raised the matter in Moscow. Aleksa noted in a Comintern memorandum that Hammer was "willing to return [to the United States] but had difficulties settling his affairs." The laundered money that Hammer had secretly distributed had gone to numerous agents of the Soviet underground in America. Had any of these agents been caught by the FBI, and if so, had they been in a position to compromise Hammer? Iosif Piatnitsky, a stout man in his late forties with an angelic halo of gray hair around his otherwise bald head, who was then chief of the Organization Department of the Comintern, was consulted. He was responsible for maintaining the security of the secret financial deals made for the foreign Communist parties and thus had direct oversight of Hammer's money laundry. Piatnitsky reported that Hammer had "compromised him-

self in the manner in which he handled his business. . . . Do not count
upon his return at an early date."[14]

As it turned out, Piatnitsky had overestimated Western intelligence.

UP UNTIL MID-1927, THE WESTERN INTELLIGENCE SERVICES THAT
had attempted to track Hammer's diverse activities were in the position of the proverbial blind men trying to describe an elephant. The
Bureau of Investigation, for example, was informed that Hammer
was receiving large sums of money from Moscow and therefore described his company "as an organization of Soviet intelligence."[15]
State Department officers, receiving a tip that Hammer was carrying
messages back and forth on his frequent trips to the Baltic states, assumed he was a clandestine "Soviet mail carrier." (They even recommended that his passport be renewed so his mail to Russia could be
surreptitiously examined.)[16] German intelligence gleaned from documents it seized in 1924 that Hammer was involved with the Soviet
trade mission in Berlin, and it assumed that he was some sort of economic agent. British intelligence traced Hammer's connections to the
Bolshevik "secret regime" and assumed he and his family were involved in its international propaganda effort.

The mosaic began to come together only on May 12, 1927. On that
afternoon, on Moorgate Street in London, British police raided the
headquarters of Arcos, the Soviet trading company, and sealed off
and occupied its offices for four days. Despite the protests of Soviet
officials, who claimed the premises were diplomatically protected, the
British used blowtorches and safecracking equipment to cut through
the steel protective doors of the vaults. They carted off several truckloads of file cabinets and boxes, which turned out to be a massive intelligence coup. The documents not only revealed the extent to which
Soviet trade missions were being used as covers for Soviet espionage
and subversive activities, but they also guided investigators through
the elaborate labyrinth of fronts used to recruit, fund, and retrieve
data for Soviet spy networks. Among the incriminating documents
were records directly linking the Hammer enterprise to Moness
Chemicals, which was servicing Comintern espionage agents in Germany and Britain. When this was reported to the Bureau of Investi-

gation, Moness's office in New York was searched, and agents found a paper trail that included what was listed on the books as $5,000 "loans" from Harry Hammer. The bureau was also able to trace the various people and causes to whom these "loans" were to be channeled. Hammer was funneling money from his Berlin office to Moness's herbal-remedy company, which was then disbursing it to Soviet secret agents. The information produced by the raid on Moness's office was augmented by information provided to U.S. intelligence by Grigory Bessedovsky, the Soviet chargé d'affaires in Paris who defected in 1929. Bessedovsky, in explaining how Moscow financed its political and intelligence operations in the United States, reported that the main cover for laundering and dispersing funds was "a small office for the purchase of medicinal herbs in New York," which fit the description of Moness Chemicals.[17]

British intelligence moved swiftly to shut down the supply system. By the end of 1927, Hammer's offices in London were closed, and Julius Hammer, who appeared to be the prime mover in the family, was banned from Britain. The U.S. Embassy in London, which was the liaison between British and U.S. intelligence, relayed to Washington in 1932 the status of the investigation: "Dr. Julius Hammer was prohibited entry into the United Kingdom as a political agent and was the controlling personage of the Allied American Corporation which was used as a cover for the transmission of Soviet funds to American Revolutionary Organizations."[18]

British intelligence further reported that Armand Hammer was operating in Europe on behalf of Soviet intelligence and that his wife, Olga, had been allowed to leave the Soviet Union to help Hammer in his clandestine activities.[19] Despite such reports, the Bolshevik scare in America had largely abated, and with the United States moving toward full recognition of Stalin's regime—although this would not be granted until 1933—there was little interest in Washington in making an issue of the Hammer case. Although the FBI continued to keep its file on him open and the State Department continued to refuse to issue him a new passport, no action was taken to prevent the return of Armand Hammer to the United States.

CHAPTER SEVEN

REQUISITE
FOR A
LEGEND

THE FUTURE FOR ARMAND HAMMER LOOKED GRIM IN 1930. HE
had lost virtually everything he and his family had. His family's pharmaceutical business, Allied Drug, was gone, sold to pay for exports
to the Communists. The asbestos-mining concession, though it served
to lure other American businesses to Russia, had proved a financial
disaster. The well-publicized wheat venture had been aborted after a
single unprofitable shipment. The Ford Motor agency, which his
father had spent years setting up, had been taken over, without compensation, by the Soviet government's trade agency, Amtorg. The
Harju Bank in Estonia, which the Soviets had insisted he buy, had
gone bankrupt, and his family had lost all the money he had invested
in it. The Allied American import-export business and Alamerico,
its Moscow subsidiary, had to be liquidated after amassing huge
debts abroad. Other businesses he had invested in, like film importing and antique exporting, never got off the ground. His pencil-
manufacturing business, though it had made huge profits in rubles in
Russia, was unable to amass sufficient hard currency abroad to pay
its foreign debt. What profits his businesses appeared to make abroad
were siphoned off by the Soviets through money laundering to finance Soviet espionage. And with the institution of the Five-Year
Plan, Stalin ended foreign concessions. The result was that Hammer
was left, at least temporarily, out in the cold.

In the early 1930s, the Hammer brothers—Harry, left, Victor, center, and Armand (with his wife, Olga)—were partners in several companies that had been set up to sell Soviet art in the United States.

Although the Soviet government proposed to compensate him for his activities on its behalf, the amount it offered was not enough to cover the debts he and his family had incurred abroad. In Germany, for example, the complicated transactions he had made to acquire machine tools for the pencil factory had resulted in a trail of unpaid bills, debts for which he was threatened with imprisonment.

Hammer was in the position of a gambler who has drawn a hand of losing cards and has only one possible strategy for staying in the game: bluffing. Hammer was a very good bluffer. He had gone to the brink before in Russia, and by not blinking first, he had managed to survive. It helped that he had the perfect poker face and knew how to suppress his emotions. Few outsiders were aware of his desperate situation. He had lavishly entertained foreigners at Brown House and ridden around Moscow in a chauffeur-driven limousine. A dazzling aura of success was attached to his various enterprises, which had offices around the world. He had a unique reputation: an American who had made millions in Russia. Maintaining this illusion remained his last and best hope for making another arrangement with the Kremlin.

At about this time, Stalin was looking for new means of earning hard currency for Soviet activities abroad. With the deepening of the Great Depression, the situation had become so desperate that he had ordered his intelligence service to counterfeit hundred-dollar bills. Soviet agents brought the bogus money to Berlin and set up a German banking front to distribute it, but the scheme was exposed before the fake currency could be put into circulation.

There was another source of funds: art. Literally tons of paintings, icons, silver, porcelain, antiques, and bric-a-brac considered to be artifacts of capitalist decadence had been expropriated during the revolution. And the contents of numerous museums and monasteries that had been closed were also available for disposal. Even though this art presumably had a considerable value in the West, the Communists had had little success exporting it, due to trade embargoes, legal actions by émigrés, and other complications. Stalin delegated the task of devising a strategy for getting around all of this to his trusted associate and future commissar for foreign trade, Anastas Mikoyan.

Mikoyan was half Georgian and half Armenian. He had served as Stalin's right-hand man since 1925 and had already displayed great ingenuity in using the state's monopoly on foreign trade "against elements of the capitalist market," as he put it. He had managed to extract hard-currency payments from all the foreign concessionaires except one—Armand Hammer.[1]

Mikoyan met Hammer in 1923 in Rostov, where he was the province's party secretary. The two of them ended up in a group photograph after Hammer delivered a consignment of Ford tractors there. When Mikoyan came to Moscow, he called on Hammer for his assistance in an extremely delicate project—the secret sale of art from a repository called the Goskhran, a Russian acronym for the Government Committee for the Care of Valuables. In February 1920, Lenin had established the Goskhran with the idea that the art and jewels seized and expropriated by the Cheka should be put under central control so that they could be eventually sold abroad. In November 1921, their administration was transferred from the Cheka to the Commissariat of Finance. Lenin ordered, "Within three days of receiving this [edict], Goskhran shall receive all valuables now at the Cheka's disposal." Known as the Diamond Fund, the Goskhran continued through the early 1920s to receive art objects and furniture taken by the Cheka from churches, museums, and the homes of private collectors. Its first curator, Moisey Yakovlevich Lazerson, watched helplessly as many of these treasures were ripped apart and stripped of their jewels and precious metals in what amounted to a mining operation.[2] The objects and pieces of objects were then smuggled abroad. The problem was that Russian émigrés in Europe, claiming that the goods had been looted from their families, filed legal claims that mired sales of the furniture and art in cumbersome and embarrassing litigation. Mikoyan needed to find a way around this.

He sought a discreet channel through which art from the Goskhran could be sold in the United States, and in 1925 he offered Hammer a 10 percent commission on what he could dispose of in this way. Hammer set up the L'Ermitage Galleries in New York to handle art sales, and he made a number of attempts to arrange other deals, including one abortive effort to sell a fake Rembrandt in Berlin. He tried to sell a da Vinci canvas from the Hermitage in Leningrad to an American syndicate, but as it turned out the price Mikoyan had placed on it proved too high. Although none of these early art deals had worked out and the gallery had done little, if any, business, Mikoyan was impressed with Hammer's efforts.[3]

In 1929, Mikoyan turned to Hammer to help facilitate a massive sale of art objects in America. The problem that had stymied the Soviet export of art up to then was the provenance of the objects. Mikoyan needed an intermediary, preferably a U.S. citizen, who could plausibly claim that he had legitimately bought the art in Russia and could then be counted on to launder the proceeds of the sales and remit them. He decided that Hammer was a perfect candidate for this role.[4] Since he could not afford to have his prior dealings exposed to U.S. authorities, the Soviets would have an effective lever of control over him.

The logistics for this new business would be relatively simple. Art objects would be shipped to Hammer in New York on consignment. He would pretend that the items were part of the personal collection he had assembled in Moscow. He would then sell them and, after taking a commission, remit the balance to Moscow. To disguise the reason for the remittances, he would enter into a contract to buy an innocuous commodity from Amtorg, the successor to his Allied American Corporation, which was now an arm of the Commissariat of Foreign Trade and was responsible for the sale of Russian art and antiques in the United States.[5] Since the director of Amtorg in New York, Pyotr Alekseyevich Bogdanov, was a close associate of Mikoyan's, he could be relied on to cooperate in this transfer of funds. The commodity that Hammer chose to buy from Amtorg at an inflated price was Russian oak staves, to be used for making beer barrels. So art and barrel staves would come to Hammer in New York, and money would go through Amtorg to Moscow.

For the scheme to work, Hammer's true relationship with the Soviet government had to be concealed. He needed a cover story that would explain how he had got the access in the Soviet Union that put him in a position to buy the art, how he had acquired it, and why the Soviet government allowed him to export it. Even before he returned to New York, Hammer began weaving these explanations into an autobiographical account of his eight years in Russia. He got some professional help from Walter Duranty, *The New York Times*'s correspondent in Moscow. A short, impish-looking man who had lost his left leg in a train accident, Duranty had been a frequent visitor to Brown House and had written a number of helpful stories about the Hammers' concessions in Russia. He also had some close contacts with the Soviet regime—too close, according to his critics, who dubbed him "Stalin's apologist."[6]

Duranty wrote a foreword to Hammer's autobiography that said that the narrative read "like a motion picture of ten thrilling years in the life of an amazing country . . . [running] smoothly from picture to picture, each illustrating a stage in the vastest and boldest experiment Humanity has known."[7] The book carefully omits any material that might connect Hammer to the Soviet government. For example, it entirely eliminates Julius Hammer, who had sent Armand to Russia, organized the business for him, and negotiated the early deals with Soviet authorities. Expunging his father from the story presented an accounting problem, of course. The source of the money for his Soviet activities was eliminated. Hammer solved this by claiming that he had made a fortune by first building and then selling the family's pharmaceutical business for well over $1 million prior to leaving for Russia in 1921. This putative windfall was pure invention: Allied Drug and Chemical, which had been teetering on the edge of bankruptcy since 1919, was liquidated in 1921, not sold, and it provided no multimillion-dollar fortune for the twenty-three-year-old Hammer.

Julius is not the only character deleted from the book. Hammer also omits mentioning his wife, Olga, his son, Julian, and Boris Reinstein, the Comintern executive who facilitated his entry into Soviet Russia. He claims he went to Russia as a doctor who wanted to fight the typhus epidemic. Only when he had applied for a visa in the summer of 1921 did he encounter his "first real Bolshevik."[8] He writes that he "would have been attached to one of the Russian relief units, would have worked there for a year or more, and then gone home. But fate ruled otherwise."

The "fate" that transformed him from an idealistic doctor into a businessman took the form of an accidental trip to the Urals, where he saw mass starvation. Moved by the sight of dying Russians, he asked a Soviet official on the train why food was not imported to alleviate the famine. The European blockade was blamed. He then spontaneously offered to "arrange it for you through a concern owned by my family." So he wrote out a contract to buy wheat for the Urals and receive trade goods in return.[9] The news of this humanitarian gesture reached Lenin. Hammer was summoned to the Kremlin. "What we really need is American capital and technical aid to get our wheels turning once more," Lenin told Hammer. "Someone must break the ice. Why don't you take an asbestos concession yourself?" And thus, Hammer found himself a capitalist in Soviet Russia.[10] He notes, "Fate was now beckoning me on to seek my fortune in this land of promise."[11]

After several chapters describing how his mercy mission—and strokes of luck—led to his amassing great wealth in Russia, Hammer discusses his acquisition of "the Romanoff treasure." Since he had considerable spare time, he filled it with the "hobby" of collecting the "art treasures and intimate household articles of the Romanoff family."[12]

> One day my brother Victor and I were eating at a small hotel in Moscow. He looked at one of the plates and called my attention to it. The plate had been turned out at the Imperial Porcelain Factory. It bore on its back the words Nicholas I, 1825. . . . We asked the manager of the hotel where he had gotten the plate. He said it was from the Palace, but he didn't like the plates because they broke too easily. We bought his supply, giving him some thicker plates which would stand harder usage.[13]

In more or less the same accidental manner, Hammer acquired priceless Fabergé eggs, icons from the czar's monasteries, and paintings. "Some articles found their way to little shops where their acquisition was relatively simple while others were in the hands of private individuals who would part with them only after considerable negotiating."[14]

By 1929, Hammer writes, his home had become "a virtual Museum, filled with relics of the by gone splendour of the Romanoff dynasty," and as he prepared to leave Russia, he requested permission to take the art with him.[15] He claimed that a contract he had signed with the Soviet government for the sale of his pencil concession included a clause that permitted him to take out of Russia his "household effects," which included his art collection:[16] "Thanks to our contract with the government for the sale of our factories, the necessary permission was granted to us."[17]

Hammer's autobiography, published in America in 1932 and entitled *The Quest of the Romanoff Treasure,* presents a version of events that was extremely useful in establishing his new business. Of course,

Hammer had not met Lenin by accident. He had not made a great fortune in Russia. He had not acquired the art "collection" from private individuals. He had no clause in his contract that allowed him to export art. But there was little possibility that anyone in the West could check on this account.

HAMMER LINGERED IN PARIS THROUGH MOST OF 1931. HE COULD not prudently move back to New York before testing the political waters. His father had been declared persona non grata in Britain, and officials of the U.S. Embassy in Germany had spent an inordinate amount of time questioning Olga. To make matters even worse, Julius Hammer was arrested in Erfurt, Germany, for the debts that the pencil factory had incurred in that country. The court refused to release him until a bond of nearly $100,000 was posted. Hammer was unable to pay this sum immediately and did not visit his father in prison because he feared he himself might be arrested. He retained a lawyer to negotiate a lower bail, but it took two months before Julius was freed.

During this dismal transition, France provided the safest temporary residence for him and his family. He had rented a small home with a rose garden in the suburb of Garches, about eight miles outside Paris, for Olga and Julian. Olga had brought a servant with her from Russia, and she spent most of her time in the company of Russian-speaking émigrés. Hammer later compared her to an exotic bird who had been confined for years, and was now suddenly released, "soaring and singing."[18] This was his way of glossing over her drinking and infidelity, which had already separated them in all but name.[19] Hammer himself lived in a one-room office at 34 rue Tronchet in the center of Paris. He slept on a sofa and kept his pillow and toilet articles in the office safe so that they would be out of the view of any associates who came by during business hours. At thirty-three, he no longer looked youthful. He had gained weight, lost hair, and developed small but distinct pouches under his eyes.

He was in a financial bind. Banks in Britain were pressing him for hundreds of thousands of pounds, and the Internal Revenue Service was suing him for corporate taxes dating back almost a decade. His main partner in his new art business, Morris Gest, had gone bankrupt and owed Hammer and his family almost $60,000. The fledgling art gallery in New York was temporarily without capital, and the promised Soviet inventory had not yet arrived. Hammer had been compensated by the Soviet government for its takeover of his pencil factory, but with postdated notes. Some of these notes would come due in six months, some in a year, and the balance in two years. Since the Soviet credit situation was extremely shaky in 1931 and Europe was in the midst of depression, it was very difficult to borrow against this Soviet paper. But putting every resource to use, Hammer sold his Soviet IOUs at a steep discount to pay his family's considerable living expenses.

When the Russian art began to arrive in New York in 1931, Hammer's art business was in deep trouble. Harry and Victor operated it out of a tawdry one-room office on Fifty-third Street in Manhattan. Listed on the crowded nameplate were myriad corporate fronts: L'Ermitage Galleries, Day Gallery, Peasant Art Inc., Importers of Antique Art, Hortense Galleries, Inc., and A. Hammer Co. Victor had been optimistic about the business's potential, but the acceleration of the Depression had severely dampened the enthusiasm of art collectors, and in 1931, two sisters of the czar obtained a court injunction preventing the Hammers from selling objects that they claimed in brochures had been "the property of the late Czar."[20] Hammer's story that he had purchased the goods from private parties was accepted by the courts, but even so the litigation was costly.

In Paris, Hammer received increasingly gloomy reports that the art, which had come straight from Soviet warehouses in Moscow, was now piling up in warehouses in New York. There was hardly enough money to pay storage fees. He had no choice but to return to the United States, but since he had no idea how he would be treated by U.S. authorities, he left his wife and son in Paris. He quietly moved into his Greenwich Village carriage house and began to take stock of the family business. Bankruptcy was looming, and Hammer needed money immediately to pay transportation fees on incoming shipments of art.

Hammer turned for help to Jacob Schapiro, who still handled the New York end of Hammer's Soviet money-laundry operations. He was also Hammer's lawyer and accountant and held the power of attorney for his business in the United States. Schapiro had recently got control of a small New York bank called the Trust Company of

North America. The United States was on the verge of recognizing the Soviet Union, and Schapiro knew that when that happened, Hammer's connections would be exceedingly useful. He established a line of credit for Hammer, which allowed him to write checks even though he did not have the money on hand to back them. The Trust Company would honor the checks, and when the Soviet merchandise was delivered and sold, Hammer would deposit the proceeds in the bank to repay the credit extended to him. This arrangement did not come cheap. Since Schapiro was taking all the financial risks, he negotiated a contract that effectively gave him nearly half of all Hammer's profits.

Though most of the money from the line of credit would be paid to Amtorg, Hammer still had to conceal the Soviet government's involvement in his art business. To create the necessary cover, he set up a second enterprise, called A. Hammer Cooperage, which explained why he was importing oak barrel staves.

As he made these new arrangements, he found that no one seemed much concerned about his past activities after all. The Bureau of Investigation did not even question him. So Hammer sent for Olga and Julian. He was ready to begin a second and very different life in America.

PART TWO

REACHING FOR ROOSEVELT

HAMMER GALLERIES

51 EAST 57TH STREET · NEW YORK

PLAZA 8-0410

The Hammer Galleries staged the first major exhibition of Russian art in America. Money made from the sale of art was funneled to one of the main sources of Soviet espionage in America.

CHAPTER EIGHT

THE
ART
DEALER

ON MARCH 4, 1933, FRANKLIN DELANO ROOSEVELT WAS SWORN in as the thirty-second president of the United States. The following week, the banks and stock exchanges were closed, not to honor the new president but because the country was paralyzed by what was perhaps the worst financial crisis in its history. Trading in the U.S. dollar was suspended in London, Paris, Berlin, and other European centers. One of FDR's key advisers, Rexford Tugwell, later wrote that the new administration was "confronted with a choice between an orderly revolution—a peaceful and rapid departure from past concepts—and a violent and disorderly overthrow of the whole capitalistic structure."[1]

The Great Depression, which had begun on Black Tuesday—October 29, 1929—had deepened to the point where nearly one quarter of the nation's workforce was unemployed, and farmers, who then constituted another quarter or so of the population, having lost more than two thirds of their income, were being bankrupted and forced off their land. Prosperity had disappeared throughout the capitalist world. In Germany, bonfires were being lit by the Nazis to mark Hitler's ascent to power; in Italy, Mussolini and his Fascists were already in control.

A crowd of one hundred thousand people had come to watch Roosevelt address the nation—and another sixty million, almost half the population, listened to his speech on the radio. FDR arrived in an open limousine. He wore a silk hat, a morning coat, and a fur-lined topcoat. He spoke with a deeply resonant and reassuring voice: "First of all, let me assert my firm belief that the only thing we have to fear is fear itself." In words that would have sounded like radical cant at any other time in American history, Roosevelt blamed bankers and financiers for abdicating their responsibility: "The money changers have fled from their high seats in the temple of our civilization," he said. "We may now restore the temple to the ancient truths . . . social values more noble than mere monetary profit." During the campaign, FDR had zealously attacked the system of capitalism that had produced the Depression, and he had won a resounding majority of the popular vote. The new commander in chief now called for "power to wage a war against the emergency, as great as the power that would be given to me if we were in fact invaded by a foreign foe."[2]

Armand Hammer had taken an early interest in FDR's campaign. In July 1932, he had contacted Henry French Hollis, who was then practicing law in Paris and was reputed to be close to Roosevelt. He knew Hollis through the work he was doing to attain U.S. diplomatic recognition of the Soviet government, a cause that Hammer believed, as he later wrote, was of "paramount" importance.[3] Hollis, a former senator from New Hampshire, suggested that Hammer make a contribution to the presidential campaign. Hammer cabled FDR, offering to raise money for him in Europe, and he had Hollis send a letter to FDR's adviser Louis McHenry Howe in which it was suggested that Hammer's advice regarding affairs in Russia and the best way to deal with the government would be extremely valuable.[4] Although little emerged from this initial effort to make contact, Hammer quietly persisted.

HAMMER HAD RETURNED TO THE UNITED STATES IN DECEMBER 1931. After eight years of business ventures in the Soviet Union, he accomplished a remarkably swift transition to the role of art dealer in America. Even though he knew very little about art, he understood the business of illusion, and just as he had managed in Moscow to make a string of business failures look successful, he now applied his skills to turning the Russian antiques, jewelry, and decorative bric-a-brac in his warehouse into treasure. Since it would be difficult to perform such alchemy in a city with as many art experts as New York, he decided to take his wares to the American hinterland. He sent letters to all the Midwest department stores describing how he had managed to acquire the so-called Romanoff treasure during his years in Russia. A brochure and his stationery were embossed with the double-headed crest of the czars. In return for exhibiting the "collection," department stores would receive half the proceeds of whatever was sold. The first store to accept the proposal was Scruggs-Vandervoort-Barney in Saint Louis. It cabled him on January 25, 1932: "Come immediately."

Unable to pay shipping costs, Hammer improvised. He found a bankrupt theatrical-supply company that had wardrobe trunks for sale and bought six of them. Then, with his brothers' help, he packed the trunks with as much as they could hold, lugged them to the train station, and checked them as personal baggage for the trip to Saint Louis. Harry remained in New York to do the bookkeeping.

In Saint Louis, Armand saw to public relations while Victor set up the exhibition. If people could be made to believe that the goods from Russia were of cultural and historic value, they would come to see them. Hammer went to local newspaper editors, told them his stories about Russia, and supplied them with photographs to, as he put it, "get their journalistic juices flowing." When the exhibition opened, some five thousand people were in line to see "the Romanoff treasure." The sale proved so successful that the department store extended the exhibition an additional week. "Our show was a smash," Hammer recalled.

The "show" then moved on to Marshall Field in Chicago, Bullock's Wilshire in Los Angeles, Halle's in Cleveland, the Emporium in San Francisco, Kaufman's in Pittsburgh, and Woodward and Lothrop's in Washington, D.C. "We put up our tent, figuratively speaking, in a department store," Hammer later reminisced. He described the operation as "a traveling circus" in which he was both the barker and the ringmaster.[5]

Hammer's circus was based on illusion. To give the illusion authority, he published the book that Walter Duranty had helped him prepare, *The Quest of the Romanoff Treasure*. No reviewer questioned its accuracy. Nor did purchasers of objects from the purported treasure trove show any reluctance in accepting Hammer's version of how he had acquired the art (even though some of the artifacts still carried labels indicating their proximate source was government warehouses and museums). The story provided buyers with a credible provenance for whatever they purchased.

The shipments that arrived from Russia included a wide diversity of items—everything from costume jewelry to Torah scrolls looted from synagogues. Little, if any of it, had been owned by the czars— or, for that matter, by Hammer. The bulk of it was tourist junk. "What the Hammers called crowned jeweled objects of art were actually the debris of Russian hotels, monasteries, shops and palaces," the art historian Robert Williams wrote later.[6] Hammer did manage to obtain from the Antiquariat, the division of the Soviet Commissariat of Foreign Trade responsible for the export of art, fifteen valuable Easter eggs that had been made by Fabergé for the czar. "We were able to convince Mr. Anastas Mikoyan, then Minister of Trade, to have the Antiquariat sell us some of the eggs," Hammer explained later.[7] He continued to receive shipments of Fabergé eggs until the late 1930s, presumably with the approval of Mikoyan. This gave Hammer access to serious collectors, such as Malcolm Forbes, Dorothy Pratt, and Marjorie Merriweather Post.

When the original inventory of things from the workshops of Fabergé and others was exhausted, the Soviets simply supplied newly made objects in the style of these artisans, with their names attached. Counterfeiting presented little problem, since in many cases the government had seized the tools and raw materials of artisans who had fled, and labor was not in short supply. Hammer himself had taken with him from Russia a set of the signature stamps of the Fabergé workshops, so he could doctor unsigned items in the back room of his New York office. He was thus able to expand vastly the supply of Fabergé, or what passed for it.[8] As a prop, he hired a penniless White Russian prince named Mikhail Gounduroff to act as a shill. Gounduroff lent "his princely tone to our business," Hammer noted. Hammer had learned during his stint as a businessman in Russia that there is little if any danger in fabricating credentials if through the fabrication you tell your audience precisely what it wants to hear. In this case, Americans wanted to hear that they could buy authentic pieces of the Russian imperial treasure at bargain-basement prices

Hammer took particular relish in writing journalists' copy, either by supplying them with press releases or by giving vivid interviews in which he spoke about his putative adventures in Russia. It was all part of what he called his "razzamatazz."[9]

By the end of 1933, Hammer had put on his art circus in twenty-three cities across America, and diminishing returns were setting in. Expenses were going up, sales were going down. The novelty of the act was beginning to wear thin for both local newspapers and customers. Hammer returned to New York, where he had arranged an "exhibit" at Lord and Taylor. Soon afterward, he liquidated his L'Ermitage Galleries and opened an outlet in the Waldorf-Astoria Hotel called the Hammer Galleries. To attract customers, he gave lectures on czarist art and occasionally showcased his wife singing Gypsy love songs. When Hammer Galleries moved to 682 Fifth Avenue, he became a more conventional art dealer.

The sale of the Romanoff treasure did not make Hammer a wealthy man. The inventory belonged to the Soviets, and he had to remit most of his profits to them. At a time when the Depression was drying up other sources of foreign trade, the Soviets derived a substantial share of their foreign exchange from the sale of art in the United States. Hammer kept for himself what amounted to a commission. Out of this, he had to support his family: his father and mother, who acted as buyers for the Hammer Galleries in Europe; his two brothers, who managed the retail end in New York; and Olga, who had a separate residence for herself and their son on Fifth Avenue. Even as late as 1936, Hammer's gallery had less than $2,000 in its bank account.[10] But at least it was above water.

His beer-barrel business was a more serious problem. He had entered into the business with Amtorg to hide the money he was sending back to Moscow. At the time, he assumed that reselling the Russian oak staves in the form of beer barrels would not be a problem. He even thought it would be profitable, especially since with the end of Prohibition there would presumably be a vast increase in beer consumption. More beer meant more beer barrels. Accordingly, he made a deal with the Anheuser-Busch brewery in Saint Louis. When the wood arrived from Russia, he had barrels assembled from it in Brooklyn. These were shipped to Saint Louis and sold. What he had not reckoned on, however, was that commodity prices would plunge during the Depression, reducing the wholesale price of wood for his competitors. The price of Hammer's wood remained fixed by his contract with Amtorg, and not only did his margin of profit disappear, but he was also saddled with grueling interest rates on the loan he had taken out from his main creditor, Jacob Schapiro's new bank, to pay Amtorg for the wood in the first place. As Hammer cut his prices on barrels to meet his competition, he was unable to pay the principal and interest on his debt. He kept up a brave front—driving a Rolls-Royce to work—but when he continued to fail to make the payments to Schapiro's bank, it moved to have a federal court put his company into involuntary bankruptcy—which would have ruined Hammer, since all his businesses were interconnected.

Hammer had faced bankruptcy before—at least five times. His father had gone through personal bankruptcy—and debtors' prison. He knew how to maneuver through a financial crisis, and in this case he gambled on Jacob Schapiro's history. Schapiro had been his financial agent in New York when he was engaged in money laundering for the Soviet underground. Schapiro's name even appeared on documents used to channel money to Jacob Moness. If push came to shove, Schapiro could not be sure how far Hammer would go in exposing their secret past. Hammer could even claim that Schapiro, not he, was responsible for the accounting that had been used to hide the payments to Moness and other Soviet intermediaries. Whether he had been a witting or an unwitting accomplice in the money laundering, Schapiro was now a successful and respected banker, and as such he had much more to lose than Hammer.

As the legal proceedings dragged on, Hammer acknowledged signing the contract with Schapiro's bank in 1932, but he argued that he was an inexperienced businessman whom Schapiro took advantage of. As incredible as these claims may have seemed, this was evidently not an area that Schapiro wanted to bring to light. So he did not contest Hammer's claim, and the bankruptcy judge allowed Hammer to continue in business temporarily and stretch out his bank repayments.

Hammer still desperately needed cash to pay Amtorg, and he arrived at an ingenious solution to his problem: preselling art. He persuaded a number of stores to pay him in advance for art objects. In return, he gave them an additional discount. Only when the goods were delivered did he have to report the sales to the Soviet government—and remit its share. The scheme was akin to kiting checks, and while it put him further in debt, it also bought him the time he needed to find another source of credit. This time it was a government agency, the Reconstruction Finance Corporation (RFC), which Roosevelt was using to aid businesses damaged by the Depression. Hammer applied for a $50,000 loan. Even though his accruing debt to the Soviets did not show up on his books, the RFC initially turned him down because of his low net worth. So he inflated on paper the value of his inventory of objects at the Hammer Galleries, thus raising his net worth enough for him to get a $75,000 low-interest RFC loan. He thus resourcefully managed not only to keep afloat but also to get a U.S. government agency to provide the funds he was funneling to Amtorg, which was still considered one of the main sources of Soviet espionage in the United States.

DESPITE HIS BUSINESS PROBLEMS, HAMMER ENGINEERED AN IMAGE of himself as a successful capitalist. He had a natural rapport with reporters. He knew how to capture their attention with details in telling a story. Not only had the colorful fables he fed the press to enhance the value of his "imperial art" gone largely unchallenged, but they had also begun to work their way into the clip files that serve as the media's institutional memory. He provided *Time* magazine, for example, with a self-serving (and untrue) story about how he had outfoxed the Communists and "wangled out of Moscow . . . the entire Russian output of proper air-dried wood."[11] His beer-barrel business, which in reality was verging on bankruptcy, was thus depicted as a triumph. Such stories served Hammer's interest both by putting a favorable spin on his relations with Moscow and by deflecting attention from his financial problems.

Moscow had a vested interest in seeing Hammer portrayed as a successful capitalist. The Soviets helped him enhance his prestige by staging the first major exhibition of Russian art in America at the Hammer Galleries. Media attention culminated in December 1933 with *The New Yorker* magazine's extensive profile of Hammer. It described how he had "amassed a large fortune by dealing in grain, furs, pencils, office equipment, pigs, camphor, chloroform, rye, typewriters, plows, tractors, promissory notes, oil well machinery, cotton, icons,

jewelry, ladies' handbags, ether, gold and silver plates, crosses, asbestos, Russian Easter eggs, and beer barrels"—an inventory drawn
mainly from his *Quest of the Romanoff Treasure*. *The New Yorker*
portrayed Hammer as a colorful yet earnest "entrepreneur":

> He drives from his Fifth Avenue apartment to his Brooklyn
> factory every day in an old Rolls Royce, and works so hard that
> he sometimes falls asleep in his clothes, too exhausted to go to
> bed. . . .
> [For recreation] he likes to play the host in a bartender's coat,
> and sometimes spends the entire evening behind the bar, mixing
> drinks.[12]

As Hammer's renown grew, so did his ambitions. Even during these
Depression years, when he came dangerously close to bankruptcy and
exposure, he was conscious of a mission that if successful would take
him to the apogee of political power in America. He aimed for
nothing less than becoming the behind-the-scenes adviser of the new
president of the United States. He embarked on a circuitous route:
through FDR's sons. Just as his father, with Trotsky's blessing, had
induced Henry Ford's son to come to Moscow, Hammer now helped
arrange a deal in which FDR's son Elliott would visit the Soviet
Union. The terms were too good for Elliott to resist. In return for his
help in getting the necessary approvals whereby the Soviet Union
could import fifty military airplanes, disguised for the purpose of the
sale as civilian planes, and for coming to Moscow to work with Soviet officials, Elliott would be given a $25,000 commission—an enor-
mous sum of money at the height of the Depression.[13] As things
worked out, the Soviet Union didn't follow through on the deal. But
Hammer had located a potential entry point to FDR.

CHAPTER NINE

SEARCHING
FOR
MRS. RIGHT

AFTER ONLY THREE YEARS IN AMERICA, HAMMER LOOKED THE
part of a prosperous businessman approaching middle age. Although
thirty-seven, there was nothing youthful about him. His waistline had
expanded, and his hairline had receded. He used an enormous
amount of energy purposefully.

Hammer needed a more suitable marital alliance for his new role.
The vivacious and beautiful Olga had served a purpose in the Soviet
Union, but her unpredictable outbursts in Russian, unconventional
opinions about American politics, and vodka-drinking binges did not
fit with the new life he was attempting to establish. In 1935, he effectively disposed of her and their six-year-old son, Julian, by shipping
them to a small house he had bought in Highland Falls, some fifty miles
north of New York City on the Hudson River. When the boy and his
mother left, Hammer explained to his son that he and Olga would be
more comfortable where they were going because there was a Russian-
speaking community there. It was almost as if he were warehousing his
family in this remote place in case he decided to return to Russia.

Armand Hammer's personal history had bequeathed him a hard
emotional shell, the better to withstand blows from a hostile world.
His father's bankruptcy and the subsequent subterfuge to conceal
from court investigators the family's remaining assets, the temporary

*Armand Hammer, left, and his second wife, Angela, with guests at
a garden party at their New Jersey estate in April 1946.*

absence of his parents when police began investigating their political connections and they left the United States, his father's imprisonment in Sing Sing—Hammer could have weakened under these blows, as his brothers did, but instead he developed an impenetrable armor that seemed to exempt him from ordinary emotional pains. And this was a form of power. He could be ruthless without hesitation. And he could control the flow of information about himself: outsiders saw only what he wanted them to see. Since his past Soviet liaisons could be exposed at any point by his Soviet associates, he had a veritable sword of Damocles hanging over his head. But the emotional armor he had developed enabled him to act as if he were free. Undeterred by sentimental attachments to people, he could focus on the job at hand: turning any transaction to his financial advantage.

Hammer had a deep thirst for social recognition. Such recognition may, at some level, have been perceived as a shield against exposure. In any case, he frequently attempted to bring himself into association with celebrated names, no matter how fleeting or meaningless the contact, as if brushes with great people would validate his standing in society. He went, for example, to great lengths to arrange an encounter with the great American actress Helen Hayes. After she played Mary, Queen of Scots, at a New York theater, he selected from his "imperial collection" several books on the subject of Queen Mary as gifts for Hayes. One of these, he wrote her, was marked by the bookplate of the czar himself (a bookplate the Soviets were using to add value to merchandise sent to Hammer). She sent a note thanking him. On March 11, 1936, after sending bouquets of orchids and roses to her dressing room, Hammer went to the theater—dressed in tails and a silk opera hat. He wrote later that he had recorded the meeting for posterity in his "diary," although he did not then regularly keep a personal diary. The published entry is similar in style to his egocentric accounts of his meetings with such celebrated figures as Lenin, Trotsky, and Henry Ford: "Even the drizzling rain could not dampen my excited, buoyant spirits."

He imagined Helen Hayes's eyes scanning the audience and coming to rest on him, just as he had imagined Olga doing the same thing when he first saw her in Russia. After the performance he went to Hayes's dressing room, where he was the presumed focus of her attention. He talked to her through a curtain while she was changing her clothes, and then they went out for a champagne dinner at the Maison Russe in the St. Regis Hotel. According to Hammer, she discussed how impressed she was with his art collection. He never went out with Hayes again, nor did he send her any more special gifts or bouquets. He did not need to: he had achieved his trophy date. With this single encounter, she, like Lenin, Trotsky, and Ford, had been willy-nilly immortalized in his curriculum vitae.[1]

Hammer's ambitions to enhance his social standing were soon rewarded. In 1938, at a literary party, he met Olga's replacement. Angela Carey Zevely was thirty-five years old, one year older than Olga. Like Olga in 1925, she was married to a man she wanted to be divorced from. She too was a professional singer; but unlike Olga she had been classically trained, had graduated from the Boston Conservatory of Music, and sang in French, Spanish, and Italian. She came from a prominent American family that moved in the same social circle as the Roosevelts. She also owned a large farm in Red Bank, New Jersey. Hammer was instantly impressed with her qualities. As he later noted, "She was a true socialite—loved parties, dinners, theater trips and horsey society." He found her "glamorous, witty and dashing." He quickly decided, as he later put it, that this "was going to be a serious affair."[2]

Hammer had just turned forty. His hair was turning gray, and his face was beginning to show the tension he lived under. But he could turn on the charm like a spigot. He launched a campaign of orchids, art objects selected from his "treasure," and well-calculated compliments. When he learned that Angela had a hearing disability—the result of an automobile accident—he offered to find specialists who could help her overcome it.

His efforts paid off. In less than a year, he had become Angela's constant companion. Although he still kept his Greenwich Village carriage house for his nights in New York, he spent most of his time at her bucolic estate in New Jersey. Taking advantage of the Depression prices on rural land, he helped her get mortgages to buy adjoining properties. Under his tutelage, and with her money, Shadow Isle, as the estate was called, gradually expanded into a five-hundred-acre property. Hammer had become a country squire.

Hammer's old friends were struck by his rapid transformation. Luba Elianoff, for example, who had given the Hammer family Russian lessons in Moscow, knew Hammer as a crude youth lacking manners. When she remet him at Shadow Isle, he was dressed in a dinner jacket, spoke in a refined, almost midwestern voice, and displayed perfect table manners. He dropped society names as if he had always been part of the gentry. When she tried to remind him of some of their mutual acquaintances in Moscow, he looked at her blankly, as if she were addressing the wrong person.

When Elianoff asked Hammer about Olga and Julian, he said he had relocated them—this time settling them in Los Angeles, where they were finding a new life for themselves. He seemed reluctant to discuss his father, whom Elianoff had been close to. She learned from Hammer only that Julius was living in Europe and traveling frequently to the Baltic states. Except for his brothers, who worked with him in the family business, there were few links to the past in Hammer's life now.[3]

DESPITE HIS NEW SOCIETY CREDENTIALS, ARMAND HAMMER HAD not been forgotten by J. Edgar Hoover. In the mid-1930s, the FBI began to receive reports from its informers in organized crime that Hammer was involved with several major racketeers in the liquor business. The focus of the FBI reports was Hammer's relationship with the mob-based Kings Brewery in Brooklyn. Hammer's beer-barrel company allegedly was providing the brewery with false invoices for phantom barrels and other services. It appeared that Hammer was helping Kings illegally inflate costs, hide profits, and launder money. Hammer reportedly also had suspicious liaisons with other breweries with ties to mobsters, but consorting with unsavory businesses was not in itself sufficient grounds for a federal investigation.

However, the FBI uncovered a potentially more sinister aspect to the barrel business. In December 1939, it received reports that Hammer had been attempting to buy used barrels in "huge quantities" from a major distillery, Schenley Whiskey, at a price well above the market rate. Presumably, he was also buying them from other sources. Since these barrels could not be profitably resold to other breweries, the suspicion developed that Hammer was covertly supplying barrels to the German navy through front companies in Mexico. Germany was by then at war with Britain and France and, faced with a blockade, was attempting to stockpile oil in Caribbean depots in order to refuel its ships and submarines. It needed Mexican oil and wooden barrels to hold it in.[4]

Hammer's business relations with Germany were unclear in 1939, although it was known that his father (who was also cited in the FBI reports) still maintained an office in Berlin. Just four months earlier, with the Molotov-Ribbentrop Pact, Stalin had made a surprise alliance with Germany that included provisions for clandestine cooperation in the Western hemisphere, and the FBI knew that Soviet agents in the United States were assisting their German counterparts in sophisticated smuggling schemes. In retaliation, the U.S. government had frozen all operations of the Soviet trading organization, Amtorg, in New York.[5] Since Amtorg was the source of much of Hammer's imported wood, the freeze would explain why he was in the market for used barrels. Was Hammer exporting the barrels to Mexico as part of a scheme to illegally circumvent the embargo on shipping matériel to Hitler? And if so, did this arrangement reflect a new phase in the pooling of Soviet and German covert resources in America?

On February 10, 1940, Hoover forwarded his information on Hammer to the director of naval intelligence, to the assistant chief of staff of the army military intelligence service, G-2, and to the undersecretary at the State Department, who was then in charge of coordinating intelligence bearing on national security. After outlining the putative German strategy to build up caches of oil barrels in the Caribbean, he said, "Information has also been received to the effect that certain individuals of the Hammer Cooperage Company, Milltown, New Jersey, had contacted the officials of the Schenley Corporation and offered them prices far above the average for used whiskey barrels."[6]

Presumably, Hammer was also using his own barrels and was buying used barrels from other whiskey companies. The FBI contacted employees at Schenley, who denied that the company had actually delivered any barrels to Hammer. Since in any case it was not against U.S. law to sell used barrels to Mexico and the FBI had more pressing espionage cases to investigate in 1940, the case was effectively closed.

But Hammer also had a problem with the State Department. Since 1932, it had adamantly refused to grant him a new passport and effectively prevented him from traveling abroad. Hammer was not told the reason for the State Department's denial, which proceeded from intelligence reports it had received from Britain alleging that Hammer had been serving as a channel for Soviet funds to its underground in the United States.

All these reports remained scattered in different compartments of the government, however. They did not impede Hammer's rapid social advancement, his courtship of Angela, or his efforts to reach Franklin Delano Roosevelt.

CHAPTER TEN

THE
FIVE-MINUTE
SUMMIT

IN THE SPRING OF 1940, STALIN WATCHED WITH CONSIDERABLE unease as Hitler's armies blitzkrieged their way across Europe. Unlike in World War I, with the opposing armies bogged down for years in a stalemate, the Allied defenses collapsed in a matter of weeks. By mid-June, Norway, Denmark, Belgium, Holland, Luxembourg, and France had fallen. Most of eastern Europe was occupied by the Nazis. Hitler's only active opponent was Great Britain, and its army, after the chaotic evacuation at Dunkerque, was in disarray.

When Stalin had signed the nonaggression pact the previous year, he could not have anticipated that Hitler would rout the Allies in such a brief time and at a cost of only a few thousand German casualties. Hitler's domination of Europe hardly made Stalin's position more secure, especially since the German army had begun moving to within striking distance of the Soviet border. Hitler had spelled out his intentions in *Mein Kampf.* He considered it necessary for Germany to destroy the Soviet state.

The issue for Stalin was not Hitler's goodwill but his strategic timetable. Could he afford to fight a war simultaneously on two fronts? If he could not, as Stalin's generals reckoned, he would have to vanquish Britain before he could attack Russia. This meant that the longer Britain pursued the war, the more time Stalin would have to prepare the Red Army for the German attack. So although the nonaggression pact theoretically bound Stalin to avoid helping Hitler's enemies, he actually had a powerful interest in seeing that Britain got the supplies it needed. Since only one country, the United States, had the capability to supply Britain, and since the United States was still officially neutral, Stalin wanted to encourage FDR, who was already morally committed to sustaining Britain, to act sooner rather than later. In this international drama, Hammer was to play an intriguing part.

Virtually overnight, Hammer transformed himself from a businessman specializing in importing art and barrel staves from Stalin's Russia to a geopolitical strategist concerned with helping Great Britain get immediate aid from the United States. He took out full-page newspaper advertisements supporting such aid. He contributed money to pro-British lobbying groups. He even retained a public relations firm to help in the campaign. Up until this point, he had been involved in behind-the-scenes political activities. Never before had he so openly attempted to influence public policy—not even on the issue of U.S. recognition of the Soviet Union. But now he emerged from the shadows, brimming with confidence.

Hammer later attributed his political activism during this period solely to his concern about Hitler. If so, this was a comparatively recent concern. It was also not clear where he was getting funds for his campaign. His businesses, according to his loan applications, were at best only marginally profitable. But whatever his motive and whoever was helping to finance him, he proved a highly effective lobbyist.

He focused on the problem of legislative impediments to emergency help for Great Britain. As he saw it, FDR was sympathetic to the idea, but "his hands were tied" by the Neutrality Acts, including the 1934 Johnson Act, which prohibited the United States from lending money to any foreign nation that had defaulted on previous obligations to the United States.[1] Since Britain had defaulted on nearly $3.5 billion of its World War I debt, it was not, under the terms of the Johnson Act, eligible to receive further credits from the United States. Nor was it in a financial position to pay off what it owed. Hammer came up with a proposal through which this impasse could be circumvented: Britain would lease aviation and naval bases to the United States in its colonial territory in the Western Hemisphere. The sum the United States would agree to pay over the life of these leases—ninety-nine years—would wipe out Britain's debt. No money would change hands, but the deal would allow Roosevelt to negotiate new credits, and these credits would finance Britain's purchase of U.S. destroyers and other military requisites.

After formulating a rough version of the idea, Hammer sounded out the British Embassy in Washington. Voicing his concern about the welfare of English children, he suggested that Britain could obtain more than a billion dollars from the sale of leases for military bases. He also arranged to meet with G.H.S. Pinsent, the chief financial and economic adviser at the British Embassy in Washington.[2]

Hammer evidently did not realize the extent to which the British had tracked his previous activities. By 1940, British intelligence had developed a lengthy dossier on Hammer. It identified him and his associates as part of the Soviet "secret regime" in the West. Earlier that year, it had even monitored the movements of his brother Victor in Egypt (then a British protectorate) on the suspicion that the Hammer Galleries were a front for the Soviet intelligence service.[3] It had also learned through its liaison office at Rockefeller Center that the FBI had received unverified reports about Hammer's possible participation in a plot to supply oil barrels to German front companies in Mexico the previous year. So it was not about to accept at face value that Hammer's motive here was his concern for Britain—or British children. Pinsent officially wrote Hammer about his leasing proposal:

> I must be completely candid with you on this subject and tell you that we do not feel that any public ventilation of this question at the present time would be of assistance to us; perhaps even the contrary. . . . We would prefer that the question should not be developed until after the [November] Elections at least.[4]

Hammer was not deterred. After all, he was acting to influence U.S., not British, policy, and the stakes were high. Since it would be difficult for FDR to undertake any new initiative on military aid in the final days of his campaign, Hammer turned to an old acquaintance in Congress, William H. King, the Democratic senator from Utah. He had first met King when the senator came to Moscow as part of a congressional delegation and visited Brown House. When Hammer had trouble getting his father's passport renewed, Senator

King intervened with the State Department in his behalf. Over the years, Hammer assiduously cultivated the relationship. Now Hammer asked him to introduce a bill in the Senate on lend-lease—a bill that would authorize the president to enter into negotiations to lease British bases and readjust the terms of the British debt. Hammer himself drafted the bill for Senator King. Although King proposed it in September 1940, it was blocked by the Senate Foreign Affairs Committee and was never voted on.

Undiscouraged, Hammer decided to go directly to the president. He had not only contributed substantial funds to FDR's reelection campaign, but he had also personally financed an extraordinary radio dramatization in which actors performed vignettes illustrating the achievements of the New Deal. When Hammer sent Eleanor Roosevelt a recording of the program, which was broadcast as a campaign advertisement, she expressed her appreciation, saying: "What a grand thing you did to help the President!"[5] Now, it was time to play his FDR card.

He requested an appointment from FDR's social secretary, General Edwin Watson, explaining that "the purpose of my desire for an interview is to enable me to inform the President of the result of a survey of public opinion I have made on the question of financial aid to Great Britain."[6] After several delays and reschedulings, Hammer got his appointment with the president on November 28, 1940. It was Thanksgiving Day. According to Hammer, FDR "shunted his own son aside to see me that day." Hammer had to wait about a half hour in General Watson's office until FDR was available. During that interval, the general proposed to Hammer that they have a dice game. Hammer recalled that he got down on the rug, pulled out his money, and started rolling. It was Hammer's lucky day. He won $300. Then Watson ushered him into the Oval Office.[7] In some sense, history was repeating itself for Hammer. Nineteen years and one month earlier, he had had a meeting with Lenin, who sought to break the isolation of the Soviet Union by making him his "path" to American business.

Knowing that FDR was keenly interested in analyses of public opinion, which was then a relatively new field, Hammer came armed with a large volume of editorials clipped from U.S. newspapers in October 1940, the fruits of a survey he had commissioned to show that newspapers heavily favored financial aid to Great Britain. He wanted to demonstrate to FDR that the president would gain, rather than lose, popular support by effecting Hammer's plan.

Even though the meeting itself lasted no longer than five minutes, Hammer believed that he had impressed the president with his logic. FDR had a special skill with people that was at once genuine and evasive. Part of his charm was his ability to convey to visitors, by nodding and smiling in agreement, the impression that he was paying close attention to what they were saying.[8] It is not surprising that Hammer believed he had made a real connection. He wrote later that FDR listened "keenly" to what he had to say. He presented a volume of clippings to the president, which FDR brought with him to a White House briefing the next day. Hammer claimed that Roosevelt favored the destroyers-for-bases idea and that he "wanted me to help" work out the plan.

To this end, Hammer noted that FDR put him together with his secretary of commerce, Harry Hopkins.[9] Hopkins had had an operation for stomach cancer the previous year that left him suffering from such severe malnutrition that he looked as if he were on the verge of death, yet he remained FDR's most influential adviser—and closest friend. He lived in an apartment at the White House, dined and traveled constantly with FDR, spent late nights analyzing alternative strategies for the president, and was directly involved in shaping and carrying out the American response to the escalating war in Europe. His advice seemed to carry such weight that he was compared by FDR's critics to Rasputin.[10] Hopkins's assignment from FDR, according to Hammer, was to come up with a "joint plan" with him on lend-lease.[11]

FDR presented another version of the five-minute meeting at his press conference the next day. When asked whether he had conferred with Hammer "on the naval defense bases," he responded flippantly, "Never talked about it." The president, who liked joking with the White House press corps, continued, "He gave me a long book here which I have not had a chance to look at yet. If you are really interested, you may look at it. It has 28,636,940 news clippings." When the reporters laughed at his description, he shrugged and said, "It is a very interesting compilation—which I haven't had time to scan."[12]

FDR's humor served a purpose. It distracted the press's attention from Hammer's access to his administration. Such a diversion was hardly imprudent given the growing FBI and British intelligence dossiers suggesting that Hammer was involved with Stalin's espionage apparatus. If it became public, this association could prove damaging to FDR, who had come under vicious attack for his earlier attempts to reach an accommodation with Stalin. At a more private level, however, such a connection might have been regarded by FDR as a useful back channel to Stalin on the issue of lend-lease—as long as it was kept quiet. In any case, FDR's subsequent actions on Hammer's proposal were anything but dismissive. He sent Harry Hopkins, who was to be his czar of lend-lease, to New York on at least two occasions in late 1940 to meet with Hammer on the plan. Then, in January 1941, Hopkins flew to London to discuss the concept of lend-lease with Churchill. Within a few months of these meetings, Hopkins negotiated the celebrated destroyers-for-bases swap with the British, which in March 1941 was approved by both houses of Congress and signed into law by the president. Although the source of FDR's unconventional lend-lease plan remained a mystery to his cabinet—his secretary of labor, Francis Perkins, for example, attributed it to a "flash of almost clairvoyant knowledge"—many elements of it closely paralleled Hammer's proposal.[13]

As it turned out, the lend-lease concept had far-reaching consequences. It provided a precedent for waiving restrictions on military aid to nations fighting Hitler, and in June 1941, when Hitler invaded Russia, Stalin was able to apply for, and receive, lend-lease aid on a massive scale.

Hammer never saw FDR again, but he maintained contact with his administration, and this subsequently led to an extremely lucrative deal.

Hammer with two of his prize Black Angus cattle in the 1950s.

CHAPTER ELEVEN

FORTUNES OF WAR

HAMMER WAS FINALLY DIVORCED FROM OLGA ON NOVEMBER 29, 1943. She settled for alimony of $75 a week and the cost of their son's schooling. Olga and Julian were relics of Armand's first life—the life in Moscow he now found it necessary to separate himself from as much as possible.

Three weeks after the divorce became final, Hammer married Angela Zevely. Since they had been living together for five years in her home in Red Bank, New Jersey, and she was already an integral part of his new life, the marital vows were little more than a formality, paving the way for her to bear him American children. The wedding itself took place in his brother Victor's Park Avenue apartment. Hammer wore a black evening jacket and smoked an expensive Havana cigar. His hair was parted in the center and slicked back. He had gained more weight in the past few years, and he now had jowls. Even though the ceremony was a small family affair, Hammer could not resist one display of his newly acquired influence. Bernard Botein, a state supreme court justice, officiated.

A few days later, the couple flew via Mexico to Havana for their honeymoon—it was Hammer's first trip out of the United States in twelve years. Since Cuba did not require a U.S. passport, Hammer's problems with the State Department were not an issue. Angela and he took the bridal suite at Havana's finest hotel, El Presidente. But as Angela observed the procession of businessmen coming in and out of the suite, it became clear to her that her new husband had another agenda on this trip. He was embarking on a major business venture.[1]

THE WAR HAD EFFECTIVELY ENDED HAMMER'S ART-IMPORTING business. Even with occasional highly publicized events—such as the sale of objects from the William Randolph Hearst Collection in 1941 —the Hammer Galleries remained only marginally profitable. Hammer's beer-barrel business was in even worse financial shape. Almost all his major customers had switched from wood to aluminum, and he needed to borrow money from the Reconstruction Finance Corporation to continue to stay financially afloat. But now, through his connections in the Roosevelt administration, he had found an opportunity to make a killing. To advance the war effort, the administration had strictly restricted the amount of grain used for distilling alcohol and had allocated almost all of it to the major distilleries that were producing alcohol for smokeless gunpowder and other munitions. By 1943, stocks of grain had been heavily depleted, and there was a severe shortage of beverage alcohol. Hammer intended to fill this gap.

His ten years in the barrel business had already brought Hammer in contact with the more powerful players in the wholesale liquor business. Many had begun their careers as bootleggers during Prohibition. Some, like those he was meeting with in back rooms of casinos in Havana, were still involved in the illicit end of the business—a black market that had flourished during the war—and preferred to continue a cash trade outside the purview of government supervision. Hammer had no compunction about doing business in this netherworld. His experience laundering money for the Soviet Union's espionage and propaganda apparatus made stealthy payments in the whiskey business seem little more than child's play.

Earlier that year, Hammer had bought a defunct Maryland liquor distributor, which he renamed Old Clover Distillery. Although it had no business of consequence, it had a license to sell whiskey wholesale. He also optioned the right to buy several thousand barrels of bourbon from the inventory of an Illinois distillery. This was stock that he could dilute up to 95 percent with lower-quality alcohol and then merchandise as "blended" whiskey. Next, he negotiated to buy an abandoned distillery in Newmarket, New Hampshire. The Nahum Chapin Distilling Company, as it was called, had gone bankrupt the previous year because it could not profitably compete with larger producers of industrial alcohol. It had then been taken over by the RFC, which was its main creditor. Hammer offered the government corporation, which also had been financing his barrel company, $55,000 for the distillery. When the RFC accepted his bid, he lined up a large supply of surplus dehydrated potatoes in neighboring Maine, which he planned to convert to alcohol.

All that he needed to complete this coup was the dispensation from the administration to produce beverage alcohol. Without it, he would have nothing more than a hopelessly bankrupt plant; with it, he would have a veritable license to print money.

Judging from Hammer's preliminary moves, it is evident that he was confident that the requisite permission would be forthcoming. He could not have otherwise afforded the risk of committing himself to buying a marginal liquor company and a closed distillery. He was counting on friends in the administration who owed him a favor. His most important contact was Harry Hopkins, who in 1943 was overseeing war production for FDR. Hopkins assumed a key role in allocating benefits among business interests in the state-run part of the war economy. He introduced Hammer to FDR's uncle, Frederic Delano, who was then on the War Production Board, and to other key officials. In May 1944, the administration approved Hammer's application to produce beverage alcohol. A few weeks later, the RFC lent him the money to reopen the New Hampshire distillery.[2]

The prior owners of the company were shocked to see their bankrupted plant turned into a money machine. *They* had lost money because, like everyone else, they had been restricted to producing industrial alcohol for the war effort. Why had Hammer, not they, been given permission to produce beverage alcohol? Why had Hammer been given RFC financing to modernize the facility? Hammer had no previous experience as an alcohol producer, and although they were not aware of it, he was being investigated on suspicion of Soviet espionage while his application was pending. They suggested that he used illicit influence to make "unconscionable" profits. In a letter to their senator, Styles Bridges, they noted:

The company understands that Mr. Hammer . . . has operated
the plant at full capacity in the manufacture of beverage alcohol; that his is the only concern in the United States which has
been permitted to make and distribute beverage alcohol, while
all other distillers had to make alcohol for industrial use only;
that this discriminatory privilege was of enormous benefit to his
associates.[3]

The reference to unnamed "associates" implied that others in the
government were benefiting from Hammer's profits.

The distillery's former owners had little chance of getting help
from Senator Bridges, who was by this time the recipient of large
cash campaign contributions from Hammer. Nor did they get any redress from the Roosevelt administration. When they protested Hammer's special treatment to the War Production Board, the response
was that Hammer's exemption from the restrictions on producing
beverage alcohol proceeded from unique circumstances. In the case
of his distillery—which of course had previously been the com-
plainants' distillery—"the difficulty of transporting its small output
to consuming points made it impractical to incorporate the unit into
the industrial alcohol program."[4] Such an explanation obviously
begged the real issue of why the refinery had been given different
treatment when Hammer got control of it.

Hammer clearly had an edge, albeit an invisible one, over the previous owners. Regardless of who had been his "associates" in providing him with it, the administration had no interest in reversing its
decision. Within months, Hammer made his first real fortune, selling
potato alcohol mixed with a splash of bourbon. It cost him less than
a penny a quart to produce and sold in department stores for five
dollars a quart as Gold Coin blended whiskey.

The key to this remarkable success story is not classic capitalism,
in which one produces and brings to market some commodity more
efficiently than one's competitors; instead, it is the version in which
one is granted an exclusive privilege by the state that makes it difficult, if not impossible, for others to compete. Hammer had been initiated into this latter form of enterprise by Lenin. The advantage
came not from a Horatio Alger work ethic but from providing government leaders with desired services or emoluments. Even though
his Soviet concessions had failed to furnish Hammer with profits

in hard currency, they had taught him something that was to prove far more valuable: the techniques for finessing and exploiting government-granted privilege—making contact at the top, ignoring sentimental considerations that may get in the way, collaborating with officials in power, obfuscating problems, and projecting the image of success.

As the profits continued to pour in from his beverage alcohol, Hammer bought established brands of whiskey—Roamer Whisky, Buckingham Scotch, Blue Grass Bourbon, and J. W. Dant. He also bought other distilleries. He incorporated all these companies into United Distillers of America, a holding company owned half by him and half by his brother Harry. By 1945, when the war ended, United Distillers had revenues of $17 million. By 1946, revenues had increased to $40 million, and United Distillers, with operations in nine states, had become the largest privately owned distiller in the United States.[5]

Hammer had also taken up big-game fishing, a predatory sport that seemed to fit his new status as a captain of industry. He particularly enjoyed chartering a boat in the Pacific and hunting down giant sailfish. He would then have himself photographed triumphantly in front of his catch. One such photograph was taken in Acapulco in January 1946. It shows Hammer in slacks and a white shirt with rolled-up sleeves. He proudly holds up his fishing rod. Behind him, hanging from ropes, are his prey—two sailfish that dwarf him. It was a way of demonstrating his superiority.[6]

Hammer made no effort to conceal his newly acquired wealth. He relocated the United Distillers headquarters to the seventy-eighth floor of the Empire State Building, which was then one of the most prestigious addresses in New York City. He acquired the seventeenth-century panels from Treaty House in the Uxbridge section of London, so named because the treaty ending the English Civil War was signed there, and used them to decorate his private office. (He gave the historic panels to Queen Elizabeth when she was coronated.) He also acquired a seventy-eight-foot yacht, which he used to commute from his home in New Jersey to his office in Manhattan. He had the ship refitted with oversize engines so that he could impress onlookers with its speed. He then bought a twin-engine Beechcraft plane and hired Fred Gross, a young aviator, to pilot it. He also made his estate a cattle-breeding showplace, stocking it with a prize-winning herd of Black Angus. He entertained lavishly, cultivating congressmen, senators, governors, prosecutors, bankers, and the social elite. An album of snapshots taken on June 29, 1946, shows a party with a dozen guests and family members playing badminton on a manicured lawn in front of the vegetable garden, dining on tea cakes under a striped tent, and relaxing in swimming suits. "Armand . . . lives by the philosophy that money can buy everything and everybody," Angela observed later, in their divorce proceedings.[7]

HAMMER CELEBRATED HIS FIFTY-FIRST BIRTHDAY CRUISING AROUND Manhattan Island on his yacht with his wife, his mother, and his two brothers and their wives. It was an occasion tinged with sadness and foreboding. The sadness came from the absence of his father, who at the age of seventy-four had died of a heart attack in October. Hammer could not escape feelings of guilt about his father. He believed that Julius had gone to prison twice on his behalf: the first time in 1920 for the botched abortion Armand was responsible for; the second time in Germany in 1930, when Armand chose to negotiate to lower the bail rather than pay what he considered an exorbitant amount. These incarcerations had taken their toll on Julius's health. To be sure, Armand had tried to make up to his father the first imprisonment by going to Russia in 1921 in his stead. And he had used his political influence, once he acquired it, to get his father's medical license restored in 1943. But even after his father's death, Hammer could not erase from his mind the image of Julius in a prison uniform, wearing thick glasses, breaking rocks with a sledgehammer. He described this specter over and over again—even years later.[8]

The foreboding on the birthday cruise was triggered by Rose Hammer's plan to depart the next day for Germany and, if it was possible, Russia. Mama Rose, as the family called her, was seventy-four. When it was her turn to give a birthday toast, she told her family that she had "some obligations to people there who were good to me when I needed them. . . . Your dad played a trick on me by leaving me at this time, so I must make the trip alone."[9] She had stated on her passport application that the purpose of the trip was business for the Hammer Galleries, but as Hammer knew, she had a very different mission. She desperately wanted to see the grandson who had remained in Russia when the Hammers had left some twenty years earlier. Even though she had received occasional letters describing Armasha, as he was called, no one in her family, not even his father, Victor, had seen him. Then in 1946, Victor received word from a Soviet journalist in Germany suggesting that it could be arranged for him to visit Armasha. Victor wanted to meet with the journalist but was denied the permit that was then necessary to travel to Germany. "National security" grounds were cited.[10] Now Rose Hammer was going to meet with the Soviet intermediary. Whether it led her to the Soviet sector of Berlin— or even to Moscow—she was determined to pursue the search.

Anti-Soviet hysteria was sweeping across America in the early 1950s. In 1947, the House Committee on Un-American Activities had brought the idea of a widespread Communist influence to the public's attention by suggesting that movie and radio performers were wittingly or unwittingly part of a conspiracy. The search for conspirators was coming perilously close to the Hammer family. Victor's second wife, Ireene Hammer, who was a well-known radio performer of children's stories, had been blacklisted from the networks because of her alleged sympathies toward Communist causes.[11] Then, in 1950, while U.S. troops were fighting in Korea, Senator Joseph McCarthy was blaming Communist agents in the State Department—205, 81, 57, the number varied with each speech—for the failure of U.S. foreign policy. His demagoguery launched an organized flight from reality during which politicians were obsessed with the issue of personal loyalty.[12] Even in this atmosphere, however, Hammer had avoided any public discussion of his life in Russia. That situation could change if his mother turned up on an unauthorized trip to East Berlin or Moscow with a Soviet Armand Hammer.

Hammer could never, of course, entirely escape his past. In 1948, a Soviet agricultural specialist who worked for Amtorg in New York contacted him at the New York City gallery.[13] He said that he knew Hammer had been interested in Soviet agriculture and that he was familiar with Hammer's postwar effort to contribute money and organize support for the United Nations Relief and Rehabilitation Administration, which had provided surplus food to the Soviet Union.[14] Hammer chatted with the man from Amtorg—and agreed to meet him again to discuss Soviet agriculture.

In recalling the meetings years later, Hammer said that the Amtorg man was a Russian agronomist who simply came into his gallery to see an art exhibition. They met there by chance, and the conversation turned to the Soviet agricultural situation, a subject of interest to him. The agronomist suggested that what the Soviet bloc needed to import was not the surplus food of the West but chemical fertilizers so it could grow its own food.

But while Hammer may have been surprised by this encounter, the Amtorg official may have had an ulterior purpose for visiting the Hammer Galleries. Hammer was no ordinary American gallery owner. In helping to organize the Soviet "path" to American business, he had helped set up Amtorg in his own company's offices. For years, he had used Amtorg as a channel for transferring money to Moscow. And he was well acquainted with some of its top officials. He could not, under these circumstances, prudently assume that a visit from an Amtorg employee was either accidental or purposeless. He knew Amtorg was an instrument of the Soviet state. Demands had been made on him in the past by the Soviets, and they could be made on him in the future. Even though he was now a respected capitalist—one who could get an appointment with those close to the president of the United States—he remained vulnerable to disclosures about his secret life. The Soviets presumably understood his vulnerability and knew that they could use it to increase their leverage with him. So whatever else he did, he could not simply dismiss his conversation with the Amtorg official and whatever suggestions he had made to him—not, at least, without carefully reckoning the consequences.

In any case, after meeting the Soviet agronomist, Hammer began looking into the possibility of leasing a plant to produce exportable fertilizer bases. He went to America's leading expert in the manufacture of synthetic nitrogen-based fertilizer, Dr. Charles O. Brown, who had built twenty-six such facilities around the world. In their initial meeting in 1949, he explained to Brown that he was planning to expand his whiskey company to include the production of ammonia, the basic component of fertilizers, and then retained him as his consultant and charged him with finding a suitable facility.[15] He also offered Brown the job of running the new ammonia subsidiary he intended to create. Hammer had committed himself to yet another new enterprise.

. . .

THE EDGE THAT THE GOVERNMENT HAD GIVEN HAMMER IN THE
whiskey business faded away as the war ended and the free market
replaced government allocations. While United Distillers was still
making money, competition had greatly reduced Hammer's profit
margins. Now he saw an opportunity to acquire another lucrative
government-granted concession.

In 1950, Brown located a huge government-owned refinery in Morgantown, West Virginia. The sprawling 850-acre complex had been
built during World War II by the U.S. government at a cost of $75
million to produce ammonia, which was then critically needed for munitions. After the war, it was modified to produce ammonia for fertilizers, which were temporarily needed in massive quantities for export
to occupied Japan and Germany. Now, as that market waned, the
U.S. Army was offering to lease the plant to the highest bidder. It fit
Hammer's purpose ideally.

According to the figures worked out by Brown, the plant's annual
production of synthetic ammonia could be increased from 36,000 tons
to 250,000 tons. If all that ammonia could be sold at its current price
of $80 a ton, the venture would gross $20 million a year. Even after
paying the army a royalty of $12 a ton and covering other expenses,
Hammer calculated that his annual net profit would be $4.8 million.
Whereas the other major contenders for the contract did not envision
a market for such a prodigious quantity of fertilizer base, Hammer
was confident that there was one abroad: the Soviet bloc. He therefore offered the army a minimum of $400,000 a year for fifteen years
for the lease. (The next highest bid was for only a two-year lease.)[16]

Even though Hammer had submitted the highest bid, he knew
from previous experience with government agencies that the logic of
economics is often made subordinate to the logic of politics. So with
the stakes this high, he moved that summer to fortify his position. He
didn't have the sort of access to the Truman administration that he
had had to the Roosevelt administration, but he had substantial allies in Congress. In most cases, he had made them the old-fashioned
way: by making cash contributions to their "campaigns" (even if they
were not running for office). He had extended this largesse to both
Republicans and Democrats. His principal contact among the Demo-

crats in the House was Albert Gore of Tennessee. In 1950, Hammer had made Congressman Gore a partner in a cattle-breeding business, and Gore made a substantial profit.

Money specifically tied to the Morgantown refinery deal was offered to other politicians. For example, Undersecretary of the Army Archibald Alexander, who was in a key position to influence the awarding of the contract, received a call from one of Hammer's intermediaries in New Jersey concerning his plans to run for the Senate after he retired that year from the army. The caller reportedly told Alexander that he would receive a contribution of $100,000 for his campaign if, and only if, Hammer received the lease.[17] With such efforts in his behalf, Hammer had every reason to assume his bid would prevail.

Instead, the army rejected Hammer's bid and awarded the contract to a chemical company that had not even submitted a bid originally. In a letter to his congressman, Hammer wrote that the army's decision "violates the elementary principle of fair play and honorable dealings which should and must exist between departments of government and private business."[18] Applying all his remaining political clout, he got the House Armed Services Committee to review the matter that October. He hoped that the army's decision could be reversed, but as the hearing proceeded, he found himself under unwanted scrutiny. The committee counsel zeroed in on an area he had gone to great lengths to keep veiled: his life in Russia. When Hammer testified, he tried to skirt any reference to the fact that in the 1920s his company Allied American was essentially a Soviet vehicle, with three Moscow-appointed directors who had a veto over anything the company did. When asked, for example, where Allied American conducted its business, Hammer answered disingenuously, "Our main office was in New York. We had branches all over Europe. London, Paris, Berlin, and other countries." Only when he was pressed further to name the other countries did he acknowledge, "Well, it had an office in Moscow."[19]

The army and the committee counsel had already been briefed on Hammer's suspected activities on the part of the Soviet Union. When Senator Bridges, who remained Hammer's point man in Congress, informally inquired about why Hammer had lost the ammonia-refinery deal, he was told that the army objected to Hammer's bid "because

of Dr. Hammer's previous connections in Russia." Based on information in Hammer's FBI file, "his company should not be given contracts, nor should it hold any position of public trust within the
Department of the Army."[20]

Senator Bridges immediately went to see J. Edgar Hoover, who was
an old friend. He asked for an off-the-record and confidential explanation of why his patron had been effectively blacklisted by the FBI.

With the onset of the cold war in the late 1940s, the FBI had
greatly intensified its surveillance of employees of Amtorg, and had
noticed several contacts Hammer had in 1948 with the Amtorg official who had discussed fertilizer exports with him. It also had a
dossier that extended back more than a quarter century and contained information on other suspicious contacts between Hammer
and the Soviets. Hoover made clear that until Hammer explained
these dealings, he would remain under FBI scrutiny.

After his meeting with Hoover, Bridges flew to New Jersey to see
Hammer and gave him a frank appraisal of the problem: the FBI had
information that Hammer had acted as a Soviet agent. He had allegedly laundered funds for the Communist underground and helped
establish Soviet espionage agents in America. As things stood, he had
no chance of receiving any government contract.

Senator Bridges then proposed a solution. He would arrange for
Hammer to be interrogated formally by the FBI. This would give him
an opportunity to refute the allegations made against him—but if the
interview went wrong, he could be charged with perjury—or worse.
Hammer instructed Bridges to make the necessary arrangements.

Hammer, age fifty-four, finds a House Judiciary Subcommittee hostile to his bid to take over the government-owned refinery at Morgantown, West Virginia.

CHAPTER TWELVE

THE DEBRIEFING

J. EDGAR HOOVER HAD BEEN SHADOWING ARMAND HAMMER FOR more than three decades. He had spotted Hammer in 1919, even before he was appointed to the Bureau of Investigation, when he helped prepare the Justice Department's deportation case against Ludwig Martens, Lenin's chief agent in New York. Hoover had followed Armand Hammer's progress through two world wars, the diplomatic recognition of the Soviet Union, and, now, McCarthyism. He had arranged to have Hammer temporarily detained in Britain and to have his mail intercepted, his office searched, his bank accounts monitored. And he continued to scribble his original assessment—"a rotten bunch"—on File 61-280, which was labeled "Armand Hammer, Internal Security—Russia."

Hoover could see from his agents' reports on the payoffs in Hammer's postwar liquor-distribution business that generating large sums of off-the-books cash was not a problem for Hammer. He realized that Hammer had his quota of members of Congress, White House aides, and political bosses who would act in his behalf, and it came as little surprise that Senator Bridges, whose state was home to one of Hammer's distilleries, was trying to help him. Hoover himself had a useful working relationship with Bridges, especially when it came to marshaling support for the FBI in Congress, and he agreed to the senator's request for a meeting. In January 1952, he arranged for Bridges to be given a confidential briefing on the secret Hammer file. Senator Bridges learned that the allegations against Hammer were serious and specific:

He had been a Soviet courier.

He had laundered funds for the Soviet Union, and at least $75,000 of Soviet funds had been transferred to him.

He had helped recruit Soviet spies and position them in the U.S. government.

He had a contract to train dogs for the Soviet police.

He had been, in the 1920s, a key link in a network that provided money to espionage rings in New York and London.

The FBI was less specific about the methods through which their information had been assembled. Some of the more damaging details had been obtained through FBI and British intelligence black-bag jobs—illegal operations that involved breaking into private safes and photographing their contents.[1]

When Hammer was apprised of these charges, he realized that there was an intrinsic flaw in them. All the events that Senator Bridges had been briefed on had occurred a quarter of a century before. Without Soviet records, which presumably would not be forthcoming, it would be extremely difficult to substantiate the accusations. Moreover, most of the key witnesses were now dead. The deceased included Boris Mishell, the Russian American businessman who had accompanied Hammer to Russia; Ludwig Martens, Lenin's agent in New York and the organizer of the asbestos concession; Boris Reinstein, Lenin's pro-paganda chief and Hammer's liaison in Moscow; Abraham Heller, his father's business associate; Gregory Weinstein, his contact in the Commissariat of Foreign Affairs; Jacob Moness, the espionage agent and go-between for the laundered funds; Charles Ruthenberg, the sec-retary of the U.S. Communist Party who had received clandestine funds from Hammer; and Genrikh Yagoda, Stalin's intelligence chief who had supervised his company's foreign activities. Most important, his father was also dead.

From what Senator Bridges told him, Hammer gleaned that the FBI had had informants in the U.S. Communist Party in the 1920s—one, in particular, code-named Finger—who might still be alive. But their reports probably amounted to little more than hearsay. Even so, Hammer knew that he was entering a veritable minefield.

By January 21, Hammer had prepared a memorandum that provided his side of the story, denying the central charge that he was an agent of the Soviet government. Senator Bridges passed the document to Hoover. "In view of the apparent desire of the subject to rebut or explain specific allegations against him, the subject is being given this opportunity to do so," Hoover telexed his field office in New York. Hammer was scheduled to appear on February 20, 1952, but at the last moment he canceled his appointment "for reasons of health" and requested that the interview be held in his office rather than in the FBI field office.[2]

Even though he had never met Hammer (and never would), Hoover knew his adversary. By attempting to move the questioning to his own office, he was trying, Hoover noted, "to dominate this situation and dictate the conditions of the interview." The move would have also allowed him to secretly record the session, and Hoover knew that a record of the questions could then be used to embarrass the FBI. "He should come to *our* office. . . . See that Sen. Bridges is ultimately advised of Hammer's attitude," he ordered in a handwritten confidential office memorandum. Hoover emphasized the word *our,* settling the matter.[3]

On March 6, 1952, Hammer went to the FBI's New York field office. Records of the interview note, with routine preciseness, that he arrived at 11:00 A.M. His FBI interrogators described Hammer as fifty-three years old, five feet eight inches tall, 190 pounds, with black graying hair, blue-gray eyes, and a ruddy complexion.

Hammer's strategy was to take advantage of the ambiguity of the fragments that the FBI had assembled from his past life. He would, like a sleight-of-hand artist, rearrange them and reject outright the pieces that didn't fit into the picture he wanted. When he could not plausibly deny something, he would divert suspicion from himself by claiming that the Hammer referred to was Julius, his now deceased father. Just as Julius had saved him from prison by taking the blame for him in the abortion case many years before, he could save him now. The deception was possible because they had lived in the same house in Russia, they ran the same business, and they were entrusted with the same responsibilities. They had often been treated as a single organic "Hammer" by Soviet intelligence, and how could the FBI be certain, more than two decades later, to which Hammer an informant had referred?

Armand depicted his father to the FBI as a soft-headed and mis-guided idealist with whom he did not agree. He told the FBI, for ex-ample, that his father had been a "joiner" of Communist front organizations and that this was a "sore subject" with him and other members of the family. He explained that he had no interest in radical politics or lost causes, such as communism. He said that he had been a businessman even before he was twenty-one and that he had gone to Russia to collect a business debt and stayed on to make money.

Hammer knew from Senator Bridges's briefing that he had to deal with the charge that the Soviets had transferred $75,000 to him, so he took the initiative in explaining this sum and advancing his creden-tials as a dyed-in-the-wool capitalist. His story was that he had been owed the $75,000 for oil-drilling machinery he had shipped to Soviet Russia in 1920, and when the Communist government failed to pay this debt, he went there to collect it—and succeeded. When asked if he had any confirmation that such a sizable transaction took place—bills, contracts, export permits, correspondence, and so forth—he replied that he had kept none. He noted that "if only a man were to save every piece of correspondence he had written or received during his lifetime, it would be easier to refute [false charges]."[4]

Hammer had also been prepared for the charge that he had asso-ciated in the 1920s and 1930s with suspected Soviet espionage agents and couriers. The FBI agents ticked off a list of six men, some of whom Hammer had been well acquainted with in Paris, Berlin, Lon-don, and New York. Jacob Moness, for example, headed the FBI's list. Moness had received substantial sums of money from Hammer in the mid-1920s. Nevertheless, Hammer categorically denied ever having "met" or even "heard" of Moness. He did the same with the others on the list.

It was a masterful performance. The interrogators' accounts of the interview show that Hammer's answers were both confident and complete and that he went out of his way to provide alternative ex-planations for the reports that appeared to connect him to Soviet in-telligence. After four hours, the FBI agents had elicited little more from Hammer than his prepared text, which stressed his commitment to American capitalism and the "principle of private property." At the conclusion, he presented the FBI with a list of personal references that included two influential judges and Congressman Emanuel

Celler, the chairman of the House Judiciary Committee, which had oversight responsibility for the FBI.

J. Edgar Hoover reviewed the debriefing with considerable interest later that March in Washington. Although Hammer had now embedded in the FBI file his version of events, crucial parts of Hammer's story were inconsistent with other evidence the FBI possessed. For example, Hammer's assertion that the $75,000 the Soviets had transferred to him was the settlement of a 1920 oil-machinery debt was demonstrably untrue. In keeping with the blockade of Soviet Russia, army intelligence closely monitored the export of oil machinery, and no such shipment had occurred. Moreover, the FBI had established (through illicit methods) that no such commercial transaction was shown on the books of Hammer's corporation—or was known to its other employees. The FBI had been able to determine from the serial numbers on the bills that much of the money was disbursed to the Soviet underground in America. Jacob Moness, the man Hammer swore in his debriefing he had never heard of, was one of the principal recipients of these funds. A burglary of Moness's office had uncovered records detailing sums of money advanced by Hammer.

The problem was, as Hoover no doubt recognized, that there was no prosecutable case here—not on the basis of thirty-year-old evidence that was mostly illegally obtained. And Hoover was not willing to expose the methods the bureau was continuing to use to trace Soviet money. More to the point, Hammer had demonstrated, as Hoover had handwritten in his file, that he had "political support." At least two influential senators—Styles Bridges of New Hampshire and Owen Brewster of Maine—and two important congressmen—Albert Gore of Tennessee and Emanuel Celler of New York—were among his supporters. Hoover, who had survived in Washington for three decades because he understood the reality of power, had no interest in challenging this congressional phalanx. He decided to take no action. Hammer had effectively stalemated him.

THE FBI INQUIRY HAD BEEN HUMILIATING FOR HAMMER, AND DEspite Senator Bridges's reassurances, he was not certain about how it would be resolved. As if to prove that he still belonged in the realm of U.S. presidents, in July 1952 he bought the summer home that had belonged to FDR on the Canadian island of Campobello off the coast of Maine. He paid the late president's son Elliott $12,000 for it.[5] This was where FDR had courted his wife and where he had been stricken with polio. The thirty-four-room mansion had fallen into ruin after the president's death, but Hammer thought of it as a kind of national shrine to FDR, who had called it his "beloved island." Now Hammer called it his permanent connection with FDR.[6]

But this period, Hammer noted in his autobiography, wasn't the best of times. To fight what he called "invasions of gloom," he turned to Dale Carnegie's self-improvement prescriptions (for example, repeating to oneself the maxim "Every day, I get better in every way"). His physical health was no better than his mental state. He complained that he was usually tired and always in pain with gallbladder and kidney stone disease, suffered from insomnia, and was almost paralyzed by pain in his right leg. He was in and out of the hospital for operations that seemed to lead inevitably to complications, not cures—as did almost every palliative he attempted in business, politics, and even family relationships.[7]

Hammer's success in making money had always proceeded from his ability to find allies in government. Beginning with Lenin, he had demonstrated great ingenuity in finding a route, no matter how circuitous, to those in power. He then managed to finesse some government-protected concession or niche, a deal that protected him from the vagaries of competition. But now suddenly the Truman administration had turned cool to his approaches, and the support he had bought in Congress was of no help. The IRS initiated a major criminal tax case against him, one that could put him out of business. The Defense Department refused to buy industrial alcohol from his companies, putting them at a severe disadvantage among their competitors. And the New York State Liquor Authority had suspended his company's wholesale license.[8] Government had turned from ally to enemy, and competing in the free market was not Hammer's strength.

The huge profits that had flowed in during the mid-1940s quickly began to ebb—and flow out of his coffers. To pay debts and get cash, he began selling United Distillers' assets—its inefficient plants, its brand names, and even its herd of breeding cattle. In February 1953, he sold almost all of what remained of his whiskey business to his chief competitor, Schenley Industries. His company became a shell, devoid of operating businesses

What funds remained in this shell were gradually siphoned off to pay Hammer's personal expenses. United Distillers had on its payroll his yacht captain, his airplane pilot, his Japanese chef, his personal lawyer, his chauffeur, his wife's maids, and even his farmhands. And it had on its books all the mortgages and loans he had taken out to pay for his yacht, plane, car, farm, and residences (including the retreat at Campobello). It also was potentially liable for millions of dollars in lawsuits resulting from claims that Hammer's cattle-breeding station had misrepresented defective bull semen it had sold.

His other business, the Hammer Galleries, had also become financially troublesome. Armand had entrusted its day-to-day management to his charming brother Victor, who had never been much of a businessman. Victor, like his mother, had become obsessed with the quest for the lost Armand Hammer in Russia, and he took expensive trips to Europe, paid intermediaries, and bought worthless art from strangers who promised to help, all to recover a past from which Armand was desperately trying to distance himself. Victor neglected the art business to such an extent that it was unable to pay the mounting expenses of the search and was slipping into debt.

Hammer's marriage to Angela was also on the rocks. To be sure, it had never been a traditional love match—not, at least, since their honeymoon, when she told him that she did not want to have a child by him—ever. After that, it was a marriage of convenience. She had given him respectability at a time when he needed it. She also provided the estate in New Jersey, which she had worked hard at developing into a major cattle-breeding center. In this regard, he found her to be, as he noted, "capable, intelligent, industrious and a delightful companion."[9] But as Hammer's interests diverged from hers, he found that she became increasingly bitter toward him. She made it clear that she resented him for spending long periods of time on his own in New York. (He stayed in the home that was exclusively his: the one-room carriage house in Greenwich Village, where he had lived as a medical student.) She became suspicious when he began selling the cattle, which she considered her own. These suspicions were overtly disruptive when she drank. That June, for example, in front of Senator Bridges, no less, she had accused Hammer of putting the/ profits of the sales into his own pocket and cheating her of her share./ She also broke into a room in the estate where he kept his private papers and took letters he had received from Lenin as well as a book of addresses, which she threatened to use to expose his past.[10] He blamed her behavior on alcoholism, complaining that "she was a steady, day-long drinker, and by the end of the day, she would have drunk herself out of control, and in those hours she might say or do anything."[11]

In early 1953, while his wife was in the hospital recovering from an operation, Hammer sent his yacht to Marathon in the Florida Keys and then flew down to join it. He was seeking an escape from his increasingly troubled life, and he was about to meet someone who was sympathetic to his needs.

CHAPTER THIRTEEN

THE
REINCARNATED
MISTRESS

IN APRIL 1953, BETTYE MURPHY HAD BEEN WORKING AS THE manager-hostess of Laney's Supper Club at the yacht basin at Marathon for nearly a year. She was twenty-nine years old, had long red hair, a lithe body, and a perky smile. She had come to Florida from Indiana. Laney's attracted a diverse clientele from the yachts that anchored in the marina, and Bettye, who was naturally inquisitive and gregarious, enjoyed talking with these people. One Friday, she noticed that a man was staring at her. Men often stared at her, but this man did not look like the usual Laney's customers, with their spiffy white ducks and sporty shirts. This man was dressed in seedy clothes—stained shirt, tattered jacket, and dirt-splattered khaki pants. His sunglasses were taped together. He looked old to her, perhaps in his mid-fifties, though not unattractive. His hairline was receding in a widow's peak, making his forehead seem disproportionately large. His jaw seemed tightly clenched, as if frozen in position. At first, she thought he must be a shrimper. But he lacked the muscle tone and suntan of someone who worked outside. He could have been a bum who had wandered in from the marina, and Bettye wondered whether he would be able to pay for the wedge of Key lime pie he had ordered.

As if he had somehow anticipated her concern, the man paid the bill and left a dime tip on the table. He remained seated, still gazing

Bettye Jane Murphy when she met Hammer.

at her, after her other customers had left. When she asked if there was anything else he wanted, he ordered an Armagnac, again raising questions in her mind about his ability to pay. Beckoning her over, he introduced himself as Doc. When she asked what kind of doctor he was, he replied "doctor fix-it," explaining that he fixed problems. He then added, "I once was a real doctor, but I never practiced medicine." He took off his sunglasses and apologized for staring, explaining that she bore an uncanny resemblance to a girl he had known a long time ago. She was, he added, his one and only true love—Marjorie.

Bettye sat down at his table. She found herself mesmerized by the sound of his voice. He told her about meeting Marjorie just after he had graduated from medical school in 1921. She was the daughter of one of his professors and had contracted tuberculosis. As a young doctor, he was confident that he could cure her if he got her into a sanatorium in time. Before this was accomplished, however, his father sent him to Russia on a business trip. By the time he returned, Marjorie had died.

"How old are you?" he asked Bettye.

She told him her date of birth: December 2, 1923.

When he heard this, he paused, nodded to himself, and then told her that Marjorie had died in the fall of 1923, just a few days before Bettye was born. He said he did not believe their physical likeness was merely a coincidence and that he believed that when someone dies before his time, his soul sometimes migrates to someone about to be born. He then began asking her about the location of birthmarks on her body.

Bettye was slightly taken aback by the personal nature of the stranger's remarks, and she was not drawn to mysticism, but he had hooked her interest. She said she did have the kind of birthmark he described. He touched her hair—which was, he said, identical to Marjorie's. "You could be Marjorie," he said.

To break the tension, Bettye began playing a bar game with the man, a sort of table shuffleboard. While they were in the midst of the game, a uniformed crewman arrived at the café. He was from the yacht that had arrived in Marathon the day before. The crewman went directly to Doc and spoke to him in a deferential manner, and it dawned on Bettye that the man she had thought was a bum was actually the owner of the yacht, Dr. Armand Hammer.

Hammer's pilot, Fred Gross, came into the café a few minutes later, and he and Hammer began discussing a trip to Cuba. "Have you ever seen Havana?" Hammer asked Bettye.

A few days later, she was in Cuba, which was then known mostly for its tall rum drinks, mambo dancing, cockfights, and gambling casinos. Hammer took rooms at El Presidente Hotel in Havana. He requested the bridal suite that he and Angela had stayed in during their honeymoon nearly ten years earlier. Bettye thought later that Hammer had been trying to relive his history. He had got it wrong the first time, but he could replicate the situation and get it right the second time around.

Hammer took Bettye with him everywhere he went on the island. The first night, they went to the Tropicana casino, where they were ushered into the private offices of the director, who treated Hammer with the same deference the yacht hand had. Hammer, it turned out, knew the owner of the casino, Meyer Lansky. The next day, they attended the jai alai games and sat in the box of the president of Cuba, Fulgencio Batista. They also went on a tour of rum distilleries, whose owners lined up outside to meet them when they arrived. At stores, they were treated like foreign dignitaries. She was given anything she pointed to, even though no money ever seemed to change hands.

Before they left Cuba, Bettye insisted they take a walk on the beach. When Hammer appeared in his business suit for the expedition, she took a pair of scissors and trimmed his trousers off at the knee.

On their return to Florida, Hammer took Bettye on a cruise on his yacht. He told her he was going back to New York and wanted her to come with him. When she said it would be inappropriate because he was married to another woman, he ordered his captain to come on deck and marry them then and there. It was a sham ceremony, but he had made his point. About a month after they met, she went with him to New York.

In New York, Bettye became part of Hammer's secret life. He showed her three different apartments he had leased under three different aliases. They were conveniently scattered around the city: in the East Fifties, in the West Fifties, and on Fourteenth Street near Union Square. He used these apartments for private meetings and other business (the West Side one had a small workshop in back for modifying art objects for the gallery). He offered her any one that suited her. She picked the Fourteenth Street apartment, which was only ten blocks from his carriage house. He arranged for his mother's maid to clean and service the apartment. He would appear there— and then disappear to go to his carriage house or somewhere else. So she wouldn't be lonely, he gave her a small parakeet, Tweet-bird, and a black poodle he named Prince Eric, after his and Angela's prize bull. He took great pride in the accomplishments of Prince Eric.

Hammer arranged piano lessons for Bettye and had a grand piano put into the apartment so she could practice. He encouraged her to go to museums and lectures and to audit classes on art. He also gave her a more practical education—in speedwriting and typing. When they ran into people whom he knew, he often introduced her as his secretary. He also put her on his payroll.

Hammer used pseudonyms when they traveled and frequently shredded and destroyed letters and other documents. At one point, she watched while he methodically burned in her fireplace an Estonian passport that he had obtained when his U.S. passport was denied. He then fed other documents into the fire. He cautioned her against ever speaking about these papers to anyone. Even though more than a year had passed since his interrogation, he still believed he was in danger of being raided by the FBI.

Late in 1953, while they were at the Fourteenth Street apartment, he collapsed, and she rushed him to Doctors' Hospital. He came close to dying from a urinary blockage that required emergency surgery. She waited all night for him to regain consciousness. When he found out that he would be spending weeks in the hospital hooked up to intravenous tubes, he told her he wanted to write his autobiography— and needed her help. He sent her to retrieve a cache of papers from his carriage house, and then, reading and ripping up documents as he went along, he began dictating to her. The problem, she realized, was that he couldn't get past one central character: his father. Every subject—medical school, business, art, Russia—would somehow involve his father. Julius had not only been his model; he had been his savior. Hammer went over and over how he had killed a woman in an abortion and how his father had taken the blame for him and gone to prison for him. He had tried to redeem himself by taking his father's place in Moscow. He became his father's proxy, signing documents next to his father's name, but he couldn't take the pressure and had had a nervous breakdown. His father had come to his aid in Moscow and rescued him again. He still could not accept his father's absence, and he described how, years after his death, he would sit alone on a bench at the cemetery and try to explain himself to his father's ghost. He said only his father could absolve him.

Bettye soon realized that the autobiography would remain stuck, like a needle on a broken record, until he could overcome his obsession with his father. After he got out of the hospital, the project lapsed. Hammer had a new project, and she was a participant in it too. It was his divorce.

HAMMER HAD BEEN SO SUCCESSFUL AT MANAGING HIS SECRET LIFE that Angela knew nothing about Bettye's presence in New York. But she had become increasingly agitated about her husband's refusal to share the accounting of their cattle sales and about the long periods when he was absent that summer. In July, she had asked him if there was another woman.

He flatly denied it. Adultery was grounds for divorce in New Jersey, but he wanted the divorce on his terms, not hers. He told her the next day that he wanted a divorce because she was an alcoholic. He warned her not to oppose him. He told her that if she resisted the divorce, he would not hesitate to ruin her.

Angela took the threat extremely seriously, as she explained in her deposition in the divorce proceedings, because she had learned during their sixteen years together that "my husband . . . is a master of psychological warfare. His nine years in Russia, at a time when that country was in a post-revolutionary state, replete with purges and liquidations, together with his medical training, causes him no pain to see the suffering of others." She also recalled that "he would boast about the way he handled people and organizations who sought in any way to block him."[1] But she didn't acquiesce to his wishes. She hated him too much.

Hammer began systematically to dismantle Angela's life. He changed the locks to his New York carriage house and told security guards at his office in the Empire State Building not to let her in. Her bank accounts were drained or frozen. Paychecks stopped coming for her household help, all of whom were on the payroll of United Distillers. He fired their longtime chauffeur, who was indispensable to her, particularly because of her progressive deafness. He hired lawyers in New York and New Jersey, including Louis Nizer, one of the most formidable attorneys in the country, and private detectives. On November 11, 1953, he formally sued Angela for divorce in New Jersey on grounds of mental cruelty. He was the plaintiff; she was the defendant.

She countersued. WIFE SUES TO NAIL $10 MILLION OF HAMMER'S $$; SAYS HE CHISELED, the New York *Daily News* reported. The accusations and counteraccusations provided grist for the gossip mill but had little bearing on the case. In *Hammer v. Hammer,* both parties wanted to be rid of each other, and the legal battle centered on money. Hammer claimed that his total wealth had dwindled to less than $2 million, much of it in difficult-to-sell assets, such as houses and art. He had very little cash in his bank account, and his tax returns showed that his total income had not exceeded $26,000 a year since 1949. Angela claimed that he had hidden funds—but she couldn't prove it. The legal depositions dragged on for more than a year.

DURING THIS HIGHLY PUBLICIZED BATTLE, BETTYE MURPHY waited in the background. Hammer had promised to marry her when it was over, in a real ceremony. But as the months passed without a more concrete commitment, she left New York and went to live with her grandparents in Illinois. Hammer begged her to come back. He told her that he wanted to have a child by her, and she relented and returned.

She was Hammer's secret ally. One night in early 1955, she had accompanied him on his yacht to the pier of Angela's farm in New Jersey. Angela was in the hospital, and he still had the keys to her house and strongbox. He said he wanted to recover two signed letters from Lenin that he knew were in her possession because she had discussed their monetary value in a telephone conversation with her sister. An old associate of his who lived in a nearby cottage on his property had bugged Angela's telephone line.[2] If she had those letters, he reasoned, she might also have pilfered more damaging papers from his files. As it turned out, he did not find the letters, but he returned to the boat with his arms full of oil paintings and his suit pockets stuffed with jewelry, all of which he said Angela had expropriated.

Bettye, with her speedwriting skills, had been given the job of transcribing the tapes of Angela's phone conversations. Hammer had already told her much about his past, but his stories always made him out to be something of a superman. Now she heard Angela's complaints about Hammer's sleeping, eating, and hygienic habits. Hammer explained to her what to pick out from the hundreds of hours of tapes. His concern was not Angela's legal strategy or her plight but what she may have found out about his past, the past he feared the FBI was still searching for.

Bettye found nothing in the tapes that would indicate that Angela knew much about this. She voiced suspicions mainly about how he may have diverted profits from their cattle-breeding business. It appeared that Hammer had ordered Prince Eric and their other breeding bulls to be injected with steroids. This had greatly increased the output of semen, which Hammer sold to breeders in Argentina, but it had also led to the birth of deformed calves, which, in turn, had resulted in lawsuits. Angela seemed anxious about the outcome of these lawsuits. She also seemed to be genuinely weary of the conflict with Hammer and ready to settle it.

Late on the evening of May 8, 1955, Bettye witnessed a sudden dramatic development in her companion's already troubled life. Hammer, who had been regularly staying at her apartment, was in his pajamas when the phone rang. It was his brother Harry, one of the few people who had her home number, and he spoke briefly to Hammer, who told him to have Olga call him immediately. Hammer sat silent until the phone rang again. He answered it and spoke to Olga, whom he had not seen in more than ten years. There was no small talk. Over and over again, he asked her to describe exactly what had happened and who had seen it happen. After he hung up, he made a call about money. He then turned to Bettye and told her that she was to fly to Los Angeles the next morning. Once there, she was to deliver to a lawyer $50,000 in cash.

She asked what had happened.

"Julian has been arrested for murder," Hammer replied.

CHAPTER FOURTEEN

LIKE FATHER, LIKE SON

WHEN HAMMER LEFT RUSSIA IN 1929, HE CONSIDERED LEAVING his wife and infant son behind. His mother forbade it: she adored Julian, who was then an extraordinarily beautiful baby, with blue eyes and blond hair. So Hammer brought them with him to Paris and then to New York. But Julian did not fit in with his second life. He didn't speak English at first and was an uncomfortable reminder of Hammer's life in Russia. Julian later recalled that he was unable to connect with his father, no matter what he did. When Julian threw a temper tantrum, his father pretended not to notice. Even before his parents separated, Julian was sent away to boarding schools. He moved with his mother from Highland Falls to Los Angeles when he was ten. He recalled that he "never saw my father at Christmas during this period," although he did occasionally visit him at "the ranch," as he called the Shadow Isle estate in New Jersey. But even then he would often be left alone while his father attended to business. When Hammer made an appointment to see his son, he would almost invariably break the date. Julian later tried to explain this away:

> I realize that my father was always a busy man and I question why he should be expected to give up a part of his life for me. In my early life there were some occasions when he would agree to meet me or take me out and then find himself dealing

Hammer and his son, Julian.

with business matters and so unable to honor his commitment to me. . . . These incidents put me in a stronger negotiating position for financial help.[1]

In retrospect, Julian realized that his relationship with his father was always a multidimensional negotiation. At one level, he tried to get something tangible—petty cash or a gift for himself; at a deeper level, the negotiation was about getting his father to recognize him as his son. It was at the latter level that his father kept rejecting him.

Even as a child, Julian saw his father, yellow pad in hand, as calculating. He always seemed to reduce even the most highly charged emotional issue—such as the pain his mother would express over the family's separation—to a cold-blooded analysis of costs and benefits. To play in this game, Julian believed that he had to create his own "bargaining chips." He used truancy, juvenile delinquency, and other self-destructive behavior as factors on the cost side of his balance sheet. Julian would then offer to negate the undesired behavior in return for a benefit, such as a fishing vacation with his father.

To please his father, Julian went to Marshall College in Huntington, West Virginia, where he drank, gambled, and took a course in journalism. He then tried to impress his father with his journalistic skills by presenting him with a twenty-page account of one of the rare vacations they had taken together, a trip to the Caribbean when he had just turned twenty-one. Entitled "Caribbean Diary: A Factual Account of the Way a Business Trip Should Really Be Taken," he dedicated it "To Dad and Angela." It is a witty and perceptive essay that ends with one of his persistent fantasies. Their private plane would crash, and the newspaper headlines would proclaim ALCOHOL TYCOON & FAMILY LOST IN CRASH LANDING OFF FLORIDA COAST. He also supplied an alternative title, TYPHOON DOWNS TYCOON.[2] Apparently, Hammer was not amused. He never acknowledged to Julian that he had read the piece.

Julian gave up journalism, dropped out of college, and enlisted in the army. Later, he attempted to eke out a living as a writer of Western adventures, and he got married, to Glenna Sue Ervin, a young divorcée. His father sent neither congratulations nor money. In fact, as Julian's twenty-sixth birthday approached, he realized that he had not seen his father in nearly three years. On the afternoon of his birthday, he ran into an old acquaintance, a soldier named Bruce Whitlock. They had briefly been roommates and drinking buddies several years before.[3] Although Julian realized that Whitlock was "rough trade," having served prison time, he had been, as he later put it, "seduced by his carefree lifestyle." What fascinated Julian about Whitlock was that "he seemed to break the rules and somehow manage to get away with it."[4] So they had a wild reunion. They drank beer, martinis, and vodka and went to a Russian restaurant, where Glenna Sue joined them for a birthday dinner. Since she was five months pregnant and didn't want to stay out all night, they went back to Julian and Glenna Sue's apartment. Glenna Sue went to sleep, and Julian and Whitlock continued drinking. At about 3:00 A.M., there were two shots—and screams.

When the police arrived at Julian's home, they found Whitlock dead in a pool of blood. Julian gave his version of what happened. He had offered Whitlock his IOU to satisfy a $400 gambling debt. Whitlock did not accept it and asked instead for Julian's car and clothes. Julian refused. The negotiation became progressively uglier, and Whitlock demanded that Julian, in lieu of the debt, allow him to have sex with his wife. When Julian tried to block his way to the bedroom, Whitlock, who had been a boxing champion, knocked him down. Julian then got his pistol from a drawer. Whitlock came at him with a broken bottle, and Julian fired twice—with dead accuracy.

Julian was arrested and arraigned on a charge of first-degree manslaughter. That was when his mother called Hammer for help.

When Hammer read the *Los Angeles Times*'s headline above the story about Julian's arrest, he could not help recalling how it paralleled a headline thirty-six years before, when his father had been arrested for manslaughter. This time it was not MILLIONAIRE DOCTOR ARRESTED, but MILLIONAIRE'S SON KILLS GI.[5] If his father had not stepped in to take the blame for that unfortunate death, he too might have been charged with manslaughter. It was now his turn to rescue his son.

Through an intermediary, Hammer retained Mitchell, Silberberg and Knupp, a high-powered Los Angeles law firm with a reputation for its connections to the California political establishment.[6] A young partner, Arthur Groman, was assigned the case. Groman was to become an important part of Hammer's life.

Arthur Groman studied the agreed-upon facts of the case: Julian had shot Whitlock twice in the chest. Whitlock, as an autopsy confirmed, had a high level of alcohol in his blood at the time. There were no witnesses to the shooting other than Julian and Glenna Sue (who could not be compelled to testify against her husband). Groman then filed a brief severely limiting the state's ability to refute Julian's account. Citing a recent ruling by the California Supreme Court that the prosecution could not impeach its own witness, it argued that since the prosecution had used Julian as its witness in preliminary proceedings to establish the facts, it could not challenge the credibility of his testimony in a future trial. It was a technical point, but it held. If the prosecutor could not undermine Julian's account, there was no point in bringing him to trial, since it is legal in California to shoot someone in self-defense. In July, the prosecutor dismissed the charges.

Three months later, Julian's son was born. Hammer had a grandson. He was christened Michael Armand Hammer.

THE INTERMEDIARY WHO HAD HELPED HAMMER WITH JULIAN'S legal defense was Congressman James Roosevelt, the eldest son of FDR. Roosevelt had begun his political career in 1937 as his father's military aide. He attracted attention for intervening in politically sensitive cases and offering his influence to financial backers of the Democratic Party. As his unabashed efforts to make money for himself grew more and more controversial, FDR had little choice but to ease him out of the White House. James then tried the insurance business, working as a broker, but was unable to make enough money to support his multiple divorces. When he decided to run for Congress in California in 1954, he explained that politics "is the only thing for which I have any fundamental training."[7] With the Roosevelt name, he had little problem getting elected.

Hammer saw an opportunity. He knew that Roosevelt needed money, and Hammer needed a point man in Congress. To be sure, he still had his connection with Senators Bridges and Gore, but they had shown that there were limits to how far they would go in his behalf. What Hammer needed was someone in Congress who would cross the line when necessary, and Roosevelt appeared to be his man. After Julian's case was dismissed, he telegraphed Roosevelt, "Your help . . . played important role. Deeply appreciative." He sent Roosevelt his private phone numbers and invited him to call him if he needed any assistance.[8]

Roosevelt bit. He told Hammer he was in deep financial trouble, "a drowning man." He urgently needed $2,500 to meet his alimony payments and debts. He inquired whether Hammer, through his gallery, could sell some of Roosevelt's only objects of value: a diamond ring, two letters to him from his father, and a letter to him signed by President Truman marked "Personal and Confidential."

Hammer sent him the $2,500, which was to be an "advance" against the sale of the objects. He then suggested that he could also help straighten out the affairs of Roosevelt and Sargent, Incorporated, a business Roosevelt had set up to sell group insurance.[9] Roosevelt, excited at the prospect of Hammer coming to his rescue, had told him that "I believe that not more than $10,000 in capital is needed in the company. . . . I would like to get a partner."[10] Hammer said that the money was not a problem and that, working through his accountant, Hammer would be Roosevelt's silent partner. He would not only put up capital, but he would also persuade corporations he was associated with to use Roosevelt and Sargent as brokers for their employee insurance.[11]

Hammer cultivated Roosevelt socially, sending his plane to pick him up and inviting him to Campobello (where Roosevelt had gone as a child, when it belonged to FDR). Roosevelt had found his patron, someone willing to solve his financial problems. Hammer had his man in Congress, someone who would prove extremely useful for his plans.

CHAPTER FIFTEEN

THE
MARITAL
EL DORADO

HAMMER'S DIVORCE FROM ANGELA CAME THROUGH ON JANUARY 19, 1956. After years of conflict, it was more of a relief than a victory for both parties. Angela got back her farm in New Jersey, a cash settlement of $30,000 (which paid her legal bills), and alimony of $1,000 a month. Hammer retained his yacht, his art gallery, his carriage house in Manhattan, a farm in New Jersey, and his freedom. Six days later, Hammer remarried. But his new bride was not his mistress, Bettye Murphy, whom he had promised to marry and who was by now five months pregnant with his child. She was Frances Barrett Tolman, a frail but dignified widow.

At fifty-three, Frances was quite wealthy. She had inherited more than $8 million from her husband, Elmer Tolman, who had died a little over a year earlier. Having no children or immediate relatives, she lived alone, with only a part-time maid, in the Holmby Hills section of Los Angeles, in a large house that had previously belonged to a movie star. She was lonely, and in early 1955 she chanced on a tabloid article describing in lurid detail the marital problems of Armand Hammer. She realized when she saw his photograph that he was someone she had met twenty years before at one of the Hammer Galleries' department-store sales. She telegraphed him at the gallery, expressing her sympathy and asking "if she could be of help."[1]

Armand and Frances Hammer in Venice on their honeymoon, July 1956.

Hammer, after ascertaining how wealthy she was, realized that there was something she could do for him: provide him with money. According to his 1955 tax return, his total income was under $27,000 a year, and that was the highest it had been in six years.[2] His yacht, plane, and country estate had all been paid for by United Distillers, which was now itself running out of money. His art gallery was heavily in debt. He had to pay lawyers for both his divorce and Julian's defense. He had to help support an ex-wife, an estranged wife, and a mistress. When he asked Frances that May to lend him the $50,000 that he needed for Julian's release, she instantly wired her bank in New York to give it to him. These were the funds that Bettye delivered to the Los Angeles lawyer (although she had no idea they had come from Frances—or that Frances even existed).[3] From that point on, his secret courtship of Frances was accompanied by secret financial arrangements with her. He promised to marry her when his divorce was settled.[4]

As Christmas approached, he told Bettye about this plan. He told her in a quiet, dispassionate voice that she was, and always would be, his true love—the reincarnation of his lost love—but that "compelling circumstances" made it necessary for him to marry Frances. Before she could speak, he outlined what he had in mind for her. It was as if he were laying down the terms of a deal. She would move to Mexico in order to maintain the secrecy of their relationship. She was to tell no one, not even their child when it was born, about him. In return, he would provide her with a house in Mexico City, a new identity, and financial support for the rest of her life. He would also provide her with a sham marriage to a Mexican national, who would be paid to go through with the ceremony so that their child would be legitimate (but not bear Hammer's name).

Bettye was stunned. She had taken him at his word when he promised that they would be married. She had come to New York with him, giving up her job in Florida. She had waited for nearly three years for him to get his divorce. She had been his accomplice in wiretapping and burglary. She was about to have his child, a child he had asked for. Now he was proposing to send her to a foreign country, where she knew no one and did not speak the language. In addition, she would have to go through yet another sham marriage. She understood the reasons that lay behind his scheme. The choice, crudely put, was between love and money—and he chose money.

Her range of choices was, on the other hand, limited by the reality of her situation. She had no job, home, or income—other than what he had provided her—and she was about to have a baby that she could not afford to raise. Bettye had seen how he had run roughshod over Angela because she opposed his will, and she accepted his terms.

In January, a few days before his wedding, Hammer's movers arrived at Bettye's apartment. They loaded her personal effects and dog into a station wagon and left for Mexico. Two days later, Hammer's pilot flew her to El Paso. Hammer's lawyer took her across the Mexican border and introduced her to a Mexican stranger who was to be her "rent-a-husband." They signed the divorce papers even before the two-minute wedding ceremony began. Afterward, the man disappeared, and she was driven in the station wagon to Mexico City.

On May 15, 1956, Bettye gave birth to a seven-pound, six-ounce girl who was named, on Hammer's instructions, Victoria—the name of Hammer's grandmother. A few weeks later, Hammer flew to Mexico to see his daughter. He had lost weight. He was now on a strict diet, and he told Bettye that he swam twenty laps a day for exercise. Suntanned and in a white sport shirt, he looked in remarkably good shape for a man who was about to celebrate his fifty-eighth birthday. His new marriage—and secret paternity—seemed to have rejuvenated him. After staying for about an hour, he put on his dark sunglasses and signaled his chauffeur. He told Bettye that he had to meet Frances, who knew nothing of his secret life in Mexico, that evening in Los Angeles, and his plane was waiting.

HAMMER COULD FINALLY TRAVEL FREELY. THE STATE DEPARTMENT, which had previously denied him a passport on unspecified national-security grounds, had issued him one on October 28, 1955, after he signed an oath stating he was not a member of the Communist Party. It was his first new passport since 1928. The change in the State Department's treatment of him suggested, as Senator Bridges had hinted to him a few months earlier, that J. Edgar Hoover had finally closed the security case against him. If so, Hammer was now free to pursue the plan to acquire an ammonia plant, which had been interrupted in 1951, when he realized that he was the subject of a government investigation.

Meanwhile in the Soviet Union, the negotiations that his mother had begun some seven years earlier in Germany to see her Russian grandson, Armasha, were bearing fruit. In early 1956, Soviet authorities arranged for Armasha, who was now twenty-eight years old and teaching school in Kazakhstan, to return to Moscow. They also invited his American family to visit him there.

Rose Hammer was absolutely set on seeing Armasha before she died. She wasted no time in renewing her passport. She added a handwritten letter to the State Department that April, pleading, "Please permit me to visit my grandson in Moscow."[5] In May, she and Victor flew to Russia.

Shortly thereafter, the long-awaited reunion took place at the Savoy Hotel, across from the Kremlin. Neither Rose nor Victor knew what Armasha looked like—the last photograph of him they had was taken when he was a two-year-old toddler—and they were surprised by his gruff appearance. He was a muscular, partly balding man with grotesque steel dentures. He introduced himself in perfect English and told of the life he had lived since he had been abandoned by his father. During the war, he had been evacuated from Moscow to Central Asia. Later he was admitted to the elite Institute of Foreign Languages in Moscow—after Victor Hammer had agreed to pay the tuition as well as his expenses. He became proficient in Spanish and English, and with the $700-a-month stipend he was receiving from America, he was able to move in the upper strata of Moscow society. After he graduated from the language institute, he had been sent to Kirgiz, where he got married and had a daughter.[6]

Armasha told them that he wanted to visit them in New York. He explained that the Soviet authorities would grant him an exit visa if he could get a U.S. visa. Victor assured him that they would get him the visa.

While Rose and Victor were reacquainting themselves with Armasha, Armand and Frances were on a honeymoon in Venice, Paris, and London. In London, they stayed at Claridge's for two weeks. During the day, they went to art museums and galleries, since Frances's hobby was copying the great masters in oils. During the evening, they went to the theater, which she also enjoyed. He wanted to please her. When they returned to Los Angeles in August, he moved into her spacious home.

Hammer had begun managing Frances's investments for her. He lent substantial amounts of her money to his own companies, United Distillers and the Hammer Galleries, to get them out of debt. He also invested in a number of other business ventures. They included a mine in Wyoming that produced ersatz jade for jewelry (and proved unprofitable), a radio network (which he quickly resold), and a small oil company in Los Angeles. On paper, the oil company looked moribund. It lost money, it had less than $14,000 in its bank account, and its revenues, which were from dying oil wells, had fallen to less than $600 a week. But Hammer wanted this company for two reasons: its stock was listed on the Los Angeles Stock Exchange, and it had a name he liked: the Occidental Petroleum Corporation.

He now had a new wife, a new residence, a new congressman, and a new corporation. Even though he was approaching his sixtieth year, he was ready for another new life.

PART THREE

THE
OIL
TYCOON

Господину А. Хаммеру
Первому концессионеру беседовавшему с В.И. Лениным
18-II-1961. С наилучшими пожеланиями Н. Хрущев

Hammer with Nikita Khrushchev.
The inscription says, "To Mr. A. Hammer, the first concessionaire
who conferred with V.I. Lenin. February 18, 1961.
With the best wishes of N. Khrushchev."

CHAPTER SIXTEEN

THE PATH REOPENED: FROM KENNEDY TO KHRUSHCHEV

ON JANUARY 19, 1961, INAUGURATION EVE, A FREEZING SNOW-storm choked Washington, D.C. The icy drifts on Pennsylvania Avenue were so high that army engineers had to use flamethrowers to cut a pathway through to the Capitol rotunda. Despite the blizzard, John Fitzgerald Kennedy was sworn in as the thirty-fifth president of the United States at noon the next day, and Robert Frost spoke movingly of "a golden age of poetry and power, of which this noonday's the beginning hour."[1] Hammer was in the grandstands, watching the young president take his oath. He had braved the storm to fly to Washington because he was determined to speak with Kennedy, seeing an opportunity, as he put it, "to play my part" in the new administration.[2]

That evening, Hammer was Senator Albert Gore's guest at one of the five black-tie inaugural balls. He could count on Gore for such invitations. He had made him his partner in the cattle-breeding business—a partnership that had proved profitable—and he had given him each Christmas over the past five years a gift of antique silver. Since Gore had been a close colleague of Kennedy's in the Senate, there seemed to be a good possibility that Kennedy might stop by his table, and Hammer sat patiently next to Pauline Gore, waiting for such a moment. But in his rush to get to the other balls, Kennedy bypassed the Hammer-Gore group.[3]

Hammer wanted to discuss with Kennedy his plan to go to Russia. That October, he had received an intriguing message from Moscow, delivered by his nephew, Armasha. After having had his trip to the United States inexplicably delayed for years by the Soviet Ministry of Foreign Affairs, Armasha had finally received his visa in 1960. On his visit, Armasha told his uncle how he was living a gilded life in Moscow, consorting with the sons and daughters of the Communist elite. He said that his friends spoke often of Hammer and that he understood from them that Hammer would be treated like a "hero" by the Soviet leadership if he visited Moscow.

Hammer did not think particularly highly of his nephew—in fact, he later expressed doubts that he *was* his nephew.[4] He would probably have regarded such talk as flattery if not for one thing: Armasha's visit had been made possible by the personal intervention of Nikita Khrushchev. By this time, Khrushchev had called for "coexistence" with the West. Was he now interested in reopening the path that had been closed for so long?

Hammer realized, as he later wrote, that relations between the United States and the Soviet Union were then "veering perilously toward confrontation."[5] Only a few months before, a U.S. U-2 reconnaissance plane had been shot down over Russia, and Khrushchev had withdrawn from a summit conference scheduled to be held in Paris among the leaders of France, West Germany, the United States, and the Soviet Union. In this tense atmosphere, Hammer had to be particularly careful to avoid the appearance that he was undertaking a trip to Moscow at the behest of the Soviets. The ideal way of protecting himself against such suspicions was to go to Russia with the imprimatur of a U.S. president. He had hoped a meeting with Kennedy would result in one. He even envisioned being able to account for his trip by saying (as later he did, anyhow, in a speech to the Foreign Policy Association of New York in 1981): "My friendship with Jack Kennedy afforded me the opportunity to return to Moscow. . . . President Kennedy asked me to see what could be done to establish better trade relations with the U.S.S.R."[6]

Since Hammer was scheduled to leave for Moscow in mid-February, the time needed to get such authorization was rapidly running out, and he now turned to the "drowning man" to whom he had earlier thrown a well-calculated lifeline, Congressman James Roosevelt. Hammer had provided Roosevelt with campaign contributions, vacation homes, and plane tickets and had made his insurance company, Roosevelt and Sargent (in which Hammer was a silent partner), Occidental's insurer. He had also arranged for Roosevelt to participate in one of Occidental's more promising explorations for oil.[7]

Roosevelt went directly to Lawrence O'Brien, the president's chief of staff and also an old friend of Roosevelt's. He told O'Brien that it would be a great favor to him if he could set up a "courtesy" meeting between Hammer and Kennedy, no matter how brief.[8] He pointedly explained that Hammer, as chairman of Occidental Petroleum, was in a position to provide the Democrats with substantial financial support in California, and this support might also prove useful to the president.[9]

Hammer's new identity as a California oilman was indeed impressive. Although Occidental was still losing money—$127,000 in 1960—it had caught the imagination of Wall Street. Between 1956, when he assumed control, and January 1961, its shares had appreciated more than 6,000 percent. On paper, Occidental now had a market value of over $10 million.

An important part of this extraordinary rise proceeded from Hammer's ability to put the best face on problematic oil-drilling results. For Hammer, this was not all that different from selling the so-called Romanoff treasure. In both cases, image counted more than substance, at least in the short run. In 1958, for example, he announced with great fanfare a major Occidental discovery in Nicaragua. The company's stock price skyrocketed even though, as was disclosed in a footnote in the annual report two years later, there was no oil. (Similarly, he announced that Occidental had found the "largest iron ore deposit in the western part of the United States" and gold in Montana—all on dubious geologic evidence.)[10]

To be sure, Hammer's skillful hype accounted for only part of Occidental's success. He also used his wife's fortune, as well as money he got from a few outside investors, to buy oil leases for Occidental—on terms that proved favorable to the company. The infusion of capital led to increases in Occidental's oil finds and greatly added to the aura of success surrounding the company.

Hammer was a resourceful businessman with an eye for talent, and he managed to get for Occidental one of the best oil drillers in California, Eugene Reid. Using his high-flying stock as currency, Hammer bought Reid's small wildcatting company and then made him head of exploration for Occidental. Hammer not only went out to the drilling sites himself at all hours, but he also relentlessly drove others who worked for him. For example, when he needed data from his chief financial adviser, Maury Leibovitz, and found that Leibovitz had gone off on a camping vacation with his family in a small motorboat on the Sacramento River, he had his secretary get the number of all 114 telephone booths at marinas along the river and call them day and night until Leibovitz answered one of the phones.[11]

Maury Leibovitz, who had a degree in psychology as well as one in accounting, found that Hammer had not only an extraordinary ability to digest information but also a keen gambling instinct. "The Doctor sees Lady Luck," Leibovitz explained in an interview. "Once he perceives she is present, he'll chase her, romance her, even make love to her."[12]

Hammer's calculated gambles were augmented by Reid's uncanny skill at hitting oil and gas in northern California. By 1961, Occidental, although still small by international standards, was a widely known, respectable-size California oil company. And Hammer was in a position to give generous financial help to Democratic candidates.

Nevertheless, Lawrence O'Brien was unable to arrange for Hammer to see Kennedy. The best O'Brien could offer him was a signed photograph of the president.

Since Hammer would not be going to Moscow under the aegis of President Kennedy, he needed another sponsor, and Senator Gore helped provide one. In late January, the senator approached Luther Hodges, the new secretary of commerce, and suggested to him that since Hammer planned to visit the Soviet Union and other countries as a private citizen, it would be worthwhile to have him report his findings about business conditions in those countries to the Department of Commerce.

Secretary Hodges had no reason to decline the request. Gore was an important Democratic senator, and it involved no commitment on his part (Hammer would be paying his own expenses and traveling on a tourist visa). Hodges took the precaution, however, of ordering that the intelligence files on Hammer be reviewed. The results did not entirely reassure him. He wrote Secretary of State Dean Rusk, "We had a security check made on Dr. Hammer which, as you probably know, was not too conclusive."[13]

By this time, Hammer was heading for Moscow. He arrived there with Frances on February 11, 1961. Frances was his full-time traveling helpmate, and she enjoyed this new role. Hammer was attentive to her and chivalrous in introducing her to others. He also went to great lengths to explain "the world according to Hammer," as she put it.[14]

As they drove into town from the airport in his ZIL limousine, Hammer could not help contrasting what he saw now with what he had seen when he had first come to Moscow in 1921. Instead of the "crumbling shacks" that had once greeted him, there were tall housing towers. Instead of horse-drawn sleighs skidding down dirt roads, there were Soviet-built taxicabs moving down modern highways. Instead of people "dressed in rags," he saw that nearly everyone wore "serviceable"—if monotonous—clothing. Instead of starving children, he saw young people "skating and skiing." When Frances and he arrived at the Sovietskaya, a hotel reserved for top party officials and foreign VIPs, he found that although it was not luxurious by Western standards, their suite was spacious, clean, and well appointed.[15] It was probably the warmest winter that Moscovites had experienced in fifty years, and there was even fresh fruit in the marketplace.

Hammer wasted little time in making contact with the U.S. Embassy. On February 14, he met with William Morrell, Jr., who was the counselor for economic affairs and reported to the Department of Commerce. (In fact, although Hammer had no way of knowing it at the time, Morrell was part of the CIA contingent in Moscow.) They went together to the Soviet Ministry of Trade, where they met the chief of trade for Western countries and his deputy for trade with the United States. They were given the more or less standard reception for visiting business VIPs, and Hammer heard the more or less standard briefing on the possibilities of expanding trade in peaceful goods between the Soviet Union and the United States.[16] When they returned to the U.S. Embassy, Hammer told Morrell that he now wanted to see Anastas Mikoyan, the deputy prime minister and the real power behind Soviet trade.[17]

According to Hammer, Morrell was taken aback by the idea that Hammer warranted such a high-level meeting. Morrell explained to him in a patronizing tone that Deputy Prime Minister Mikoyan did not see U.S. businessmen. What Morrell evidently did not realize was that Hammer was no ordinary American businessman. Hammer already knew Mikoyan. He had met him during the NEP days, when they were both in their twenties. Mikoyan was Stalin's protégé when Hammer was considered to be the Soviet Union's "path" to U.S. business, and their careers kept intersecting. Mikoyan was commissar for trade; Hammer was a conduit for foreign trade. Mikoyan was in charge of fitting foreign concessions into Soviet strategy; Hammer was a concessionaire. Mikoyan headed the project for selling art to the West; Hammer was the Soviet Union's dealer in New York. Hammer later said that he never met "a smarter man at any level of political office, anywhere," than Mikoyan.[18]

The day after Hammer's meeting with Morrell, a Soviet limousine picked him up at his hotel and drove him to the Kremlin to meet with Mikoyan. Mikoyan's interpreter was the only other person at this meeting, which began promptly at 5:00 P.M., according to Hammer's very abbreviated version of it, "with reminiscences of our meeting 35 years ago." It ended, an hour and thirty-five minutes later, with Hammer offering to send Mikoyan "one of my bulls as a gift."[19] The portion of the discussion that Hammer chose to relate to the Commerce Department concerned the usual Soviet complaints about the unfairness of U.S. trade policy. Whatever else was said can only be speculated on, but in less than forty hours, Hammer was back in the Kremlin. He had been summoned there by Khrushchev himself. Earlier that morning, February 17, Khrushchev had ratcheted up the cold war a dangerous notch by threatening to counter in Berlin what he characterized as "extensive military preparations" by the West German government.[20] Any Soviet move to put pressure on Berlin, which was cut off from the rest of West Germany, could force Kennedy into a military confrontation. But Khrushchev had a more amicable—and mutually profitable—alternative in mind: an expansion of trade, for which Hammer could be a vehicle.[21]

ALTHOUGH FOUR YEARS HAMMER'S SENIOR, KHRUSHCHEV HAD never met Lenin. In the mid-1920s, he had become a commissar in the Ukrainian coal mines, then survived Stalin's purges, and by the time of Stalin's death was the secretary of the Communist Party's Central Committee. He was both crude and cunning—a 1959 CIA psychological study noted that he also could be "deadly and dangerous."[22]

Hammer was struck by "the continuity" between his Soviet summits. He wrote later that "Khrushchev repeated many of the points Lenin had made to me when he drew his chair near to mine in 1921. . . . Like Lenin, Khrushchev admired American technology. . . . Like Lenin, he believed that American industry could profit from trade with the USSR."[23] There was another parallel he did not note: just as Boris Reinstein, Lenin's Americanologist, had sat in on Hammer's original Kremlin meeting, now Anatoly Dobrynin, the head of the Central Committee's U.S.A. Department and Khrushchev's chief Americanologist, sat in on this one.

The session with Khrushchev lasted two hours and five minutes. Afterward, as if to commemorate the reopening of the path, Dobrynin arranged for Hammer to visit his former pencil factory—now the Sacco and Vanzetti Pencil Manufacturing Factory—for the ceremonial presentation of a pencil. The *Moscow News* carried the story—and Hammer's photograph.

He departed with Frances for London the next day. The Soviets had provided a new jetliner that had no other passengers on it. From London, he wrote Secretary Hodges that "in view of the fact that there were many things stated in my interview with both Mikoyan and Khrushchev which could be conveyed better in person, I have decided . . . to return to Washington to make a personal report to you, and any other interested member of our government."[24]

Hammer got the requested meeting with Hodges on February 25, 1961. After recounting Khrushchev's concerns about modernizing Soviet food production, he reeled off the litany of complaints about the restrictiveness of the U.S. trade policy. Khrushchev had argued that if the United States improved its terms of trade, the Soviet Union would buy more U.S. goods and thus help the economy and create jobs for workers. Khrushchev had further suggested that such mutually beneficial trade could be greatly increased if the United States made credit available to the Soviet Union—so it could buy now and pay later.[25]

Hodges listened courteously, but he had heard this argument before. What Hammer did not tell Hodges—or discuss in any of his other reports to the Department of Commerce or to the U.S. Embassy in Moscow—was his own proposed role in expanding the Soviets' petrochemical capacity. The plan, which was still in an early stage, would eventually involve Hammer's using U.S. financing to acquire for the Soviet Union the means to produce massive quantities of phosphate fertilizer.

OCCIDENTAL PETROLEUM WAS THE VEHICLE THROUGH WHICH THE various parts of the vast fertilizer project would be assembled. Occidental was perceived on Wall Street as a quintessential capitalist company, dedicated to moneymaking. The discovery of natural gas at its Lathrop Field in California in December 1961 further advanced the value of its stock, which was Hammer's currency for acquiring other companies.

In order to carry out the complex international project, Hammer needed to take absolute control of Occidental. He was the company's chairman and president, but he owned only 10 percent of Occidental's 3.5 million shares at that time, which meant that his directors, representing the other 90 percent of its ownership, could, in theory at least, resist his plan to move the company into the fertilizer-exporting business. To make sure that this did not happen, he began calling on Occidental's directors. He told them that if they wanted to continue serving on his board, they must give him a signed but undated letter of resignation. With these letters in his pocket, he could at any point in the future remove them from the board without prior warning. One by one, the directors complied with this extraordinary request. Technically, this coup violated the Securities and Exchange Commission's disclosure rules for publicly traded companies (since obviously it deceived stockholders, allowing them to believe their board of directors had independence), but since no one outside the boardroom knew about the letters, Hammer was able to do whatever he wanted with Occidental. He sought out the appropriate acquisitions to transform Occidental from a California oil and gas company to a producer of fertilizers that could be exported.

Hammer's plan would work only if the Kennedy administration moved to relax the policies that had effectively closed down trade with the Soviet bloc since the onset of the cold war in the late 1940s. The

Export Control Act of 1949 required all U.S. businesses to obtain export licenses before they could sell to the Soviet Union any product that could conceivably enhance its industrial or military capabilities. Since these licenses were seldom granted, the policy amounted to an undeclared embargo. The United States had also pressed its NATO allies and Japan to join a ban on "strategic exports" to the Soviet bloc, which was enforced by NATO's Coordinating Committee on Export Controls. If any other nation, even one that was neutral, sent proscribed goods to the Soviet bloc, it faced economic retaliation by the United States and its allies. The United States further reduced the possibility of the Soviet Union's obtaining the means to import Western goods by prohibiting the institutions that ordinarily financed international trade from providing the Soviet Union with any credit. The Soviet Union was also denied most-favored-nation status, which meant that it had to pay a much higher tariff than most other nations on products it exported to the United States. By the late 1950s, preventing trade with the Soviet bloc had taken on the rationale, if not the zeal, of a theological crusade: if communism was an unmitigated evil, then trading with Communist countries was like trading with the devil. In this atmosphere, labor unions were successfully encouraged to refuse to handle Soviet goods on the grounds that they had been produced by Communist "slave labor." At the outset of his presidency, Kennedy had shown a willingness to ease, if not abandon, these measures.

Since Occidental's move into the fertilizer business involved considerable risks—for example, a sudden change in foreign relations could leave the company with no overseas market for fertilizer—Hammer kept in close contact with the Soviet government. He provided a plausible context for his frequent communications with the Soviet missions in New York and Washington, D.C., by arranging for a Soviet art exhibition in the United States. He also wrote to the Soviet Embassy about the logistics of sending two prize Angus heifers and two Angus bulls to Khrushchev, sending copies of the correspondence to the State Department. He suggested that the shipment be handled by Amtorg, the Soviet agency he had helped set up in the 1920s.[26] He met with Soviet Ambassador Mikhail Menshikov and even held a dinner party for him. Since the ambassador reported directly to Dobrynin, he served as a convenient channel.[27]

In June 1963, with all his ducks in a row, Hammer made a four-day trip to Moscow. His timing couldn't have been better. Khrushchev, in desperate trouble over the failure of the agricultural component of the Soviet Union's Five-Year Plan, had made the development of a massive agrochemical industry an urgent priority. Hammer received the encouragement he needed to proceed.

From Moscow, Hammer announced that Occidental was purchasing the Best Fertilizer Companies of California, which had developed a new technology for concentrating phosphates in sulfuric acid. The result was a powerful fertilizer base, called superphosphoric acid, or SPA, that was ideal for exporting to Russia. When Hammer returned to America, he began assembling the necessary components for merchandising fertilizer. He bought International Ore and Fertilizer Corporation, the world's largest exporter of fertilizers, which provided a ready-made network for warehousing, shipping, and trading the requisite components. He bought Jefferson Lake Sulfur, the third-largest producer of sulfur in America, which provided the sulfuric acid needed for the SPA. He bought huge phosphate deposits in Florida. He also bought Nordac Limited, a British company that held important patents on SPA technology. Occidental was suddenly a new entity: its fertilizer division accounted for over 90 percent of both its revenues and its earnings. Hammer now had the exportable-fertilizer capacity that the U.S. Army had denied him a decade earlier.

Hammer did not want to be blocked again by a suspicious government. Ever since he had returned from Russia in 1961, he had pushed, without success, to associate himself publicly with President Kennedy. He even had Senator Gore propose that he act as the president's intermediary in Berlin when another crisis occurred there.[28] The White House did not respond to that offer, so Hammer donated the former Roosevelt home on Campobello to the U.S. government and proposed that Kennedy, who he assumed would want to identify himself with FDR, attend the dedication ceremony. But the White House again declined, offering only to have Kennedy "send a message."[29] Now, after consummating the fertilizer acquisitions, Hammer sent Kennedy a telegram:

MY COMPANY RECENTLY ACQUIRED LARGEST INDEPENDENT SUP-
PLIER OF AMERICAN FERTILIZER MATERIALS IN THE WORLD WITH 23
BRANCHES OPERATING IN 59 COUNTRIES AND DOING TURNOVER OF

$65 MILLION. I BELIEVE OUR ORGANIZATION WILL BE ABLE TO FUR-
NISH AMERICAN KNOW-HOW TO HELP HUNGRY PEOPLE THROUGH-
OUT THE WORLD TO RAISE THEIR STANDARD OF LIVING WHICH IS
THE BEST ANSWER TO COMMUNISM AND OTHER OPPRESSIVE SYSTEMS
ENDANGERING PEACE. HAVE ASKED JIMMY ROOSEVELT TO REQUEST
MEETING WITH YOU IN WASHINGTON NEXT WEEK TO EXPLAIN MY
PLAN MORE FULLY.[30]

Even after recasting his enterprise as an antidote to communism,
Hammer did not receive his requested meeting. On September 25, he
learned from Roosevelt that Kennedy could not see him in the foreseeable future because he had scheduled "a trip to several states in
connection with conservation problems."[31] Nor would another opportunity present itself before Kennedy was killed in Dallas on
November 22.

Nevertheless, Hammer went ahead with the fertilizer project. In
May, he wrote Khrushchev a formal request for a meeting (supplying
a copy to the Commerce Department). He noted, as if Khrushchev
had not been already informed, "We now have the largest fertilizer
company in the western part of the U.S.," and "I am hopeful I can be
of some assistance in bringing our two countries together in helping
to supply your needs in fertilizer plants, etc."[32] A month later, he was
in Moscow meeting with Khrushchev, Mikoyan, and Menshikov (who
had recently taken over the U.S.A. Department in Moscow while Dobrynin went to Washington as the Soviet ambassador).[33] Khrushchev
had already committed himself to a crash program to raise the annual
Soviet production of chemical fertilizers from five million tons to one
hundred million tons by the end of the decade. And Hammer now
possessed the technology to contribute to this expansion. According
to Hammer's memorandum of the meeting, Khrushchev predicted
that "if you are successful in this [fertilizer project], it will be much
bigger than building the first pencil factory."[34] To this end, Hammer
had brought to Moscow some of Occidental's top technicians, but it
took most of the summer for them to work out the details.

An Agreement in Principle was officially announced in Moscow on
September 26, 1964. To provide a historical context for this deal,
Izvestiya reprinted the chapter from Hammer's 1932 book, The Quest
of the Romanoff Treasure, that describes Lenin asking him to "break
the ice" between Russia and America. The plan called for Occidental

to create from scratch a state-of-the-art agrochemical industry for the Soviet Union. It envisioned building ten new fertilizer plants in the Krasnoyarsk region of central Siberia that would process the SPA concentrate that Hammer would ship over from America and Africa in specially built tankers. It would cost well over $1 billion and would produce enough fertilizer—some 50 million tons a year—to change the face of Soviet agriculture.[35]

If it worked out as planned, Hammer would have what was tantamount to a monopoly on importing phosphate bases for Soviet fertilizers. He would have achieved this by again applying the rules he had learned in the Leninist era. He had started at the top. He had collaborated with Mikoyan in developing a project that would help fulfill the Soviet Five-Year Plan. He had cloaked the purpose of the project in altruism, suggesting that it was designed to "help hungry people throughout the world to raise their standard of living" and was "the best answer to communism." And now that the project was out in the open, he made it look like a success.

The day the plan was announced in Moscow, Hammer held a press conference in London, where he was hoping to borrow money for the project. He explained that "our know-how is what the Russians want." When a journalist asked about possible political ramifications of what amounted to an unprecedented transfer of technology at the height of the cold war, Hammer answered, "I am a businessman not a politician, and this is business."[36]

But it was the sort of business that was not so easily divorced from politics, as events demonstrated. Just two weeks after Hammer's press conference, Khrushchev was abruptly removed from power, and shortly thereafter the Soviet fertilizer project, which had been closely identified with the deposed leader, was temporarily suspended. By the time Khrushchev's successor, Leonid Brezhnev, was prepared to resume the project, in 1965, the escalating war in Vietnam brought the rapprochement between the United States and the Soviet Union to a screeching halt. Despite Hammer's prodigious efforts, his path was at least temporarily blocked.

THE FBI HAD BECOME AWARE OF HAMMER'S NEGOTIATIONS WITH the Soviets in 1961, when it began picking up calls and letters from

Hammer to the Soviet Embassy. When Hammer scheduled a meeting with the Soviet ambassador in May of that year, his activities were brought to the attention of William Sullivan, the assistant director in charge of domestic intelligence. Sullivan, who was J. Edgar Hoover's number-three man at the bureau, reviewed all politically sensitive investigations. He saw that Hammer had "numerous contacts among high [U.S.] government and social circles."[37] On July 14, 1961, he passed on to Hoover a memorandum that summed up the situation. It characterized Hammer as "a type who would do business with the devil if there was a profit in it." And it noted that "in all probability the latest project in which Hammer is interested and which he apparently has successfully interested Representative Roosevelt and Senator Gore is some business deal proposed with the Soviets. . . . This situation has political overtones, and, accordingly, we should not become involved in it."[38]

Hoover had retained his power through six presidencies by remaining alert to just such "political overtones." He concurred with Sullivan's assessment. Aside from taking the defensive measure of informing his nominal superior, Attorney General Robert Kennedy, about Hammer's contacts with the Soviet ambassador (which may have accounted for the cool reception Hammer's requests for White House meetings later received), he decided that the FBI would not pursue the matter any further.[39]

The search into Hammer's murky past had not ended, however. In early 1963, the FBI liaison with the CIA, Samuel Papich, received a request for Hammer's file. It came from James Angleton, the CIA's powerful chief of counterintelligence. Angleton was not a man to be ignored.

Ghostly thin, with prematurely silver hair and a finely sculptured face, Angleton had already become something of a legend. Before joining the intelligence service, he had edited the poetry magazine *Furioso* and had worked closely with such poets as Ezra Pound, T. S. Eliot, and e. e. cummings. He was dazzlingly erudite on a wide range of subjects, including orchids, mushrooms, and gems. The counterintelligence mission he had taken on a decade earlier had now become in his fertile mind nothing short of a search for a holy grail: the grand design of Soviet intelligence. He had also become so obsessively enigmatic regarding this quest that many of his colleagues had begun to doubt that what he sought actually existed. Angleton's theory that the KGB had a strategic plan for deceiving the CIA was reinforced in 1962, when a new Soviet defector, Anatoly Golitsyn, was debriefed. Golitsyn offered to supply Angleton with the missing pieces to the design. One of the more curious pieces involved someone Golitsyn called the Capitalist Prince, whom Soviet intelligence had recruited in the 1920s.[40]

Although Golitsyn did not give the name of this person, he provided several clues to his identity. He was the son of an American millionaire. He had come to Russia on business in the NEP period. He had returned to the United States in the early 1930s. He had left a son behind in Russia, whom the Soviets used as leverage in dealing with him. He had been reactivated in the late 1950s. And the Soviets had aborted the production of a fictional play about a capitalist prince in 1960 for fear of exposing their agent.

Angleton's research chief, Raymond Rocca, put together a list of American businessmen who had gone to Russia during the NEP period and were still alive in 1961. The most prominent name he came up with was that of W. Averell Harriman. He was the son of a millionaire railroad tycoon. He had obtained a manganese concession in 1925 and the next year had gone to Russia to look after it. He had served as FDR's ambassador to the Soviet Union during the war. He had been elected governor of New York. He had been an assistant secretary of state. Indeed, it would be difficult to find a more prominent American.

Angleton, who had a tendency to go after the grandest conceivable conspiracy—and one involving someone of Harriman's stature would qualify—launched Project Dinosaur, an investigation to determine whether Harriman could be Golitsyn's Capitalist Prince. None of Harriman's activities in Russia fitted Golitsyn's clues, however, and it quickly became clear that Angleton was on the wrong track.

Even while Project Dinosaur was careening toward its inevitable dead end, Rocca began reviewing the file he had received from the FBI on the next candidate on his list, Armand Hammer. He knew that Hammer had been of some interest to the British MI-5 and that Angleton had requested his British dossier in 1959. Rocca noticed four intriguing parallels between Hammer and the anonymous Capitalist Prince.

First, Hammer's return to America (in 1932) coincided with that of the man Golitsyn described.

Second, Hammer was known in Russia as the son of a millionaire. In the communiqué he had sent other party leaders in 1921, Lenin had identified him as the son of "the American millionaire Hammer."

Third, Hammer had left behind a relative in Russia—Armand V. Hammer—under confusing circumstances. While Hammer now claimed this was his brother's son, according to his FBI file he had represented him as his own son in 1942, when he was applying for a U.S. visa on his behalf.[41] Even if Hammer had done this simply to expedite the visa (which was denied), he may have confused the Soviets about the paternity of the Russian Armand Hammer.

Fourth, Hammer appeared to have been involved in an active Soviet espionage ring in 1927, which would fit the time frame for the recruitment of the Capitalist Prince. According to the file on the Arcos raid furnished to the CIA by British intelligence, partly burned financial records established Hammer's business as the conduit through which thousands of dollars were provided to the espionage agent Jacob Moness. Moness, in turn, was at the heart of a well-delineated "military espionage" organization operating in Berlin, London, and New York.

While Hammer's profile seemed to match that of the elusive Capitalist Prince, it did not provide Angleton with the big fish that he was seeking. Unlike Averell Harriman, who had worked at a high level in every Democratic administration since FDR's, Hammer was a relative minnow in terms of access to the U.S. government. If he was indeed the Capitalist Prince, what was his mission? Angleton, who had been known to wait seven years for one of his prize orchids to propagate, was an almost pathologically patient man. Instead of informing the FBI about the Capitalist Prince, he elected to watch— and to wait for this piece to fit in with other still missing pieces of Golitsyn's puzzle.

In June 1964, Angleton's counterintelligence staff sought more information on Hammer. The CIA station in Tripoli reported that he was in Libya.

Omar Sheli with King Idris of Libya in 1966.

CHAPTER SEVENTEEN

THE GEOPOLITICS OF CRUDE

IN THE EARLY 1960S, THE INTERNATIONAL OIL BUSINESS WAS AL-
most exclusively the preserve of a cartel of seven powerful oil companies known as the Seven Sisters. The arrangement could be traced
to a weeklong grouse shoot on the moors surrounding Achnacarry
Castle in Scotland in September 1928. The sponsor of the event was
Sir Henri Deterding, the chairman of Royal Dutch/Shell, an Anglo-
Dutch consortium that owned, aside from major oil concessions, a
large share of the world's oil tankers. Among his guests were the
heads of the world's two other largest oil companies: Walter Teagle,
the chairman of the Rockefeller holding company, Standard Oil of
New Jersey (which became first Esso and then Exxon), and Sir John
Cadman, the chairman of Anglo-Persian Oil (which became British
Petroleum). These three men, whose oil companies produced almost
four fifths of the oil in the world in 1928, stood together in their plus-
four tweeds and shot birds during the day and then retired to the castle to eat them in the evening. Under the pretext of engaging in blood
sport, they conspired to eliminate competition in the world oil market. At the heart of the deal they struck was an agreement not to dis-
turb the highly profitable status quo. Instead of bidding against one
another for the right to develop the oil that might be found in the
Middle East, Latin America, or elsewhere in the world, they would

cooperate in offering bids to develop new oil finds. They would then apportion among themselves the oil discovered, according to a formula that guaranteed each oil company the same relative share of the market it had in 1928. Once they had established this as-is principle, as it was called, they expanded the arrangement to include Standard Oil of California (now Chevron), Standard Oil of New York (now Mobil), Texas Company (now Texaco), and Gulf Oil. The seven companies agreed to share their oil tankers, refineries, pipelines, and marketing facilities. They agreed that the cartel would operate everywhere in the world except in the United States, which has strict antitrust laws.

From that point on, whenever oil was discovered in any developing country, the Seven Sisters set up a local consortium that would offer to explore, drill, and market it. Since no one but the cartel's members had the tankers, pipelines, and other wherewithal to get the oil to the market, the governments had little alternative but to accept the offer. If a government ever attempted to renege on the deal, the cartel could shut down oil exports by withdrawing its tankers, closing its pipelines, and refusing access to its refineries. The effectiveness of these measures was amply demonstrated in 1951 in Iran. When Premier Mosaddeq attempted to nationalize the consortium's oil concession, the Seven Sisters closed down the country's access to the world oil market, paralyzing the Iranian economy. The Mosaddeq government was then overthrown by the shah's supporters, with the help of the CIA, and control over the country's oil was restored to the Seven Sisters. The cartel extended its control over the world's supply of exportable crude through these methods into the 1960s. There was only one potential weak spot in its formidable system: the Kingdom of Libya.[1]

Libya had been created under the auspices of the United Nations in December 1951 by joining three former Italian colonies in North Africa and appointing a tribal leader as its king. It had the historic distinction of being the first (and only) monarchy created by the United Nations. The new monarch, King Idris, who had spent much of his life in exile in Egypt under British protection, found little to rule over in his new nation. Although Libya is vast—occupying an area larger than that of France, the United Kingdom, and Germany combined—it was almost entirely a trackless desert, with only two populated enclaves on its Mediterranean coast. The new kingdom had a population of about one million people, according to the United Nations census, 94 percent of whom could neither read nor write. Virtually its entire civil service—including the four justices on the new supreme court—had been recruited from foreign countries.[2] Its economy was minimal. What little farming the Italians had attempted to introduce to the area had been decimated, if not entirely eradicated, by droughts and by plagues of locusts. The only industry that existed was scavenging the tanks, planes, barbed wire, and minefields left over from the desert battles of World War II for scrap metal, which was then exported to Europe. The new government was financed almost entirely by subsidies it received from Great Britain and the United States in return for granting them the right to build naval and air bases on its territory. Despite such dependence, the country did not have a national airline or even telephone lines to the outside world.

As late as the mid-1950s, Libya's meager private economy depended heavily on the construction by the United States of Wheelus Field Air Force Base, a $100-million project that was designed for ten thousand U.S. troops and technicians. "It was our only sure industry at the time," as one former Libyan official put it.[3] A major source of income for the new Libyan bureaucracy was systematically collecting kickbacks from the project's subcontractors, making the government, in the eyes of one U.S. diplomat, "the most corrupt in the world."[4]

The kingdom had one hope: oil. A geologic survey commissioned by the United Nations showed highly promising oil-bearing formations under its great desert, and when oil companies expressed interest in exploring for oil there, the government devised a system of concessions that was unique in the Middle East. Instead of giving a single consortium a nationwide concession for developing its oil, Libya divided its oil prospects into eighty-five separate concessions. The government's Petroleum Act of 1955 allowed oil companies to bid separately for each concession but restricted the number that any one company could acquire. Moreover, it introduced a number of subjective criteria, such as "national interest," on which the bids would be decided. The purpose of this novel system was to prevent the Seven Sisters cartel, which had just three years earlier closed down the oil fields of Iran, from gaining exclusive control of Libya's oil. "We did not want to cede total control to the cartel, but we also needed access to the markets it controlled," Mustafa Ben Halim, the official responsible for drafting this law, explained.[5] His strategy was to encourage independent U.S. and European oil companies to compete with the cartel.

The first concessions were awarded in 1955. They went to four Seven Sisters companies—Esso, British Petroleum, Texaco, and Standard Oil of California—and seven independent oil companies. Initially, the drilling yielded little oil, and it appeared that despite the UN survey Libya might be as poor in oil as it was in other resources. Then, on April 12, 1959, Esso made a major strike at Zelten, a desert oasis about one hundred miles from the Mediterranean. As it became apparent that there was a vast sea of high-quality oil under the desert, a rush began.

Only a few generations before, Tripoli had been an Arabian slave market. Now oil transformed it into an influence bazaar for scores of independent oil companies seeking concessions. According to the 1955 Petroleum Act, the original concessionaires had to cede to Libya half their territory, which would be re-awarded in 1965. Oil-company representatives jammed the city's modest hotels and coffee-houses, seeking access to influential government officials. Swarming around the oilmen, like flies around honey, were intermediaries of diverse nationalities—Arab merchants, Bedouin nobles, Swiss lawyers, American wheeler-dealers—who offered their services for a fee. "It was becoming increasingly dirty," Ben Halim noted.[6] At stake was a prize potentially worth many billions of dollars. It was a prize that greatly interested Armand Hammer.

HAMMER HAD GRAND PLANS FOR OCCIDENTAL THAT WENT beyond the fertilizer business. He wanted to break into the global crude oil business. He was determined, with a ferocity of purpose and unrelenting focus that many of those who worked under him could not always deal with, to make the company an international success, one, as he put it, that "the whole world will recognize."[7] He was an outsider to the clubby fraternity of the Seven Sisters, and to succeed, he had to find a crack in their control of the system. Libya presented him with an opportunity to do that.

"By opening his oil lands to bidders, Idris created a commercial pandemonium," Hammer later observed. The second round of concessions would be awarded in 1965, and "I wanted to get in this game from the moment I caught sight of it."[8] The problems of obtaining an oil concession from an autocratic government like Libya's were not all that different from those he had experienced in getting concessions in Leninist Russia. In both countries, power was concentrated in the hands of relatively few men who, despite their fiery rhetoric, had pragmatic objectives. Just as Lenin had attempted to use competition driven by capitalist greed to achieve his higher purpose—the development of the socialist state—so the Libyan monarch was attempting to use the would-be concessionaires to develop Libya's economy. This was familiar territory to Hammer. In January 1961, he incorporated a subsidiary in Tripoli called Occidental of Libya. He then rearranged the schedule of his trip to the Soviet Union that February so that he would have a two-day stopover in Tripoli.

Hammer arrived in Tripoli on February 9. He was somewhat taken aback by the primitive accommodations—he had to go through a stable to reach his hotel—and he got some sense of the business environment there when he met with Abdullah Abbad, a three-hundred-pound Libyan swathed in tribal robes and carrying a jewel-encrusted dagger. Abbad, who was better known in Tripoli as the Black Prince, claimed to be distantly related to King Idris and in a position to get Hammer an oil concession. He explained that Hammer would have to pay a bribe. He also explained the mechanism for bribery in Libya. The bribe would take the form of an "overriding royalty," which represented a percentage of the value of the oil taken out of the concession, usually 3 percent. If, for example, a concession yielded one million barrels of oil, the overriding royalty of 3 percent would be the value of thirty thousand barrels of oil. This would be deposited, usually in dollars, in a Swiss bank. Even though the oil companies affiliated with the Seven Sisters cartel had consistently refused to pay such bribes—if only because they did not want to set a precedent that could be cited in other countries in which they had concessions—Abbad suggested that smaller companies would not receive favorable consideration in the 1965 bids unless they made such arrangements with key officials in the royal court. He then offered to serve as the conduit for the bribe.

Hammer listened with interest but did not make a commitment. The Black Prince, with his dagger and flamboyant dress, did not inspire confidence. Hammer realized that winning a Libyan concession would require a long and arduous pursuit, and he knew he had the time—nearly four years—to find the right route.

Later that February, in a report made to Secretary of Commerce Hodges, Hammer warned about the dangers of influence peddlers in Libya, but he did not mention his own involvement with such agents.[9] In fact, Hammer had set his sights on the potentially richest concessions in Libya, blocks 42b and 44. Since both areas were extensions of two oil fields that had been awarded to Seven Sisters companies, they presumably contained large quantities of oil and would be hotly sought after by other bidders. To get these concessions for Occidental, Hammer sought the right influence peddler to give him the needed edge. In 1962 he retained no fewer than three different intermediaries in Tripoli, each of whom claimed connections to the royal court. He gave them the coded names Warren, Sam, and the White family. All three promised they could reach the same highly influential man, Omar Shelhi.

Shelhi, a short, well-built man with shrewd eyes, was then only thirty-two but already a legend in the oil bazaar. As a child, he had been in exile in Egypt with the royal family, and after his father was assassinated, he had been adopted in all but name by King Idris, who had no children himself. He was even regarded by many as a possible royal successor. In any case, he clearly had the ear of the elderly king, and through his brothers and other family members he held great sway over the military and the police. He was also reputed to have great influence over, if not total control of, the Petroleum Concession Committee.

By 1964, however, neither Warren, Sam, nor the White family had managed to produce the collaboration with Shelhi that Hammer sought. At this point, Herbert Allen, the founding partner of the New York investment bank Allen and Company, entered the picture. He introduced Hammer to three men who claimed they had the right relationship with Shelhi and could get the concession. They were an unlikely threesome: a Frenchman, a Serb, and a Libyan. The Frenchman introduced himself as General de Rovin (he subsequently turned out to be a swindler whose real name was François Pegulu). The Serb was Ferdinand Galic, a socialite who claimed to have access to the royal court of Libya. The Libyan was Taher Ogbi, who had served for a short time as labor minister in King Idris's government and claimed an active relationship with Shelhi. Although Hammer had no way of evaluating their bona fides at the time, he lunched with them at Claridge's in London on September 17, 1964, and was apparently satisfied with their claims of influence. The next day, he signed a letter of agreement with Ogbi. It stated that if Ogbi and his confederates succeeded in getting Occidental the two specified concessions it wanted, Occidental would pay into Ogbi's shell corporation either 3 percent "of gross income derived from the sale of this oil" or, if Ogbi preferred, a onetime payment of $1.5 million.[10] In a separate arrangement, Hammer agreed to give Allen and Company a percentage of the profits Occidental derived from the oil.[11] The deal was predicated, of course, on Ogbi's ability to make the necessary arrangements with Shelhi to get the concessions.

While his new agents were attempting to open a back channel to Shelhi, Hammer himself sought to meet King Idris. Just as his meeting with Lenin had paid off with the Communists, he hoped that a meeting with the king would impress Libyan officials. He had learned from U.S. diplomats in Tripoli that agricultural reform was a subject that personally interested Idris, and he informed Libyan officials in late 1963 that Occidental was prepared to build a modern fertilizer plant in Libya. When they expressed interest in such a facility, he requested a meeting with King Idris so that he could formally present the proposal. Although both the Libyan officials and U.S. diplomats tried to convince him that the king did not discuss such matters, he doggedly persisted and finally got his summit in October 1964. By then, however, the royal imprimatur had lost much of its value. Arab nationalists, who had become progressively more anti-Western in the 1960s, had so weakened the monarchy that King Idris was spending most of his time at a residence near the British naval base at Tobruk so that he and his court could be evacuated at short notice by British troops. Although King Idris was the nominal ruler, he had little power, even over his own government. Hammer still needed a connection with Shelhi.

The deadline for the submission of bids for oil concessions was July 17, 1965. That spring, Hammer became concerned that his new intermediaries were no better than his old ones. Despite their promises, he still had no deal with Shelhi. In fact, after four years in Libya, he had not even met Shelhi. That April, in sheer desperation, he demanded that Ogbi make arrangements for him to meet Shelhi outside Libya. When Ogbi stalled, Hammer began to suspect that he was being duped.[12] "The whole thing looked like a big promotional swindle," he later said.[13]

In May 1965, Dorman Commons, the newly appointed vice president for finance at Occidental, advised Hammer to cut his losses in Libya and seek opportunities for Occidental in domestic oil. The company had no experience in exploring for desert oil, and with its minuscule net worth stood little chance of being selected in the July bidding. "Anyone else would have given up," Commons recalled, "but not Hammer: he wanted all or nothing." Hammer was, to the point of obsession, determined to succeed in Libya.[14] He sat down with his top executives and Libyan consultants and had them recount, case by case, how other small companies had obtained concessions in the first round of bidding. His interest focused on Wendell Phillips, an American archaeologist who had managed to win one of the most sought- after concessions.

Phillips, then in his mid-thirties, was an extraordinary adventurer. Tall, blond, and given to dramatic gestures, he had led an expedition to Arabia in 1951 to uncover the queen of Sheba's capital. He enjoyed wearing desert robes, riding camels, and living in Bedouin tents. The following year he went to Oman, where he acted as a Lawrence of Arabia–type adviser to the sheikh of Oman, who gave him a valuable oil concession.[15] When Phillips arrived in Libya in 1955, he had little experience in the oil business, and the company he set up for the bidding, Middle East American Oil, was little more than a shell corporation. Yet he had prevailed over the companies of the Seven Sisters cartel. Hammer wanted to know what magic he had used to do this.[16]

By the time Hammer tracked down Phillips in Amman, Jordan, where he was living, it was June 1965, and less than six weeks remained before the bids had to be submitted in Libya. He offered to pay Phillips's expenses if he would fly to Paris and suggested in a telegram that they meet on June 13 at the Hôtel Ritz "to discuss an important matter of possible mutual interest."[17] Phillips had not heard of Armand Hammer—or of Occidental Petroleum—when he received the cable. But after checking out Hammer's credentials, he decided it was worth a trip to Europe.

Hammer met with Phillips at the Cavalieri Hilton in Rome on June 22. He got right to the point: he said that he planned to submit bids for two of the most sought-after concessions in Libya, and he asked Phillips directly whether he could help him reach Shelhi.

Phillips told Hammer he might be able to do something, but if he did, he expected a piece of the deal for himself and for two associates who had the means of reaching Shelhi. Hammer agreed that everyone would be taken care of. Phillips then introduced Hammer to one of his associates: Hans-Albert Kunz.

Kunz was a large man in his early forties with a bulldoglike head and a massive jutting jaw. Even with his glasses, his poor eyesight caused him to tilt his head and peer almost menacingly. He spoke English with a heavy guttural accent. He was a Swiss citizen who had gone to Egypt as a young man and entered the catering business. He used his charm to cultivate Arab sheikhs, and through the connections that he made with these sheikhs, he became a facilitator for Western companies exploring for oil and building pipelines in that part of the world. He catered meals for their crews and also provided their employees with visas, import permits, and whatever else they needed from recalcitrant government officials. As he became more successful, he set up a corporation in Geneva called IMEG Management that provided services to other companies. His partner, Kemal Zeinal Zade, had the all-important connection with Shelhi.

Zade, who was then thirty-three, was born in the Soviet Union. His father was Azerbaijani; his mother, Chechen. He had gone to England on an Iranian passport and attended the London School of Economics. While in London, he worked as a translator for the BBC and befriended Busairi Shelhi, the older brother of Omar Shelhi. Through contacts provided him by the Shelhi family, he made business deals in Libya on behalf of a German steel company. He then moved to Düsseldorf, where, aside from attending to his business deals, he ran a Russian restaurant. Since he had a fear of flying, he depended on Kunz for most of the arrangements in Libya.

Kunz suggested that Hammer go with him to Düsseldorf to meet with Zade. Although Hammer had already been stung at least a half dozen times by promoters who claimed a connection with Shelhi, it was a measure of his determination that he was on the plane with Kunz the next day.

In Düsseldorf, Hammer, Kunz, and Zade dined at Zade's Russian restaurant. While Gypsy musicians played violins in the background and huge portions of caviar were brought to the table, Hammer found that he and Zade had much in common. They both had lived in Moscow, and they could converse in Russian about the situation there. Both had left relatives behind in Russia—Hammer, his nephew; Zade, his sister. They both boasted of having important Soviet connections. Hammer was in contact with Mikoyan; Zade, with Geidar Aliyev, who had headed the KGB in Azerbaijan and would become deputy prime minister of the Soviet Union. They both liked Russian food and music. They then talked business.

Later that same night, Zade called Shelhi. He told him that a man named Hammer, whom he had just met, was planning to bid on blocks 42b and 44. Shelhi responded by laughing out loud at the man's brazen nerve in bidding against Seven Sister companies for the two prize concessions. Up until this point, he had never heard of Hammer. He told Zade that he was wasting money on the telephone call since Hammer's company was not even under consideration for the concessions. Zade replied that Hammer understood that he stood little chance of winning—without help. But if he did win, he was willing to pay $2.8 million in cash to his silent partners the day he was awarded the concessions and would also give them an overriding royalty of 3 percent of the value of the oil. If these blocks contained as much oil as the adjacent fields, the royalty would amount to a staggering sum. Zade then vouched for Hammer, saying that he was a "serious man."[18]

Shelhi understood that Zade had put himself on the line. And he was his brother's friend. Shelhi needed to go to Germany in any case to see an eye doctor, and he agreed to meet Hammer there the following week.

One week later, Hammer arrived on schedule at 9:00 A.M. at Shelhi's suite in the Königsberg Hotel in Bonn. He was older than Shelhi expected. His skin was pale and dotted with liver spots. His eyes were shielded by heavy horn-rimmed glasses. His suit was rumpled, as if he had traveled in it all night. But he strode into the room with confidence and had a firm handshake.

Hammer wasted no time with small talk. He told Shelhi he wanted to do business in Libya. He took out his pad and a pencil and asked Shelhi what was required of him.

Shelhi was taken aback. He told Hammer that the competition for concessions was unrestricted war and that he did not appear to have the resources to wage it. "You have no credentials," he said. "Zero."

Hammer was oddly unfazed. He gazed straight at Shelhi and told him that he would do whatever was necessary to win the war. He explained that he could act swiftly and decisively since he did not have to seek the approval of anyone else in his corporation. "There are no committees, no auditors," he explained. "You're looking at Oxy." He then said that he could break the Seven Sisters' monopoly if he gained access to Libyan oil, and if Shelhi helped him, he would make him "the richest man in Europe." Shelhi was impressed. Even if this were all fantasy on Hammer's part, he seemed willing to act and take the consequences. Hammer was different from the other oilmen with whom Shelhi had dealt.

As Shelhi began describing the situation surrounding the second round of bidding—now only days away—he realized that Hammer was an extraordinarily good listener. One by one, Hammer homed in on the key problems. More important, as his questions reflected, he was able to see them in terms of Shelhi's, as well as his own, needs. The problem for Shelhi was not arranging for Hammer to be awarded the concession; it was arranging it in such a way that his role did not surface. To avoid a scandal, Hammer needed to provide an ingredient to the deal, even if it was only a fig leaf, that would plausibly explain to others why Occidental, a company with virtually no experience in international oil, had been chosen over more seasoned companies. Hammer suggested such a ruse: Occidental would offer to drill for potable water in the drought-stricken al-Kufrah region, where King Idris's father was born. Shelhi said that no other oil company would make such an offer, and the committee could thus justify granting Occidental the concessions on the grounds that Libya's national interests were being addressed.

As Shelhi described what should be included in the offer, Hammer furiously scrawled notes on his pad and enthusiastically approved each of Shelhi's requests. He also made clear that he would obediently expedite them. For instance, to show how a river of water could be produced from the underground springs at al-Kufrah and used to irrigate the desert, he told Shelhi that he intended that very evening to charter a jet to fly American hydraulic engineers and agricultural experts to the region. "Don't worry, Omar," he said in his gravelly voice; "they will be in Libya before you get back to Tripoli."

Hammer acted with a clarity of purpose that Shelhi had never seen before in a businessman. The water-drilling program would involve only trivial added expenses for Occidental, but it would provide the rationale that would allow him to be Hammer's secret partner.

After this discussion, they went to a quiet restaurant in Bonn overlooking the Rhine. Hammer seemed to have an answer for everything. He was also flattering, telling Shelhi, "You are like my son." Before the meal concluded, Shelhi stressed to Hammer that their collaboration had to remain a deep secret. No one, other than Kunz and Zade, was to be told. If Hammer needed to send him a message in Tripoli, he was to use a code name, and they agreed on Dr. Dardenne (the name of Shelhi's eye doctor in Germany).[19]

The next day, Hammer met with Kunz and Zade to work out the details of when and how the 3 percent royalty was to be paid. They had to pay Wendell Phillips a finder's fee, and they settled on giving him a .335 percent share, which, to keep Shelhi's involvement discreet, would be paid directly by Occidental. The balance of the royalty— 2.665 percent—was to be paid by Occidental on a quarterly basis to an account that was jointly controlled by Zade and Kunz at the Union Bank of Switzerland—UBS—in Zurich. They would then transfer to Shelhi his share, which was half the money they received. Even though his name was not on the UBS account, Shelhi was not concerned about receiving his money: his influence in Libya was vital.

Hammer no doubt realized that 3 percent of the gross proceeds was a stiff price, but he had little choice. Time was running out. At this point, he had to fish or cut bait. When he got back to London, he moved with great dispatch to get out of the deal he had made with his other intermediaries. He telegraphed Ogbi in Tripoli and Allen in New York, notifying them that he had canceled the agreement he had made with them the previous September.[20] (Allen and Company later sued Occidental for breach of contract but was unable to prove that a valid contract existed.)

On July 26, Hammer flew to Tripoli to supervise the official presentation of the bid that Occidental had submitted the week before.

It was rolled in sheepskin and bound with red, black, and green silk ribbons—the colors in Libya's new flag. Aside from the usual terms for developing an oil field, which gave the Libyan government 40 percent of the earnings derived from the oil, it also contained the offer to search, without charge, for water in the al-Kufrah area.

Although the results of the auction were not to be announced by the Libyan Oil Ministry until February 1966, Hammer was confident enough of the outcome to buy a converted U.S. A-26 bomber so that he could shuttle between Tripoli and Rome.[21] But as February came and went and more time passed without a definitive word from Shelhi, he became concerned. He had reason to worry. Occidental was not doing well financially. Its oil and gas fields in California were being depleted. Its heavy investment in fertilizer for Russia was stymied. It had also suffered multimillion-dollar losses from investments Hammer had made in California real estate. He was able to conceal the real estate losses from shareholders and banks in 1966 by vastly inflating the value of the company's unsold real estate,[22] but this accounting legerdemain was under SEC investigation and could provide only temporary cover at best. Occidental desperately needed a flow of cash, and the Libyan concession was the salvation on which Hammer depended.

In September 1966, Hammer demanded another meeting with Shelhi. This took place at the Intercontinental Hotel overlooking the Lake of Geneva.

When Shelhi arrived at Hammer's suite, Hammer seemed unusually agitated. As if delivering a sales pitch, he pounded away, point by point, at the resources he had already committed to the Libyan project. He had even commissioned, he said, a Swiss pharmaceutical company to develop an antitoxin that would neutralize the sting of poisonous scorpions in the Libyan desert. But he had to know about the status of the concession.

Shelhi could see the lines of tension on Hammer's face as he spoke, and he attempted to reassure him. "Be patient," he told him, explaining that the Concession Committee had to go through the motions of deliberating on the merits of all the bids, and that took time in Libya, especially in the summer, when most officials went on vacation. He assured Hammer that at the end of the process Occidental's bid would prevail.

When several more weeks passed and several of Hammer's messages for Dr. Dardenne went unanswered, he had Zade call Shelhi repeatedly. He then surprised Shelhi by turning up at the tearoom of the Hilton Hotel in Rome. Hammer acted as if he had accidentally run into Shelhi, but Shelhi later suspected that this was not the case. He assumed Zade had informed Hammer of his whereabouts. When they had tea, Hammer talked extravagantly about his plans to help the king develop Libya. He seemed almost intoxicated with the idea of gaining behind-the-scenes power. It was not what Shelhi wanted to hear, but the die was now cast.[23]

On February 26, 1967, as Shelhi had promised, Hammer's company was awarded the two concessions, which were renumbered 102 and 103. Occidental was chosen over fourteen more-experienced companies. By December, they had struck oil, which was not surprising since both concessions bordered highly promising oil-bearing formations, but the quantity of oil surpassed all expectations. According to estimates by the engineering firm of De Golyer and Mac-Naughton, the two fields contained three billion barrels of low-sulfur oil. Hammer had hit an enormous jackpot.

In public statements, Hammer attributed his success in getting the Libyan concessions to altruism—specifically, his promise to explore for water for the Libyans. In his autobiography, without ever mentioning Kunz, Zade, Shelhi, or the underside of the deal, he claimed that his bid "differed dramatically from the conventional offers of the other companies. . . . We offered to explore near the desert village of Kufra—the birthplace of the King and Queen and the site of the King's father's tomb. The absence of water, more than the lack of oil or foreign exchange, had imprisoned Libya in its medieval poverty. . . ."[24]

This story, which has all the elements of a fairy tale—a good king, a kingdom imprisoned by lack of water, and a wise man who shows the king how to lift the curse from his kingdom—became the conventional account of how a small, inexperienced American oil company got the richest prize in Libya.

Immediately after winning the concession, Hammer instructed Occidental's controller, James Murdy, to pay $2.8 million into the UBS account in Zurich controlled by Kunz and Zade. Murdy balked at making such a large payment to a secret account until Hammer showed him the contract with Kunz and Zade, a contract that Hammer argued was so secret it had to be kept in his safe-deposit box at the City National Bank in Los Angeles, and no copies could be made of it. On April 5, 1967, the first installment of the payoff was transferred to the UBS account.[25] This was only the down payment. If the estimates of the size of the oil reserves were accurate, the 3 percent royalty Hammer had promised amounted to a king's ransom: the conspirators would eventually get the price of ninety million barrels of oil. In 1967, oil was selling at about one dollar a barrel, which meant that the override would be worth $90 million. Even at these prices, Occidental could expect to gross nearly $3 billion from the concession—and, after paying the Libyan government its share and the expenses of getting the oil to market, still reap a rich profit.

HAMMER ACHIEVED CONSIDERABLE POWER IN THE BUSINESS OF politics as well as the world of oil in the mid-1960s. In Washington, D.C., he set up a subsidiary, Occidental International, to conduct his "government relations," and he staffed it with some of the best lobbyists, politicians, and public relations men that money could buy. He cultivated key senators in both political parties and helped fill the campaign coffers of some two dozen congressmen through substantial cash contributions (which, before the Campaign Finance Act of 1972, were legal).

Initially, in 1964, Lyndon Baines Johnson's White House was unreceptive to his requests for access to the president. LBJ's national security adviser, McGeorge Bundy, who had asked for and reviewed Hammer's FBI dossier, recommended against it. When a presidential aide informed Bundy that "Congressman Roosevelt keeps calling. [Hammer] is obviously a big contributor to him," Bundy replied that Johnson "should not have to see him."[26] When Roosevelt was told that LBJ did not have time to see Hammer, he fired off an angry letter to the White House, saying that "Dr. Hammer is not only in a position to be, and will be a five figure contributor to the Democratic Party, but has been in the past. It seems rather incredible that the President's schedule would be so tight that he could not give Dr. Hammer 5 minutes."[27]

By 1965, Hammer had got a foot in the White House door by establishing a rapport with LBJ's chief of staff, W. Marvin Watson. He would later hire him as Occidental International's vice president of government relations. Just before a White House reception for King Faisal of Saudi Arabia in June 1966, Watson wrote a terse note to LBJ, saying that "Hammer was in today. He says he has 25 he would like to do without."[28] This was Watson's shorthand for $25,000. Whatever the purpose of the offer, Hammer had little problem getting the access to the White House he wanted after he made it. When the president was too busy to see him, he could always see Watson or other top advisers. LBJ even invited him to his Texas ranch. Hammer took great pride in his elevated status. The relationship with LBJ, as far as Hammer was concerned, was one of the "easiest" ones he had yet enjoyed with a president.[29]

While Hammer was cultivating LBJ, and just as he struck oil in Libya, a blackmailer threatened to expose part of his secret life. In December 1966, he received in the mail a set of photographs. They showed Hammer and Bettye Murphy in bathing suits at the beach at Acapulco; Hammer and Bettye on Hammer's yacht; Hammer holding in his arms his illegitimate daughter, Victoria, who was now ten. The photographs were followed by telephone calls to Hammer's home. The blackmailer demanded $25,000 in cash.

Hammer had gone to great lengths to keep his liaison with Bettye secret. After he had arranged the fake wedding and new identity for her and a notional father for Victoria, he camouflaged the money he was providing them every month by channeling it through a chain of anonymous lawyers. He had also insisted that Victoria not be told who her benefactor was. But now somehow his secret had seeped out. If the existence of Bettye and Victoria was revealed, Hammer's carefully constructed public image would be damaged, and his marriage to Frances, which had been so useful for financing his business, could very well be ruined.

When he told Bettye over the phone about the blackmail threat that December, he chose his words carefully, saying that "whatever happens, I have the means to resolve the problem." He then asked her, after a deliberately long pause, whether she knew who the blackmailer was.

She told Hammer that she did. He was Raymond Glen Howerton, who had lived with her briefly. After he moved out, she found that he had stolen a shoe box full of photographs, including the ones Hammer had seen. He had also taken jewelry from her.

Hammer said, "Don't worry. Just leave it in Papa's capable hands." And he did not waste any time in acting against the blackmailer. He employed detectives to locate Howerton, who was living in a motel near Houston. Hammer then met Bettye at the airport there. He was wearing a wrinkled suit but looked in good shape for a man who was nearing seventy. Two men in sunglasses soon approached them, and Hammer told her that they worked for a federal drug agency, and with their help he planned to "set up" Howerton by planting evidence against him. Even though the men did not display their badges, Bettye did as Hammer asked and described Howerton to them. A few days later, her jewelry was returned to her. When she asked Hammer what had happened to Howerton, he answered tersely, "Three guys went fishing, and two came back." The blackmail threats ended.

Hammer's fishing story suggested to Bettye, as no doubt it was supposed to, that his mysterious associates had done away with Howerton, and indeed she knew from the actions he had taken against his ex-wife that he could be extremely ruthless. But as she later found out, Howerton had not been murdered. He moved to a small town in Texas, where he died of natural causes in 1972.[30]

Around this time, Hammer also had to suppress a potentially damaging story that connected him to Israel. The version that appeared in the *Arab Oil Review* in March 1966 described his Jewish background and the efforts he had made in the 1950s to raise money for Israel—which was essentially accurate—and then went on to allege that he had traveled to Israel and acted as an Israeli agent, which was untrue. Hammer assumed that this mixture of fact and falsehood was deliberately being spread by a competing oil company that hoped to undermine his position in Libya. He suspected Esso. To prevent the story from gaining any currency in the Arab world, he decided to deny all aspects of it—and even adopt another religion. He joined a Unitarian church in Los Angeles and asked its minister to write a letter identifying him as a practicing Unitarian. He then wrote Shelhi, enclosing the *Arab Oil Review* article:

My only thought is that the editor of this magazine may be trying to play the game of the major oil companies who are, of course, angry at the way that concessions were awarded.

To new companies . . . the February issue also criticized the government for not granting concessions to Esso. You will note in this connection that Esso is supporting the magazine.

Hammer went on to defend himself against the "malicious lie" that he was Jewish and a supporter of Israel:

I enclose a copy of a letter from my minister in the Unitarian Church which speaks for itself. . . . I have never been in Israel and never have been a member of any organization that collects contributions for Israel, nor have I or any company I have been associated with had any business dealings with Israel. Therefore you can see how sinister this unfounded rumor is.[31]

He later told Shelhi that Jews were conspiring with Esso to discredit him. He talked of "evidence," which he never provided. Hammer's abandonment of his religion did not increase his stature in Shelhi's eyes. Even so, Shelhi had an interest in protecting the Hammer concession. He called local editors and made sure that the story was spiked in Libya.[32]

The instant conversion to Unitarianism was a typical ploy by Hammer to invent the persona needed to carry out the deeds at hand. He had given up living with his Russian wife and child to become an American businessman and denied a decade's worth of work in the Soviet Union to improve his chances of getting contracts from the U.S. government. Denying his Judaism was also expedient.

BEFORE OCCIDENTAL COULD GET ANY MONEY FOR ITS LIBYAN OIL, it had to build a pipeline to transport it 130 miles across the desert to the Mediterranean coast. It also had to construct floating docks at the port of Ez Zuetina so that the oil could be loaded aboard tankers. In 1966, Occidental had a net worth of less than $50 million and could not pay for this massive construction. But Hammer made a deal with the Bechtel Corporation in San Francisco to both build and finance the entire project. In return, Bechtel would be paid $153 million from the proceeds of the oil.[33]

Bechtel began constructing the pipeline—which at forty inches in diameter was the largest in Libya—in August 1967. It was completed by February 1968. Less than a month later, Occidental's oil was loaded onto tankers and shipped to Europe.

In April 1968, Hammer staged an extravagant affair in the Libyan desert to dedicate his oil field. Occidental's engineers had worked for three weeks erecting a fifty-foot-high canvas pavilion from which hundreds of red, green, and black flags fluttered. Most of the eight hundred Libyan guests wore white tribal robes. Red carpets were laid across the sand for the king. *Fortune* magazine reported that "camel troops patrolled the dunes around the installation, scarlet-coated bandsmen stood in formation with their instruments shining in the midday sun and the blood of sacrificial lambs stained the desert sand."[34]

Hammer flew in with Frances and Senator Gore, who was leaving Congress at the end of his term to work full-time for Occidental. On the podium, Hammer stood shoulder to shoulder with King Idris and renamed the concession Idris Field. Afterward, an immense feast was served in two adjacent tents. Although the show cost Occidental over $1 million, Hammer thought he had got his money's worth. Like his meeting with Lenin, it was a validating experience. He claimed that King Idris had privately told him, "Allah sent you to Libya!"[35]

While the royal imprimatur was an important ingredient in Hammer's recipe for success—and one he enjoyed—he also needed the continued collaboration of Shelhi. Less than a month after the ceremony, Hammer arranged for Shelhi, along with Kunz, to come to Los Angeles (Zade's fear of flying prevented him from attending the meeting). When they arrived at his home, Kunz brought up the 3 percent royalty. Payments had been delayed, and he wanted to pin Hammer down in front of Shelhi. But Hammer was elusive, saying that Occidental's auditors, Arthur Andersen and Company, still had a few technical questions about the agreement.

Before anything could be resolved, Hammer insisted that they view a film, which Occidental's public relations department had produced, about King Idris's participation in the inauguration of Occidental's oil fields. They were joined by Frances. Afterward, Hammer took them to Trader Vic's restaurant in Beverly Hills. The next day, he left Los Angeles, but he sent his limousine to take the visitors to Disneyland.[36]

ON WALL STREET, OCCIDENTAL STOCK, WHICH WAS BEING HEAVily traded, soared to more than $100 a share. The frantic bidding reflected not the company's meager earnings but its projections for the sale of billions of barrels of Libyan oil. No other independent company had ever obtained a concession of such magnitude. Hammer did little to discourage the speculation. He was using the stock as a sort of private currency, albeit a highly inflated one, to buy other less well valued companies. The more than a dozen companies he acquired in this manner promised to diversify Occidental, providing sources of income beyond the oil field in Libya. The largest of the acquisitions was Island Creek Coal, the nation's third-largest coal producer, which Hammer made Albert Gore chairman of.

As Occidental became an industrial giant, Hammer, who took full credit for its achievement, began to get the recognition he had so long sought. He was continually in the limelight as the company's driving force. Profiles of him appeared in *Fortune, Forbes, BusinessWeek, The New York Times,* the *Los Angeles Times,* and elsewhere. They were generally favorable, portraying him as a "shrewd and daring" entrepreneur possessing an almost magical "Midas touch," someone who had the "boldness" to take on, like some David challenging Goliath, the most powerful oil companies in the world.

If these qualities are seen as measures of risk taking, the descriptions were accurate. Hammer had arranged for Occidental to go more than $700 million into debt, mainly to pursue his gamble on Libyan oil. He had successfully challenged the giant Seven Sisters cartel. He had personally arranged an enormous bribe that competing oil companies had been either unwilling or unable to engineer. He had pursued an all-or-nothing strategy, and he won the prize. The resulting attention from the press seemed to give him new energy and confidence.

Even when Occidental's Libyan oil began to come in, the company's cash-flow problem was not immediately solved. The world was awash in oil, prices were low, and Occidental had enormous expenses. Unlike the Seven Sisters, which owned their own fleets of tankers, Occidental had to charter tankers, and because of bad timing, Hammer paid top rates for them. He had also committed five cents a barrel to exploring for water at al-Kufrah. On top of this, Occidental had to pay Libyan taxes on every barrel of oil it exported. While the company still had a gross profit of fifty-six cents a barrel, after these deductions it needed almost all of that to repay the $153-million loan from Bechtel. Occidental indeed was so pressed for cash in 1968 that its accountants began looking hard at the money Hammer was paying into the UBS account. In his haste to make a deal with Shelhi, he had agreed to pay the 2.665 percent royalty on the gross value of the oil, not on Occidental's net proceeds. Writing to Wendell Phillips, Kunz said Hammer had told him that the royalty from the bribe would make "more money than [Hammer's] company will make per barrel, considering that he has to pay taxes and royalties to the Libyan government."[37] Now that the concession was his and the oil was flowing, Hammer decided to revise the deal, calculating the royalty on a net-price basis, which meant that Shelhi and his associates would get only about half of the $3.8 million that was due them in 1968.

That July, Shelhi married the daughter of the Libyan prime minister in a ceremony in the palace. King Idris was his best man and appointed him the minister for palace affairs. Both Kunz and Zade came to Libya for the wedding banquet. Afterward, Shelhi told them that he would not tolerate Hammer's cheating them on the payments. As far as he was concerned, the agreement he had made with Hammer was crystal clear: Hammer was to pay them 3 percent of the total value of the oil, not 3 percent of his net proceeds. He made clear to them that if Hammer did not honor his word, the concession agreement could be reviewed by the palace.[38]

Kunz was concerned that Shelhi might try to sabotage the concession. When he returned to Switzerland, he wrote Phillips: "You know how Arabs are, he does not care about the future. He now thinks he has been cheated and is capable of doing the worst. . . . He is not only mad, he went berserk about the situation." Kunz wanted Phillips to apprise Hammer of the precarious situation. He suggested in the letter that they act together to put "pressure on Armand to settle this satisfactorily and within the shortest time possible." If not, he warned, there would be "a disaster . . . for all of us."[39]

The pressure evidently worked. Rather than risk everything, Hammer reversed himself and deposited the additional $1.9 million in the UBS account.[40]

Hammer was now gambling that Occidental's financial bind would be relieved by an expanded flow of Libyan oil. He had been told by his technicians that the extraction of more than six hundred thousand barrels a day could prematurely destroy the field, but he needed the extra oil to repay his debts, and he ordered them to increase pumping so that the field would produce eight hundred thousand barrels a day by the end of 1969.[41]

What he had not reckoned on was that in September 1969, just as his concession was reaching its full capacity, the Libyan monarchy would be abruptly overthrown by a twenty-seven-year-old sublieutenant in the Libyan army named Muammar al-Gadhafi.

CHAPTER EIGHTEEN

AVOIDING JUDGMENT DAY

GADHAFI'S COUP CAUGHT THE WORLD BY ALMOST TOTAL SUR-
prise. Gadhafi belonged to a tribe of Bedouin nomads who grazed
their goats very close to Zelten, where the underground sea of oil was
discovered in 1959. At the age of seventeen, he formed a secret society, the Free Officers, dedicated to creating a pan-Arab state. He enrolled in the army's newly formed officer corps and through his
personal magnetism and messianic style recruited other cadets to his
cause. Even when he was sent to Britain in 1966 to train as a military
engineer, he continued to organize his group. When he returned to
Libya in 1968, he began to organize a revolution. In August 1969,
King Idris left Libya on his summer vacation, taking with him four
hundred pieces of luggage. Shelhi and his bride accompanied him to
Bursa, Turkey. Most of the other important government officials
were also on vacation outside Libya.

On September 1, Gadhafi acted. Though he could count on just a
handful of young officers—and his total arsenal consisted of only five
service revolvers and forty-eight bullets—he managed to seize the
military headquarters in Tripoli. The soldiers there, dissatisfied with
the weak (and now absent) monarch, rallied around him. He then
took command of Libya's only radio station and personally broadcast communiqué 1, proclaiming the new Arab republic. Except for
one soldier who was shot accidentally, it was a bloodless coup.[1]

*George Williamson and his wife with Armand and Frances Hammer
at a banquet in London in 1970. Williamson was Hammer's
new man in Libya.*

Gadhafi—who immediately promoted himself to the rank of colonel and created a Revolutionary Command Council to run the country—reassured Western countries that he would honor previously made commitments to supply Europe with oil. At the same time, he ordered the United States and Great Britain to close their military bases on Libyan soil. He also began making secret arrangements to acquire Egyptian and Soviet arms, suggesting that he was far more dedicated to breaking with the West than Western diplomats had assumed.

As his oil adviser, Gadhafi brought to Tripoli Abdullah Tariki, a former oil minister in Saudi Arabia who had lost favor in his own country for speaking against the Seven Sisters. Tariki was savvy about the oil business. He realized that what had prevented Saudi Arabia from taking control of its oil was that the oil companies maintained a unified front there in the form of a single consortium, Aramco. If the Saudi government attempted to take the nationwide concession away from Aramco, the country would be effectively shut down, as Iran had been shut down in the 1950s. The other oil-producing countries on the Persian Gulf faced the same situation. But Libya was a different story: it was the only country in the Middle East in which the Seven Sisters did not have exclusive control of the oil. Instead, a company that was not part of the cartel, Occidental, held the largest concession. Tariki recognized that Occidental was vulnerable, since unlike most other international oil companies, it had no major source of oil other than its concession in Libya. When Tariki began slowly but firmly asserting the new government's power, Occidental became a prime target.[2]

Gadhafi further turned the screws on Hammer by having his public prosecutor conduct an investigation of how Occidental had obtained its rich concession. This was no minor issue. Shelhi had been tried in absentia for corruption and sentenced to death by a revolutionary tribunal. Gadhafi then expropriated the concession of a small American investment group, Chappaqua, on the grounds that it had been obtained through the intervention of Shelhi.[3] If Gadhafi took the position that Occidental had also got its concession from Shelhi, it would be similarly vulnerable.

The investigation was headed in exactly that direction. The night of the coup, Omar Shelhi's brother Aziz had been arrested in Tripoli. He was repeatedly interrogated, as were other officials involved in awarding concessions. All the Occidental documents in Tripoli were subpoenaed. By early 1970, the Libyan interrogators had extracted the full story of Hammer's bribe.[4] The only real issue by May 1970 was how Gadhafi would use his leverage with Hammer.

The day-to-day job of placating Gadhafi's government fell to George Williamson, Occidental's new representative in Tripoli. Williamson, though only thirty-four, had ten years' experience in the oil business in Libya working for the Texas oil billionaire Nelson Bunker Hunt. He was a charming Texan who had befriended many Libyans, including some in Gadhafi's inner circle. He had been approached by Hammer in September 1969 with a generous offer to work for Occidental—nearly double what he had been earning from Hunt—and he accepted it. Even though he saw Hammer as an "outsider" in the oil patch—a Jew from New York with little evident experience in oil—this didn't bother him. He liked mavericks. Hammer was also willing to take on an Arab fanatic at a time when more experienced oilmen, including Hunt, were preparing to pull out of Libya. Williamson was concerned at first about Hammer's age. He was over seventy, and Williamson wondered how long he would be able to run a business. But he found that Hammer's mind remained quick and agile, so quick that Hammer saw and solved problems before Williamson—who spoke with a slow Texas drawl—had finished his sentence. Hammer also impressed him with his raw determination. He assumed he could maneuver around all the obstacles in his path, even the Libyan revolutionary government. But now, as Williamson watched the investigation unfold, he was concerned that Hammer was on a collision course with Gadhafi, a course that left little room for maneuvering.

Hammer thought of Gadhafi as "very cunning and very intelligent."[5] He could do little to change the outcome of the investigation, but he did see an opportunity to profit from a grim situation. Shelhi was in exile in Geneva, where without any influence in the new Libya he was useless to Hammer. But Hammer did have a use for the millions of dollars that were to flow into the UBS account and that were earmarked for Shelhi under the terms of the original contract. He might very well need those funds to buy influence in Gadhafi's regime.

Occidental's financial-control officers, in particular Dorman Commons and James Murdy, had already advised Hammer that, given the force majeure in Libya, he would be justified in cutting off the payments to Shelhi and his associates.[6] No more money need flow into the UBS account. Hammer told them that he would go to Switzerland and discuss the matter. In Zurich, Hammer sent Shelhi a terse message: payments were being terminated because Shelhi was no longer able to help in Libya. He added that if Shelhi ever got back in power, he "would be happy to do business" with him again. Shelhi stoically accepted this. He was on Gadhafi's death list, and Hammer would not want Occidental to be associated with him. He was not surprised to see himself cut off in this way. "I never expected more of Hammer," he reflected later.[7]

When Hammer returned to Los Angeles, he gave Murdy and Commons a very different account of what had transpired in Switzerland. He said that Shelhi had agreed to reduced payments, based on the net rather than the gross price of the oil, and that he believed that Occidental was both legally and morally bound to continue making these payments to Shelhi by means of the UBS account.[8]

Commons was mystified by the sudden insistence on adherence to the contract. "Hammer had never shown any moral inhibitions before about breaking contracts," he said later. "He had high-priced lawyers to handle those problems. We couldn't understand why he was now honoring a contract that wasn't worth the paper it was written on." But Commons understood also that opposing Hammer's wish was tantamount to resigning.[9]

What neither Commons nor Murdy—nor possibly anyone else at Occidental—knew was that Hammer had made a new arrangement with Zade and Kunz while he was in Switzerland, one that would give him control over most of the money.

Hammer made clear to them that they had little choice in the matter, noting in a letter to Kunz that "if this matter should go to litigation, it could well be that you would be risking everything because, if this agreement was declared by U.S. courts to be invalid, there would be nothing due to you."[10]

Kunz and Zade replied to Hammer on January 7, 1970: "It is sad to see you, once more, trying in such an unbecoming way to back out from your undertaking."[11] But they knew Hammer held the trump card. If they wanted Hammer to continue the payments, they would have to accept his new rules.

Shelhi would receive nothing—and would not be told of the new arrangement. His share would be used as a reserve fund by Hammer. Zade and Kunz would continue to get their share, which was half the money paid into the UBS account. They would now work for Hammer as "consultants" in Iran and other oil-producing countries. Their company, IMEG Management, would also get lucrative contracts from Occidental to build pipelines.

For their part, Zade and Kunz verified for Occidental's auditors, Arthur Andersen and Company, that they received the money paid into the UBS account. Neither the auditors nor other Occidental executives were aware of the deception. Only Hammer knew that Shelhi's share had been diverted to a reserve fund.

Meanwhile, Gadhafi ratcheted up the pressure on Occidental. His real threat was not nationalization, in which case Occidental might seek redress in the courts for the violation of its contract, but further cutbacks in production to conserve the oil field, which Libya could legally make. Hammer had no choice but to go along with this, since the alternative—abandoning the concession—would ruin Occidental. On June 3, 1970, the Revolutionary Command Council ordered Occidental to cut its production of oil by an immense amount—nearly 40 percent. The company was now producing just enough to fulfill its contracts with European refineries.

Gadhafi delegated his second in command in the Revolutionary Command Council, Major Abdul Jalloud, to deal with Occidental. Jalloud was a wiry, energetic thirty-year-old who had been a friend of Gadhafi's since childhood, and who now headed both Libya's intelligence service and its oil industry. He skillfully conducted a war of nerves against Occidental's executives, which included having the border guards strip-search them each time they entered the country. At one point, Hammer suggested that it was "too dangerous" for George Williamson to remain in Tripoli, but Williamson stayed, and he dealt with Jalloud on an almost daily basis. He also dined with him on occasion. He found that Jalloud could switch in a split second from warm charm to fanatic zeal and then, just as quickly, return to his former demeanor.[12]

In early July, Jalloud informed Williamson that there would be another 10 percent cutback in August and that on September 1, the first anniversary of the revolution, which he called Judgment Day, Occidental's concessions might be nationalized.

Hammer was in Los Angeles when Williamson gave him the news. He calmly and patiently went over the timetable as if he were discussing nothing more than some future vacation. Then he asked—in detail that amazed Williamson—about all of Jalloud's strengths and weaknesses. He even asked about his taste in food, drink, and women. When Williamson was finished, he said, "Tell Jalloud, I'm coming to Libya."

Before he made the trip, Hammer made a final gambit. He flew to New York to meet with J. Kenneth Jamieson, the chief executive of Esso. Jamieson saw Hammer as an upstart and an opportunist, someone who made up his own rules in a game that Jamieson had been on top of for years. Several months earlier, Hammer had attempted to undermine the Seven Sisters cartel in Iran. He had gone to Tehran and offered to give the Shah a "better deal" for Iranian oil than the cartel was providing.[13] The Shah turned him down, but tensions between the Shah and the cartel increased.

Now Hammer was asking a favor of Esso. He told Jamieson that Gadhafi was pressuring Occidental to grant the government a major measure of control over the pricing of its Libyan oil. He said that while he was resisting these demands, Occidental "was having serious difficulty in fulfilling contracts for delivery of oil" and that if Gadhafi imposed any further cutbacks, it "was in danger of being wiped out." He asked whether Esso would be willing to supply Occidental with the oil it was losing in Libya, at cost, from its concession in Saudi Arabia. Hammer was making the implicit threat that unless Esso did so, he would capitulate to Gadhafi's demands, which would open the way for Arab leaders to make the same demands on other oil companies. Jamieson, a man of considerable reserve, listened politely but was not about to be extorted to save Hammer's neck. Later that month, Jamieson informed Hammer that if Occidental wanted oil from Esso, it would have to pay the market price. It was now clear to Hammer that the enemy of his enemy was not necessarily his friend. The Seven Sisters would not be coming to Occidental's rescue.[14]

What was at stake for Hammer was not just money—he owned only a small percentage of Occidental's stock—but his reputation as a powerful tycoon, which he had assiduously built over the past decade. This had been significantly enhanced by the abundant oil strike in Libya, and he was not about to see it all disintegrate on Gadhafi's Judgment Day. He had to prevail in Libya, as he had done before in Russia, by collaborating with those in power rather than opposing them. Jalloud was the key to this strategy.

Hammer arrived in Tripoli in his private plane on August 25, one week before Judgment Day. Williamson was waiting at the otherwise deserted airport. As they drove into town in Williamson's Mercedes limousine, Hammer, who had not been in Libya since before the coup, was surprised by the number of roadblocks. There seemed to be one every mile, manned by troops with automatic weapons. The city was an armed camp with few civilians on the street. Hammer found Jalloud waiting for him at the presidential palace, a .45-caliber revolver buckled at his waist.[15]

Jalloud quickly got down to business. His position was straightforward: Libya should get an increased share from each barrel of oil Occidental exported as well as retroactive compensation for oil Occidental had already exported.

Hammer, of course, had been well briefed by Williamson on these demands. But he was impressed with the resolve with which Jalloud presented them. Jalloud was intelligent, and had a commanding presence. Hammer admired the way he did business. "I only wish I could hire him," he told Williamson, who accompanied him to all the sessions.[16]

Each day after the negotiations, Hammer flew in his Gulfstream from Tripoli to Paris. Although it was nearly a three-hour flight, he preferred to spend the night in the comfort of the Hôtel Ritz. He would return to Tripoli in the morning, refreshed and brimming with energy.[17]

A number of top Occidental executives had wanted Hammer to take a hard line in the negotiations, even if that meant closing down the oil fields and battling Libya in court, but he had decided on another strategy: turning Occidental's vulnerability into a virtue. He sought to persuade Jalloud that Occidental's dependence on Libyan oil would work to make Occidental a better ally for Libya than the Seven Sisters oil companies, and that Occidental's survival was in Libya's long-term interest. On most of the specific points, he acquiesced to Jalloud's demands. By September 1, 1970, he had signed an agreement whose terms were unlike any ever before agreed to by a Western oil company. Libya would now get 55 percent of Occidental's profits from its oil and, even more important, would have power over the future pricing of the oil. Once Occidental had agreed to these terms, the other oil companies in Libya, including the Seven Sisters, would be asked to follow suit. If they did not agree, they would be shut down. Within three weeks, they had all acquiesced. With the stroke of a pen, Hammer had acknowledged the ultimate sovereignty of an oil-producing nation over its oil—and had forever changed the geopolitics of oil.

After this, the Middle Eastern dominoes began to fall. Once the oil companies had agreed to Libya's terms, they came under pressure from Iran, Iraq, Saudi Arabia, and other Persian Gulf nations. The Shah of Iran, for example, demanded—and received—an even better profit-sharing arrangement. Libya then had Hammer and the other Libyan concessionaires match Iran's terms. In a matter of months, the control of oil had begun an ineluctable shift from the Seven Sisters cartel to the oil-producing nations. These nations then began coordinating their actions through a group they had previously set up in Vienna, the Organization of Petroleum Exporting Countries, or OPEC. As one oil executive put it, "The oil industry as we had known it would not exist much longer."[18]

To ensure Hammer's continued cooperation in these tumultuous times, Major Jalloud, who had assumed control of Libyan intelligence, sought one further prize: a confession. In December 1970, he dispatched a young French-trained prosecutor, Sassi al-Haj, to New York to find out about Hammer's role in the bribing of Libyan officials.

Hammer had no choice but to submit to the prosecutor's questions. He met Sassi in his lawyer's office accompanied only by his translator, Hakim Burshan. He listened quietly with his best poker face as Sassi reeled off the evidence he had found that showed that Hammer had authorized the payment of bribes to government officials. Hammer was linked not only to Shelhi but to other influence peddlers in Libya. Sassi had also obtained, possibly from the interrogation of Omar Shelhi's brother Aziz, the precise schedule of payments to the UBS account.[19]

Sassi assured Hammer that his purpose was not to prosecute him—or even to release the information to the public. He explained matter-of-factly that the Libyan Revolutionary Command Council had decided that it was not in Libya's interest to prosecute American businessmen—if they demonstrated that they were willing to cooperate in the investigation. As a sign of such cooperation, he wanted Hammer to sign a document acknowledging that Occidental had won its concession through corrupt practices. If he signed, Sassi promised no further action would be taken.

Hammer understood the bind he was in. If he refused this deal, he would be deemed uncooperative, and as the public prosecutor made clear, the investigation would continue in a more public forum. It might even result in the expropriation of the Occidental concession. If that happened, Hammer would lose everything he had created, including his reputation. If, on the other hand, he signed the document, he would give Gadhafi future leverage.

Given Hobson's choice, Hammer signed the document. He had managed to live a secret life before, with the Soviets holding a sword above his head, and survive. Now he was willing to gamble that it would not be in Gadhafi's interest to expose him. Whether or not Hammer knew it when he signed the document, Gadhafi's strategy for completing the takeover of the West's oil concessions depended in large measure on keeping Occidental in the game.

Hammer's strategy of collaboration paid off handsomely. Not only did Occidental continue to profit from Libyan oil for the next fifteen years, but the company received $136 million in compensation from Gadhafi for the nationalization in 1973 of 51 percent of its concession. Occidental was the only foreign company in Libya to receive such compensation. Gadhafi also favored Occidental in a number of other ways, including allowing it to earn interest on money due Libya.[20] Hammer later wrote in his autobiography that he had often been attacked by executives of other oil companies for his role in Libya. His answer to those critics was: "I survived, they didn't."[21]

While Hammer was coming to terms with Gadhafi, Omar Shelhi was attempting to overthrow him. He planned a raid on Tripoli and recruited mercenaries to carry it out. But Shelhi's countercoup failed in 1974 after word of it leaked to Libyan intelligence.

AT CIA HEADQUARTERS IN THE EARLY 1970S, JAMES ANGLETON and his staff followed the progress of Hammer in Libya with increasing interest. By then, Gadhafi had surreptitiously expanded his contacts with the Soviet bloc, arranging for East German advisers to instruct his security service and contracting for arms shipments; and U.S. intelligence had correspondingly increased its monitoring of Libyan communications. Most of the electronic eavesdropping and other sophisticated surveillance was carried out by the National Security Agency (NSA)—and then passed on to the CIA.

Although the NSA could not decipher the diplomatic cables that were transmitted between Moscow and Tripoli, it could determine when transmissions increased or abated. When Angleton's staff analyzed this information, it found a pattern that corresponded to the movements of Armand Hammer. Just before each of Hammer's trips to Tripoli between 1970 and 1972, the volume of secret transmissions from Moscow to its embassy in Tripoli abruptly increased, and after he left Libya, it abruptly fell off. This pattern did not hold for any of the other oil executives who went to Tripoli. Was the fit with Hammer merely a coincidence? Angleton pondered. Or were the Soviets taking an interest in Hammer's negotiations?

Angleton's staff turned to the NSA's interceptions of the unencoded phone calls that Hammer and his Occidental executives had made to their representatives in Libya. They noted that from 1971 onward, Hammer was supposedly acting in concert with the international oil companies and had access to their strategy. Yet from the CIA's analysis of this material, it appeared that in conversations with Occidental employees in Tripoli over open telephone lines, Hammer's top executives were revealing fully, and almost daily, the oil companies' unified negotiating strategy. Since Soviet intelligence had the means to eavesdrop on these conversations, and presumably was doing so, it could pass the information on to the Libyan negotiators. In any case, the Libyans were able, time after time, to anticipate successfully the moves the oil companies made.

Angleton was not surprised, therefore, when Hammer acquiesced to Gadhafi's nationalization of over half of Occidental's Libyan oil subsidiary, a step that foreshadowed escalating oil prices throughout the world.

7/24/79

AH:

Enclosed are (1) the original microcassette of the recording made in
your office on July 23 and (2) an
"insurance copy" of the same recording on a standard cassette (which
I used to make the verbatim transcript I gave you on August 6).

In keeping with the confidential
nature of this recording the labels
are written in Russian.

There are no other copies either of
the recording or of the transcript.

                                    -jh

A note to Hammer from his son, Julian.

CHAPTER NINETEEN

THE ART OF BRIBERY

ON NOVEMBER 18, 1969, TWO MONTHS AFTER GADHAFI TOOK power in Libya and while Occidental was still operating at full throttle, Hammer attempted to get a concession in the Persian Gulf through a very direct means: cash. He took an attaché case packed with $217,000 from his suite at Claridge's and, walking down the corridor to an even larger suite, delivered the money to Sheikh Sultan al-Mualla, the oil minister of the tiny emirate of Umm al-Qaiwain. Sheikh Sultan was the son of the emir of Umm al-Qaiwain and an important ally if one wanted to do business in the emirate, as Hammer did. The $217,000 was the cash portion of the nearly $1.7 million that Hammer had agreed to pay to get the concession to drill for oil in the emirate's offshore waters. Mecom Oil, a Texas company that had previously held the concession, got $1 million of the balance, and a remaining $454,000 went into the emirate's national treasury. This, however, was not the total price of the deal. Hammer arranged for an additional $200,000 to be paid to Sheikh Sultan's personal bank account in Switzerland through Patentia Anstalt, a trust that Hammer controlled in Liechtenstein. Protected by Liechtenstein's strict secrecy laws, the trust made this and other such sensitive transactions difficult to trace, even by Occidental's most tenacious auditors.[1]

This surreptitious payment by Hammer to a government official was not an isolated incident. In 1978, an investigation by Occidental's board of directors that was initiated in response to shareholder lawsuits found that between 1969 and 1975, Hammer had authorized questionable payments, either directly or through intermediaries, to scores of government officials in fourteen different countries in Africa, Asia, and Latin America. In addition to the specific payments the investigators were able to trace, they found that $8.7 million in phantom commissions had been paid by Occidental to foreign nationals through anonymous bank accounts in Switzerland and offshore banking centers. Because of the banking laws in those places, it was impossible to determine the ultimate recipient of the funds.[2]

Up until 1977, when Congress passed the Foreign Corrupt Practices Act, it was not a felony in the United States to bribe a foreign government official. But it was almost invariably a crime in the country in which the bribe was carried out. Moreover, if an oil company obtained a concession through illegal means, it could be revoked without compensation and leave the company no effective legal recourse, as Libya dramatically demonstrated when it nationalized Western concessions. Since such a revocation could expose investors in a company to potentially catastrophic losses, even before the Foreign Corrupt Practices Act became law, a publicly traded company had a legal obligation to disclose to its shareholders that it had used bribery or other illegal practices abroad if doing so could materially affect the prospects of the company. The failure to disclose such information could constitute securities fraud and provide a basis for shareholder lawsuits (as happened at Occidental). At best, then, bribery was a gray area.

Hammer was willing to operate in this gray area because he believed, as he explained in 1971 to one of the intermediaries delivering the cash, "money talks."* He castigated his competitors in established oil companies as "bureaucrats with MBAs" who needed to justify their actions to "special committees of the board of directors" and

---

* Hammer used a concealed microphone in the study of his home to make surreptitious tapes of his conversation about payoffs with this intermediary in November 1971. They are among a number of such tapes, now in my possession, that Hammer made secretly in various situations over an eighteen-year period. He apparently did not tell his business associates about the existence of the tapes. Their purpose remains a mystery.

"layers of accountants."[3] They had little incentive to risk soiling their reputations by competing in the influence bazaar, especially in the 1960s, when their companies had more oil than they could profitably sell on the world market. Hammer himself suffered from no such constraints. He ran a one-man show. According to Occidental's vice president for finance at the time, Hammer overrode financial controls whenever they got in his way and brushed off accountants' questions as if they were "annoying flies."[4] He summarily fired executives who resisted his orders, and treated Occidental's directors—all of whom he handpicked and whom, it will be recalled, he made sign undated letters of resignation—as nothing more than rubber stamps to validate his actions. When he wanted to expedite a deal, he did not even have to inform his board. He could draw on cash reserves without the authorization, or even the knowledge, of any other officer of the company. Few other executives, at least of publicly owned companies, were capable of bribery on the scale that Hammer practiced it.

The act of bribing seemed to enhance Hammer's sense of personal power—and control. Sir John Foster, who was one of England's shrewdest queen's counsels and who advised Hammer on his Middle East ventures during this period (and subsequently served on the board of directors of Occidental), observed that "Hammer enjoyed the directness of it all. He liked to see people jump up when he came into a hotel room with an attaché case full of cash. He liked to see the gleam of anticipation in their eyes when he opened it. He liked it even better if they quivered a bit. He liked to see people hooked on his money."[5] Hammer had a plaque mounted in his office that read, HE WHO HATH THE GOLD MAKES THE RULES. Getting someone to do what he would not do otherwise by dangling cash in front of him and seeing the cash nexus in action tended to confirm his base view of human nature. Hammer could induce the recipient of a bribe to do his bidding even if that meant—as it often did—that the bribed person had to violate the law of his country and risk his career and freedom. The more the recipient compromised himself in this process, the more vulnerable he became to future demands.

BRIBERY ALWAYS REQUIRES SOME ELEMENTARY PRECAUTIONS IN order to minimize the risks of exposure. First, the briber needs a source of well-laundered, if not completely untraceable, funds. Second, he needs an intermediary who can stand between him and the bribed official. Third, he needs a cover story to help obscure the favoritism he has obtained by trading money for influence. Hammer clearly understood these rules.

Having perfected the techniques of money laundering decades earlier in Russia, Hammer masterfully assembled off-the-books funds in the 1960s that gave him absolute control over a continual supply of virtually untraceable money. In some cases, he set up a shell company outside the United States—beyond the purview of its laws—that was not owned by Occidental and therefore not subject to the scrutiny of its auditors. He would generate a profit for this supposedly independent shell company by directing subsidiaries of Occidental to sell it oil at an artificially low price and then repurchase the oil from it. The profit that would accrue to the shell company from these manipulated transactions would provide him with a slush fund.

Consider, for example, the ease with which Hammer created a company called OTAG in May 1968. He had a lawyer set it up in Switzerland for a nominal fee of less than $1,000. Hundreds of such entities are incorporated in Switzerland every week, many with names composed of letters randomly drawn from the alphabet, and another such corporation would attract virtually no attention. Hammer subsequently had the ownership of OTAG transferred to a shell company named Oil Findel, which he had set up in Luxembourg and was nominally owned by a Luxembourg lawyer. OTAG made money by buying oil from a European subsidiary of Occidental at about 1 percent below the market price and then instantly reselling it at the market price to a Belgian utility company that had previously contracted with Occidental for the oil. These transactions took place entirely on paper—no oil went to OTAG; it simply received money from the Belgian utility, retained the 1 percent difference as its profit, and then passed the balance of the money back to the Occidental subsidiary. Occidental's accountants had little reason to be suspicious since the lower price OTAG received could be justified by daily fluctuations in the price of oil. Through this scheme, hundreds of thousands of dollars were diverted from Occidental to OTAG. After paying Swiss taxes on the transactions, OTAG would transmit the balance of the money as dividends to its nominal owner, Oil Findel, in Luxembourg, which would then deposit the funds in bank accounts in Switzerland that were controlled by Hammer. He would withdraw cash from these accounts and have it brought to Los Angeles, where it was placed in a safe-deposit box at the City National Bank that had been rented by his executive assistant.[6]

According to Dorman Commons, Occidental's vice president for finance, Hammer had many other schemes, some even more convoluted than that involving OTAG, through which he diverted funds from the treasury of Occidental and its subsidiaries to myriad offshore accounts outside the purview of Occidental's accountants and auditors. "Hammer had access to as much discretionary cash as he needed," Commons explained.[7]

For example, in the fall of 1971, Hammer stunned Commons by suggesting to him that he had set aside funds to pay off Major Jalloud and other principals in Gadhafi's government. He discussed this calmly and with moral detachment, as if he were discussing a new corporate pension plan, assuring Commons that the money could not be traced to Occidental. Commons did not know the source of the mystery funds destined for Gadhafi's men. He later learned that Hammer had found a way of diverting the money that he and other members of Occidental's board believed had been sent to Shelhi.[8]

Hammer also had no problem recruiting the necessary intermediaries for his bribes. Since he had never considered himself part of the American system, he had a natural affinity for the freebooting financial soldiers of fortune who operated outside the conventional rules of established business. These were usually peripatetic businessmen, often of mixed nationality, who had multiple passports, Swiss bank accounts, and proprietary shell corporations in Liechtenstein, Monaco, Liberia, or some other place that could protect their anonymity. Their principal activity was searching for lucrative liaisons with government officials in underdeveloped countries.

Often, these liaisons were formed in shadowy circumstances. During the latter part of the 1960s, Hammer employed no fewer than twelve such intermediaries. They reported only to him and were, in effect, his private staff. Indeed, they were so discreet that when two of them met in 1969, neither told the other he was working for Hammer.[9] They went wherever Hammer needed to acquire influence: Venezuela, Nigeria, Cameroon, Angola, Argentina, Mexico, Guatemala, Iran, or

Peru. Although, like Kunz and Zade in Libya, they called themselves consultants, they were in fact the cogs in a secret system that delivered laundered money from Occidental to the pockets of local officials who helped get Occidental oil concessions. They had virtually no contact with the geologists, engineers, drilling crews, and executives who constituted the overt side of Occidental's search for oil, since they were prospecting at a different level. Even top Occidental executives did not know of their affiliation or, possibly, of their existence. Hammer had set the dual regime up so that only he had a full picture of its activities. This also, of course, gave him the burden of coordinating, as well as keeping discrete, the two sides of the equation.

Others might have found running parallel secret and public enterprises an intolerable strain, but Hammer had no such problem. Even as a child, he had separated what he could say to outsiders from what he kept secret about his father's radical politics. In Russia, where he had two different identities—as a high-profile U.S. businessman and as a covert facilitator for Soviet intelligence—compartmentalization became a requisite for survival. He became so good at it that he could even seal away from his public life his secret family.

The intermediaries also provided Hammer with a safety net. If things went wrong in a foreign country and the authorities learned that one of his intermediaries had tendered a bribe, Hammer could maintain that he had retained the intermediary only as a consultant and that he had never authorized him to make payoffs. So long as this buffer was not breached, he could insulate himself from the consequences of the bribery, as was demonstrated in Venezuela in the early 1970s.

Hammer had become interested in obtaining concessions in the Lake Maracaibo region of Venezuela. Up until then, Esso and the other Seven Sisters had treated Venezuela as if it were their private preserve. Now, however, the Ministry of Oil was opening the bidding for concessions to independent oil companies, not necessarily because it expected them to prevail but because it wanted to pressure the Seven Sisters to increase their production. Hammer realized that to win any concessions under these conditions, he would need help from inside the ministry. He retained John Askew, an entrepreneur from Arkansas who claimed to be well versed in the intricacies of business in Venezuela.

Hammer made a deal with his new consultant. He transferred $3 million through a Swiss bank account to a shell company Askew had in the Bahamas called Noark International. Askew, after further laundering the money through a Panamanian bank, used it to pay off key officials in Venezuela on Hammer's behalf. Askew, though he was to receive 1 percent of the profits derived from the oil Hammer got in Venezuela, had no illusions about his role. He later described himself as "a conduit and agent" for Hammer.

To avoid the stigma of working with foreign oil companies, Venezuela announced that the new concessions would be in the form of "service contracts" with its national oil company, CVP. The foreign company would receive 90 percent of the oil extracted in return for prospecting, drilling, and producing it and would further pay the standard 52 percent income tax to the government as well as a 16.67 percent royalty. The fields contained an estimated three billion barrels of recoverable oil.

Hammer, in serious trouble in Libya with the rise of Gadhafi, needed a share of this oil and had no qualms about paying $3 million under the table to get service contracts for three of the five concessions. The winners of the concessions were announced on December 1, 1970, but in the fall of 1971 a potentially deal-breaking problem developed. The Venezuelan oil-concession committee objected at the last moment to Hammer's proposal to have his Liberian subsidiary, Occidental World Wide Corporation, sign the service contracts. The committee insisted that Hammer establish an Occidental subsidiary in Venezuela for this purpose. Hammer could not go along with this because, as he explained to Askew, the Liberian subsidiary was a crucial element in his strategy of keeping Occidental's foreign oil earnings overseas, where they need not be reported to the Internal Revenue Service or come under the scrutiny of U.S. authorities. Hammer feared that a Venezuelan subsidiary would undermine that strategy.

With only days remaining before the service contracts were to be signed, Hammer summoned Askew to his home in Los Angeles, where he secretly recorded their conversation. On the tape, Hammer can be heard suggesting that Askew fly back to Venezuela and "work behind the scenes" with government officials to get them to acquiesce to his Liberian subsidiary. When Askew expresses doubts that they will relent, Hammer explodes. "You talked to the minister, didn't you?" he says. "He's getting paid, isn't he? . . . Then why the hell doesn't he deliver?" Hammer suggests to Askew that "maybe you're not paying the minister enough." As the discussion progresses, Hammer decides to review—and records on his secret tapes—the entire $3-million bribe scheme. "Who gets what?" he asks.

Askew dutifully goes through the list of payoffs targeted at influencing the administration of Rafael Caldera, the leader of the COPEI Party and recently elected president (who again holds that office, as of 1996). Askew explains that he distributed $500,000 in cash to some officials of COPEI, provided $500,000 for officials of the Ministry of Mines and Hydrocarbons, and $1 million to Pedro Tinoko, a powerful banker who became finance minister and then head of Venezuela's central bank. After adding up these bribes, Hammer says, "I lose a million dollars somewhere here. I haven't got beyond two million," and he presses Askew for a further reckoning. Askew then describes another $750,000 in payoffs, including a $50,000 payment to a minor official who provided data about the proposed bids of rival oil companies. When Hammer determines there is money left over, he instructs Askew to "take a quarter or half million away from other people. Go to Caldera." At this point, as the tape recording makes clear, Hammer is in full control of the scheme, even micro-managing it. He suggests that Askew go to a key official in the ministry, and tell him, "Look, there is another quarter million dollars." If necessary, he urges, increase the offer to $500,000. He explains that this official could go directly to President Caldera to solve their problem.[10] In this netherworld of offshore cash payments, Hammer had no way of verifying whether any of the $3 million he had transferred into Askew's Bahamian company ever reached the targeted officials in Venezuela. The funds could be traced from the shell company to anonymous accounts in Panama and then to cash withdrawals. After that, the trail disappeared. Whoever got the money, Occidental was awarded the three potentially valuable service contracts Hammer sought.

Before the company could profit from the oil, Venezuela elected a new president, Carlos Andres Perez, who nationalized all service contracts in 1974. Although the government compensated the other foreign oil companies for their losses, it refused to compensate Occidental, on the grounds that Occidental had unlawfully obtained its contracts through bribery. Government investigators had uncovered a few payments that Askew made—and they displayed on television a check from Askew to the father of a minor official in the Ministry of Mines and Hydrocarbons—but they were unable to develop any evidence that any Venezuelan government official had received money from Askew, nor had they been able to link Hammer to Askew's payoffs. (They did not know about the taped discussions of the bribes. The tapes remained in Hammer's possession until his death.) Hammer meanwhile denied that he had authorized any bribes. He acknowledged that $3 million had been paid to Askew but claimed that it was part of a legitimate deal to buy back a portion of Askew's interest in the service contracts. Hammer maintained that if Askew had used the money to make payoffs, it was done without his knowledge. He even persuaded the State Department that his company was being victimized in Venezuela, and the U.S. Embassy in Caracas intervened in Hammer's behalf.

Hammer's buffer held. Even though Askew was arrested in 1976 and it was clear that officials had taken money from him, no one could prove that Hammer was involved in the scheme. In 1989, after more than a decade of litigation, a Venezuelan court ordered the government to pay Occidental $42.2 million in compensation for losses it incurred because of the nationalization of the service contract.

HAMMER WAS ADEPT AT SUPPLYING THE REQUISITE COVER STORIES for his subterranean activities. These stories did not have to be believable in every detail or able to withstand direct scrutiny; they needed only to add enough ambiguity to the circumstances so that officials not disposed to finding corruption could point to an alternative explanation. The stories provided the bribed officials with an important measure of protection after a concession was approved. Hammer frequently suggested that decisions in his favor proceeded from recognition by authorities that he and his company could help address specific humanitarian concerns. Early on in his career, he found that this particular cover worked very well. When he had returned from his first trip to Russia, he had used the story that Lenin had been moved by his concern for the famine in Russia and had consequently granted him an asbestos concession. He discovered then that even ordinarily skeptical businessmen like Henry Ford accepted his explanation that good deeds pay off—especially since it was in their interest to do so. His later experiences only confirmed the advantage of attributing altruistic motives to self-interested acts.

In the 1960s, when Hammer visited underdeveloped countries that had potentially lucrative resources, he had the U.S. embassies there, which were usually alerted to his arrival by cables from influential senators like Albert Gore, arrange formal audiences with top government officials, followed by press conferences. In these meetings, he cited the possibility that Occidental might help alleviate problems that afflicted the country: it could build fertilizer factories to help relieve food shortages; it could drill wells to relieve droughts; it could provide state-of-the-art pesticides that would eradicate scorpions. In the press briefings, he made a point of always referring to himself with his medical title, so that he was not just a businessman but "the doctor." Even though the promised humanitarian ventures rarely went beyond the talk stage (with the exception of drilling for water at the oasis of al-Kufrah in Libya), they provided a convenient smoke screen for the behind-the-scenes activities.

Hammer, of course, could not have been as effective as he was in promulgating his cover if it did not in fact project a persona that had real meaning for him. He wanted to be recognized as the humanitarian doctor.

ALTHOUGH HAMMER HAD MASTERED THE ART OF BRIBERY, NOT all his bribes produced profitable oil concessions. In Nigeria, for example, Occidental obtained a concession through the efforts of Hammer's Monte Carlo–based intermediary, Salvador Amon, who stood to receive $2 million if it worked out. But the concession failed to yield oil, and Amon had to settle for $137,000.[11] And even though Occidental struck oil at the concession it obtained in the Persian Gulf off the coast of Umm al-Qaiwain, the concession became entangled in a territorial dispute with another emirate, one supported by Iran, and it had to be abandoned. Such failures were, however, part of the game. The successful concessions that Hammer engineered, such as the bonanza in Libya, had, by the mid-1970s, transformed Occidental into a significant—and profitable—international oil company. The oil that was flowing, and the money it produced, provided Hammer with the means to achieve something he had committed himself to nearly a half century before: opening up a path between U.S. business and the Soviet Union.

CHAPTER TWENTY

TO
RUSSIA
WITH MONEY

THE INAUGURATION OF RICHARD MILHOUS NIXON AS THE THIRTY-seventh president of the United States on January 20, 1969, had a profound effect on East-West relations—and on Armand Hammer. Up until then, the United States had pursued a cold-war strategy of attempting to deny trade opportunities to the Soviet Union. Kennedy's attempts to soften the trade policy at the beginning of his term in the early 1960s had been quickly abandoned when the war in Vietnam expanded. His successor, Lyndon Johnson, who had to contend with both the war in Vietnam and the Soviet invasion of Czechoslovakia, did little to change this policy. But when Nixon took office, he decided to approach Soviet trade with a more opportunistic eye.

Despite his extraordinary personal reticence and almost unimaginable unease with intellectuals, Nixon was a surprisingly bold adventurer in the realm of geopolitics. According to Henry Kissinger, who served as both his national security adviser and his secretary of state, no other U.S. president, with the possible exception of Theodore Roosevelt, matched Nixon in his instinctive grasp of Realpolitik. He believed that a nation's security interests, not idealistic principles, have primacy in determining its foreign policy. Nixon was determined to place the issue of Soviet trade in this Machiavellian context.

*Hammer with the Soviet minister of culture, Yekaterina Furtseva,
on his yacht in Florida in the 1970s.*

He viewed the withholding of technology, tariff preferences, and credit from the Communists not as a moral imperative but as a tactic aimed at extracting a political advantage. They were bargaining chips. If the Soviets were to acquire the resources and technology they needed to modernize their economy, they would have to pay a political price in other areas, such as Vietnam. "The idea," as Kissinger later explained, "was to emphasize those areas in which cooperation was possible, and to use that cooperation as leverage to modify Soviet behavior in areas in which the two countries were at loggerheads. That . . . was what the Nixon administration understood by the word *détente*."[1]

Détente was initiated in November 1971, when a trade mission headed by Secretary of Commerce Maurice H. Stans was sent to Moscow. Stans, who had been a major fund-raiser for the Republican Party before joining the administration, was Nixon's most prominent liaison with corporate America. His trip was artfully timed to coincide with a conference in Moscow whose participants included the top executives of such giants of the American corporate world as IBM, General Electric, Westinghouse, and Du Pont. When he went to the Kremlin to discuss the relaxation of trade restrictions, he sent a clear signal to these businessmen that the cold-war ice was finally cracking.[2]

While Nixon assumed that he would be able to use trade policy to control the dealings that U.S. capitalists had with the Soviet Union, those in the Soviet hierarchy had a different perspective. They believed that capitalists controlled the U.S. government and that it was their economic agenda that would determine the government's trade policy. Brezhnev and his colleagues saw détente as a convenient way to appeal directly to capitalists to pressure the United States to abolish trade restrictions.[3] To this end, Nikolay Patolichev, the Soviet minister of foreign trade, dangled billions of dollars in potential contracts in front of the assembled businessmen at the Moscow conference. In addition, he offered them a model and a guide for doing business in the Soviet Union. "I know you wonder if a capitalist can do business in a Communist country," he said, and then cited the success of "one of your richest men"—an American who in the 1920s had manufactured pencils in the Soviet Union, pencils that Patolichev himself had used in school. The model capitalist was of course Armand Hammer.[4]

. . .

THE SOVIET MINISTER'S WORDS DID NOT FALL ON DEAF EARS.
Hammer was keenly attuned to every nuance of détente. He had
watched it unfold with, as he put it, "the sharpest interest and enthusiasm."[5] He knew that the Soviet minister had a purpose in mentioning his name to the American businessmen. The message was that
he was no longer "compromised," as he had been when he left Russia in 1929. For decades, he had been uncertain how much the FBI
knew about the services he had performed for Soviet intelligence in
the 1920s. His brief liaison with Khrushchev had flickered, then died.
Now it appeared that the Soviets wanted him to be associated publicly with détente. "My connection with the Soviet Union, more or
less dormant since Khrushchev's fall from power, flourished afresh,"
he wrote.

Hammer was now in his early seventies. His face was wrinkled
and reptilian, his hair had thinned noticeably, and his hearing and
vision had weakened. But he had lost none of his focus. He was determined to play the role in détente for which he was designated.
"No policy could have been framed closer to my own beliefs and at-
titudes," he noted.[6]

He was again headed east. Occidental had much richer opportunities in a dozen other countries, but in these countries Hammer would
be merely another businessman, one who could be derided by multinational corporate executives like Kenneth Jamieson, investigated by
bureaucrats like J. Edgar Hoover, and extorted by petty tyrants like
Abdul Jalloud. In Russia, he had a mission. He had been assigned
this mission personally by Lenin, and it had been approved by Stalin.
It had allowed him to enter the inner sanctum of the Kremlin—a
privilege that few other foreigners would ever experience—and to act
in a way no other businessman could.

Hammer had been preparing Occidental for détente for nearly a
decade. In the early 1960s, he had attempted to modernize the Soviet
fertilizer industry. Although he had been unable to get the necessary
financing or U.S. cooperation for the project, Occidental had acquired in the process a half dozen companies that possessed the technology to concentrate and ship massive amounts of chemicals from
the United States to the Soviet Union. Now he saw that all the in-

gredients were coming together for the fertilizer deal that he had prepared for so many years.

In the interim, Hammer had greatly expanded Occidental's financial capabilities. His deal with Gadhafi had provided Occidental with a huge cash flow. And after Nixon articulated his plans for détente, Hammer laid the groundwork for business in Russia by buying controlling interest in a small American company called Tower International, which had been quietly developing a blueprint for investments in the Communist world. The man behind Tower International was Cyrus Eaton, an extraordinary eighty-eight-year-old American industrialist. Tall and gaunt with white hair, he had been described by the conservative *National Review* as "the most fearsome living incarnation of the old-time competitive capitalist spirit."[7]

Born in Pugwash, Nova Scotia, Eaton learned about business from none other than John D. Rockefeller, whom he worked for as a golf caddie, bodyguard, and office assistant. While still in his twenties, he had sallied forth on his own, investing borrowed funds in Canadian and U.S. public-utility companies and then merging them in an enormous syndicate called Continental Gas and Electric Company. He survived the 1929 stock-market crash and during the Depression bought iron, steel, rubber, and transportation companies. He founded Republic Steel, which became the third-largest producer of flat rolled steel in the United States, and he gained control of the Chesapeake and Ohio Railroad, which dominated the transportation of commodities in the Midwest.

Having made fortune after fortune through capitalist entrepreneurship in the 1940s and early 1950s, Eaton decided to use part of his immense wealth to improve U.S.-Soviet relations. In July 1957, he organized the Pugwash Conference of Nuclear Scientists at his bucolic estate in Nova Scotia. He paid the expenses of the two dozen scientists who attended. The Russian delegation included such figures as Dmitry F. Skobeltsyn, a leading physicist; Aleksandr M. Kuzin, an award-winning biochemist; and A. V. Topchiev, the secretary general of the Soviet Academy of Science. The American delegation had equally prominent scientists, including Leo Szilard, one of the fathers of the nuclear bomb; Hermann J. Muller, a Nobel Prize–winning biologist; and Eugene Rabinowich, the editor of the *Bulletin of Atomic Scientists.* The group slept in Pullman cars provided by Eaton's

Chesapeake and Ohio Railroad and met every morning at six o'clock for a week. Soviet scientists had an opportunity to discuss kings and cabbages—and the state of nuclear science—with their U.S. counterparts. At a less philosophical level, the conference provided an opportunity for the KGB, which had handpicked the interpreters for the conference, to gain access to a number of prominent U.S. scientists.[8] The first Pugwash Conference was deemed such a success that it became a greatly expanded annual event.

Eaton soon found himself the toast of the Communist world. He was praised as a capitalist with dedication to the idea of peaceful coexistence. He was escorted around Moscow by Khrushchev like a head of state. He was showered with gifts by Mikoyan. He was awarded the Lenin Peace Prize by the Politburo. His photograph appeared on the front page of *Pravda*.

Despite such public accolades, the Soviet leaders eventually decided that Eaton was not the appropriate focal point for the new détente. Ironically, he had greatly reduced his value to them by identifying himself too closely with Soviet interests. His blunt criticism of U.S. cold-war policies had caused members of Congress to question his loyalty, and an FBI report described him as "a consort of the Soviets, under the pretense of being an apostle of peace." Since the Soviets assumed that they needed the cooperation of the Nixon administration to make détente work, they could not afford to be associated with such an outspoken and controversial character. Eaton had served his purpose with Pugwash, but he had outlived his usefulness as a conduit to Western business.[9]

Eaton was too shrewd an operator not to realize that he had been cut out of the Soviet strategy for getting U.S. investment. Although the Soviets had encouraged him in the early 1960s to develop real estate and energy projects, including a high-rise trade center in the heart of Moscow and a natural-gas pipeline across Siberia, he found that they were now avoiding him and avoiding any commitments that advanced these projects. When Hammer visited Eaton's office in Cleveland in early 1969, he clearly had been briefed on Eaton's work. It was then that he suggested that Occidental was a more suitable vehicle than Tower International to undertake the projects, and he offered to buy a majority interest in the company. Eaton evidently had little choice but to acquiesce: Hammer, not he, was now the designated player in this game. He came to an agreement with Hammer in which Occidental assumed the debts that Tower International had incurred over the years preparing projects in the Soviet bloc. In return, Hammer agreed to give Eaton 45 percent of any profits that ensued from their projects.

Hammer further widened his access to the Soviet hierarchy through Yekaterina Furtseva, the minister of culture. Trained as a textile weaver, Furtseva had joined the Communist apparatus in 1930, when she was only nineteen.[10] A favorite of Stalin's, she rose rapidly in the party and was appointed to the Politburo in 1950—the first woman in Soviet history to achieve this position.[11] When Hammer met her in 1964, he was attracted by both her toughness and her comeliness.[12] Mikoyan had assigned her the responsibility of arranging art exchanges with the United States, a program that Hammer had been involved in since the mid-1930s. When Hammer learned that Furtseva admired the works of Grandma Moses, he offered to arrange an exhibition at the Pushkin Museum of Fine Art in Moscow. Furtseva had proposed sending the Red Army Chorus on a tour of the United States, but the State Department objected to the propagandist aspect of such a tour. Hammer had promised—but failed—to use his influence with the Johnson administration to overcome these objections.[13] Furtseva admired his efforts, and throughout the late 1960s, Hammer assiduously cultivated the relationship. Furtseva, meanwhile, began to live noticeably better in Moscow—building, for example, a $160,000 vacation home for herself—leading to rumors that Hammer was the source of her newfound wealth. In any case, Hammer could count on her as an ally.

By 1972, Hammer had all his pieces in place. "I wanted Occidental to take the lead in the new policy of détente," he explained. "The corporation was better placed for this role than any in America."[14] The Soviet business arena was opening to Hammer once again, but he was far wealthier and far more powerful than he had been, and he planned to do business on a monumental scale. Among the advantages he now held was the promise of a very special channel to the Kremlin.

YURI ANDROPOV MADE SURE HAMMER HAD THIS ACCESS. ANDROPOV headed the KGB and was a powerful Politburo member, one who would in time succeed Brezhnev as the general secretary of the Communist Party. He had the responsibility of implementing the Soviet détente strategy, and in January 1972, he selected Mikhail Bruk to be Hammer's personal "ambassador"—and facilitator—in Moscow.[15]

Bruk was born in Moscow in 1929. His father was Jewish; his mother, Russian. He attended schools usually reserved for the children of the Communist elite, the so-called *nomenklatura,* and then enrolled in the Communist Party. He perfected his English in the late 1940s at the Institute of Foreign Languages, a facility that served as a training center for the top prospects for Soviet intelligence. In the late 1950s, he was dispatched to Cyrus Eaton's Pugwash Conferences as a technical interpreter. There, he distinguished himself by using his charm to cultivate relationships with a number of leading Western scientists, including Leo Szilard. Bruk also traveled around the United States as a Soviet journalist, although with his perfect English he was often mistaken for a British journalist. During these years, he built on his slight friendship with Szilard and began contacting other American nuclear scientists, an activity that quickly brought him to the attention of the FBI. He then found he had problems renewing his visa, and he returned to Moscow.[16]

Bruk had been acquainted with Hammer's nephew Armasha at the Institute of Foreign Languages, and when Hammer came to Moscow in 1964, Bruk interviewed him at length for a Moscow newsweekly. He continued to maintain an interest in Hammer from afar during the late 1960s. Now, with Andropov's backing, he was to have an open connection with him. By mid-January 1972, he had set up a headquarters for Hammer on the top floor of the Hotel National, across from the Kremlin. He was Hammer's official expediter.

Hammer assumed from the outset of this relationship that Bruk was a Soviet intelligence officer. When a top Occidental executive asked about Bruk's business experience, Hammer answered nonchalantly, "Mike's KGB." He explained, "We can't do business in Russia without the KGB, and it's better to have a KGB man we know about than one we don't."[17]

That winter, Bruk received a wish list from Hammer. At the top of it was a request that Hammer be permitted to fly to Russia in his Gulfstream jet. When Bruk explained that no private jet had ever been allowed to fly in Soviet airspace, Hammer explained in return that he needed to demonstrate to other American businessmen that he, and he alone, had the necessary connections in Russia to obtain unique privileges. But obtaining the permission for Hammer was no easy matter, even for Bruk. He had to clear the request with the head of KGB counterintelligence, the general in command of Soviet air defense, the minister of civil aviation, the Moscow Airport Authority, and the national security adviser to the general secretary of the Communist Party, a process that took, even with Andropov's backing, nearly four months. Bruk also managed to arrange the permission for Hammer to enter and leave Russia without going through the usual customs and passport control, a privilege ordinarily accorded only to visiting heads of state. He filled other items on Hammer's wish list as well, such as arranging for him to import his Mercedes limousine to Moscow and to reside in the Lenin suite in the Hotel National—the rooms in which Lenin had slept during the early days of the revolution.[18]

Bruk had more than these matters of protocol to coordinate that spring. Hammer was negotiating three ventures that, for political reasons, the Soviets wanted to announce soon after the summit meeting in Moscow between Nixon and Brezhnev, which was scheduled for late May. The first and most advanced project was an expanded version of the fertilizer deal that Hammer and the Soviets had unsuccessfully attempted to launch in the mid-1960s. A massive swap of U.S. phosphate for Soviet ammonia, potash, and urea was to continue through 1998—Hammer's one-hundredth birthday. For its part, Occidental would mine over fifty million tons of phosphate rock from deposits in northern Florida—more than 6 percent of the nation's total production. The phosphate would be dissolved in sulfuric acid, concentrated, and shipped in heated tankers to Russia, where it would be piped to a petrochemical complex that Hammer would build. In return, the Soviets would provide Occidental with a commensurate quantity of natural gas, which would be converted into ammonia and other chemical products and exported to the United States and Europe.

The second project, though unformed at this point, was even grander in concept. It involved Occidental's developing a vast natural-gas field in the Yakutsk region of east-central Siberia and then transporting more than one hundred billion cubic feet of gas a year through twelve hundred miles of pipeline that would be constructed over the frozen wasteland to the port of Olga on the Sea of Japan.

The natural gas would then be liquefied under tremendous pressure and loaded onto specially constructed tankers, which, like giant thermos bottles, would carry it to Japan and the United States.

The third project, which had been developed by Eaton's Tower International, was for the construction in the heart of Moscow of four modern skyscrapers that would house a world-class International Trade Center. The complex would include a six-hundred-room hotel, a sixteen-story office building, a sixteen-story apartment building for foreigners, a two-thousand-seat conference center, five international restaurants, and an eighteen-hole golf course (the only golf course in the Soviet Union). The Soviets believed that such a facility was necessary to encourage Western businessmen to come to their country.[19]

Nixon's weeklong summit in Moscow—the first visit of any U.S. president to the Soviet capital—ended on June 1, 1972. The next month, Hammer held his own summit. He arrived in Moscow on July 14 in his private plane. He was accompanied by Sargent Shriver, the Kennedy brother-in-law who had served as the founding director of the Peace Corps and then as ambassador to France. Shriver would be nominated later that year as the Democratic candidate for vice president of the United States. He was now acting as Hammer's legal adviser.

Hammer's entourage also included David Karr, a man of considerable mystery. Karr's real name was David Katz. Born in Brooklyn in 1918 to Russian and Latvian parents, he had been a political activist during his youth and at the age of twenty had joined the staff of the *Daily Worker*. In 1941, he moved to Washington and joined the Office of War Information. In 1945, his Communist background became an issue. He changed his name to Karr and became the assistant to Drew Pearson, who was then one of the most powerful newspaper columnists and radio commentators in America. Through the contacts he made as a journalist, Karr became involved in corporate public relations and then in corporate takeovers. He reemerged as a wheeler-dealer in Paris in the early 1960s and set up a Bahamian-chartered company, Financial Engineers, that specialized in arranging commodity and technology deals in the Soviet bloc. Karr's principal contact in Moscow was Dzhermen Gvishiani, the well-connected son-in-law of Premier Aleksey Kosygin and the deputy chairman of the State Committee for Science and Technology of the Soviet Council of Ministers. Since this was the agency that Hammer had to deal with, Karr had come along on the trip.

Hammer meant this to be a high-profile mission. Along with Shriver, Karr, and a half dozen Soviet journalists, he attended a ceremony sponsored by the Committee for Science and Technology, at which he signed a "preliminary agreement" for the fertilizer project. (Despite the fanfare and photographs, it was in fact only a tentative agreement to negotiate further.)

On July 17, Hammer flew to London, where he called a press conference to announce that he had concluded "a wide-ranging agreement" with the Soviet government, according to which Occidental's technology would be exchanged for Soviet raw materials. Describing it as "one of the first fruits" of the Nixon summit, he said that "in my 51 years of dealing with the Soviet government, I have never found the grounds more favorable for the rapid expansion of East-West trade than exists at present." Though the deal was hardly in concrete form and, even if completed, would hardly impinge on the U.S. energy situation, he told reporters that the venture would, among other things, help solve "growing oil and gas shortages in the United States."[20] Hammer's announcement sent Occidental shares up 19 percent, adding in a matter of hours over $200 million to the market value of the company before the flood of buy orders forced the New York Stock Exchange to halt trading of the stock temporarily.

In Washington, Peter Peterson, the Nixon administration's secretary of commerce, quickly ascertained that Hammer had not reached any sort of binding deal with the Soviets. His intelligence indicated that the negotiations between Occidental and the Soviets were in a very early stage. Peterson found Hammer's grandstanding disturbing, especially since the Soviets, by not denying his claims about the putative deal, seemed to be cooperating with Hammer in the deception. This posed a threat to the administration's policy of linking U.S. economic investment in Russia to the cooperation of Soviet leaders in the matter of Vietnam and other areas. If other American businessmen believed that Hammer was locking up lucrative contracts for Soviet natural gas and other valuable resources, they might rush in to seek their own deals. Such a stampede to Moscow would make it difficult, if not impossible, in an election year for Nixon to resist pressures to relax trade restrictions before the Soviets had accommodated the United States by acceding to its political demands.[21] Whatever Hammer's intention, his actions were undercutting Kissinger's détente strategy. Yet there was little Peterson could do about it. Hammer had crafted links to Maurice Stans—who by now had left the Commerce Department to become the finance chairman of Nixon's reelection campaign—that led to the White House.

Some six weeks before Nixon had departed for the May summit in Moscow, Hammer personally delivered to Stans $46,000 in well-laundered money—cash that had come from one of Hammer's off-the-books slush funds in Switzerland. It was the first part of a $100,000 contribution he was making to Nixon's reelection fund. Stans made clear to Hammer that his cash commitment made him a member of the exclusive Hundred-Thousand-Dollar Club, a group of Nixon backers that presumably would have some access to the Oval Office. When Hammer returned from London on July 19, he called Tim Babcock, a former Republican governor of Montana who now was vice president of Occidental International, Hammer's lobbying arm in Washington. Hammer had hired Babcock because he was a friend of Nixon's, and he acted as Hammer's ambassador to the Nixon administration. Hammer told Babcock he needed to brief the president on his Soviet deal. Babcock called H. R. Haldeman, Nixon's chief of staff, and the meeting was set for the next day.

Hammer arrived at the White House in the early afternoon. "I had just returned from the Soviet Union, where I had signed the first trade agreement since the Nixon/Brezhnev summit," Hammer later claimed, "and Nixon naturally wanted to hear all about it."[22]

Haldeman, who sat in on the meeting, recorded a somewhat different version of the encounter in his diary:

> July 20th, 1972. The P[resident] and I met with Armand Hammer today. Ostensibly for him to report to the P[resident] on his trip to Russia and the big oil deal with the Soviets. . . . Hammer is hysterical, came in with an envelope full of art books and his own story of Russia.
>
> Told us about his background in Russia, and everything, which was really quite fascinating, but he is obviously quite entranced with himself, and not much of anything else.[23]

Hammer did, however, speak of matters other than himself. He pointedly said to Nixon, without knowing that his conversation was being recorded by the White House taping system, "I'm in the 'Hundred-Thousand-Dollar Club,' " and suggested that he was prepared to furnish further assistance.

Nixon wanted more from Hammer than money. Occidental was then employing Marvin Watson, who had been a senior aide to LBJ and briefly served as Johnson's postmaster general. He was also one of the Democratic Party's best political organizers. Nixon had asked Watson to run a campaign to get conservative Democrats in the South to vote for him. Watson had agreed to take on the assignment if Hammer would rehire him when the campaign was over. Haldeman put it to Hammer: "We have to have him." Hammer, knowing he needed Nixon's help to complete his Soviet initiatives, readily granted this favor.[24]

Later that same week, Hammer tested his standing in the Hundred-Thousand-Dollar Club. He met with Stans and complained that Pete Peterson was publicly casting aspersions on his Soviet venture. Soon afterward, Peterson's negative comments to the press stopped, and Hammer was given a "channel" to the White House in the person of Helmut Sonnenfeldt, the senior deputy on Kissinger's national-security staff. Sonnenfeldt had reservations about Hammer, whom he found both "crafty" and "self-aggrandizing," but there was little he could do about it since Hammer evidently had support at the highest levels of the Nixon administration.[25]

AT OCCIDENTAL HEADQUARTERS IN LOS ANGELES, MEANWHILE, Dorman Commons completed his analysis of the financial implications of the Soviet ventures. As the company's chief financial officer and director, he had a responsibility for protecting the stockholders' interests. Despite the recent excitement about the company on Wall Street, Commons knew that Occidental's profit margins had been severely squeezed by the deal Hammer had made with Gadhafi—as well as by Hammer's continuing insistence on funneling a percentage of the Libyan money into the Union Bank of Switzerland account. In the first six months of 1972, Occidental had gross revenues of $1.2 billion, but it had earned only $4 million in profit. Commons reckoned that these meager earnings were barely enough to finance the company's plans to expand its oil business. Yet Hammer was now moving to commit the company to billions of dollars' worth of projects in the Soviet Union.

For the least grandiose of these projects, the Moscow International Trade Center, $110 million would be required to build the hotel and apartment buildings alone and, even using the most optimistic assumptions about occupancy, would not yield Occidental a return on its investment in the foreseeable future. Commons estimated an investment of $1 billion would be necessary for the fertilizer project, which would involve, among other things, constructing four highly advanced ammonia plants on the Volga River, a six-hundred-mile pipeline to the port of Odessa on the Black Sea, a terminal, and four oceangoing tankers. He estimated that the largest of the projects, the Siberian natural-gas project, would cost over $4 billion.

All of these projects involved enormous risks for Occidental. The International Trade Center would become a white elephant if there was not at least a tenfold increase in the number of foreign businessmen visiting Moscow. The fertilizer project would fail—and Occidental could lose its entire investment in it—if Occidental was unable to deliver the quantity of phosphates specified in the agreement. Even if the U.S. government did not block the transfer, Occidental's own geologists doubted that Occidental's Florida phosphate deposits contained the necessary quantity of phosphate. The Siberian project required not only that a pipeline be built across some of the most inhospitable terrain on earth but also that public utilities in Japan and the United States sign long-term contracts to buy the Soviet gas.

Commons met with Hammer on the last day of July to present his analysis. He told Hammer, point by point, his reservations about the Soviet projects. Hammer took copious notes on a yellow pad as Commons spoke and then attempted to assuage his doubts by asserting that Commons had seen only preliminary drafts of the deals. He assured Commons that the risks would be brought under control in the final contracts with the Soviets. But Commons was not convinced. He asked Hammer one more question: how could the risk of détente breaking down be controlled? If it did break down, Occidental might have to write off its entire Soviet investment.

Hammer stared at him without replying—a long stare that even years later caused a chill in Commons when he thought about it. Hammer then said that Commons would have his answer the next day.

When Commons arrived at Occidental's headquarters the following morning, he found that the files on the Soviet project had been removed from his office. He was told that Hammer wanted to see him. Without speaking, Hammer handed him a letter. It was the signed letter of resignation that Commons had given Hammer when he had assumed his position. It had been undated. Now he saw that the date of his resignation had been filled in by Hammer. It was that day, August 1, 1972. He had been fired.[26]

ON FEBRUARY 11, 1973, HAMMER AGAIN WENT TO MOSCOW. Four months earlier, he had got the imprimatur of the Soviet leadership in a meeting with Mikhail Andreyevich Suslov, the chief ideologist of the Communist Party and the second-highest-ranking member of the Politburo. Brezhnev, who declined to meet with Hammer then, sent him a letter crediting him with "a highly significant role" in "the present positive turn in Soviet-American relations." Now Hammer wanted to meet Brezhnev in the Kremlin, as he had met Lenin and Khrushchev.

The meeting took place on February 15. Hammer described Brezhnev as "a man of great humanism and vast warmth. . . . His eyes quickly filled with tears when his sentiments were stirred." At one point, according to Hammer, Brezhnev spontaneously reached in his pocket and gave Hammer his own gold watch as a gift. "Brezhnev was eager to open up Soviet trade," he recalled. He "liked my formulation 'détente through trade,' and he was ready to put his weight and muscle behind the deals I wanted to make for Occidental."[27] Brezhnev himself described the relationship with Hammer differently, and less sentimentally, in a television interview: "I help him; he helps me. It's mutual. We do not discuss secrets—just business."[28]

Hammer wasted little time in attempting to exploit his contact with Brezhnev. On his way back from Moscow that February, he stopped off in Tehran to see the shah's chief minister, Asadollah Alam, who considered Hammer, as he noted in his diary, "a lively old man." Hammer explained that through him the Soviets were offering a "tripartite deal" that involved a vast quantity of natural gas. Iran would trade its natural gas to the Soviet Union, which would deliver an equal amount of Siberian gas to Alaska, which Occidental would sell in the United States. In this exchange, the United States would wind up paying Iran for its gas.[29] Hammer's plan turned out to be economically infeasible, however. It is logistically impossible to ship Soviet gas across the Arctic to Alaska, an Occidental executive pointed out later. He concluded, "Hammer was simply trying to impress the Shah with his Soviet connection."[30]

Although the tripartite idea was dropped after Hammer returned to the United States—Hammer never even informed his board of directors of it—he advanced two of the more conventional "business" arrangements he had discussed with Brezhnev. In April, Hammer signed a twenty-year contract for the delivery of phosphate to the Soviet Union. Hammer himself described the accord as "the breakthrough in Soviet-American trade."[31] Then, in September, Hammer signed the contract to build the International Trade Center in Moscow. The third proposed deal, the Siberian gas pipeline, whose cost had escalated to $17.5 billion, was quietly shelved.[32]

But initiating even the two projects required an enormous infusion of capital into the Soviet Union. Since Hammer knew that Occidental was not in a position to provide this capital on its own, he turned to the U.S. Export-Import Bank, the agency that had been set up by Congress to finance U.S. trade with the underdeveloped world. Hammer proposed that the bank make a twenty-year $180-million loan to the Soviet government to help construct processing plants, pipelines, and other facilities for Occidental's fertilizer project. The interest rate on this proposed loan would be about half the prevailing commercial-bank rate. Hammer was confident that if the Export-Import Bank provided money on these favorable terms, he could raise another $180 million at conventional rates from a syndicate of banks, led by the Bank of America, that wanted to do business in Russia. This sum, he reckoned, would at least be enough to set the project in motion.

Before the loan could be granted, Hammer had to overcome a serious barrier: Congress had prohibited the Export-Import Bank, which before 1973 had never even considered an application for a loan to the Soviet Union, from making loans to the Soviet Union unless the president determined that it was in the national interest. Hammer needed a letter from Nixon.

Hammer had continued to support Nixon with cash contributions even after the president was reelected. On March 13, 1974, he wrote Nixon that the "fertilizer transaction" was under consideration by William J. Casey, the newly appointed chairman of the Export-Import Bank, and that its approval "could be very important at this time." He noted that the "transaction is a particularly important one for the United States, affecting as it does the farmers, our balance of payments, unemployment, and the energy shortage." He ended the letter warmly, asking whether he could "be of any service to you and our country," and adding that "unless you are successful, mankind indeed will take a step backward."[33]

Though the deal took months more to negotiate, Nixon in the end came through for Hammer. On May 20, the president wrote Casey that he had concluded that Hammer's "transaction . . . makes exactly the kind of contribution to the national interest which I envisioned when I made the determination . . . that it is in the national interest for the Export-Import Bank to finance U.S. exports to the Soviet Union."[34] The next day, Hammer's seventy-sixth birthday, the Export-Import Bank approved the $180-million loan. It was the largest loan that the bank had ever made to a Communist country.[35] Shortly after this, the Export-Import Bank lent the Soviet government another $36 million, which was earmarked for Hammer's International Trade Center.

Even with these low-interest loans, the Russian deals were far from profitable. The Soviets had neither the equipment nor the experience to handle efficiently the volatile phosphoric acid that Occidental began shipping to Odessa; and by the time Occidental received the Soviet ammonia in return, the world markets were glutted with ammonia, and the price had collapsed. Occidental executives struggled without success to make economic sense of these deals for the next two decades. Zoltan Merszei, Hammer's chief executive officer, had twenty years' experience in the chemical-commodities business at Dow Chemical. Even so, he found there was little he could do to salvage Hammer's massive phosphate-for-ammonia exchange. The contract that Hammer had signed with the Soviet Ministry of Trade neglected to take into account the wide fluctuations in the prices of the underlying commodities. From the point of view of making money, this was not a sound deal. But even after Merszei pointed out the defects in the contract, he found that Hammer was determined to proceed with it. "The key to Hammer was that he did not care about money," Merszei later reflected. "He cared about power."[36] For Hammer, the Kremlin represented one of the world's principal centers of power. By accommodating the Soviet leadership on this and other matters, he sought access to this power.

By the summer of 1974, Hammer had a personal net worth of $20 million. He had total control of Occidental Petroleum and the millions of dollars that had been diverted into slush funds. He employed twenty political lobbyists, including Marvin Watson and Tim Babcock. Senators and congressmen depended on his largesse. And he had access to both Brezhnev and Nixon.

Armasha Hammer, Armand's nephew and namesake, was left behind in the Soviet Union when his father, Victor, returned to New York in 1928. In 1960, with the help of Eleanor Roosevelt, Armasha obtained a visa to visit the Hammers in America. His mother, Vava, is on Roosevelt's right, and his Russian wife is on her left.

Although Hammer claimed to have had several meetings with John Kennedy, this is as close as he ever got to him. Hammer is at the rear of a group gathered at the White House, where Franklin Roosevelt, Jr., then the Undersecretary of Commerce, was making an announcement.

In 1952, Hammer bought Campobello, the Roosevelt summer home off the coast of Maine. He later donated it as a memorial park, and in 1964 there was a dedication ceremony attended by Lady Bird Johnson, in the foreground. Hammer is behind her. Senator Edmund Muskie of Maine is at the far right, next to FDR, Jr.

Hammer with King Idris of Libya in 1968, when the Occidental Petroleum Corporation's Libyan pipeline was dedicated.

Hammer in Los Angeles with Kemal Zeinal Zade, who had served as a go-between in setting up Occidental's Libyan oil deal. Nearly $3 million was deposited into a secret Swiss bank account controlled by Zade and his colleagues when the deal was made.

Armand and Frances Hammer with the Pope in 1980.

Hammer with his grandchildren, Michael and Casey Hammer.

Martha Kaufman, a freelance writer, met Hammer in 1974. She became his mistress and the curator of his art collection. When his wife became suspicious about their relationship, Hammer had Kaufman change her name to Hilary Gibson. She also changed her appearance, wearing wigs and new makeup so that Frances wouldn't recognize her. As Hilary Gibson, she became the director of planning for the Armand Hammer Museum of Art and Cultural Center.

Armand and Frances Hammer having caviar and champagne on the Oxy One, *Hammer's private plane.*

Hammer and Rosamaria Durazo, whom he introduced as his private physician, with President and Mrs. Bush at the White House in April 1990, a few months before Hammer died.

Hammer talking to his granddaughter, Casey, at the opening of the Armand Hammer Museum of Art and Cultural Center in November 1990.
It was his last public appearance.

CHAPTER TWENTY-ONE

WATERGATE CRIMES AND MISDEMEANORS

IN THE AUTOBIOGRAPHY HAMMER PUBLISHED IN THE LATE 1980S, he wrote that in 1975, "all of my worst nightmares had come to life."[1] He was referring to the very real possibility that he would be arrested and taken to prison in manacles, just as his father had been. The cause of this nightmare was Watergate. The same unrelenting investigation that had forced the resignation of President Nixon in August 1974 had zeroed in on Hammer's role in providing cash for the cover-up.

Three years earlier, in June 1972, Hammer had paid little attention to the news story concerning the arrest of five burglars in the suite occupied by the Democratic National Committee in the Watergate complex. The break-in had happened when Hammer was in London laying the groundwork for his Moscow deals. The only reason he had even noticed the story was that he also maintained a suite in the Watergate and was concerned about the lapse in security.[2]

The men arrested in the Watergate were not hapless burglars, of course. They were clandestine operatives employed by Nixon's campaign to plant electronic listening devices in the Democrats' headquarters. The men assumed that the charges lodged against them would be quashed, and they refused to divulge anything to the authorities who had arrested them. In return, the Nixon reelection committee paid them in cash every week for their silence.

*Hammer with President-elect Nixon in Palm Springs, California,
on December 7, 1968.*

As the months dragged on, large amounts of cash were required. Maurice Stans, the Nixon campaign's principal fund-raiser, found himself under increased pressure to provide, as he put it, "safe money" obtained "out of channels."[3] His problem was compounded by the Campaign Finance Act that had gone into effect on April 7, 1972, which made it a federal crime to contribute money anonymously to political campaigns. Stans thus had to search for contributors who had special qualifications. They had to have available to them safe money, preferably hundred-dollar bills that could not be traced to their source, and they had to be willing to evade the Campaign Finance Act and keep their contributions secret.

Hammer qualified on both counts. He had a large cache of safe money. By July 1972, he had diverted more than $2.8 million of Occidental's money to the Union Bank of Switzerland account administered by Kunz and Zade. He was a member of Stans's Hundred-Thousand-Dollar Club, and he happily made an anonymous contribution of $54,000 in laundered hundred-dollar bills, though he was not told what the money would be used for. He had Babcock deliver the cash to Stans in three installments. The first brown envelope was delivered on September 8, 1972; the last, on January 17, 1973. Since the election was over by the latter date, Hammer's money surely went into the fund controlled by the White House that was used to pay for the Watergate cover-up.

When the cover-up began collapsing in 1973, Nixon's reelection committee came under increasing pressure to reveal the names of all its contributors. Hammer was in trouble, but he believed he could slip out of it. Tim Babcock, once the governor of Montana and now an Occidental executive, was dependent on him for his livelihood. Babcock had little choice but to follow Hammer's instructions if he wanted to retain his position. Hammer therefore had Babcock report that he had made the late donations on behalf of himself and four businessmen in Montana. The problem was that if Babcock and his friends were asked where they had obtained the $54,000 in cash, they did not have a plausible source for it. So Hammer provided one. In June 1973, he contacted his consultant in London, who then specialized in, as the consultant himself later put it, "solving sensitive problems outside the corporate structure." Before he had become involved with Hammer in 1964, he had been a successful and well-respected businessman in his own right. But Hammer offered him an opportunity for something that conventional business lacked: international adventure. For him, at the age of fifty, it was a new life, one in which he traveled through underdeveloped African countries and barren sheikdoms in the Middle East to reconnoiter the routes to officials in a position to award oil concessions. In helping Hammer devise means of influencing these officials, he gradually became engaged in a dimension of finance that involved setting up numbered Swiss bank accounts owned by Liechtenstein foundations and shuttling money through them in a way that produced virtually untraceable cash. Hammer was a complete master of these machinations. "He was the most devious man I ever met or could imagine," the consultant later reflected. "I shouldn't have stayed with him, but I was fascinated." When he had helped Hammer generate cash in September 1972, he had no idea that it would be used as a postelection contribution to Nixon and go to help finance the Watergate cover-up. Now Hammer asked him to provide a cover story for where Babcock and his friends had gotten the cash to make their putative contribution. Hammer asked him to take responsibility for the $54,000. He was to say that he—not Hammer—had lent the cash to Babcock the previous September. Hammer also asked him to write out a backdated promissory note. Without realizing the purpose of this maneuver, he accommodated Hammer. Marvin Watson then flew with the note from London to Washington and had Babcock sign it.[4]

With the paperwork for this elaborate cover-up in place, Hammer denied all responsibility for the illegal contributions. When he was interviewed by two FBI agents on August 23, 1973, he told them that his only contribution to Nixon's campaign was the $46,000 he had delivered in March 1972. This sum, which had already been disclosed by Stans as Hammer's contribution to the Committee to Re-elect the President, was legal, since it had been delivered before anonymous contributions were prohibited by the new Campaign Finance Act.[5] Hammer did not tell the FBI about the additional $54,000 in cash he had donated, which was not legal. Two weeks later, the Senate select committee investigating the Watergate affair asked Hammer about his contribution. He again stated that his only contribution was the $46,000 he had given in March.

Although his hastily improvised cover-up might have withstood a superficial examination of campaign contributions, Hammer had not reckoned on the Watergate scandal—and one of the most intensive investigations in the history of the country. One by one, Hammer's dominoes toppled. The four businessmen in Montana admitted to the FBI that they were sham donors recruited by Babcock. Hammer's London consultant, after being given immunity from prosecution, admitted that he had never actually lent the money to Babcock and that he had backdated the promissory note. Watson, in a deal with the prosecutor, admitted he had taken the backdated promissory note to Babcock in June 1973 and had him sign it. Babcock, confronted with this evidence, broke down and admitted that he had lied in his FBI statements. He identified Hammer as the true source of the illegal $54,000 and the organizer of the cover-up.

The Watergate prosecutors now moved against Hammer. If Babcock's chronology was accurate, Hammer had arranged for six people, including himself, to lie to FBI agents, mislead a Senate investigation, and create false documentation. Such a concerted obstruction of justice was a serious matter.

Hammer had retained the legendary trial lawyer Edward Bennett Williams as his Washington attorney. Williams straightforwardly told Hammer how serious his legal situation had become. The prosecutors had two of Hammer's top executives, Watson and Babcock, pleading guilty to criminal misconduct. Both men would testify that Hammer had ordered them to arrange the cover-up. In addition, they had Hammer's own statements to the FBI and the Senate select committee that he had contributed only $46,000—not $100,000—which would indicate that Hammer himself had acted to further the cover-up. They also had the sham promissory note and the London consultant, who could testify that it had been fabricated at Hammer's instructions. They had a solid case for charging Hammer with multiple counts of obstruction of justice.

Williams explained that even if Hammer persuaded a jury that he had given the entire $100,000 to Babcock before the April 7 deadline and that Babcock for his own reasons had delayed giving $54,000 of the money to Stans until after the deadline, he still could be convicted on the more serious charges of obstruction of justice and be sentenced to years in prison. And if a jury believed that his employees acted on his behalf, he would almost certainly be convicted. Williams advised Hammer to make a deal with the prosecutors that would not require the case to go to trial. He suggested that Hammer offer to

plead guilty to the lesser charge of making an illegal campaign contribution.[6]

Hammer found the idea of admitting his guilt abhorrent. He had
spent five decades trying to wash away the stain of his father's conviction. Could he now accept such a stain on his own record? He believed, as he later noted, that "guilt lives on in the mind of the
criminal and in the society in which he moves, where he will always
be suspected and distrusted."[7] Yet he also realized that there was no
easy way out of this dilemma. If he pleaded guilty, he faced public
disgrace and the possible loss of control of Occidental. If he did not
plead guilty, the FBI investigation of the laundered funds contributed
to the campaign would only intensify. With hundreds of agents at its
disposal, the bureau was capable of cutting through the veils on his
offshore-banking activities with the power of a buzz saw, and it could
expose the UBS account and lead to Zade and Kunz. Hammer's diversion of millions of dollars from Occidental—an unauthorized
diversion that could result in embezzlement charges against him—
would likely be discovered then. He could not permit that to happen.
He had no choice but to authorize Williams to make a deal.

Williams, who was experienced in dealing with the Watergate prosecutors, carefully assessed the situation. He saw that the prosecutors
had little interest in going on with the Watergate investigation after
Nixon resigned. They appeared in their discussions with him to consider the Hammer case an annoying loose end that they still had to
resolve. Williams thus offered them a way of both ending and justi-
fying the investigation. Hammer would plead guilty to misdemeanor
charges of making an illegal campaign contribution, which would
mean that he would be put on probation and fined rather than sent
to prison. In return for this admission of guilt, the prosecutors would
not bring felony charges against Hammer for obstruction of justice.
Williams persuaded them that this solution would best serve the public interest, since there was little point in spending large sums of tax-
payers' dollars to put a seventy-six-year-old man in prison. And they
would get full credit for humbling a wealthy industrialist. While
agreeing to the deal in principle, it took the prosecutors until August
1975 to work out the exact charges. Finally, on September 1, 1975,
Hammer pleaded guilty in federal district court in Washington, D.C.,
to three counts of making illegal campaign contributions. (Each

count involved a separate cash contribution after the April 7 dead-line.) The presiding judge, William B. Jones, appointed a court pro-bation officer, James Walker, to assess Hammer's contrition for the crimes before he passed sentence.

Hammer found it almost unbearably painful to admit his guilt be-fore the world. About this period, he wrote in his autobiography, "Nothing in life meant more to me than my good name and reputa-tion. And now here I was about to be sentenced."[8] "I cannot describe the anguish I am suffering by being placed in this humiliating posi-tion," he wrote to his probation officer just before he was due to be sentenced. "It is as if a whole life of usefulness is being wiped out by the making of an anonymous political contribution of my own money, an act which was concededly perfectly legal prior to April 7, 1972." He then went on, in this extraordinary twenty-page letter, to deny the very thing he was supposed to admit: his guilt. "The fact is that I was the victim not the principal," he wrote. He asserted that he was pleading guilty not because he believed he was guilty of the crime he had been charged with but because he was too infirm to endure a trial. He claimed that the worst he might be guilty of was a lapse of memory, noting that "in the hectic life I lead, with problems of global scope often engaging me day and night, this matter could conceivably have been overlooked."[9]

Williams reviewed the letter, aghast. It undercut the deal he had negotiated with the prosecutors, and he strongly advised Hammer not to send it. But Hammer could not resist trying once again to do what he had done so successfully in the past: manipulate information to his advantage. He overrode his lawyer and sent the letter to the court.

As Williams feared, Judge Jones found the letter to be inconsistent with the agreed-upon guilty plea. He ruled that if Hammer believed he was not guilty, he could not plead guilty. Stunning Hammer, he ordered the guilty plea withdrawn. The prosecution then announced that since the terms of the plea bargain had been violated, it would convene a grand jury to indict Hammer on two additional felony charges of obstruction of justice. Williams abruptly withdrew from the case.

"Now I had the worst of all possible worlds," Hammer reflected later.[10] The nightmare, rather than ending, intensified. Although Occidental was paying Hammer's legal expenses, these were now approaching $1 million, and the expenditure would almost certainly invite shareholder lawsuits. In addition to the Watergate Special Prosecution Force, Hammer now had to contend with the Securities and Exchange Commission, which had begun its own investigation of allegations by former Occidental employees that Hammer had bribed foreign leaders. The SEC obtained an order for Hammer to appear in court with his records and testify about cash payments made to intermediaries in these alleged transactions. If he complied with the order, he would find himself in an investigatory cross fire that could expose his Swiss banks accounts.

Unable to cope with these pressures, Hammer fell back on the dying-man strategy. "The inescapable facts are that I am 77 years old and I suffer from coronary heart disease and associated vascular and heart problems," he wrote the court. He then had himself admitted to the Cedars of Lebanon Hospital in Los Angeles. In January 1976, no fewer than six medical specialists employed by Occidental furnished opinions that Hammer was medically unable to appear before the SEC or stand trial in Washington. His Los Angeles attorney, Arthur Groman, stated that Hammer's doctors had concluded that Hammer was unlikely to recover from his heart condition. In view of this "terminal" condition, the prosecutors agreed to transfer the case to federal court in Los Angeles, where the presiding judge, Lawrence Lydick, allowed Hammer to again plead guilty to the three misdemeanors.

Hammer attempted one last time to avoid a public admission of guilt by requesting that Judge Lydick sentence him in Cedars of Lebanon, suggesting that he might die of a heart attack if he left the hospital. Judge Lydick turned down this request but allowed Hammer to be attended by a medical team in the courtroom.[11]

The long-delayed day of reckoning came on March 23, 1976. Hammer arrived in federal court in a wheelchair. His face, usually tan, was ashen; his eyes were downcast; his body quivered. Two doctors attached dozens of wires to him so that they could monitor his heart in an adjoining room. Attendants stood by with an oxygen tent and other emergency paraphernalia.

This courtroom spectacle was staged for an event that took only a few minutes. Judge Lydick recited the three misdemeanor charges.

After each one, Hammer replied in a weak but alert voice, "Guilty." Judge Lydick then charged Hammer a $3,000 fine and sentenced him to one year's probation.

On leaving the courtroom, Hammer had, as his lawyer delicately put it, "a miraculous recovery." He checked out of the hospital, discarding, like the props they were, his wheelchair, electrocardiograph, and emergency oxygen tent. The next day, he was back in his office at Occidental. He also now arranged to end the SEC investigation— by signing a consent decree in which Occidental agreed to disclose past questionable payments. (Occidental subsequently appointed a special committee to investigate these payments, and it issued a report of its findings in 1976.)

"Hurrah. . . . The ordeal is over," Frances Hammer wrote the next week.[12] She had been a dutiful wife for the past twenty years, making her Los Angeles home and her financial resources available to her husband. She had accompanied him on a half dozen trips to Russia although she found them physically tiring. She had stayed at his side throughout his three-year legal nightmare. That January, she had delayed the celebration of their wedding anniversary while he retreated to the hospital. Now, with Hammer back home, she invited the other members of his family to a small gathering. The guests were his son, Julian, who had recently divorced his wife, and Victor Hammer and his wife, Ireene. Harry was now dead, Armasha lived in Moscow, and Frances did not know of the existence of Victoria, Armand's twenty-year-old daughter.

Hammer looked exceedingly fit. He had lost forty pounds on a high-protein diet and regained his suntan. He eloquently toasted Frances for the support she had given him during his years of legal difficulties, saying that he felt as if he had come back from the dead. He smiled broadly.[13]

IN JUNE 1976, HAMMER RETURNED TO MOSCOW. HIS REPUTATION had not been tarnished there. On the contrary, it was, if anything, enhanced by his perceived ability to prevail over the U.S. government. In the Soviet Union, he was still Lenin's great capitalist. His fertilizer project was described by the Soviet press as the "deal of the century" and valued at $20 billion, which represented roughly 90 percent of all foreign investment in the Soviet Union at the time. With the money he had procured from the Export-Import Bank and a syndicate of U.S. commercial banks, a giant complex of high-tech ammonia plants was being erected along the Volga. With subsidies he had got from the U.S. Maritime Administration, a fleet of tankers was being built in American shipyards to carry phosphoric concentrate to Russia. The first ship was to be named the *Julius Hammer*. With other credits Hammer had obtained from American banks, the ground had been broken for the skyscrapers in his International Trade Center project. The first building would be called Hammer House. With oil prices quadrupling on the world market—an explosion due in part to Hammer's deal with Gadhafi—Occidental was now a highly profitable corporation that could easily afford to finance the uncompleted elements of these projects.

Later that summer, Hammer arranged for the Soviet government to grant him yet another privilege: his own apartment near the Kremlin. It was not as spacious as Brown House, his former residence in Moscow—now the Australian Embassy—but it was a luxurious five-room suite equipped with Western amenities and its own staff of servants. "No other capitalist had ever been accorded such privileged status," Mikhail Bruk, Hammer's Moscow facilitator, recalled. His housewarming party that October was attended by elite members of the Soviet hierarchy, including Brezhnev's national security adviser, Andrey Aleksandrov-Argentov. Urbane and cultured, Aleksandrov-Argentov had the primary responsibility for coordinating information concerning Soviet foreign policy. After meeting Hammer, he told him that Brezhnev had granted him an audience, and he took Hammer to the Kremlin, where they met with Brezhnev for ninety minutes.[14] In that meeting, Brezhnev made a point of discussing U.S. foreign-policy issues, such as the Strategic Arms Limitation Treaty, so that Hammer could carry a message back to Washington.

During the next year, Hammer commuted regularly among America, Russia, and other Communist countries. He negotiated major projects for the development of petrochemical and energy industries in Poland, Romania, Czechoslovakia, and China. To further advance détente, as well as to restore his own tarnished image at home, he launched the Armand Hammer Conference on Peace and Human

Rights in Oslo, Norway. Funded by Occidental Petroleum, it became an annual event. Like Cyrus Eaton's Pugwash Conferences, Hammer's gatherings brought together leading Soviet and Western intellectuals for a week's discussion of ways to further peaceful coexistence.

By 1978, Hammer had become the recognized channel through which U.S. corporations sought business opportunities in the Soviet bloc. Hundreds of companies—ranging from the *Reader's Digest,* which wanted to publish a Russian-language edition in Moscow, to DeLorean Automobiles, which wanted to manufacture components of its aluminum sports cars in Soviet factories—worked through Hammer. What Lenin had described as a small path to American business had now expanded to a superhighway. In recognition of his achievements, Brezhnev honored Hammer on his eightieth birthday by giving him the Lenin Order of Friendship, an award that no other foreign businessman had ever received—or would ever receive. Whatever his crimes in the United States, Hammer was a hero in the Soviet Union.

Hammer with his mistress, Martha Kaufman (later Hilary Gibson).
His wife, Frances, stands behind them. The painting is Rembrandt's Juno,
which the Armand Hammer Foundation acquired in 1976.

CHAPTER TWENTY-TWO

OLD MASTERS AND YOUNG MISTRESSES

HAMMER DESCRIBED THE ART WORLD AS A "JUNGLE" DEFINED BY "vicious jealousies and ruthless combat between dealers and collectors" where he had to fight "tooth and nail for pictures." In this respect, he found it similar to his experiences "walking in the jungles of business."[1] He first saw this side of the art world in Moscow in 1927, when he was struggling to keep his family's business afloat in a sea of debt. Stalin's right-hand man, Anastas Mikoyan, offered him the opportunity to earn the foreign currency he desperately needed through the sale abroad of selected pieces of art from the Goskhran, the government committee responsible for the national treasure. Since the export of the national treasure was a capital offense, such an enterprise could not be undertaken without the sanction and full support of the Soviet state.[2] The role that Mikoyan had proposed for Hammer was that of an intermediary: the Soviet authorities would remove art from the Hermitage and other Soviet museums and provide it, along with documents attesting to a plausible provenance, to Hammer, who would then offer it to collectors in Germany, France, and the United States. Mikoyan told Hammer, "You can have the old masters now. . . . But we are making a revolution in our country and we will get them back."[3] For his assistance in acting as a go-between, he would earn a 10 percent commission on each sale.[4]

In March 1927, Hammer was given his first "masterpiece" to dispose of. It was an oil painting, twenty-four inches by thirty inches, depicting the circumcision of a child surrounded by angels. According to the Soviets, it was a work by Rembrandt entitled *The Circumcision of Christ,* an extraordinary subject, since it called attention to Christ's Jewish heritage. The picture was purportedly a "lost" Rembrandt that had been sold to a Russian collector in the nineteenth century. It then supposedly remained in his family's collection until the Russian Revolution. Hammer was to claim that he had acquired it from an art restorer who had bought it from the family.

Hammer contacted an art collector in Berlin who had already expressed an interest in the lost Rembrandt and offered to sell him the picture for $500,000 (the equivalent of roughly $4 million today). The collector insisted that the painting be authenticated before the negotiations proceeded, and on April 8 Hammer sent his brother Victor to Berlin with the painting. *The Circumcision of Christ* was then taken to Max Friedländer, the director of the Berlin Museum and one of the leading experts on Rembrandt.

In Friedländer's initial examination, the age of the paint appeared to match that of other Rembrandts of the period, and the brushwork appeared to be the work of the master. But further testing and a chemical analysis revealed that the paint had been manufactured in the twentieth century. Friedländer then reported to Victor that the painting was a clever (and recent) forgery.[5]

Hammer found himself caught in the midst of a major art fraud. Whether or not they realized it, the Soviets had provided him with a forgery. He could not admit that he had fronted for the Soviets in the deal: that not only would jeopardize his other business dealings in Russia but also might expose his laundering activities in the West. Since he had offered the Rembrandt for sale as a painting he owned, he appeared to be the perpetrator of the fraud. Although no action was taken against him in Germany, the story of the fake Rembrandt quickly circulated and effectively discredited Hammer as a dealer in old masters. He was now of little further use to Mikoyan as an intermediary in the trafficking of museum-quality art.[6]

Despite his public humiliation, Hammer had learned an important lesson. A collector had been willing to pay a fortune for the painting when he believed it was an authentic Rembrandt but would pay nothing for it when he realized that it did not come from the brush of the master. Thus, when Hammer marketed the so-called Romanoff treasure, he went to great lengths to embellish its history. The treasure was of recent manufacture and imaginatively labeled as having belonged to the czars. Still later, Hammer specialized in selling art from the collections of celebrities. He proposed in 1941, for example, to sell to the general public rather than to private art collectors the art collected by William Randolph Hearst. He suggested that if the art were sold at R. H. Macy's in New York, it would be "the greatest department store promotion that's ever been pulled off."[7]

Hammer's cynical manipulation of the authenticity of works of art reached its height with objects attributed to the Fabergé workshops. When he returned to New York in 1931, the Soviets provided him with a set of Fabergé signature stamps so that he could "sign" reproductions. As late as 1954, when Hammer brought Bettye Murphy to the Hammer Galleries workshop on West Fifty-seventh Street in New York, he was still using these stamps to simulate the Fabergé imprint. His face beaming with pride, he demonstrated to Bettye how the nineteenth-century tools provided the appearance of an authentic Fabergé signature. He told her how collectors who fancied themselves experts on Fabergé were duped by the forgeries. He would let them discover the "signature" on their own and then, if they told him about it, act surprised. Hammer thus enjoyed not merely the monetary profit from the sale but a sense of superiority in outwitting the art buyer. To him, collecting was a confidence game in which he supplied the necessary authentication, which took the form of a label, genuine or fake.[8]

Hammer treated forgeries as a sort of private joke. In his home in Los Angeles, he hung imitations of the paintings he had acquired. Some of these were painted by Frances, who had always been interested in art and who had allowed Hammer great leeway in investing part of her wealth in paintings. In building the Armand Hammer Collection during the 1960s, Hammer focused on acquiring works of the old masters. This strategy led him to buy things of dubious quality, especially since a low price often took precedence over any other consideration. Nevertheless, Hammer considered himself a shrewd buyer.[9]

He collected his bargains relentlessly, and by 1970, he had acquired over eighty paintings. He attempted to arrange an exhibition of his collection at two museums in Washington, D.C.—the National Gallery of Art and the National Collection of Fine Arts—but both declined. Finally, in March 1970, he persuaded the Smithsonian Institution to exhibit the collection in its National Museum of Natural History. He spared no expense in making the opening-night gala an event. He invited congressmen, senators, Supreme Court justices, and White House officials as well as most of the diplomatic corps. While the party was a success, the collection itself was ridiculed by critics.[10] For example, Paul Richard, the arts reviewer for *The Washington Post,* described the paintings as both trivial and ugly and, adding injury to insult, suggested that some might be forgeries. He scathingly wrote, "Never have so many major masters been represented in this city by canvasses so poor," and took them as evidence that even the greatest artists had "bad days."[11]

After having invested millions of dollars of his own and his wife's money in the collection, Hammer found himself exposed to derision from the very art establishment he had hoped to enter. But rather than admitting defeat, he decided to improve the collection's credentials. "I needed a jolt like that," he later reflected. "It was hard for me to believe that great artists had bad days."[12] He went straight to the group that had scorned him, asking John Walker, director emeritus of the National Gallery of Art, to take a look at his collection.

Walker was appalled. Much of the collection was mediocre, and some of the work was probably not authentic. He advised Hammer that at least half of the paintings should be discarded.[13]

To Walker's surprise, Hammer not only took his advice but retained him as a consultant. Walker was impressed by Hammer and by the way he learned from his mistakes. "With his brilliant mind, [Hammer] quickly grasped why he had erred," Walker recalled later. "He had been a colossal bargain hunter."[14]

With Walker's assistance, Hammer now set out to build a more serious collection. He instructed Walker that the new collection should include only art up to the standards of "the finest museums in the world."[15] These new acquisitions required sums of money that went beyond Hammer's—and his wife's—resources. To pay for them, Hammer used the Armand Hammer Foundation, which he had set up as a tax shelter in 1968. He had Occidental make substantial donations to the foundation, and later he also channeled substantial funds into it from the secret Union Bank of Switzerland slush fund.[16] He justified using corporate funds to finance his personal art collection by telling Occidental's board of directors that his name was so closely associated with Occidental's that whatever enhanced his own prestige enhanced the corporation's. The board, which Hammer controlled, had little choice but to acquiesce.[17] Hammer saw art as a powerful form of public relations, a means of creating a brand name for himself. To this end, he arranged to send the Armand Hammer Collection to the Soviet Union in early 1971, through the good offices of Mme. Furtseva. It would be exhibited at six Soviet museums, including the Hermitage in Leningrad and the Pushkin Museum of Fine Art in Moscow. It would also be sent that year to London and Dublin. The cost of these and other international exhibitions of the collection, as well as the cost of the lavish receptions that attended them, were fully paid by Occidental as a corporate public relations expense.

Although these world tours of the Hammer Collection may have added to the prestige of Occidental, they also benefited the Hammer Galleries, which dealt in the art that the Armand Hammer Foundation bought partly with Occidental's money. The same year he initiated his prestigious art exchanges with the Soviet Union, Hammer extended his art-dealing operations by buying for $2.5 million a 75 percent interest in M. Knoedler and Company, America's oldest art gallery. He also had himself elected a trustee of the Los Angeles County Museum of Art by promising to bequeath his collection to it. He now wore four hats simultaneously: the director of the museum that would display the collection, the head of the foundation that paid for the collection, the chief executive of the oil company that funded the foundation, and the dealer who, through Knoedler and Company and Hammer Galleries, bought paintings for the collection. By this time, his collection was ranked by Walker with the most important in the country. Through it, Hammer had achieved a large measure of the recognition he wanted in the art world.

Hammer, with the help of Maury Leibovitz, his financial adviser (whom he made a 25 percent partner in the art business), attempted to build Knoedler Galleries into a major force in the art world. During the next few years, Hammer hired a number of top people to run it, including John Richardson, who had previously headed Christie's

Fine Art Department. Richardson remembers Hammer as a wizened man who, with his leathery skin and hooded eyes, reminded him of an old tortoise. He was impressed by Hammer's energy but realized that he had no eye for art and no scruples. This became evident when Hammer took him to his home and showed him a painting that he claimed was Modigliani's *Woman of the People.* Richardson recognized the work as a howling fake but, guessing that he was being set up, tactfully said, "Interesting." Hammer chose to take Richardson's laconic comment as a sign that he believed the painting was genuine and exclaimed with great glee, "That painting fools all you experts. It's a copy by Frances." (Richardson also noticed that Hammer's putative Rembrandt engraving of the goddess Juno had Frances's face in place of Juno's.)[18]

Richardson found that Hammer crossed the same line between art and illusion in his business relations. "It did not take me long to discover that Hammer knew and cared as much about art as Al Capone," he later wrote, explaining:

> So long as one was not too closely involved, working for Hammer—above all, watching him fabricate something out of nothing—was entertaining. The boasts, the lies, the corners he cut! It was an education in chutzpah, in abracadabra—like being backstage at a conjuring show and seeing how the tricks were done.[19]

Richardson was appalled at the way Hammer used the prestigious firm of Knoedler to further his tax-avoidance maneuvers. He used paintings once attributed to great artists but now recognized as copies as devices by means of which would-be tax dodgers—the prospective buyers—could attempt to get deductions. The tax-avoidance scheme worked fairly well, Richardson recalled, until the IRS began retaining outside experts to assess the value of suspicious art donations. Hammer himself was sued by the IRS for taking excessive deductions and was forced to pay $237,000 in back taxes and penalties.[20]

Richardson also witnessed Hammer's skills—and connections—in exchanging art with the Soviet government. In 1972, Hammer bought for the Knoedler Galleries a minor painting by Goya for $60,000, the relatively low price reflecting its inferior quality. He recognized that its illustrious signature might be used to advantage in the name game even if it lacked artistic value. Such an opportunity arose later that year, when Mme. Furtseva informed him that the Soviet Union would greatly appreciate a gift of a Goya. Hammer arranged this through a complex set of transactions that served to conceal the profits he derived. First, he had his gallery transfer ownership of the Goya to a shell corporation based in Zurich. It was nominally owned by a Liechtenstein foundation but controlled by Hammer himself through his London consultant. Thus, it would not look as though he were selling his own painting. He then had the Armand Hammer Foundation buy the painting from the Zurich corporation for $160,000, generating a windfall profit of $100,000 in cash. Next, he had his foundation donate the painting to the Soviet Union while announcing in a press release, with his characteristic hyperbole, that this represented a "million-dollar gift from my private collection." He and his London consultant then flew to Leningrad with an attaché case containing $100,000 in cash to attend the opening of the exhibition at the Hermitage featuring the Goya. Two days later, they flew on to London without the attaché case. In return for Hammer's largesse, Furtseva arranged for him to be given a major painting. Hammer subsequently received a painting by the modern master Kazimir Malevich, which he then turned around and sold to a German buyer for $750,000 that went into his personal account. So while his foundation lost money (and his gallery lost a bargain-priced Goya), he made a tidy profit.[21]

By the mid-1970s, Richardson was no longer "entertained" by Hammer's magic. When he objected to the liberties that Hammer took in "upgrading" Knoedler's inventory by "trading it like baseball cards," he found that he had fallen from favor. Soon afterward, he resigned.[22] By this time, Hammer had found a more compatible art adviser: Martha Wade Kaufman.

Kaufman, an attractive freelance writer with flaming red hair, had first met Hammer in August 1974. She had been commissioned by a publisher of magazines for airlines to write an article on Hammer's art, and Occidental's public relations department had arranged for her to meet Hammer at nine in the morning in his sixteenth-floor office of their Wilshire Boulevard headquarters. When she arrived that morning, he was not there. She elected to wait, sitting in a cubicle outside his door most of the day. When he finally arrived, at five in the afternoon, he profusely apologized for the eight-hour delay and ordered his secretary to bring them both iced tea.

He was heavier than she expected (he then weighed 206 pounds) but walked with a robust spring to his step. She noticed that he was dressed in an immaculately tailored gray suit, a white shirt, and an elegant tie. He also had a deep tan. He looked remarkably vigorous for a man she knew was in his mid-seventies. He was also taken with her. He later would tell her, "You didn't stand a chance."

She began the interview by asking him his motive for collecting art: was it another business or a profound passion? Instead of answering her questions, he abruptly changed the subject to a painting in his collection by Rubens. "It could be you," he said, looking at her with a fixed gaze. He then explained that Rubens's mistress was the model for the painting, and he told her that her colors perfectly matched the flesh tones in the painting. He looked at his watch and told her he had an appointment with his barber and asked her if she minded continuing the interview while he was getting his hair cut. But at the barbershop, instead of the discussion about art she expected, he interviewed her about her marital status. She was flattered by the attention and told him that she was married to a USC professor and had two daughters but did not get along with her husband. She explained that she wanted to learn more about art, and that was why she had chosen to write the profile of him.

When his haircut was complete—after only a few minutes—he pulled her by the hand toward his waiting limousine. He told her he was on his way to the airport, and would fly to Moscow that evening. He told her that it would be his eleventh flight to Moscow that year. He asked her to write her home telephone number on his yellow pad. A moment later, he was gone, and she realized she had not got the answers she needed to write the article. Except for redheads and nudes, he had not even discussed art.[23]

Hammer called her a few weeks later. In a very businesslike way, he told her he was back in Los Angeles, had thought about her questions, and now wanted to complete the interview. He suggested that she meet him that afternoon at a private suite at the Beverly Hilton, which he said he used when he did not want to be disturbed by routine office business.

He opened the door for her when she arrived and seated her on a sofa across a table from him. When she took out her pad to take notes, he told her that what he was saying was not for publication, but he wanted her to hear him out. She was slightly mystified by the request but put down her pad.

Hammer told Kaufman that art for him was neither a business nor a passion; it was a means to achieve an end: immortalizing his name. He wanted to leave behind such an unrivaled collection that future generations would associate the Hammer name with greatness. To do this, he intended to spare no expense in buying masterpieces. He would exhibit the collection in the great museums of the world during his lifetime, and after his death it would be housed in a separate building in the Los Angeles County Museum of Art, where it would stand forever as a monument to him. He told her he had already made the preliminary arrangements with the museum, but he still had to improve the collection and create a global reputation for it. He then told her the real purpose behind this meeting: he wanted her to leave journalism and work closely with him in realizing this prodigious ambition. She would act as his personal art consultant, curator, and liaison with museums around the world. She would have her own office at Occidental and would travel with him on his private jet. He then leaned close to her, suggesting this would be more than a professional relationship, and told her he was offering her a new life. If she accepted, she would, as he put it, "never have to worry about money again."

She was overwhelmed by this sweeping proposal and the confident manner in which he had delivered it. "Why me?" she asked.

He replied that he had felt himself "drawn to her" from the moment they met. He said he could sense that she wanted to learn from him. "I want to take care of you," he said, embracing her.[24] He then led her to the adjoining bedroom and began a relationship with her that would continue for more than ten years.

After Hammer left the suite, Kaufman saw that he had left five one-hundred-dollar bills on the table for her. She was insulted, and she left them behind. But his message was clear—if crude.

On September 22, 1974, Kaufman was put on the payroll of Occidental. She nominally worked for Occidental's public relations department, but in reality she could come and go as she liked. She met Hammer in Venezuela, Peru, Mexico, Japan, Great Britain, and other countries where he mixed business and art over the next decade. When Hammer traveled with Frances on the corporate jet,

Kaufman would take a commercial flight to the same destination. Officially, her role in these countries was to arrange exhibitions of the Armand Hammer Collection—which now included more than 160 paintings—at local museums. She would also organize a gala reception, to which officials, socialites, and journalists would be invited. Hammer justified the expenditure on the grounds that his art served as a "goodwill ambassador" for Occidental. In some countries, such as Venezuela, the art-related events also diverted public attention from the secret machinations and intermediaries through which Hammer was actually winning oil concessions.[25]

Hammer made the terms of their deal clear to Kaufman. As she later described the relationship, she would serve as his "confidante, friend, business associate, cohabitant, consultant, nurse, mistress, and lover." She would "submit" to his sexual demands. In return, he would provide her with employment, support, and a lifetime income from a secret bank account in Switzerland. The account was, as she understood it, where he put the income from secret deals he made, and it would grow to $10 million.[26]

Kaufman saw another side to Hammer's art collecting when he became fascinated by the work of the nineteenth-century caricaturist Honoré Daumier. In this case, Hammer actually became interested in the artist's work. Daumier had a cynical view of the political order: those who have power suppress those who lack it to increase their personal wealth. With his sharp pen, he mercilessly savaged the French establishment, depicting its leading figures—magistrates, bureaucrats, cardinals, bankers, and businessmen—as brutish, greedy, arrogant, and grasping men with bloated stomachs and evil faces. Hammer, who himself had fought the oil establishment, appreciated, as he put it, Daumier's "courage to stand up to authority."[27] He also saw parallels between the crusading spirit of Daumier and his father, Julius. As he observed to Kaufman, both men used their wit and intellect to oppose the ruling class. Like Julius, Daumier had spent time in prison. He had been found guilty in 1832 of maligning the French government and offending King Louis-Philippe with a caricature. The more Hammer learned about Daumier, the more he wanted to collect his work—and flaunt it in the face of the establishment.[28]

Hammer's opportunity came in 1975, when he heard about the availability of the George Longstreet Collection, which contained more than six thousand Daumier lithographs. Longstreet had collected these over a half century, and he now wanted to see them housed in a suitable institution. He had tentatively agreed to sell his collection to the Los Angeles County Museum for the relatively low price of $250,000, which is how Hammer, a trustee of the museum, learned it was for sale. Hammer had a simple philosophy in situations such as this: "When you see an opportunity, grab it by the forelock."[29] He decided to attempt to buy the Daumiers himself even though this meant bidding against a museum of which he was a trustee.

California law requires a trustee to put the interest of the institution he or she represents above personal interest, and since Hammer was doing the opposite, the museum's board could have legally forced him to withdraw from the bidding. Hammer offered the museum an attractive deal: if it would allow him to buy the Daumier collection for $250,000, he would deliver it to the museum as a donation within six months of the purchase date. This arrangement would allow him to take a large tax deduction, and the museum would get the collection at no cost. Hammer insisted that the deal not be put in writing so as to maximize his tax advantage (which would otherwise be limited to the actual purchase price of $250,000 rather than the assessed fair-market price of the collection, which could be many times that amount). The board of trustees agreed to what seemed a mutually beneficial arrangement. Hammer bought the Daumiers.

Six months passed, and Hammer did not donate them to the museum. Despite letter after letter from the museum's director, Hammer found that he was unable to suppress his desire to own the collection. He told Kaufman he could not "bear to part with the Daumiers." He wanted them displayed around the world under his control—and under his name. He wrote to the museum, denying that he had made an agreement with it. He possessed the Daumiers, and he correctly assessed that without a contract the museum would not take him to court. He now promised to bequeath the Daumiers to the museum on his death, but since wills can be changed at any time, the pledge had no legal force. (And as it turned out, he changed his will so the museum never got the works.)[30]

In June 1976, Hammer got an opportunity to buy a world-class Rembrandt: a portrait of the Roman goddess Juno (a copy of which, with Frances's face instead of Juno's, John Richardson would later notice in Hammer's home). The portrait had hung for years in the Metropolitan Museum in New York. It belonged to William Middendorf, a prominent investment banker and former secretary of the navy, who had retained the Knoedler Galleries to sell it to the highest bidder. Although the company had failed to find a suitable buyer, it retained the right of first refusal, which meant Hammer could match any offer that Middendorf accepted and get the Rembrandt. When Middendorf himself found a buyer, the J. Paul Getty Museum, and agreed to sell it to that institution for $3 million, Hammer immediately stepped in with his right of first refusal. As he wrote, "I managed to put one over on Paul Getty." Exercising the option given to Knoedler, he demanded that Middendorf sell him the Rembrandt for the same price the Getty Museum had offered. Not wanting to involve himself in litigation with Hammer, Middendorf acquiesced, and Hammer sent an Occidental executive over to his house to retrieve the Rembrandt in his pickup truck.[31]

There was now one name Hammer needed in order to complete his collection: Leonardo da Vinci. Hammer learned in 1980 that a 470-year-old Leonardo notebook was coming up for sale at Christie's in London. The book, called the Leicester Codex because it had been owned by the earls of Leicester since the eighteenth century, consisted of eighteen sheets with four panels on each sheet. Scribbled on them in Leonardo's handwriting are his notes—on subjects that include astronomy, hydraulic engineering, and the color of the sky—and some 360 sketches. The notebook had great "historic value," as Hammer put it, and it was the only Leonardo manuscript in private hands. When it came up for auction in December 1980, Hammer got it for $5,280,000 (plus a 10 percent commission to Christie's), a record for a manuscript.[32]

On December 3, 1980, Hammer called a special meeting of the four directors on Occidental's Executive Committee and asked that the company make a secret "appropriation" to the Armand Hammer Foundation of up to $6 million to cover the cost of acquiring the Leonardo. Zoltan Merszei, who was on the committee, found the request for a "charitable donation" to be unusual, but as he later explained, the members of the committee had no choice but to approve it if they wanted to remain in Hammer's good graces.[33] The minutes of the Executive Committee note that "such a contribution is deemed a worthwhile and appropriate expenditure of corporate funds."[34]

Hammer renamed Leonardo's manuscript the Codex Hammer and arranged to have the small Italian town of Vinci, where Leonardo was born, confer honorary citizenship on him. He became, ceremonially, Armand Hammer da Vinci. He also had the Armand Hammer Foundation contribute funds to UCLA to establish the Armand Hammer Center for Leonardo Studies and Research.[35]

After Hammer took physical possession of the codex, he had it dismantled and cut into seventy-two separate pages. He then had each page mounted in a separate freestanding display case so it could be prominently exhibited. When criticized by scholars for cutting up the manuscript, he replied that Leonardo had originally intended it as a " 'loose sheet' configuration" and that by separating it, he was able to "make a presentation which is almost overwhelming in its power and detail."[36]

Hammer announced that he had retained a squad of elite commandos trained in Asian martial arts and armed with Uzi machine guns to guard the codex day and night. Though there were then no actual commandos guarding it—and it had once been left unattended in two crates on his plane at an airport—the purported security arrangements caught the interest of the media.[37] With great fanfare, the Codex Hammer traveled to fifteen museums in nine countries and attracted more than a million viewers.

With the Leonardo in his possession, Hammer could claim to be a twentieth-century Medici. The roster of great artists in his collection spanned the history of Western art since the Renaissance. By 1983, an impressive list of halls and galleries had been named after him in such great museums as the Metropolitan Museum in New York, the Corcoran Gallery in Washington, and the Musée Jacquemart-André in Paris. He had been decorated by President Reagan with the National Arts Medal and given the Legion of Honor by the French minister of culture, Jack Lang. Yet he wanted art to serve, as he put it, as his "ticket to immortality," and for this purpose he needed more than the usual plaques and medals. He needed his own museum.[38]

Hammer had envisioned the Los Angeles County Museum giving him a separate building, one in which no other patron's name would be mentioned and for which he or his foundation would appoint the curator and control the exhibits. But when that idea fell through in 1987, he decided to build, with Occidental's funds, the Armand Hammer Museum of Art and Cultural Center. There would thus be a permanent job for his longtime mistress Martha Kaufman (who had changed her name by then to Hilary Gibson to deflect the scrutiny of Frances). He would attach it to Occidental's headquarters, and his name would be carved in letters three feet high on two sides of the building, like some ancient stela. He would spare no expense constructing it. To strengthen the association between himself and Leonardo, he would import the white marble for its outer walls from the same quarry in Italy that had supplied Leonardo with his marble five centuries earlier. He would also transfer $36 million from Occidental's treasury to the museum as an endowment to pay its operating expenses. There would be a seven-foot-high portrait of him in the entrance, and inside there would be the Codex Hammer and the Armand Hammer Collection, including the Daumier collection. It would be art displayed, as *Newsweek* later described it, "more like a mausoleum than a museum."[39] For Armand Hammer, there was little difference.

CHAPTER TWENTY-THREE

THE
GO-BETWEEN

JUST BEFORE NOON ON JANUARY 20, 1981, RONALD REAGAN, THE
president-elect, and Jimmy Carter, the outgoing president, took their
respective places at the podium on Capitol Hill, and Reagan was
sworn in as the fortieth president of the United States. Hammer, who
had attended every president's inauguration since FDR's in 1933,
watched the performance with great interest a few feet away from the
principals. He was the guest of Albert Gore, Jr., the freshman senator from Tennessee (and future vice president). At five previous in-
augurations, he had been the guest of Gore's father, Albert Gore, Sr.,
who now headed Occidental's coal division and earned more than
$500,000 a year. Hammer, despite his advancing age, still moved
about with great energy, flailing his hand to greet other VIPs. His po-
sitioning was excellent. He was seated in the section of the stands reserved for the one hundred senators of the United States. That
evening at the inaugural ball, he placed himself strategically at the
side door through which the new president was scheduled to make his
entrance and waited patiently to greet him. But when Reagan arrived, he brushed past Hammer, giving him the cold shoulder.
Though it was a minor insult, Hammer was too much of a realist not
to see that the political winds were changing—and in a threatening
direction.[1]

The Hammers and the Reagans.

Hammer had cause for concern. During the 1980 presidential campaign, Reagan had made his position on the Soviet Union crystal clear. He viewed the Soviet regime, to which Hammer had hitched his star, as an "evil empire." He denounced the Soviet leaders who had decorated Hammer as "liars and cheats." He opposed the policy of détente—to which Hammer was dedicated—as a license for the Soviets "to pursue whatever policy of subversion, aggression and expansionism they wanted anywhere in the world." He advocated ratcheting up the pressure on the Soviet economy instead of relieving it.[2]

If Reagan turned his campaign rhetoric into U.S. foreign policy, Hammer could suffer enormous losses. He had invested a large part of Occidental's money in Soviet projects. On one single project, the export of superphosphoric acid, Occidental had spent nearly $750 million. The company had constructed a gigantic plant in Jacksonville, Florida, to convert phosphorous ore mined nearby into highly concentrated superphosphoric acid (SPA). The Jacksonville facility, which had the capacity to produce one million tons of fertilizer base a year, was built for a single customer, the Soviet Union, which was the only country that used SPA as a fertilizer base. Occidental had also had to build tankers, storage tanks, and other facilities for delivering the fertilizer base to the agricultural areas of the Soviet Union, and these construction projects had delayed deliveries until 1978. Then, in December 1979, the Soviet Union had invaded Afghanistan, and Afghan rebels launched a guerrilla war against the Soviet occupation. The United States began supplying these guerrillas with guns and other armaments. President Carter placed an embargo on exports to Russia. The SPA shipments were suspended indefinitely. Occidental's other projects in the Soviet Union were also frozen.

At first, Hammer used accounting tricks, as one executive described them, to conceal the amount of money Occidental was losing in the Soviet Union because of this interruption. But unless the embargo was lifted soon, Occidental's auditors would have no choice but to recognize the huge loss, one that could easily exceed $1 billion.[3] Hammer had written Brezhnev on January 23, 1980, offering his services as a go-between in the conflict with the United States over Afghanistan. He said, "I believe, I can make a positive contribution to the easing of the tension which has arisen in relations between our two countries."[4]

Less than a month later, he was in Moscow. He went directly to the Soviet Ministry of Trade to explain the potentially disastrous consequences of the embargo. After he described the losses that Occidental was already suffering, a Soviet deputy minister asked, "Is there anything we can do to help?" Hammer shot back, "You can sue Jimmy Carter, but that won't do any good."[5] He knew that a political solution was necessary.

Hammer proceeded to the Kremlin, where he had an appointment with Brezhnev. In their hour-long meeting, Brezhnev gave Hammer the Soviet line on the invasion of Afghanistan. He claimed that the Soviet Union had intervened in Afghanistan for purely defensive reasons after it had received intelligence that the CIA, with the assistance of Pakistan's intelligence service, was plotting a coup d'état in Kabul.

Brezhnev now wanted Hammer to undertake a mission that would relieve the growing strain of the Afghan war on Soviet resources. He suggested that Hammer broker a deal with Washington that would leave the Soviet-backed Communist regime in power for at least five years. The United States would cut off military support for the Afghan guerrillas. In return, the Soviet Union would withdraw its troops from Afghanistan over a period of five years, and then free elections would be held.[6]

"For most of the rest of 1980," Hammer noted in his autobiography, "I shuttled around the world trying to pull together a political settlement of the crisis."[7] According to his flight log, he traveled 307,596 miles that year in his newly acquired Boeing 727 jetliner, the *Oxy One,* which had been outfitted with additional fuel tanks to give it an intercontinental range. High-tech telephone equipment allowed him to call almost anyplace in the world from the plane.[8]

As the head of a multibillion-dollar corporation, Hammer had connections with businessmen, lawyers, financiers, and politicians who could open doors for him in most of the countries pertinent to the settlement. He was able to arrange meetings with the top officials of a half dozen European countries in a matter of weeks. His initial objective in this self-styled shuttle diplomacy was to find an internationally respected statesman who would champion his peace plan. He made this strategy clear in tape recordings he dictated during his mission, on which he referred to himself in the third person, as "A. H.," and described the officials with whom he had met, their political position on Afghanistan, and their reaction to his proposal.

By early April 1980, Hammer had settled on a possible candidate to advance his plan: Valéry Giscard d'Estaing, the president of France. Edgar Faure, a former president of the French senate who was a close associate of Giscard's, was hired as an "attorney" for Occidental in France. Hammer reported in his taped diary that "this [relationship] will enable A. H. to keep a close connection with the president."[9] And it did. Faure arranged for Hammer and his wife to lunch with Giscard at the presidential palace on April 2. Hammer notes on the tape that Giscard was an impressive figure with "aristocratic bearing," "very fine features," and "very stylishly cut clothes." He had learned that Giscard wanted to be invited by Brezhnev to Moscow for a Franco-Soviet summit. Presumably, he wanted to play a grander role on the international stage, and Hammer suggested that he had Soviet connections that could facilitate such a summit. He graphically described (with considerable hyperbole) his 1921 meeting with Lenin and then turned the discussion to Afghanistan. He suggested that a deal with the Soviets could be worked out if the United States agreed to cease its support of the rebels and "not try to overthrow the government even if it is Marxist."

Giscard d'Estaing and Hammer had, as Hammer described it, a "warm and heated" discussion. Hammer noted: "At first, the president didn't agree with A. H. He said, 'We don't want a Marxist government there. . . . We must let the Afghanistan people decide themselves what kind of government they want.' " Hammer persisted. He told Giscard that "Brezhnev was sincere" in wanting peace and argued that "we've got to be realistic and face the fact that since the revolution of 1978, there has been a Marxist government, and the Russians are not going to pull out so easily and let [in] an unfriendly government." Hammer reports that his argument seemed to persuade Giscard. "He seemed more inclined to agree with A. H. that for the time being we should not try to overthrow the present government or encourage the rebels to do this."

Hammer saw an opening to advance his "mission," as he called it. "Why don't you play a role in this thing?" he asked Giscard, saying that the Russians trusted the French more than they did the Americans. He noted that the Soviet foreign minister, Andrey Gromyko, had scheduled a trip to Paris the following week and proposed that "we get [Secretary of State Cyrus] Vance over at the same time and have you mediate between the two of them and start the talks going." Although Giscard did not agree to this approach, he showed interest in discussing the peace plan with Brezhnev (especially after Hammer suggested it could lead to an invitation to Moscow).

After the meeting, Hammer reported on tape that he was making progress. He was also elated with his performance: "Before the luncheon was over, A. H. had won [Giscard d'Estaing] over completely. In fact, Frances said, 'You certainly scored, you accomplished your mission with him.' "[10]

Hammer still had to persuade President Carter to consider his peace plan for Afghanistan, but he had not been able to get an appointment. He blamed Zbigniew Brzezinski, Carter's hard-line national security adviser, noting on tape that "he was the man who had been blocking A. H.'s appointment with President Carter."[11] Brzezinski had indeed opposed Hammer's access to the White House that spring. Deeply suspicious of Soviet intentions in Afghanistan, he regarded Brezhnev's plan to be, as he later explained, "inconsistent with the foreign policy aims of the U.S." As he saw it, the United States had committed itself to reversing the Soviet invasion of Afghanistan, which meant getting rid of the regime in Kabul. The key to achieving this objective was supplying weapons to the guerrillas. If the United States cut off this aid as part of a deal with Brezhnev, the rebellion would probably collapse. Brzezinski assumed that part of Brezhnev's motive in making the proposal was to sow divisive seeds between the United States and its allies.[12]

Hammer managed to find another channel to Carter later that spring. Realizing that the Democratic Party needed early funds for the 1980 campaign, he approached Carter's top political operatives and offered to make a much-needed $100,000 contribution. Soon afterward, Carter agreed to meet with Hammer, who attributed his success to "pressure from Hamilton Jordan [the president's chief of staff], Jody Powell [the president's press secretary], . . . Robert Strauss [the head of the president's reelection campaign], and others." He further reported that "Lee Kling, who is now treasurer of the campaign and is very well disposed to A. H., apparently had a lot to do with arranging the meeting with Carter."[13]

At 11:45 A.M. on June 5, 1980, Hammer arrived at the Oval Office. "Mr. President, it's been a long time I've waited for this meeting," he said. He mentioned his $100,000 "donation," explaining that he had been asked to delay it and that he believed that Carter could be re-elected if he were known as "the president for peace, as distinguished from Reagan, who would be known as the president for war." But he was unable to persuade Carter to consider his peace plan. When, for example, he suggested that if the United States ended its intervention in Afghanistan, "in five years there would be free elections," Carter coolly responded, "I don't think we can wait that long."[14]

Although rebuffed by Carter, Hammer did not give up. Since Pakistan was the principal staging area through which U.S. arms were funneled into Afghanistan, and since Pakistan's intelligence service was the main mechanism for organizing, training, and directing the guerrilla bands opposing the Soviet army in Afghanistan, he next turned to Mohammad Zia ul-Haq, the president—and military dictator—of Pakistan.[15] He realized that without Zia's active cooperation, the United States would have little choice but to seek a negotiated solution along the lines that Brezhnev had offered. Zia was "a pivotal figure" in settling the Afghanistan crisis.[16]

Eager to gain Zia's confidence and cooperation, Hammer flew to Islamabad in August 1980 and met with him at his home. Although Zia was a military man who lived austerely, without any visible trace of personal indulgences, he had grand ambitions for developing Pakistan, one of which involved finding oil so as to reduce the country's dependence on oil imports. Hammer used this. Even though he had heard from Occidental's executives that there was "no economic logic" to justify investing in Pakistan, Hammer had his own political logic. He offered to develop a major oil industry in Pakistan. He told Zia that Occidental had the resources and ability to find along Pakistan's coast quantities of oil large enough to satisfy the country's domestic needs and even make it an exporter. He also offered to construct a state-of-the-art oil refinery in Pakistan and a pipeline to the country's interior. Since such projects, if carried out, could cost Occidental hundreds of millions of dollars, Hammer told Zia that they would start only after peace had been restored to the area.[17]

After making clear to Zia that he was prepared to be Pakistan's benefactor, Hammer outlined his peace plan. To his surprise, Zia seemed willing to consider a key element of it: allowing the pro-Soviet government to remain in power in Kabul after Soviet forces pulled out. Though Zia may have been merely treating a potential benefactor politely, Hammer pursued the perceived opening. He flew to Moscow and reported the development directly to Brezhnev. As it turned out, Hammer had misread Zia. Soon afterward, Zia made clear through diplomatic channels that he was not willing to undercut the Afghan rebels. Even so, by the fall of 1980, Hammer was confident that "reason would prevail" after the presidential campaign was over. He assumed that Carter would go along with the deal to end the war in Afghanistan, thus restoring détente with Moscow.

But it was Reagan, not Carter, who won the election. Hammer set out to approach Reagan that November to discuss his peace plan but found that the path had been firmly blocked. Not only could he not see Reagan, but Richard Allen, Reagan's designated national security adviser, refused even to respond to his calls. Hammer then learned that the icy treatment he was receiving could be traced to events surrounding a former colleague of his, the mysterious power broker David Karr.[18]

IN THE EARLY 1970S, HAMMER HAD FOUND KARR TO BE A USEFUL intermediary. In the Soviet Union, he helped Hammer negotiate a number of deals with the State Committee for Science and Technology, and in France he helped Hammer extract Occidental from unfavorable contracts to charter tankers. But when Karr demanded that he participate as a partner in the Soviet deals, Hammer abruptly dispensed with his services. In retaliation, Karr began leaking information to SEC investigators about Hammer's business dealings, including an unsubstantiated charge that Hammer had bribed officials in the Nixon administration. Hammer characterized these allegations as "pure trash," but in 1978 he attempted to placate Karr by agreeing to allow him to participate in a potentially lucrative arrangement in which the Soviet government would give Occidental and its partners the exclusive right to sell gold coins commemorating the Olympic Games scheduled to be held in Moscow in the summer of 1980.[19]

This did not quiet Karr. Testifying before the SEC in June 1979, he alleged that Hammer had made substantial payoffs to Soviet officials, including a $100,000 bribe to Yekaterina Furtseva (who had died in Moscow in 1974 after coming under investigation for corruption).[20] Karr's allegation suggests that he may have learned about the final destination of the attaché case that Hammer brought to Leningrad in 1972.

Soon after a report of Karr's testimony appeared in *The New York Times,* the sixty-year-old Karr was found dead in his apartment on the avenue Foch in Paris. Although his doctors concluded that the cause of death was a heart attack, his wife, who had been in New York, suspected that he had been murdered. She obtained a court order that stopped the funeral and cremation ceremony while it was in progress. Karr's body was taken to the Institut Médico-Légal for an autopsy, which failed to turn up any evidence of foul play.[21]

The concern over Karr's abrupt death did not end, however. Since he had been in Moscow less than twelve hours before he died and complained there to his daughter about severe stomach pains, France's equivalent of the CIA, the External Documentation and Counterespionage Service (SDECE), began investigating the possibility that Karr had been administered an exotic time-delayed poison in Moscow that simulated the symptoms of a heart attack. Since such a poison was believed to be available to the KGB, the SDECE developed the theory that Karr was murdered by Soviet intelligence. Before going to Moscow, he had dangled before the CIA a tidbit about money Hammer had paid a high Soviet minister and other Soviet officials. SDECE officers had an interest in this that went beyond the circumstances surrounding Karr's death. If Soviet officials had taken bribes from Hammer, they also could be vulnerable to recruitment for intelligence purposes. The SDECE began amassing a dossier on Hammer, the man in the middle of the putative payoffs.[22]

On November 21, 1980, Colonel Alexandre de Marenches, the head of the SDECE, met with President-elect Reagan at his transition headquarters in California to brief him on the French assessment of Soviet intelligence threats. An imposing man with a flamboyant mustache, Marenches spoke flawless English. In discussing Soviet "agents of influence," a term that he didn't precisely define, he warned Reagan that there was one man of whom he should be particularly wary: Armand Hammer. He explained that French intelligence had investigated Hammer's contacts with Soviet officials and had reason to believe that he acted as a vehicle through which they extended their influence. He then recommended that Reagan avoid Hammer.[23]

Reagan was taken aback by this extraordinary warning. He told Marenches that although he was not acquainted with Hammer, he had recently found that every time he went to his barbershop in Beverly Hills for a haircut, Hammer was seated in the chair next to him. Marenches replied, with a knowing nod, "See what I mean."[24]

EVEN BEFORE THE INAUGURATION, HAMMER HAD LEARNED THAT Reagan had been told that he had acted on behalf of the Soviet Union, but he was determined to gain access to the White House nonetheless. To do this, he had to find some means to dispel Reagan's suspicions about his loyalty. He knew from his unreturned calls that Richard Allen and the National Security staff would not be helpful, so he sought alternative routes.[25]

One path was the president's wife, Nancy Reagan. Almost immediately after the inauguration, Hammer set out to cultivate her through her extensive social and civic interests. To begin with, he contributed $20,000 that January to the redecoration of the White House, a project that she was personally supervising. He then invited her to host the reopening of the Corcoran Gallery, a museum to which he had donated $1 million. She accepted and appeared with him at the gala event. He also won favor with her by establishing a scholarship in honor of her father at the American College of Surgeons and by donating $50,000 to her Just Say No campaign against drug abuse.[26] He invited her to a dinner he was hosting for Prince Charles, whom she had expressed an interest in meeting, and he seated her between himself and the prince. On this and other social occasions, Hammer expounded on his commitment to capitalism and his admiration for her husband's policies.[27]

Hammer also attempted to approach President Reagan directly. He used Occidental's government-relations office in Washington, which in 1981 employed men with a wide range of political connections, including William McSweeny, a former high-level aide in the Johnson administration; Jerrold L. Schecter, the former spokesman for the National Security Council in the Carter administration; Rear Admiral Tazewell Shepard, Jr., a former aide in the Kennedy administration; Gordon Reece, a former public relations adviser to Prime Minister Margaret Thatcher; and Jack King, a former spokesman for the National Aeronautics and Space Administration. They spent much of their time in 1981 arranging for Hammer to attend political functions at which Reagan was expected to appear. In one instance, when Reagan went to Ottawa to sign a trade treaty, Hammer got himself invited to a reception given by Prime Minister Pierre Trudeau. When he arrived, he determinedly worked his way through the crowd of Canadian officials and security men to where Reagan was standing. His face beamed as he approached. Thrusting his hand out to Reagan and introducing himself, Hammer reminded the president that they had previously met in the barbershop in Beverly Hills (without realizing that this had become a sensitive subject for Reagan after his conversation with Marenches). Reagan quickly turned away to speak to a Canadian official, and Hammer did not get a chance to resume the conversation.[28] Though Hammer had flown all the way from Los Angeles to see Reagan, he was not discouraged by the fleeting encounter, since he had at least demonstrated to Reagan that he was treated seriously by the Canadian government.

Less than a week later, Hammer was in London at a black-tie dinner given by Prime Minister Thatcher for the Reagans. Even though it was little more than a repeat of the scene in Canada, Hammer was determined to insinuate himself into Reagan's presence, over and over again if necessary, until he was accepted.

During this time, Hammer opened a less direct path to the White House, through David Murdock. A high school dropout who had made a fortune buying and reorganizing industrial companies, Murdock had also become one of the chief fund-raisers in the Republican Party in California, and what was of more interest to Hammer, he had powerful ties to Reagan's top aides in the White House.[29] Hammer recognized that Murdock's political connections could be useful to him, and he sought to cement a bond between them.[30] He knew that Murdock was an avid collector of Arabian horses. He had also gleaned from a casual conversation with him that Murdock desperately wanted to obtain a stallion from a Russian strain of Arabian horses but had not been able to get the necessary permission from the Soviet authorities. Hammer, with his contacts in Moscow, was in a position to solve this problem.

In early February 1981, he called Murdock, who had his offices diagonally across the street from Occidental's on Wilshire Boulevard, and offered him a champion Russian Arabian stallion, Pesniar. He explained that he could arrange to get permission to export the stallion through his connection with Brezhnev. In return, he asked to be partners with Murdock in breeding the horse.

Murdock jumped at Hammer's offer and two months later went with Hammer on *Oxy One* to Moscow. They then flew to Pyatigorsk, on a plateau on the northern slopes of the Caucasus Mountains, to visit the Tersk Breeding Farm, a facility ordinarily not open to foreigners, to see Pesniar. They would pay $1.4 million for the stallion; Murdock estimated that they would earn at least $15 million from the breeding rights.

Once Murdock had become interested in Pesniar, Hammer offered him a deeper financial alliance. Murdock owned 19 percent of Iowa Beef Processors, the nation's largest beef-packing company, which made him that company's largest stockholder. Hammer told Murdock that once the trade embargo was lifted, he could make the meat company vastly more profitable by selling millions of tons of frozen beef directly to the Soviet bloc. In light of Hammer's success in obtaining Pesniar, Murdock had no reason to doubt that Hammer had the connections in Moscow to benefit Iowa Beef. Hammer proposed that Occidental, with Murdock's support, buy Iowa Beef for $800 million, which was about 30 percent more than the market value of the company (and would give Murdock a sizable profit on his shares). To avoid negative tax consequences, Hammer further proposed that Occidental pay in stock, which would make Murdock the largest shareholder in Occidental. It would also make Murdock, who was only fifty-eight, the logical successor to Hammer, who was then eighty-two. Under these conditions, Murdock eagerly supported the merger, which was consummated later that year.

While this alliance was still being negotiated that winter, Murdock accommodated Hammer by using his "good offices," as he put it, to clear up "misunderstandings" about Hammer at the Reagan White House. He made the case that Hammer used his contacts in Moscow only to benefit his business interests.[31]

By the spring of 1981, Hammer detected cracks in the barricade that had been erected around him at the White House. He had established a warm relationship with White House aide Michael Deaver (whom he later offered to employ at Occidental at three times his government salary). Nancy Reagan began putting Hammer on the White House invitation list, and even Richard Allen could no longer cold-shoulder him at receptions.

On April 25, 1981, Reagan ended the embargo on Soviet trade, a decision that proceeded mainly from concern about American farmers losing their share of the grain market. Hammer wrote Reagan, commending his "courageous decision" and asserting that renewed trade with the Soviet Union was in the national interest.[32] It certainly was in Occidental's interest. Occidental had lost $383 million because of the sixteen-month interruption of its Soviet business, and it instantly prepared to resume shipments of SPA to Odessa.

The day after he heard the news that the embargo had ended, Hammer canceled all his scheduled engagements and departed for Moscow.[33] As on Hammer's other thirty flights to Russia in the past five years, his jetliner stopped in London to take on two Soviet navigators. When the plane landed at Sheremetevo Airport outside Moscow, it taxied directly to a new terminal building, where two Soviet protocol officers were waiting. Without going through customs, they escorted Hammer through the VIP lounge to a waiting Chaika limousine, which took him directly to his Moscow apartment. He was met there by Mikhail Bruk, his suave Soviet aide, and General Aleksandrov-Argentov, Brezhnev's national security adviser. He had been dealing with both these men for nearly two decades, and they had just helped him acquire Pesniar for Murdock.[34]

Hammer told them that despite all his efforts, even including an approach to Kurt Waldheim, the secretary general of the United Nations, the Reagan administration had effectively rejected a negotiated peace in Afghanistan along the lines that Brezhnev had proposed and that there was little more he could do to restore détente in the present confrontational atmosphere in Washington.

General Aleksandrov-Argentov had the responsibility in the Kremlin of coordinating information about the United States that was received from different Soviet ministries and intelligence agencies. He was fully aware of the poor state of relations that existed. Even so, he encouraged Hammer to proceed with his projects in the Soviet Union on the assumption that the ice jam in U.S.-Soviet relations could be broken. When Hammer flew back to America two days later, he learned that Reagan had rejected a U.S.-Soviet summit in the near future. Hammer believed that without such a summit, the prospects for restoring détente remained gloomy.[35]

Despite Hammer's misgivings about détente, his mission to gain acceptance by the Reagan White House was progressing. On October 4, 1981, Reagan made Hammer the chairman of an unpaid advisory board called the President's Cancer Panel. Although the appointment was an honorary one, Hammer skillfully used it to portray himself as an insider in the Reagan administration. He also used it to dispel lingering doubts about his loyalty by claiming that he had received "FBI clearance" for it, although, in fact, his appointment neither required nor received any FBI scrutiny.[36]

Hammer benefited from Richard Allen's departure as national security adviser in 1982. Allen was replaced by Judge William Clark, a California lawyer in Reagan's inner circle whom Hammer knew from Los Angeles. Unlike Allen, Judge Clark felt no antipathy for Hammer.

Hammer won further favor from Nancy Reagan by giving some paintings that the president admired to the White House, including one of Reagan's favorite paintings of the West, Charles Marion Russell's *Fording the Horse Herd*. He also pledged $1 million to the construction of the Ronald Reagan Library. By July 1983, he was able to describe President Reagan as a "good friend."[37] Though Hammer's access to the Reagan White House was mainly at the social level during the mid-1980s, it served his purposes as a go-between.[38]

HAMMER NEVER LOST SIGHT OF HIS GEOPOLITICAL OBJECTIVE: GETting détente back on track, but he found, as he later wrote, that "the road back to Moscow was long and winding."[39] There were also a number of detours. In short order, three Soviet leaders died: Brezhnev, in November 1982; his successor, Yuri Andropov, in February 1984; and then Andropov's successor, Konstantin Chernenko, in March 1985. Hammer flew to Moscow to attend each of their funerals. Shortly after the funeral of Andropov, General Aleksandrov-Argentov brought Hammer to meet Chernenko. Then, in December 1984, Hammer, along with Aleksandrov-Argentov and Bruk, had an extraordinary one-and-a-half-hour meeting with the new Soviet leader. Hammer was surprised to find that Chernenko, who had been rumored in the press to have been in feeble health, looked robust and confident. After presenting Hammer with the gift of a vase as a token of appreciation for his services, Chernenko asked Hammer to give him his assessment of Reagan.

Hammer spoke in English with Bruk translating for him. He told Chernenko that by now he knew Reagan well, and he was convinced that despite the president's anti-Soviet rhetoric, he was driven by a powerful desire to go down in history as a great leader. He also said that Reagan received further impetus in this direction from his wife, who desperately wanted her husband, as she had confided to Hammer, to win the Nobel Peace Prize. Hammer suggested to Chernenko that Reagan would be amenable to holding a summit.[40]

Chernenko authorized Hammer to convey to Reagan that he was ready to meet, and Hammer fired off letters to members of the National Security staff, apprising them of this. When he did not receive a favorable reply that December, he decided that he was not going to get to the president by going through channels. Reagan "was not being fully informed by some members of his circle, who were almost as suspicious of the Soviet Union as some members of the Politburo were of the USA." Hammer had hoped that through Nancy Reagan, to whom he spoke with increasing regularity, he would be able to set up a direct line of communication between himself and the president. But he made little headway in 1985. "Despite my constant knocking," he wrote about this period, "the doors to the Oval Office in the White House remained jammed."[41] His frustration increased when Chernenko died after less than a year in office. It was as if he had to begin the entire process over. Again he went to Red Square and stood in a blizzard. To guard against the bone-chilling wind, Hammer wore cashmere undergarments, wool-lined galoshes, a fur hat, and a mink coat. He again heard the sad strains of Chopin's "Funeral March." He again watched as the designated successor delivered a long eulogy from atop Lenin's Tomb. But there was a dramatic difference this time: the successor was Mikhail Gorbachev. He was articulate and vigorous, and appeared to be attuned to the values of capitalist countries.

Later that day, Hammer met Gorbachev at a reception. He was struck, as he later wrote, by how "his face brightened with charming warmth." He recognized that this affability would greatly facilitate his task of bringing about a summit.

Events moved quickly in that direction. By the next spring, Reagan and Gorbachev had agreed in principle that a summit would be useful, and U.S. and Soviet diplomats were negotiating the logistics of where and when it would take place. On June 12, 1985, Hammer was back in the Kremlin, accompanied as usual by Aleksandrov-Argentov and Bruk. They met Gorbachev in his office at the building that housed the Communist Party Central Committee, the same office in which Hammer had met Chernenko six months before. Hammer found Gorbachev commanding, "a man of enormous intelligence." But as the discussion turned to Ronald Reagan, Gorbachev seemed "disturbingly limited" in his understanding of the U.S. system.[42] Hammer attempted to explain to the Soviet leader, with help from Aleksandrov-Argentov, the competing pressures that influenced Reagan. He argued that delaying the summit would strengthen the hand of the faction in the Republican Party that wanted to derail détente. He urged Gorbachev to move quickly to expedite the meeting.[43]

When he returned to Washington, Hammer asked if he could brief Reagan on what Gorbachev had told him, and an appointment was arranged for June 23. It was the first time he had been invited to the Reagan Oval Office. During the fifteen-minute meeting, he described Gorbachev's demeanor and tried to persuade Reagan to "set a date and go to Moscow."[44] He implored him not to allow any problems of protocol to delay the summit. He said, with a touch of calculated flattery, "You're too big a man to stand on pride. You are the President of the most powerful country on earth and the most powerful man in the world."[45]

The summit took place that November in Geneva. Even though Hammer did not attend it, he took satisfaction that his efforts as a go-between had helped bring it about. It was a role for which he expected to be rewarded.

CHAPTER TWENTY-FOUR

BALANCE OF POWER

IN THE EARLY 1980S, HAMMER BECAME FASCINATED, ALMOST TO the point of obsession, with Marlon Brando's portrayal of a Machiavellian oil tycoon, supposedly modeled on him, in the film thriller *The Formula.*[1] This fictional tycoon, Adam Steiffel, successfully masterminds a conspiracy to artificially inflate the price of world oil.

Though Steiffel is ruthless, power hungry, and engaged in criminal activities, Hammer spoke publicly about this homage to himself. But he was not entirely satisfied with the character's physical appearance. "I was disappointed," he told *People* magazine. "Brando was trying to characterize me without any hair and wearing a hearing aid. Well, I still have my hair, and I've never used a hearing aid."[2] On another occasion, he complained in a speech to the American Petroleum Institute that Brando wore "rimless specs" in the film, whereas he always wore horn-rimmed glasses.[3] He also complained that Brando looked overweight in the film, whereas he was lean and fit.[4] But he took as a tribute to himself the immense power attributed to Steiffel. Hammer recognized that Steiffel derived this power not from his position in a corporate hierarchy but from his extraordinary ability to perceive human weakness and exploit it. This corresponded closely with his own view of power. To Hammer, power was principally an intellectual quality. One controlled others by calculating precisely what they wanted or feared.

...ner contemplating a bust of Lenin in Moscow.

Hammer had long prided himself on his ability to exercise power behind the scenes. When Bettye Murphy asked him in 1953 if he ever dreamed of becoming president of the United States, he replied, "I don't need to become president. I make presidents."[5] Some thirty years later, when Hammer was asked during an interview for a newspaper whether he had "more power than the President of the U.S.," he smiled silently and nodded affirmatively.[6] Such claims exaggerated the reality of his power, but they clearly reflected his ambition to control the actions of those at the highest levels of government. In pursuing this ambition, he assumed that virtually anyone, even a president, could be moved with the appropriate incentive. In some cases, this might involve no more than an offer of access to special medical treatment for a worrisome ailment, as with Israeli Prime Minister Menachem Begin. In other cases, it might take something more sinister, like supplying secret funds to Libyan leaders after the Gadhafi coup d'état.[7]

To research the needs, fears, and vanities of those he wished to influence, Hammer hired specialists: private detectives, former employees of the FBI, CIA, and foreign intelligence services, and even criminal informants. One such specialist was Herbert Itkin, who had been used by the FBI and other law-enforcement agencies to penetrate organized crime by pretending to collaborate with criminals. Itkin then entered the federal witness-protection program and worked for Hammer under assumed names.[8] Over the years, Hammer developed a wide network of such operatives. For him, information was power.[9]

Hammer's quest for data that could be used as leverage became almost an end in itself. At one point in the late 1970s, he attempted to widen his access to the records of politicians in financial distress by buying a controlling interest in the First National Bank of Washington, D.C. After spending almost $5 million to buy 5.2 percent of its holding company, Financial General Bancshares, he attempted to persuade a foreign financier who was seeking to do business in the United States to join him in the takeover attempt. The financier could not see the point of the deal. Hammer looked at him as if he were naïve and explained that the bank had outstanding loans to more than one hundred U.S. senators and congressmen. When his prospective partner still failed to see the point,

Hammer explained that all these congressional borrowers had sub-mitted statements to the bank that revealed their precise financial status, including their debts, earnings, real estate holdings, and other assets. He suggested that this data would be worth more in terms of influence than the entire investment they would need to make. The financier declined to participate when he realized that Hammer had blackmail in mind.

Hammer did not succeed in the takeover, and he sold his interest in the bank in 1981 for an $8-million profit. The group that bought him out secretly represented the infamous Bank of Credit and Commerce International, or BCCI, which subsequently was convicted of one of the largest banking frauds in history.[10]

Hammer found numerous other ways to acquire strategic informa-tion about members of Congress. As one of his chief public-affairs officers in Washington concluded, "When it came to most politicians, Hammer had little problem in finding just the right button to press."[11] He also used superior information to dominate his subordi-nates at Occidental. "When my executives talk with me, I already know as much as—and often more than—they do," he explained in a magazine interview in 1981.[12] His seemingly uncanny ability to an-ticipate their precise objections to projects he favored gave him an unsettling psychological edge in meetings. Not uncommonly, he would interrupt them in midsentence with a sudden wave of his hand and then complete their thoughts for them, indicating that he had taken into account their objections, or "quibbles," as he often char-acterized them. He would then end further discussion of the issue with a wilting stare.

Even Occidental's chief executive was not exempt from such treat-ment. A. Robert Abboud, a Lebanese-born banker whom Hammer had brought in to replace Zoltan Merszei in August 1980, found that he was often subject to this type of petty humiliation. On one occa-sion, in March 1981, Abboud was on the telephone with Occidental's representative in London, discussing strategy for dealing with a British plan to increase taxes on the company's oil concession. Ham-mer walked into the room and signaled him to put his hand over the receiver. In front of a roomful of people, Hammer then stood behind Abboud and, treating him more like a stenographer than the com-pany's president, told him, sentence by sentence, what he should say.

He demonstrated to everyone present that he was fully versed in, and in control of, the issue.[13]

Although Hammer made a point of attributing his knowledge of corporate activities to "intuition," he derived at least some of it from surreptitious internal investigations. At times, these involved planting concealed microphones in subordinates' offices and cars. When he did not want even Occidental's security people to know about this "James Bond stuff," as he referred to it, he used his son, Julian, to install the electronic devices. Hammer's purpose, as Julian understood it, was "to keep absolute control over Oxy."[14]

Up until 1982, Hammer had little problem achieving this objective. Even after the SEC had forced him in 1972 to end his practice of getting signed, undated letters of resignation from the members of the board of directors, he continued to select board members on the basis of their allegiance to him. They included lawyers and financiers who depended on him for a large share of their business, company executives who depended on him for their tenure, and longtime allies who had demonstrated their unswerving loyalty to him. Whatever their views, he made it clear that he expected them all to accept one thing: Occidental was a corporate extension of Armand Hammer.[15] He insisted that the annual shareholders' meeting be held on his birthday, and he peremptorily rejected the idea of creating any corporate identity for the company that was separate from himself. Advertising and public relations campaigns had to focus on him.[16] The justification for this policy was that foreign leaders considered their deals to be with Hammer, not with a faceless American corporation. The board of directors so rarely challenged his authority that Hammer was able to brag as late as 1980 that it had always "voted unanimously."[17] This unanimity ended when, as a consequence of Occidental's acquisition of Iowa Beef, David Murdock entered the picture.

In making Murdock vice chairman of the Occidental board in 1982, Hammer had assumed that Murdock would prove as useful an ally in business as he had in advancing Hammer's political designs. He had made a great effort to help Murdock, getting him Pesniar and other Arabian stallions at bargain prices and arranging for Occidental to buy his shares in Iowa Beef at a premium price. He now expected Murdock to show his appreciation, as other directors had done, by voting for the measures he favored.

But Murdock was not cut from the same cloth as Hammer's other directors. He was far wealthier than Hammer and a generation younger, and more to the point, he was the largest shareholder in Occidental. Murdock had a shrewd and independent understanding of the situation. On one occasion in 1981, while showing two guests his private club atop Murdock Plaza, he pointed to Hammer's helicopter taking off from the roof of the Occidental Building across the street and commented, with an acid tone in his voice: "That's my partner Doc Hammer up there. His private helicopter is going to take him to his private jet, which is going to fly him to his private apartment in Moscow, all paid for by the shareholders of Oxy. Now I don't have a helicopter, private jetliner, or any of those corporate amenities, but I own four times as many shares in Oxy as Hammer—though one wouldn't know it from the way he talks about the company."[18]

As it turned out, Murdock was also concerned with Hammer's reasons for flying to Moscow. He now had access to Occidental's financial data and found that the company had used dangerously optimistic accounting assumptions in evaluating its Soviet projects. In the case of the fertilizer deal, for example, it had assumed that it could sell the ammonia it received from the Soviets for artificially high prices. When more realistic assumptions were applied to the data, it appeared that Occidental would suffer multibillion-dollar losses in Russia. Whatever Hammer's purpose had been in making these grandiose deals, they had not produced any tangible benefit for the company, and Murdock was not prepared to allow Hammer to bleed Occidental any further.[19]

Hammer was then pressing forward with a scheme to develop a giant open-pit coal mine in the interior of China. The plan involved mining some fifteen million tons of coal a year—which would have made it the largest coal mine in the world—transporting the coal by rail to a port in the Sea of Japan, and then exporting it by ship to utility companies in Japan and South Korea. To finance the mine, Hammer proposed that Occidental guarantee bank loans of $345 million, which would be repaid through the sale of the coal.[20] Even though the price of coal on the world market was "sinking," Hammer said that this "does not concern me a great deal." He took the "long-term point of view." He explained, "I feel now about China as I felt when I first went to Russia in the time of Lenin."[21]

Murdock was not moved by such nostalgia. If coal prices were falling, he wanted Occidental to get out of the coal business. Hammer argued that even if the coal venture lost money, it would help Occidental get oil concessions in China. Murdock scoffed at this logic, suggesting that the only connection between the two endeavors was that they would both lose money. And he rubbed salt into the wound by comparing the proposed China ventures with Occidental's money-losing Soviet-fertilizer venture.

Hammer bristled at this opposition. "As soon as he got on the inside, David Murdock began to throw his weight around," he wrote later, "opposing most of our corporate strategies and, in particular, criticizing me in board meetings." Murdock also asked that his personal representative be installed in Occidental's executive offices to monitor Hammer's activities. And even though he had agreed to limit his holdings in Occidental to 5 percent, he began pressing the board for permission to buy a larger stake. As Hammer put it, "It was getting nasty."[22]

In April 1982, Murdock invited Hammer to lunch at his club. The meal remained amiable until dessert, when Murdock looked Hammer straight in the eye and told him, "I think you should resign. I think you're too old to be running Occidental."

Hammer described the discussion that ensued in dramatic detail. Initially, he was taken aback by Murdock's aggressive request. He noted that "very few people on earth would have the nerve to speak to me like that." Yet "Murdock was as cool as a cucumber."

But Hammer was not about to give up the base of his power. He told Murdock, just as coolly, "I'm going to finish my term."

"You and I are at war," Murdock said. ". . . I never lose."

Hammer, getting up from the table, shot back, "I never lose either."[23]

Despite his bravado, Hammer realized that it was a war that he *could* lose. Murdock had an impressive track record of taking over companies from the inside. It was indeed his specialty, and he was now vice chairman of Occidental's board. Even with the support of a majority of the board, which Hammer could still count on, he could not dismiss Murdock until his term expired, in 1984. And this gave Murdock plenty of time to stage a coup d'état. It could take the form of a proxy battle for shareholder support, or it could take the form of a takeover of Occidental by another company allied with Murdock.

Shortly after confronting Hammer, Murdock persuaded Abboud, who had day-to-day responsibilities for running Occidental, to remain neutral in the power struggle. Hammer suspected that Abboud was already in Murdock's camp. In any case, Abboud's decision meant that Hammer could not rely on aid from Occidental's management.

Even so, Hammer had other resources at his disposal. He still controlled secret bank accounts. He had funneled over $20 million into the Union Bank of Switzerland account during the past twelve years, and while Occidental's auditors believed this money had been going to pay off the commitment to Omar Shelhi and his associates for obtaining the Libyan oil concession, much of it was still available to Hammer. He also had his connections in Moscow and the network of intermediaries that he used to facilitate deals around the world. He assumed that information, especially negative information, would be a decisive weapon in this war. By mid-1982, he had mobilized a half dozen investigators, including Herbert Itkin, to research Murdock's life. He used his contacts to gain access to private as well as public databases. He had undercover agents approach Murdock's former acquaintances and surreptitiously attempt to extract information from them. He even had intermediaries go to Mafia informers in the hope that they could supply stories and theories. Hammer sought allegations that could embarrass or even intimidate Murdock. For this purpose, the charges did not have to be substantiated—or even true. Since his investigation was conducted outside Occidental, he brought in Martha Kaufman, who now worked for him at the Armand Hammer Foundation, to organize the material. Though she had been his mistress and confidante for eight years, she had not fully grasped his need for total control. He would subsequently force her to completely change her identity to conceal his secret liaison. She now saw that he was a master at acquiring other people's secrets. He could penetrate even the confidential files of law-enforcement agencies. By early 1983, he had assembled a half-inch-thick document he called "The Murdock Dossier."[24]

Hammer's philosophy was that "you had to play out every card in your hand before you walked away from the table."[25] He asked Murdock to come to his office and, when he was seated, handed him the dossier. As Hammer told the story, Murdock opened the file, slammed it closed, and left the office. Hammer had accomplished his purpose: he had shown him his "stick" and that he could wield it. He then proceeded to offer Murdock a carrot.[26]

Hammer had sized up Murdock as a calculating businessman who would prove more interested in the "quick buck" than in corporate power.[27] He now offered him an opportunity to avoid a potentially nasty fight and make an instant profit. He would have Occidental buy back all Murdock's common and preferred shares at a price well above the market price. The size of the premium that Occidental would pay Murdock was negotiable, and since it would come from Occidental's treasury—not out of Hammer's own pocket—Hammer expected they could reach agreement on it.[28]

There were reasons for Murdock to consider the deal. The Reagan administration was rapidly moving toward instituting an embargo on Libya, and if that happened, Occidental's earning power would be damaged, and his five million shares of Occidental stock would drop in value. Under these circumstances there was little point in engaging in a mudslinging contest with Hammer: the prize, Occidental, was no longer worth it. So Murdock decided to cash in his chips.

After prolonged negotiations, Hammer agreed that Occidental would give Murdock a rich premium over the market price for his shares, one that would amount to a $60-million payoff. After the deal was ratified, in July 1984, Murdock resigned from the board.

Hammer had one piece of unfinished business to take care of. In August 1984, he announced that Occidental was to have a new president, its third in four years. Ray Irani, the executive vice president loyal to Hammer, would replace Abboud. He attributed Abboud's departure to "honest differences." In an interview with the *Los Angeles Times,* Murdock said that Abboud's

> desire to pay down the debt, stay out of new adventures and bring more conservative operating methods to the company was in the best interests of the shareholders. But unfortunately this was in conflict with Dr. Hammer's more flamboyant method of operation. As in the past, no one has ever dared stand against his singularly autocratic rule.[29]

. . .

FOR HAMMER, POWER MEANT GETTING WHAT HE WANTED AND keeping it. He had no small appetite—and no plan to abdicate: "I want everything life has to offer right up until my last moment on earth."[30] Even as he was approaching ninety, he was fully capable of applying his power in ways that made younger executives cringe or even resign. Consider, for example, how Hammer dealt with a threat to his rule that came from terrorists in the jungles of Colombia in the late 1980s.

In 1984, after spending $50 million on exploration, Occidental had discovered a "monster" oil field, as Hammer described it, thirty miles east of the Andes in northern Colombia. By early 1985, geologists had estimated that the Cañon Limón Field, as it was named, contained a billion barrels of oil and once it reached full production would generate 250,000 barrels a day, a quantity equal to almost one tenth of all Alaskan oil production. In addition, the oil was light, low-sulfur crude, which was much in demand by refineries in America.

The enormous strike could not have come at a better time for Hammer. Occidental and other U.S. companies had been advised to withdraw all their American personnel from Libya, and it was clear that embargo was imminent. By this time, Occidental had other sources of oil, including an offshore platform in the North Sea, but most of its reserves were in Libya. Hammer realized that the Cañon Limón discovery could go far in making up for the expected loss of Libyan oil. It could also help alleviate the growing burden of debt that stemmed in part from the company's projects in Communist countries. When Hammer went to Bogotá to sign an agreement with President Belisario Betancur, he boldly announced that he intended to have the field in production by 1986. Since the oil had to be transported over the Andes to the Caribbean port of Covenas, a 286-mile pipeline had to be built over extremely difficult terrain at a projected cost of $400 million.[31] To help organize the "crash program," Hammer retained IMEG, the consulting firm of his longtime associates Kunz and Zade, who were still acting as the custodians of the secret UBS account through which the Libyan payments were funneled. Zade later told an associate that Hammer expected them to kick back part of their fees on the pipeline to the Armand Hammer Foundation.[32] Hammer retained Bechtel to build the pipeline. Drilling and engineering contractors were flown in from around the world to ready Cañon Limón for production while Hammer's intermediaries in Bogotá obtained the construction permissions and environmental waivers.[33]

Oil flowed on schedule from test wells in Cañon Limón in late 1985, but it could not be brought to market because of an unforeseen problem. Armed guerrillas had interrupted work on the pipeline. They were part of the formidable People's Liberation Army, a Marxist group that derived part of its income from cocaine trafficking and held de facto control over the jungle terrain through which the pipeline went. Throughout 1985, the Colombian army had proved to be either unable or unwilling to protect the pipeline in these areas. Even though it was against Colombian law to negotiate with guerrillas, Hammer decided he had no choice. He focused on finding the appropriate inducement for their cooperation.

Hammer retained, at $2,000 a day, a former CIA officer who had experience dealing with revolutionary movements in Latin America. He also hired local mercenaries who had contacts with the cocaine traffickers. By early 1986, he had opened channels to the People's Liberation Army. Its leaders needed cash, presumably to pursue their revolution, and Hammer needed oil to pursue his corporate goals. The two parties had little problem arriving at an arrangement: in return for protecting Hammer's pipeline, the People's Liberation Army would receive regular payments in laundered dollars.[34] The payoffs, which reportedly amounted to more than $3 million during the first year of the arrangement, did not sit well with James Sutton, Occidental's security chief in Latin America. Sutton had worked for the FBI before joining Occidental, and he considered the payments "immoral, improper, ill-advised and illegal actions." When he vocally opposed them, Hammer fired him.[35]

Hammer himself described the payoffs in relatively innocuous terms. "We are giving jobs to the guerrillas," he explained. "We give them catering jobs . . . and they in turn protect us from other guerrillas."[36] Of course, the money also helped the guerrillas expand their violent activities to other parts of the country. But whatever the collateral costs, Hammer had again succeeded: his oil, worth more than $1 billion a year, was flowing to the sea. With the proceeds, Occidental could continue to expand.

. . .

FOR HAMMER, POWER AND SECRECY WERE OPPOSITE SIDES OF THE same coin. He had developed early in his career a remarkable ability to compartmentalize his machinations. So long as the seals between these compartments held fast, he alone knew how the contents fit together. Omar Shelhi, who had once believed he was Hammer's partner in Libya, discovered, but only in 1995, how Hammer had used this technique to blind him—and Occidental's board of directors—to a diversion of more than $20 million over fifteen years.

In May 1995, Shelhi was still in exile in Geneva, living in a modern high-rise apartment with his wife, the daughter of the former Libyan prime minister, and their two sons. By now, his abortive attempts to overthrow Gadhafi had exhausted his wealth. The only signs of his previous power were a series of framed photographs showing him with King Idris. On his desk was a sheath of documents, including cable transfers and financial statements. They came from Box 9 of the 120 boxes of auditor's records of Occidental Petroleum that the SEC had subpoenaed in the late 1970s. The records had remained under seal at the SEC repository in Maryland until 1992, when a Freedom of Information Act lawsuit pried them open.

Shelhi had always considered himself a sophisticated player in the game of intrigue. Before Gadhafi's coup in 1969, he had been the power in Libya. The CIA dealt with him, British intelligence dealt with him, and the Seven Sisters oil giants dealt with him. So did Hammer, then a virtual unknown in the oil business. His intervention had provided Hammer with his first real success: two of the most coveted concessions in Libya. Without his help, he reflected, "Hammer would be zero." Hammer had agreed to pay Shelhi and his associates, Kunz and Zade, a royalty of 2.665 percent of the value of the oil that came from the concessions—money that was to be deposited on a quarterly basis in the UBS account in Zurich. By September 1969, Shelhi had received $1.4 million as his share. Then, when Gadhafi took over, Shelhi received no more money. Hammer informed him that the board of directors had decided the company had no further obligations to him and that no further payments would be made to the UBS account.

Shelhi had accepted this pronouncement as one of the consequences of having lost power. He was now in exile. He had lost his country, his palaces, his family members: why should he expect to keep this payoff from a distant oil company? For the next three years, deeply involved in plotting a countercoup, he gave little thought to the lost royalties.

In 1972, however, he ran into Hans Kunz on a flight from Geneva to Düsseldorf. In discussing old times, Kunz let it slip that he and Zade, the other intermediary in the Occidental deal, were still receiving payments from Hammer. When Kunz realized the implications of his slip, he stopped in midsentence.

Shelhi was stunned. He had assumed that Kunz and Zade had been cut out of the deal when he was. They were, after all, his front men. Why, if the deal was abrogated, would they still be receiving money from Hammer? Had he been double-crossed? When he questioned Zade, who had been a family friend, about whether payments were still flowing into the UBS account, Zade denied that they were and told him that Kunz had misspoken. Kunz then changed his story. Shelhi suspected both men of stonewalling him and consulted a lawyer, who advised him that without documentation there was nothing further he could do.

But now Shelhi had the documentation. The cable transfers to the UBS and the accompanying royalty statements in Box 9 left no doubt that Hammer had lied when he said that Occidental's board had discontinued the secret 2.665 percent royalty. In fact, Occidental had paid the money into the account four times a year during the years covered by these documents. According to other documents now available to Shelhi, some $20.7 million had been put into this account during the time he was told it had been shut down.

"As far as Occidental's treasurer and auditor knew, for those sixteen years I was getting money due me for arranging the concession," he explained. "But as far as *I* knew, the deal had been terminated, and I didn't receive anything."

So what happened to the $20.7 million that went into the UBS account?

After Gadhafi took power, Hammer held all the cards in the game. He could end the payments and save Occidental's shareholders millions of dollars, or he could continue them and build up a secret slush fund. For the latter course, which he elected, he needed the cooperation of Kunz and Zade, whose names were on the account. If they wanted to continue to get their share, they had to play Hammer's game and cut Shelhi out. Shelhi was Gadhafi's enemy, and Hammer needed Gadhafi's cooperation. So Hammer had rearranged the pay-offs.

"I trusted Hammer. I got him the concession that made him wealthy, and he embezzled my money," Shelhi said with genuine sadness in his voice. He unfurled one of the Box 9 financial statements: a May 30, 1975, statement describing money transferred from Occidental to the UBS account.

Most of the UBS money had disappeared into other accounts, but some reemerged as gifts to charities: $2 million went to the Armand Hammer United World College, $100,000 went to rehabilitate Ford's Theater in Washington, and $500,000 in cash went to the Armand Hammer Foundation. Shelhi found it difficult to accept that "Hammer stole my money so he could give it away."[37]

But Hammer's life at this point was not about money. It was about reputation. Power and money were only means to a higher end— recognition.

CHAPTER TWENTY-FIVE

THE QUEST
FOR THE
NOBEL
PRIZE

To celebrate his ninetieth birthday in May 1988, Armand Hammer and Occidental Petroleum spared no expense in staging an extravagant event. Hammer invited eight hundred people to the John F. Kennedy Center for the Performing Arts in Washington: cabinet members, congressional leaders, Supreme Court justices, corporate heads, and foreign dignitaries. Following a caviar and champagne dinner with an inner circle of three hundred VIPs, Hammer moved to the presidential box, which President Reagan had given him permission to use that night. He sat with his special guests, who included Senator Edward Kennedy and Helen Hayes, as glowing tributes were paid to him by the ambassadors of a dozen nations, including China, Israel, and the Soviet Union (where a laudatory hour-long television documentary on him had been aired two nights earlier). After the black-tie audience toasted Hammer, it was entertained by some of the world's most accomplished artists. Violinists Isaac Stern and Yehudi Menuhin dedicated a Bach duet to him, and the diva Kiri Te Kanawa sang Mozart arias and "Happy Birthday." At the conclusion of the evening, Hammer himself went to the podium. He looked remarkably fit and elated. Baton in hand, he led the National Symphony Orchestra in "Stars and Stripes Forever." When the festivities were over, he flew on to Moscow, where he had been invited by Gor-

*Hammer with Prince Charles, who is launching a ship
in Greenwich, England, in 1979.*

bachev to be an "observer" to the Reagan-Gorbachev summit—the only private citizen in the world so honored.[1]

Hammer saw an advantage in old age. "It is possible to see with absolute clarity what matters and what is unimportant," he wrote the previous year. "I know very clearly what I want to achieve in the time remaining to me."[2] His goal was not to increase his wealth. He had found that "riches by themselves do not bring happiness."[3] To be sure, money was useful for buying the influence of government officials, rebel guerrilla armies, and others whose services or offices he needed, but it was no more than a means to an end. He wanted acclaim, a kind of recognition that went far beyond the civic awards that are ordinarily granted to wealthy men in return for their philanthropy. He wanted an honor so brilliant it would obscure all his past offenses: his money laundering for Soviet intelligence, his bribing of government officials, and his personal use of corporate funds. He had set his sights on the Nobel Peace Prize.

The peace prize was established in 1901 through the terms of the will of Alfred Bernhard Nobel, a Swedish pacifist who, paradoxically, invented dynamite, blasting gelatin, and smokeless gunpowder. Unlike the Nobel prizes for science and literature, which are awarded by the Swedish Royal Academy of Sciences, the Royal Caroline Medico-Chirurgical Institute, and the Swedish Academy, the Nobel Peace Prize is awarded by a five-person committee of the Norwegian parliament. Among its past recipients are some of the most illustrious figures in modern history. They were chosen by the committee either because they were statesmen who had negotiated an important peace, as did, for example, Theodore Roosevelt, Woodrow Wilson, Dag Hammarskjöld, and Henry Kissinger, or because they have been leaders in the quest for human rights, as were Dr. Martin Luther King, Jr., Bishop Desmond Tutu, Mother Teresa, Andrei Sakharov, and Albert Schweitzer.

Hammer did not fit into either category. Moreover, no businessperson had ever received the prize. When this was pointed out to Hammer in 1981, he answered, unfazed, "If necessary, I'll make my own categories." Some executives at Occidental feared that he had lost contact with reality, but he was genuinely confident that he could—and would—qualify as a serious Nobel Peace Prize candidate.[4]

Hammer had laid the foundation three years earlier, when he inaugurated the Armand Hammer Conference on Peace and Human

Rights, which dealt with the two categories for which the peace prize was given. The stated purpose of the conference, which was paid for by Occidental, was to encourage a dialogue between the Soviet bloc and the West. Hammer had little problem winning the support of the Soviet government for these gatherings. If nothing else, they provided (as did the Pugwash conference earlier) opportunities for its operatives, who often acted as interpreters, to acquaint themselves with Western scientists, intellectuals, and diplomats. Mikhail Bruk played a major role in organizing the Soviet side of the conferences for Hammer.

But Hammer also had his own agenda, which he made clear when he staged the initial conference in Oslo on December 22, 1978. That same week, only walking distance from Hammer's conference, the nominating committee for the Nobel Peace Prize was meeting to review possible candidates for the 1979 award. To get even more attention, Hammer had brought the Armand Hammer Collection to Oslo that week, and he pointedly invited all the members of the Norwegian parliament who were serving on the nominating committee to the gala reception for it. "This is merely the first step towards getting . . . my name in nomination with the Nobel Committee," he told Carl Blumay, who was then his public relations consultant.[5]

The Armand Hammer Conference on Peace and Human Rights was staged five more times over the next six years, in Poland, France, and Spain and at two sites associated with FDR: the Roosevelts' summer retreat on Campobello (which Hammer had donated to the U.S. government) and their former estate at Hyde Park, New York, where FDR was buried. At each conference, Hammer described efforts he had made to negotiate peace settlements and win the release of high-profile political dissidents. He augmented his image as a peacemaker and defender of human rights during this period by having Occidental's press officers arrange interviews with him or inspire news stories that developed these themes. He had the film division of Occidental, Armand Hammer Productions, follow him around with film crews and photographers. The dozens of meetings he attended with world leaders all became part of his campaign.[6]

Hammer had to find a prestigious person to nominate him for the prize. Initially, after Rosalynn Carter attended a ceremony at which he received a civic organization's Man of Conscience award, Hammer focused his efforts on inducing President Carter to place his name in nomination, but Carter refused.[7] Undaunted, Hammer turned to an equally prestigious potential nominator, Prime Minister Margaret Thatcher of Great Britain. He was convinced that Prince Charles would be able to persuade Thatcher to nominate him and would himself support him.

Hammer had met Charles in May 1977 at an opening of an exhibition of paintings and drawings by Sir Winston Churchill at the Knoedler Gallery in London. Hammer had offered him a Churchill painting as a present for the Queen's Silver Jubilee Fund. This gift was, as Hammer described it, "the beginning of a deeply cherished and wide-ranging friendship."[8] As soon as he learned that one of Charles's hobbies was painting in watercolors, he retained the American watercolorist Bob Timberlake to give the prince lessons and offered to exhibit his paintings at Knoedler. Hammer's staff, meanwhile, made lists of the philanthropic projects Charles supported. They found that he had shown a special interest in the World Wildlife Fund, particularly its effort to protect whales; the Transglobe Expedition, which had undertaken a mission to circumnavigate the world from pole to pole; and the Mary Rose Trust, which was financing the effort to raise the British ship *Mary Rose,* which sank in 1545. Even though Hammer considered some of these endeavors "odd," he made major contributions to them. He also made it clear to the prince that there was virtually no limit to his generosity—or what he would do for him. On one occasion, he pointed to a window in Buckingham Palace and told Princess Diana that "if [Charles] asked me to jump through that window there, I think I'd jump through the window"[9] (the same metaphoric feat he had earlier stated he would perform for Lenin). Hammer soon found the cause that meant the most to Charles. It was an unconventional educational enterprise called the United World Colleges.

The first United World College was established in Wales in 1962. A two-year preparatory school based on the ideas of Kurt Hahn, the German-born founder of the Outward Bound survival program, it sought to give students from different nations a combination of rigorous physical and academic training. Selection committees were set up in forty different countries, additional campuses were maintained in Singapore and Victoria, Canada, and an international advisory counsel was convened. Prince Charles had become involved in the movement through his great-uncle, the earl of Mountbatten, Britain's last viceroy of India, who as president of the United World Colleges' International Council had tried unsuccessfully to raise money to establish a campus in the United States. When Mountbatten was killed by terrorists in 1979, Charles committed himself to realizing his great-uncle's unfulfilled plan for the school. Hammer, seeing an opportunity to "cement" his friendship with Charles, offered to finance the U.S. campus the prince so dearly wanted.[10] In 1981, Hammer purchased an imposing structure in the tiny town of Montezuma, New Mexico (pop. 200). Known as Montezuma's Castle, it had been developed by the Santa Fe Railroad as a resort hotel a century earlier. The building had an unfortunate history, having been gutted twice by fire and fallen into bankruptcy. It stood on a 110-acre piece of property and most recently had been used as a Jesuit seminary, which closed in 1972. When Hammer took it over, it had been abandoned for nearly a decade and was in severe disrepair. He put his executive assistant, James Pugash, in charge of the project and gave him a deadline of one year in which to have it in shape to operate as a preparatory school for two hundred students. Contractors worked around the clock to convert broken-down buildings into classrooms, offices, and dormitories. Even though the college would not be accredited in the United States, Hammer used his political influence to get the Immigration and Naturalization Service to waive the usual visa requirements for the first batch of foreign students that was to be admitted. In September 1982, Prince Charles flew to New Mexico on Hammer's plane to open the Armand Hammer United World College of the American West.

It took nearly $5 million to realize Prince Charles's "impossible dream," as Hammer called the school. To help subsidize the project, he drew large sums of money from the funds that remained in the Union Bank of Switzerland account. The Libyan concession had now ended, and so had the diversion of the royalty to the UBS, but several million dollars remained in the account. The money was delivered to the college by Hammer's colleague Zade.[11] The balance of the funds came from Hammer's own foundation (which had also been a recipient of money from the UBS account) and from star-studded benefits that Hammer staged for the school, such as the one in Palm Beach in November 1985 at which Prince Charles and Princess Diana appeared as guests of honor.[12] Hammer had done his part: he now expected Prince Charles to show his appreciation by helping him win the Nobel Peace Prize.

THOUGH THE PEACE PRIZE IS AWARDED IN OSLO, THE NOBEL Foundation is based in Stockholm. (Norway and Sweden had been united at the time of Nobel's death.) To survey the scene, Hammer had himself invited to the ceremonies for the science and literature awards, and he arranged an exhibition of the Armand Hammer Collection to coincide with the event. He invited the Swedish royal family and other dignitaries to the opening, and got an impressive turnout. He also contributed substantial amounts of money to the Swedish Academy and retained local public relations specialists to help him find and contact the key players in the selection process for the peace prize. He relentlessly cultivated people who he thought could help him, inviting them to dinner and offering to assist philanthropies they favored. In some cases, he subtly dangled before businessmen the prospect of lucrative deals with Occidental. In other cases, he directly lobbied people connected with the administration of the prize, recounting, for instance, the story of his effort to restore peace to Afghanistan. He concluded one such presentation by saying, "I must tell you in all candor. I have dedicated my life and my fortune to the greatest goal I can imagine—world peace."[13] He also used his secret funds for this campaign. According to his London consultant, he spent some $5 million buying himself awards and honors that he believed would favorably influence his selection.

During this period, Hammer learned of a serious problem: the Nobel Prize had never been awarded to a convicted criminal (with the exception of political dissidents), and Hammer had pleaded guilty to three crimes in 1976. Even though the crimes were misdemeanors and Hammer had served his year on probation, he was told that his record would weigh against him, if not entirely preclude him from consideration for the peace prize.

Hammer felt that he had to expunge these blemishes from his record. In 1977 he had donated $5 million to Columbia University in return for its naming the Health Sciences Center after his father and himself. He now had to clear his own name. "Once convicted, a human being can never be free again," he had observed, ". . . until the world acknowledges his innocence."[14] For Hammer, the task was especially difficult since, unlike his father, he had pleaded guilty.

In 1984, Hammer retained Bruce Kauffman, a former Pennsylvania Supreme Court justice, and a team of top Washington lawyers to apply for a pardon on his behalf from President Reagan. Although almost all presidential pardons are based on a finding of compassion, Hammer insisted that his should be based on a "finding of innocence," making Kauffman's job far more difficult. Hammer also pressed Kauffman to move as fast as possible, explaining that his consideration for the Nobel Prize depended on it. Kauffman filed the application with the Department of Justice on November 6, 1984. In his petition, Kauffman asserted that "the need for rectification is urgent because, among other things, . . . the Nobel Prize will be decided [soon]. It is reliably reported that Dr. Hammer is under consideration for such honor, but will be impeded by this unjust blot on his otherwise unblemished record."[15]

While his application was pending, Hammer made a direct appeal for assistance in the matter to Edwin Meese III, Reagan's newly appointed attorney general. He stressed to Meese the need "to clear my name from the unjust blemish received in the aftermath of the Nixon Administration." In response, Meese promised Hammer that after he had received the pardon attorney's recommendation, he would make his report to the White House. Hammer took Meese's interest as an indication that Reagan would sign his pardon. He made a point of inviting Meese and others in Reagan's inner circle to his gala ninetieth birthday party and he made a large contribution to the Presidential Dinner, which helped fund the Republican Party and other causes backed by the administration.

Hammer's application still had to go through the legal machinery of the Department of Justice, which involved reviews by dozens of investigators, lawyers, and administrators. The FBI began the process on December 1, 1984, as it did with any other convicted criminal applying for a pardon: by checking its central files and other appropriate computer databases to determine whether the applicant had been investigated for any crimes after his probation had ended. The only pertinent information the search turned up was that

Dr. Hammer was the subject of a Corruption of Public Officials investigation initiated in October 1979, following the receipt by the FBI of allegations that Dr. Hammer and his associates entered into a conspiracy to bribe members of the Los Angeles City Council to . . . permit oil drilling off the coast of Pacific Palisades, California.

The allegations were that Hammer had secretly transferred $120,000 to Herbert Itkin, the former FBI informant in his employ, who had then used part of the money to bribe and blackmail public officials. This investigation—the FBI's sixth major investigation of Hammer for bribery since 1938—ended inconclusively in 1980. The FBI reported to the pardon attorney that "the results of the investigation were insufficient to warrant a presentation of testimony and evidence to a Grand Jury."[16]

The balance of the FBI review was largely routine. Agents interviewed Hammer, who told them, when they asked him if he had traveled to other cities since the date of his conviction, that he had traveled "approximately 3 million miles."[17] They interviewed the three character witnesses he had named, including William McGill, a director of Occidental, who told them that students at the Armand Hammer United World College of the American West "view Hammer as a Saint."[18] They also went door-to-door in the exclusive Holmby Hills area in which he lived, asking neighbors whether they had observed Hammer associating with people of questionable character or abusing alcohol or drugs. None had. When the FBI completed its work in January 1985, Hammer's pardon application went to the Justice Department's criminal prosecution division, where it ran into problems.

Attorneys there who had been involved in the original case strongly objected to the president granting Hammer a pardon based on a finding of innocence, since it implied that an innocent person had been coerced into pleading guilty. They believed that this was not the case. Hammer had voluntarily agreed to admit his guilt to misdemeanors in return for the government dropping the more serious felony charges of obstruction of justice, charges that prosecutors believed they could easily substantiate in court. Hammer had avoided prosecution on a felony charge through a plea bargain. By now claiming he was innocent of the misdemeanor charges the government had substituted for the felony charge, he was violating the agreement. Whereas Hammer may have believed that this maneuver was necessary for him to win the Nobel Peace Prize and that he had the political clout to get away with it, the prosecutors refused to sign off on the pardon, and without such approval Meese refused to send it on to the White House—and risk an explosive leak.[19]

Hammer thus did not find his name on President Reagan's list of pardons in 1985. In 1986, he pledged $1 million to the Ronald Reagan Library, which would stand as a monument to Reagan when he left office. This made Hammer the largest single pledger of funds for the project.[20] But he did not receive his pardon in 1986 or in 1987. Despite these disheartening delays, Hammer wrote in 1987, by which time he had increased his commitment to the Reagan Library to $1.3 million, "I hope to be vindicated."[21]

Reagan granted thirty-two pardons at the end of his final term of office, but once again Hammer's name was not on the list. (Hammer subsequently left his pledge to the Reagan Library fund unfulfilled.)[22]

When George Bush took the oath of office on January 20, 1989, Hammer was at the inauguration. Even with the benefit of makeup, he appeared ashen and frail. The week before, he had been hospitalized in Los Angeles and was in considerable pain. But he insisted on attending the inauguration and was accompanied to Washington by Rosamaria Durazo, his close friend and now an anesthesiologist at UCLA. At his side during the inauguration was Howard Baker, Reagan's former chief of staff, who was also close to Bush when he served as vice president. He was now helping Hammer in Washington. After spending most of that week attending inauguration parties, Hammer moved to bolster his credentials within the Republican Party by contributing $110,000 to its National State Election Committee.

Hammer, now ninety-one, realized that he no longer had the time to wait for complete vindication. To get his application through the bureaucracy of the Justice Department and into the White House, Hammer had his lawyers modify the request so that President Bush could base the pardon on compassion rather than a finding of innocence. The prosecutors did not object. On August 14, Bush granted Hammer his pardon.

The Nobel Peace Prize, Hammer's personal Mount Everest, seemed finally within striking distance. But somewhere along the long path toward this goal, Prince Charles's enthusiasm for Hammer had cooled, and despite all of Hammer's efforts, Charles declined to support his nomination. Nevertheless, Hammer had found another impressive nominator, Prime Minister Menachem Begin of Israel, who himself had won the Nobel Peace Prize in 1978 and who was allowed to nominate others for the award.

That Hammer now turned to Begin for help was not without irony. Hammer had shunned Israel during most of his life, denying even that he was Jewish until he was past seventy. He made his first public trip to Israel only in September 1984. He had feared that any association with Israel might incur Gadhafi's "wrath," and up until then he had been dependent on Gadhafi for oil. But in 1984, Begin was suffering from a life-threatening urologic blockage that required surgery, to which he was resistant. Hammer flew over Dr. Willard Goodwin, a top American urologist, who persuaded the prime minister to have the necessary operation. He also established his credentials in Israel, pledging "to develop at least one hundred million dollars in business ventures to boost the Israeli economy."[23] The first project he proposed, called Israel Drilling Partners, involved finding oil deep under the Negev. "If we can find oil in Israel," he said, ". . . we can transform Israel into a self-sufficient state."[24] The second project was his Elders of Zion aircraft deal, which if it succeeded, promised to make Israel a major international aircraft manufacturer.

Begin, who had enthusiastically endorsed both these projects, was willing to be Hammer's sponsor for the peace prize. In 1988, he wrote a letter to the selection committee nominating Hammer. Meanwhile, Hammer had Occidental's Washington office contact other world leaders and send them selected material about his life with which they might support his nomination. As it turned out, the 1989 Nobel Peace Prize was awarded to the Dalai Lama in recognition of his work toward ending China's domination of Tibet. Hammer intensified his efforts, hoping he might be chosen for the 1990 prize.

His campaign ended abruptly on October 12, 1990. On that day, X rays revealed that cancer was rapidly spreading through Hammer's bones.

EPILOGUE

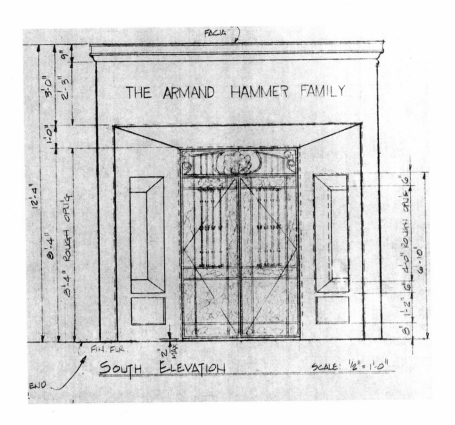

THE ARMAND HAMMER FAMILY

SOUTH ELEVATION

SCALE: 1/2" = 1'-0"

The architect's plans for the entrance to Hammer's mausoleum in Los Angeles.

POSTMORTEM

ARMAND HAMMER DIED ON DECEMBER 10, 1990. THE NEXT NIGHT, some five hundred people in formal attire gathered in the grand ballroom of the Beverly Hilton for what now was a posthumous bar mitzvah. Months earlier, they had been invited to honor Hammer for his "years of devotion to the Jewish renaissance in Israel, the Soviet Union and the United States." His bar mitzvah, at the age of ninety-two, was to have symbolized, according to the invitation, "the miracle of Jewish renewal." Though the guest of honor would now be missing, the event would take place on schedule in dramatic affirmation of the maxim "The show must go on." The audience included the former White House chief of staff Howard Baker, who had helped Hammer get his presidential pardon; Tom Bradley, the mayor of Los Angeles; former governor Edmund Brown; Governor John Deukmejian; Governor-elect Pete Wilson; Senator Alan Cranston; Robert Maxwell, a partner in the Elders of Zion deal; and stars from the entertainment world such as John Denver, Merv Griffin, Shelley Winters, and Ted Turner.

The two-hour-long ceremony was hosted by the actor Elliott Gould, who stood in front of a giant blowup of Armand Hammer at the age of thirteen, the traditional bar mitzvah age. Gould introduced each of Hammer's three special guests: Ida Nudel, Alex Goldfarb, and Nicholas Daniloff. Hammer had intervened with the Soviet government in a very public way to help with their particular problems in Russia during the period in which he was lobbying for the Nobel Prize. Each paid a tribute to Hammer. Finally, Michael Hammer, standing in for his grandfather, received a seven-foot-long fountain pen. It was a joke on the traditional bar mitzvah gift.

At four o'clock the next day, Julian Hammer and his two children, Michael, who was now thirty-five, and Casey, now thirty, arrived at the law offices of Arthur Groman. Groman, who had been Hammer's lawyer for more than three decades, read the will. When he finished fifteen minutes later, Julian sat in shocked disbelief. His father had not kept any of the promises he had made to him shortly before he died. He had made no provision in his will to pay off Julian's mortgage and other debts. He had not provided him an employment contract with Occidental. He had not provided a multimillion-dollar inheritance. Instead, he had left him, his only son, $250,000, which was not even enough to pay off the mortgage.[1] Casey and Michael fared no better.

It turned out that there was no great Hammer fortune. Far from being the billionaire the obituaries portrayed, Hammer had an estate worth about $40 million. Against this sum, the estate had potential liabilities that included personal debts, legal bills, estate taxes, and commitments of millions of dollars to various charities. There was also the pending $440-million lawsuit filed by Frances's estate, which could wipe out any money that remained.

The funeral service took place at 11:00 A.M. in a small chapel at Westwood Memorial Park on December 13. Hammer had chosen this cemetery because it was only a few hundred yards from Occidental, and he had wanted to be able to see his mausoleum from his office window. The event was an anticlimax to the jubilant bar mitzvah two days earlier. And indeed, it was more notable for who did not show up to pay their last respects than for who did.

Hammer's only son did not come. Julian was still feeling the effect of his father's betrayal. Julian's entire life had revolved around being the son of Armand Hammer, and in the end he was barely recognized as that. Who would he be now? He stayed at home with his wife, Jean.

Nor were the families of Hammer's brothers, Harry and Victor, represented. After Harry died in 1970, Armand had got into an argument with the family of his deceased wife, Bette Barber, over the Barber family's homestead in Vicksburg, Mississippi. It had been in the family for six generations, and they pleaded with Hammer, who was the executor of Harry's estate, to return it to them. But Hammer sold it to a stranger for $22,000, ending his relationship with the family.[2]

Hammer had got involved in an even more vicious fight with his brother Victor's family after Victor's death in 1985. Victor had left an estate of some $700,000, of which Hammer was executor. Instead of disbursing the money to Victor's invalid wife, Ireene, who was in a nursing home; his Soviet son, Armasha; and his adopted daughter, Nancy Wicker, Hammer himself filed a claim of $667,000 against the estate, saying he had lent Victor the money to pay his medical expenses. Since Hammer's claim would have virtually wiped out the family's inheritance, Nancy not only resisted Hammer's orders to sell the family house in Stamford, Connecticut, but threatened to make the ugly dispute public. In a preemptive strike, Hammer cut off the monthly payments to the nursing home taking care of Ireene and confronted Nancy with the possibility that her mother would be rendered destitute. As the dispute leaked to the press, Hammer abruptly changed his tactics and gave up most of his claim against Victor's estate in return for Nancy's agreeing not to say derogatory things about him in public.[3]

Victor's son, Armasha Hammer, had his own reasons for not attending the funeral. Armand Hammer had given him his name but little else of value. He blamed Hammer, not his father, for his abandonment in Russia.[4] When they were reunited, Armand Hammer treated him as if he were nothing more than "just an old stupid mistake," as Armasha wrote.[5] Hammer had almost never inquired about his wife or children, and in recent years he had prohibited him from going to the offices of Occidental in Moscow. Why should he go to his uncle's funeral?

Among those attending the service, Ray Irani, in a somber dark suit and tinted glasses, stood with the other twelve directors of Occidental in the front row of the chapel. He was Hammer's successor. When the directors returned from the funeral that afternoon, they would officially elect him chairman, president, and chief executive officer. His first order of business would be to disassociate Occidental Petroleum from the image of Armand Hammer. He would begin by destroying the cult of personality. He would have the portraits and statues of

Hammer removed from Occidental's headquarters. He would scrap the planned biography of Hammer on which Occidental had already spent $200,000. He would shut down Armand Hammer Productions, the film unit dedicated to Hammer's image building.[6] He would liquidate Occidental's interest in the company that manufactured Arm & Hammer baking soda, an investment that Hammer had made based solely on the coincidence of his name and the brand name. He would terminate the Arabian horse-breeding business, which had been little more than a personal indulgence of Hammer's. He would revise the Occidental annual report so that it contained no photographs or obituaries of Hammer and no homages to him. The only reference would appear in small print: "In Memoriam, Dr. Armand Hammer, 1898–1990."[7]

Irani would also eliminate most of the projects that Hammer had used to advance his personal agenda of opening a "path" to the Communist world. The giant coal mine in China would be abandoned. The petrochemical ventures in Eastern Europe would be sold or closed. The multibillion-dollar barter deals with the Soviet Union would be phased out. In his reassessment of them, Irani would find that Occidental had sunk into these projects vast sums of money that could never be recovered. While Hammer had used accounting license to conceal the magnitude of the losses, Irani, in closing them down, would have to recognize the real losses of the Hammer projects—a staggering $2.5 billion.[8]

At the funeral, Hilary Gibson stood alone in the row immediately behind Irani and the board of directors, already feeling a sense of isolation. She had not fared well in the corporate machinations that had preceded Hammer's death. She had been Hammer's art consultant, friend, and mistress, and he had promised her lifetime security. She had worked night and day for a year getting the Armand Hammer Museum ready for its grand opening. Hammer had been carried in on a wheelchair, a fading shadow of his former self. It was the last time she saw Hammer alive. Although most of Occidental's executives did not recognize her with her new wig, voice, and wardrobe, Irani made it clear to her that he was fully aware of both her identity and her relationship with Hammer, telling her that "information is my business."

During these final months, she had become aware that the museum was causing Occidental problems. Some of Occidental's largest institutional investors had filed a suit against the company for using $96 million in corporate funds for the project. Representatives for California's public employees' pension fund argued that "what we have here is a so-called charity whose purpose it is to memorialize Armand Hammer."[9] These suits had become a monumental embarrassment to Irani and other members of the board, and now that Hammer was dead, they would move quickly to settle them. Gibson knew that Irani had begun maneuvering to cut Occidental's connection with the museum and turn its management over to an outside party. As she watched Irani at the funeral, she could see "the handwriting on the wall." She had already lost her identity, and next she would lose her job at the museum and be put through "total hell."[10] The Armand Hammer Museum would be turned over to UCLA to manage for ninety-nine years.[11] UCLA would envision a mission for the museum that was very different from the one Hammer had wanted. It would move to convert the facility from a repository for Hammer's most prized collections to a multidisciplinary culture center where university students and local residents could attend lectures, film festivals, poetry readings, and exhibitions of contemporary paintings.[12] The huge portrait of Hammer would be taken down.[13] The Codex Hammer, the Leonardo da Vinci notebook that Hammer had renamed after himself and had made the centerpiece of his museum, would be sold at auction for $32 million. Its new owner, William Gates, the founder of Microsoft Corporation, would erase Hammer's name from its title, calling it, as it had been called before Hammer had acquired it, the Leicester Codex. The museum would still have Hammer's name on the exterior—its contract with Occidental specified that the name Armand Hammer must appear on the building in three-foot-high letters in perpetuity—but it was not the personal memorial he had so desperately wanted.

Michael Hammer, now very much in charge, presided over the brief ceremony at the chapel, but he would not follow in his grandfather's footsteps at Occidental. That year, he would resign his position as vice president and corporate secretary. He would also agree that when his term on the board expired, he would not seek reelection. In return for signing a confidentiality agreement, he would be paid a severance bonus of $1.5 million.[14]

Michael Hammer would remain president of the Armand Hammer Foundation. The endowment established by his grandfather included an extraordinary "golden casket" arrangement, under which Occidental was committed to pay Hammer's salary of $1.8 million a year to the foundation for ten years after his death. But Michael Hammer would not be able to devote his full time to the foundation's charitable work. Also the executor of his grandfather's will, he would soon be caught up in dealing with lawsuits against the estate that proliferated at an incredible rate. Within a year, more than one hundred charities, museums, family members, and other individuals would make claims. These reflected the bitter legacy of Armand Hammer's life. The list of claimants included the Ronald Reagan Presidential Foundation, which asserted that Hammer had failed to deliver $640,000 he had pledged in 1986, 1987, and 1988 (the years he was trying to win a presidential pardon); the Danielle Mitterrand Foundation, which asserted that Hammer still owed $250,000 in return for the attendance of the wife of the French president at the dinner celebrating the opening of his museum; the Salk Institute, which asserted that Hammer owed it $1,447,200 for unfulfilled pledges he had made as part of his war on cancer; Jean Stone, who said Hammer owed her $90,000 for her work on his unfinished autobiography; and the National Symphony Orchestra, which asserted that Hammer still owed it $250,000 for playing "Happy Birthday" to him at his ninetieth birthday party.[15]

Julian Hammer would never fully recover from his father's death and what he saw as the loss of his own identity. He would never speak to his son Michael again. He would devote a large part of the next five years to investigating the dispersal of his father's funds and the circumstances surrounding his death. He would die in March 1996. Casey Hammer would also sever relations with her brother, and then, after her father's death, she would initiate a legal search for funds that she believed her grandfather had hidden overseas.[16]

Hoping to preserve some of the estate, Michael Hammer would cede pieces of what Hammer had intended to be his posterity. He would agree, for example, to allow the Metropolitan Museum of Art to permanently remove Hammer's name from the prestigious gallery on its main floor—a dedication that Hammer had arranged for himself in exchange for pledging $2 million to the museum—if the museum forgave $1 million still outstanding on the pledge.[17]

The battle between the Frances Hammer and Armand Hammer estates would end in 1994. After five years of litigation, the court dismissed the suit filed by the estate of Frances Hammer. But there was an appeal, and in the ongoing struggle, legal expenses would consume a substantial part of both estates.

There was a raven-haired woman at the funeral service in Los Angeles whom no one recognized. She wore black, but she had no tears for Hammer. She was his thirty-four-year-old daughter, Victoria, whom he had kept a secret from the rest of his family. In his will, referring to her only as "a person known as Victoria Varella," he had specifically disinherited her. This was the final insult as far as she was concerned. He had forced her mother to enter a fake marriage and live in a foreign country, and he had exerted control over her by doling out money through anonymous lawyers on the condition that she follow his rules. Even though he rarely saw her, he intervened in her life like some remote god, and now it turned out that the promises he had made to take care of her meant nothing. She had come to the funeral not out of respect for him but to avenge the wrong he had done her. She would sue his estate. Her mother, Bettye Murphy, who was standing at her side, would also sue.[18]

Rosamaria Durazo was standing in the background. Many there believed she was Hammer's doctor, which was the way Hammer had often introduced her. She had been closer to him during that past year than anyone else, and she had met some of the most powerful men in the world while traveling with him. She would go back to her own life.

Casey Hammer was in tears. She had been distraught to find that the casket was closed. She had wanted to see her grandfather and place a photograph of herself in his jacket pocket after the service. She asked that the casket be opened, but her brother, Michael, refused her request.[19]

The pallbearers were Hammer's chauffeur, male nurse, and other retainers. They carried the sealed casket past the board of directors and other mourners, who then filed away. Michael and Casey Hammer accompanied the casket to the Armand Hammer family mausoleum. The marble vault contained four other caskets: those holding the remains of Julius Hammer, Rose Hammer, Victor Hammer, and Harry Hammer. Michael and Casey stood by as the casket of Armand Hammer was placed inside the vault, and they watched as the doors were sealed shut.

SOURCE NOTES

The surveillance of the Hammer family, first by the antisubversive unit of the New York City Police Department, the "Red Squad," and then by the U.S. Army and government agencies, dates back to the first decade of the twentieth century. By the time Armand Hammer was twenty-five, files were being kept on him by no fewer than five American and British agencies. Although he was probably not aware of this activity in the parallel universes of intelligence, it continued almost up until his death, when he was investigated by the FBI after he had requested a presidential pardon for campaign-contribution violations. Government agents gleaned many details that helped me fill in the jigsaw puzzle of his life. Soviet intelligence was also keeping track of Hammer and his family, and Soviet records furnished another crucial window on Hammer's early activities. From his later life, legal proceedings, including bankruptcy filings, divorce suits, probation reports, contract disputes, Securities and Exchange Commission (SEC) inquiries, stockholder class-action suits, criminal trials, and pardon pleas, provided an almost continuous paper trail. The documents I accumulated from these sources are deposited in my archives in the Special Collections section of the Boston University Library.

Hammer was not publicity shy. He gave hundreds of interviews about his achievements, wrote and rewrote his autobiography, and even commissioned a screenplay about his life. He also allowed a number of reporters, including me, to travel with him for weeks at a time. Much of the material he provided in this manner was self-serving. I use quotations from such sources to show Hammer's perception—and projection—of himself. His 1987 autobiography, written with Neil Lyndon, strongly reflects the way he wanted to be viewed by history—and as such is an important part of his biography. In terms of its factual content, however, it must be approached with caution. Lyndon himself is a first-rate and talented journalist, but Hammer controlled the final product. And while Lyndon made diligent efforts to verify Hammer's stories, many of them, especially those concerning his stays in the Soviet Union, were not checkable.

Complete references to published sources cited in the following notes can be found in the Bibliography.

PROLOGUE: THE DEATH MARCH

The chronology of Hammer's last year is derived primarily from the daily appointment schedules prepared by his staff at Occidental Petroleum. These records often include an hourly itinerary for Hammer as well as a list of the people he was scheduled to meet, his hotel accommodations and travel plans, and the times of massages and haircuts. In addition, I had access to the diary kept by his driver and night nurse, Nick Butcher, which provides confirmation of the schedule. A number of Hammer's relatives, including his granddaughter, Casey Hammer, also kept diaries during this period. I was able to fill in gaps by interviewing Butcher; Hammer's son, Julian; Casey Hammer; Hammer's assistant, Catherine Kosak; and the collaborators on his writing projects, Jean Stone and Neil Lyndon. I also looked at some of the notes that Hammer himself took during this period on yellow legal pads. They provide a running, if sometimes abbreviated, account of his activities.

The progress of Hammer's illness comes mainly from his medical record at the University of California Medical Center in Los Angeles, including his nurses' reports and laboratory reports (hereinafter cited as UCLA Medical Records).

Another major source was the litigation surrounding Hammer's death. Hammer's maneuvers concerning his estate are reflected in the various revisions of the codicils and provisions of both his will (Superior Court, Los Angeles, California, Case BP004635 [1995]) and the Armand Hammer Living Trust (author's archives). In addition, an enormous amount of material emerged in the suit filed by his wife's heir, Joan Weiss, against him (*Estate of Frances Hammer v. Armand Hammer,* Superior Court, Los Angeles, California, Case B005480, File 3550; hereinafter

called the Weiss lawsuit). Joan Weiss and Hammer's lawyer, Jay Goldberg, provided me with perspectives on this suit.

The FBI's extensive dossier on Hammer's activities (Armand Hammer
File 61-280) includes reports dating back to 1921. I obtained this file
under the Freedom of Information Act (FOIA).

The description of the Elders of Zion deal was provided by Samuel
Pisar, a Paris-based lawyer who represented Hammer in a number of his
international negotiations. I also obtained working documents from
Hammer's staff pertaining to the scheme.

Hilary Gibson, Hammer's art consultant, provided me with an extensive file concerning the development of the Armand Hammer Museum,
and she shared her observations on Hammer's activities in art and philanthropy.

The description of Hammer's relationship with Bettye Murphy is
based on my interviews with Murphy, who also gave me a chronological
record of her contacts with Hammer.

1. The description of the events at the Kluge party comes from Nick
   Butcher and interviews with other guests, including Alfred Taubman.
2. Kosak interview.
3. Pisar interview.
4. Report on Armand Hammer, 1981, FBI File.
5. Kosak interview.
6. UCLA Medical Records on Frances Hammer.
7. Goldberg interview.
8. Deposition by Hilary Gibson, Superior Court, Los Angeles, California, Case BP004635 (1990).
9. Gibson interview.
10. *Hilary Gibson v. Musick, Peeler and Garrett,* Superior Court, Los
    Angeles, California, Case BC118207, p. 5.
11. Ibid.
12. Julian Hammer interview; Kosak interview.
13. Casey Hammer, diary entry, October 17, 1990.
14. Kosak interview.
15. Gibson interview.
16. Julian Hammer interview.
17. Murphy interview.
18. Hammer, *Quest of the Romanoff Treasure,* p. 127.
19. Volkogonov, *Lenin,* p. 429.
20. Hammer, *Quest of the Romanoff Treasure,* p. 131.
21. Volkogonov, *Lenin,* p. 437.

22. Considine, *Remarkable Life,* p. 144 (photo section). Hammer also made the claim about President Hoover in a speech he prepared for the Brussels Roundtable on April 21, 1981 (State Department Files, released under FOIA).
23. Lyndon interview.
24. Goldberg interview.
25. Butcher interview.
26. Julian Hammer interview.

CHAPTER ONE: THE MATRIX

Julius Hammer came under government surveillance as early as 1905 because of his radical politics. His role in helping to organize the Russian Soviet Government Bureau, Lenin's apparatus in New York, resulted in files being kept on him by the Bureau of Investigation, the precursor of the FBI (National Archives, Record Group 59, Subject 2272); the Office of Counselor at the Department of State, a precursor of the CIA, which coordinated and disseminated foreign intelligence in the 1920s and 1930s (National Archives, Record Group 59); the Military Intelligence Division of the War Department (National Archives, Record Group 165); the FBI (file on Julius Hammer, released under FOIA); and British intelligence. In addition to records from these sources, I obtained Julius Hammer's passport file from the State Department under FOIA. A file on Julius Hammer's parole from Sing Sing State Prison in 1923 is in the New York State Archives, Albany.

A number of his colleagues in the socialist movement described Julius Hammer's activities in their memoirs—most notably, Benjamin Gitlow (*I Confess*) and Bertram D. Wolfe (*A Life in Two Centuries*). The description of Daniel De Leon comes from L. Glen Seretan's *Daniel De Leon.* The material on Ludwig Martens comes from the Justice Department's deportation file on Martens, released under FOIA. The description of Hammer's childhood comes mainly from interviews conducted with Armand and Victor Hammer in 1981 and from Hammer's 1987 autobiography, *Hammer,* written with Neil Lyndon.

1. Receiving blotter, Sing Sing State Prison, Ossining, New York, 1920, entry 71516.
2. Howe, *World of Our Fathers,* p. 291.
3. Wolfe, *A Life in Two Centuries,* pp. 167–168.
4. Hammer with Lyndon, *Hammer,* p. 52.
5. Ibid., p. 55.

6. Ibid., p. 58.

7. Ibid., p. 60.

8. Socialist Labor Party Papers, 1916, State Historic Society, Madison, Wisconsin.

9. Hammer with Lyndon, *Hammer,* p. 54.

10. Columbia University yearbook, 1919.

11. Wolfe, *A Life in Two Centuries,* pp. 167, 168.

12. Gillette, "American-Soviet Trade."

13. Gitlow, *I Confess,* p. 26.

14. Ibid., p. 59.

15. Surveillance report on Julius Hammer, June 2, 1921, Bureau of Investigation files, 1909–1921 (Microfilm 202600-795).

16. Parole file on Julius Hammer.

CHAPTER TWO: THE JOURNEY EAST

The primary source on the activities of Armand Hammer and his family in the Soviet Union in the 1920s is the three-thousand-page archive I obtained from the Commissariat of Foreign Trade (hereinafter referred to as the Soviet Archive). It includes documents from other agencies of the Soviet government, including the National Bank of the Soviet Republic and the Soviet intelligence service. I also received a number of valuable documents, including the Reinstein Report to Lenin, from the President Archives in the Kremlin (hereinafter, the President Archives). The principal source for the description of Hammer's contacts with Communist agents outside the Soviet Union is the Comintern Archives, which include the U.S. Communist Party material stored in Moscow (hereinafter called the Comintern Records). Professor Harvey Klehr, who researched these records, provided me with the material relevant to Hammer.

Details about Hammer's arrangements for his trips to Russia come mainly from passport applications, which in 1921 required extensive information and supporting affidavits. I received Hammer's passport applications—as well as those of his family—under the FOIA. Joseph Mishell provided me with a file of his father Boris's letters and clippings that cast light on this transitional period in Russia. The description of Hammer's trip to the Urals comes from Abraham A. Heller's account in *The Industrial Revival in Soviet Russia.* Walter Duranty, *The New York Times*'s correspondent in the Soviet Union in the 1920s who assisted Hammer with his 1932 memoir, described the general atmosphere in Moscow in *I Write As I Please.*

Hammer later discussed with Bettye Murphy his role in performing the illegal abortion. The description of Sing Sing is taken from *I Confess* by Benjamin Gitlow, an associate of Julius Hammer's who was in Sing Sing with him. Hammer's reaction to his brief detention in Britain comes from his own account of the event in his 1932 autobiography, *The Quest of the Romanoff Treasure.*

The assessment of American trade relations with the Soviet Union comes from Philip S. Gillette's unpublished Harvard Ph.D. dissertation, "The Political Origins of American-Soviet Trade, 1917–1924," as well as from discussions with Professor Gillette.

Biographical information about Comintern leaders is taken from the 1986 edition of Branko Lazitch's *Biographical Dictionary of the Comintern;* Harvey Klehr, John Earl Haynes, and Fridrikh Igorevich Firsov's *The Secret World of American Communism;* and Anthony Cave Brown and Charles B. MacDonald's earlier analysis, *On a Field of Red.* Alexander Mikhailovich Orlov, a defector from Soviet intelligence, provided a picture of the way in which trading organizations were used by Soviet intelligence between 1921 and 1929. His account was rendered by John Costello and Oleg Tsarev, a former KGB officer, in *Deadly Illusions.*

The Russian intelligence service underwent numerous name changes and reorganizations. The Cheka, as the All Russian Extraordinary Commission for Combating Counterrevolution and Sabotage was called, created in December 1917, was replaced by the GPU (State Political Directory) in February 1922, which the following year was renamed the OGPU or Unified State Political Directory. In 1934, it was renamed the GUGB (Chief Directorate for State Security) and became part of the NKVD (People's Commissariat for Internal Affairs). In 1941, it was renamed the NKGB (People's Commissariat for State Security); in 1946, the MGB (Ministry for State Security). In 1947, its foreign activities were assigned to the KI (Committee of Information), and in March 1954 the remaining elements of the MGB and KI were merged into the KGB (Committee on State Security). In 1920, the Soviet general staff also established a foreign intelligence service, the GRU (Chief Intelligence Directorate), whose intelligence work paralleled that of the civilian intelligence service. To avoid unnecessary confusion, I use the umbrella term *Soviet intelligence* to cover the activities of these different agencies.

In reconstructing Lenin's activities, I used Dmitri Volkogonov's *Lenin*—which is based on Volkogonov's access to previously sealed Kremlin files—as well as Mikhail Heller and Aleksandr M. Nekrich's more general Soviet history, *Utopia in Power.* The quotations from Lenin all come from volume 45 of his *Collected Works.*

Finally, Hammer later dictated a number of his recollections about this period on tapes (hereinafter called "Hammer tapes").

1. Murphy interview.
2. Wixen, "Mogul Who Refuses to Retire," pp. 60–62.
3. Victor Hammer interview.
4. Hammer, *Quest of the Romanoff Treasure,* pp. 4–5.
5. The mole was Jacob Nosovitsky. For a fuller account of the development of this "special relationship," see Costello, *Mask of Treachery.*
6. Joseph Mishell interview.
7. Duranty, *I Write As I Please,* p. 110.
8. Hammer, *Quest of the Romanoff Treasure,* pp. 32–34.
9. Heller, *Industrial Revival in Soviet Russia,* p. 51.
10. L.C.K. Martens, Biographical Memoir, 1958, no. 5, Istoricheskii Archive, Moscow.
11. Quoted in Volkogonov, *Lenin,* pp. 64, 110, 119.
12. Quoted in Cave Brown and MacDonald, *On a Field of Red,* p. 18.
13. Heller and Nekrich, *Utopia in Power,* p. 128.
14. Liberman, *Building Lenin's Russia,* p. 117.
15. Gershman, "Selling Them the Rope," p. 35.
16. Reinstein Report, p. 18, President Archives; Lenin, *Collected Works,* vol. 45, p. 337.
17. Lenin, *Collected Works,* vol. 45, p. 338.
18. Ibid., p. 340.
19. Ibid., p. 347.
20. Hammer, *Quest of the Romanoff Treasure,* pp. 60–64.
21. Hammer Tapes, April 11, 1980, side 1.
22. Reinstein Report, p. 3, President Archive.
23. Reinstein Report, p. 12, President Archive.
24. Lenin, *Collected Works,* vol. 45, p. 368.

CHAPTER THREE: LENIN'S PATH

J. Edgar Hoover's investigation of Armand Hammer is reconstructed from reports in Hammer's FBI file and from the records of the Bureau of Investigation and the State Department stored in the National Archives in Record Groups 59, 84, and 800. The Starr and Bannerman Reports are also in Record Group 800, vol. 11–332 (November 29 and December 29, 1921).

The account of contacts that Armand and Julius Hammer had with Henry Ford is based in part on letters, cables, and other documents pro-

vided by the Ford Archives and Library at the Henry Ford Museum in
Dearborn, Michigan. An overview of Ford's strategy is drawn from
Allan Nevins and Frank Ernest Hill, *Ford;* Peter Collier and David
Horowitz, *The Fords;* and Mira Wilkins and Frank E. Hill, *American
Business Abroad.* Seth Schapiro provided information about the role of
his father, Jacob Schapiro, in the Ford deals.

The description of the secret Soviet-German alliance comes from John
Wheeler-Bennett's *The Nemesis of Power* and from Gerald Freund's *Unholy Alliance.*

1. *New York Times,* December 18, 1921; *New York World,* December
   17, 1921; also, Seth Schapiro interview.
2. Quoted in *Soviet Life,* April 1985, p. 7.
3. Telegram from Armand Hammer, January 10, 1922, Soviet
   Archives.
4. Ibid.
5. Lenin, *Collected Works,* vol. 45, p. 321.
6. Williams, *Russian Art and American Money,* p. 213.
7. Dubrowsky confirmed this assessment when he defected to the FBI.
   Dubrowsky testimony, September 23, 1939, U.S. House of Representatives, Hearings before the Special Committee on Un-American
   Activities, 75th Congress, "Investigation of Un-American Propaganda Activities in the U.S., 1938–1943," vol. 8, p. 5207; also, U.S.
   Embassy, London, file on Julius Hammer, October 21, 1926, State
   Department records, Group 84, National Archives, Record Group
   800B.
8. Wilkins and Hill, *American Business Abroad,* pp. 208–212.
9. Seth Schapiro interview.
10. Hammer with Lyndon, *Hammer,* p. 137.
11. U.S. Embassy, London, file on Julius Hammer, November 9, 1926.
    State Department records, Group 84, National Archives, Record
    Group 800B.
12. Gitlow, *I Confess,* p. 388.
13. Wheeler-Bennett, *The Nemesis of Power,* pp. 96–103, 128.
14. Letter from Reinstein, January 1922, Soviet Archive.
15. Memorandum from Armand Hammer to People's Commissariat for
    Military Affairs, April 11, 1922, Soviet Archive.
16. Ibid.
17. Lenin, *Collected Works,* vol. 45, p. 523.
18. Ibid., pp. 542–544.
19. Reinstein Report, pp. 13–17, President Archives.

20. Lenin, *Collected Works,* vol. 45, p. 559.

21. *New York Times,* June 14, 1922.

22. Joseph Mishell interview.

23. OGPU Report, 1923, Soviet Archive.

24. Hammer, *The Quest of the Romanoff Treasure,* pp. 113–117.

25. Ibid., pp. 46, 112–113.

26. Joseph Mishell interview; Victor Hammer interview.

27. Parole file on Julius Hammer, including letters from Victor Hammer and Boris Mishell to Julius Hammer.

CHAPTER FOUR: THE PRODIGAL FATHER'S RETURN

I interviewed a number of people who lived with or knew Hammer during this period: Luba Elianoff, a family friend who tutored Hammer in Russian; Joseph Mishell, whose father was a close associate of Hammer's; Isaac Don Levine, a journalist; Jay Lovestone, a political associate of Julius Hammer's; and Victor Hammer. A fragmentary picture of Hammer's lavish style also emerges in the memoirs of the journalist Eugene Lyons, *Assignment in Utopia.* Julius Hammer provided information on his son's Russian activities in his application for early parole. The main sources for Armand Hammer's business activities are the Soviet Archive and Comintern Records, cited in Chapter Two.

1. Application for parole, in parole file on Julius Hammer.

2. Letter of April 3, 1923, ibid.

3. Letter from Julius Hammer to George Carlson, June 20, 1924, Soviet Archive.

4. Lyons, *Assignment in Utopia,* p. 297.

5. Elianoff interview.

6. Mel Gussow, unpublished article on Al Hirschfeld written for *The New Yorker,* June 1992.

7. Lovestone interview.

8. Reinstein Report, President Archives.

9. Letter 38, from Boris N. Stomonyakov to Moisey Ilych Frumkin, December 22, 1922, Soviet Archive.

10. Supplement to the Report on the Asbestos Concession, signed by Julius Hammer, August 4, 1923, Soviet Archive.

11. Letter 1148, from Julius Hammer to Ludwig Martens, May 10, 1923, Soviet Archive.

12. Duranty, "Soviet Concession to American Firm."

13. Allied American Contract, 1923, Soviet Archive.

14. Klehr, Haynes, and Firsov, *The Secret World of American Communism,* p. 14.

15. Costello and Tsarev, *Deadly Illusions,* pp. 30–32.

16. Letter 38, from Stomonyakov to Frumkin, December 22, 1922, pp. 8–9, Soviet Archive.

17. A. S. Rosh Report, October 5, 1925, Soviet Archive.

18. Letter 314595, from Lev Mironov, October 7, 1925, Soviet Archive.

19. Letter 1102, from Julius Hammer to Frumkin, November 28, 1925, Soviet Archive.

20. Letter 38, from Stomonyakov to Frumkin, December 22, 1922, pp. 8–9, Soviet Archive.

21. Letter 1020, from Julius Hammer, October 3, 1925, Soviet Archive.

22. Letter from Leon Trotsky to Frumkin, August 21, 1925, Soviet Archive.

23. See O'Toole, *Honorable Treachery,* p. 323.

CHAPTER FIVE: THE LAUNDERER

Raymond Rocca, the research chief of the CIA's counterintelligence staff, provided me with insights into the Moness case. The State Department's B (for Bolshevik) files in the National Archives which contain reports from U.S. embassies on Soviet intelligence activities, especially Record Group 800B, vol. 16 (U.S. Embassy, London), include foreign-intelligence reports on Moness.

The State Department assessment of the Harju Bank deal comes from material in the National Archives (Record Group 2114), especially reports from F.W.B. Coleman in the U.S. legation in Riga in May 1924 (hereinafter, the Coleman Report). The archives also have translations of stories in local newspapers, such as *Revala Bote* (May 5, 1924) and *Aba Maa* (April 24, 1924), that depict the public atmosphere.

1. Hilary Gibson interview.

2. Bettye Murphy interview.

3. Letter from Julius Hammer to Armand Hammer, December 4, 1925, Comintern Records.

4. Klehr, Haynes, and Firsov, *The Secret World of American Communism,* p. 37.

5. Letter 313779, from Genrikh Yagoda to Moisey Ilych Frumkin, September 21, 1925, Soviet Archive.

6. Letter from Charles Ruthenberg to Piatnijitsky, June 8, 1925, Comintern Records.

7. Ruthenberg Text, July 11, 1925, Comintern Records.

8. Ibid., September 8, 1926, Comintern Records.

9. Ibid., November 15, 1925, Comintern Records.

10. Letter 313779, from Yagoda to Frumkin, September 21, 1925, Soviet Archive.

11. Summary of Alamerico Import Deals, August 17, 1925, p. 2, Soviet Archive.

12. Coleman Report, May 24, 1924.

13. Letter 1243, from Armand and Julius Hammer, March 20, 1926, Soviet Archive.

14. Poroshin Report, June 24, 1925, Soviet Archive.

CHAPTER SIX: THE PENCIL MAKER

The information concerning Hammer's manufacturing activities and financial problems comes from the previously cited Soviet Archive. The description of the Arcos raid, which linked Moness to Hammer, and of the continuing investigation of the Hammer family comes from the assessment of the raid declassified by the British government and from Record Group 800B, vol. 16 (U.S. Embassy, London), in the National Archives. I also obtained, under FOIA, the complete FBI file on Victor Hammer, which helped me reconstruct Armand's activities in Russia.

1. Hammer, *The Quest of the Romanoff Treasure,* p. 1.

2. Luba Elianoff interview.

3. Hammer with Lyndon, *Hammer,* p. 186.

4. Bettye Murphy interview.

5. Elianoff interview.

6. Ibid.

7. Victor Hammer interview.

8. Elianoff interview.

9. Paper 71184227, Attachment 2, November 19, 1929, Soviet Archive.

10. *New York Times,* November 22, 1927.

11. Paper 71184227, November 19, 1929, Soviet Archive.

12. Passport-application file on Armand Hammer.

13. Hammer, *The Quest of the Romanoff Treasure,* p. 19; Victor Hammer interview.

14. Memorandum from Z. Angoritia (Zigmas Aleksa) to the Secretariat, December 6, 1930, p. 2, Comintern Records.

15. Report on Armand File, April 1924, FBI File 61-280.

16. Note 850, from Power to Brist, May 26, 1923, passport-application file on Armand Hammer.

17. Bessedovsky, "How Moscow Finances the Communist Movement."

18. File on Julius Hammer, Document 266, April 12, 1940, State Department records, National Archives, Record Group 800B.

19. FBI file on Victor Hammer, 1940.

CHAPTER SEVEN: REQUISITE FOR A LEGEND

The description of the Soviet art business in the late 1920s is derived from Robert C. Williams's seminal book on the subject, *Russian Art and American Money.* The description of Hammer's maneuvers in this business comes from the Soviet Archive.

Julian Hammer provided me with his recollections of his family's residence in Paris and with photographs. Luba Elianoff, who visited Julius Hammer in a German prison and Armand Hammer in Paris, described the second imprisonment of Julius Hammer. Victor Hammer provided the description of Armand's return to New York.

1. Williams, *Russian Art and American Money,* pp. 16–17.

2. Larsons, *An Expert in the Service of the Soviet;* Habsburg, "When Russia Sold Its Past."

3. Letter from Sameuli to Anastas Mikoyan, June 20, 1929, Soviet Archive.

4. Commission for the Supervision of Antique Value Realization, May 3, 1929, Soviet Archive.

5. Williams, *Russian Art and American Money,* p. 18.

6. Taylor, *Stalin's Apologist,* p. 175.

7. Hammer, *The Quest of the Romanoff Treasure,* p. 211.

8. Ibid., p. 14.

9. Ibid., p. 48.

10. Ibid., pp. 64–65.

11. Ibid., p. 110.

12. Ibid., p. 215.

13. Ibid., pp. 215–216.

14. Ibid., p. 215.

15. Ibid., p. 218.

16. Ibid., p. 211.

17. Ibid., p. 219.

18. Hammer with Lyndon, *Hammer,* p. 200.

19. Elianoff interview.

20. Habsburg, "When Russia Sold Its Past," p. 128.

CHAPTER EIGHT: THE ART DEALER

The description of the economic situation in 1933 comes from Edward Robb Ellis, *A Nation in Torment*. Hammer's communications with FDR are from the correspondence between Henry French Hollis and FDR in the Franklin D. Roosevelt Library, Hyde Park, New York. Hammer's view of his role in marketing Russian art objects derives from his own writings, including his 1987 autobiography, as well as from interviews of Hammer I conducted in 1981. Robert C. Williams, who traced the provenance of Hammer's Russian art, provides a more objective assessment in *Russian Art and American Money*. Documents from the previously cited Soviet Archive support his point of view. The account of how Hammer used Fabergé signature stamps comes from Bettye Murphy, for whom Hammer demonstrated the process. Hammer's financial situation is revealed in the applications he made for loans from the Reconstruction Finance Corporation, which I found in that agency's files from 1933 to 1943, in the National Archives (hereinafter, Reconstruction Finance Corporation).

1. Quoted in Ellis, *A Nation in Torment,* p. 268.
2. Quoted in Freidel, *Roosevelt,* pp. 92–94.
3. Hammer with Lyndon, *Hammer,* p. 202.
4. Ibid., p. 203.
5. Ibid., pp. 205–207.
6. Williams, *Russian Art and American Money,* p. 221.
7. Armand Hammer, 1979 draft of a preface to *Fabergé Eggs,* a book authored by the firm of Faberzhe, in author's archives.
8. Murphy interview.
9. Hammer with Lyndon, *Hammer,* pp. 207, 214.
10. Hammer loan application, 1936, Reconstruction Finance Corporation.
11. *Time,* August 21, 1933.
12. Hellman, "The Innocents Abroad," pp. 18–21.
13. *Time,* October 19, 1936; Collier with Horowitz, *The Roosevelts,* pp. 374–375.

CHAPTER NINE: SEARCHING FOR MRS. RIGHT

Julian Hammer provided the description of Hammer's paternal role in the 1930s as well as photographs from his family album. In his 1987 autobiography, Armand Hammer provided the entry from his diary. Hammer's suspected activities in Mexico are chronicled in his FBI file.

1. Hammer with Lyndon, *Hammer,* pp. 217, 218.
2. Ibid., p. 249.
3. Elianoff interview.
4. Letter from P. E. Foxworth to J. E. Hooover, December 7, 1939, FBI file on Armand Hammer.
5. Cave Brown and MacDonald, *On a Field of Red,* p. 508.
6. Letter from Hoover to Adolf Berle, February 10, 1940, FBI file on Armand Hammer.

CHAPTER TEN: THE FIVE-MINUTE SUMMIT

The account of Stalin's strategy against Hitler in 1940 and 1941 is from Barton Whaley's analysis of intelligence documents in *Codeword BAR-BAROSSA.* Hammer's version of his role in lend-lease is based on his own writings and on documents he gave me. Material in the Franklin D. Roosevelt Library confirms that he communicated with FDR on the issue.

1. Hammer with Lyndon, *Hammer,* pp. 263–265.
2. Ibid., p. 265.
3. FBI file on Victor Hammer, April 12, 1940.
4. Hammer with Lyndon, *Hammer,* p. 265.
5. Quoted in Finder, *Red Carpet,* p. 81.
6. Quoted ibid., p. 82.
7. Hammer with Lyndon, *Hammer,* pp. 266–267.
8. Goodwin, *No Ordinary Time,* p. 78.
9. Hammer with Lyndon, *Hammer,* p. 267.
10. Goodwin, *No Ordinary Time,* pp. 88–99, 204, 459.
11. Hammer with Lyndon, *Hammer,* p. 267.
12. Quoted in Finder, *Red Carpet,* p. 83.
13. Quoted in Goodwin, *No Ordinary Time,* pp. 193, 212.

CHAPTER ELEVEN: FORTUNES OF WAR

The terms of Hammer's first divorce settlement come from the Hammer divorce proceedings, *Hammer v. Hammer,* 8th Judicial Circuit of Nevada, Clark County, Case 19039 (1943). The description of Hammer's second wedding comes from Julian Hammer, who attended the ceremony. Hammer himself told Bettye Murphy about his honeymoon when he took her to Havana. She related the story to me. The reference to Hammer's second divorce is from *Hammer v. Hammer,* Superior Court,

Chancery Division, Monmouth County, New Jersey, Docket M107554 (1953–1956).

Information on the resumption of contact between the Hammer family and Soviet officials comes from the passport-application files on Rose Hammer, Victor Hammer, and Armand Hammer and from the FBI files on Victor Hammer. Nancy Wicker, Victor Hammer's stepdaughter, also provided me with a picture of Hammer's activities during this period.

Hammer quoted from his diary in his 1987 autobiography, *Hammer,* but he did not make the diary available to me.

1. Murphy interview.
2. Reconstruction Finance Corporation, records, 1941–1943. Also, Wicker interview.
3. Quoted in Weinberg, *Armand Hammer,* p. 96.
4. Quoted ibid., p. 98.
5. Ibid., p. 99.
6. Julian Hammer interview.
7. *Hammer v. Hammer* (1955), C-1712.
8. Murphy interview.
9. Hammer with Lyndon, *Hammer,* p. 282.
10. FBI file on Victor Hammer.
11. Weinberg, *Armand Hammer,* p. 106.
12. Rovere, *Senator Joe McCarthy,* pp. 5–8.
13. Victor Hammer interview.
14. Finder, *Red Carpet,* p. 89.
15. U.S. House of Representatives, Hearings before the Committee on Armed Services, p. 62.
16. Ibid., p. 112.
17. Weinberg, *Armand Hammer,* p. 110.
18. U.S. House of Representatives, Hearings before the Committee on Armed Services, p. 6.
19. Ibid., p. 131.
20. From Mark Galusha to Styles Bridges, November 27, 1951, Styles Bridges Papers, New England College, Henniker, New Hampshire; also, Weinberg, *Armand Hammer,* p. 109.

CHAPTER TWELVE: THE DEBRIEFING

The account of Hammer's debriefing comes from the 1952–1953 reports on Armand Hammer in FBI File 61-280. I also interviewed a number of

FBI officers about this file, including William Sullivan after he retired from the FBI.

1. Sullivan interview.
2. Summary report, February 21, 1952, FBI file on Armand Hammer.
3. Memorandum from Hoover to A. H. Belmont, February 27, 1952, FBI file on Armand Hammer.
4. Quoted in report of March 28, 1952, p. 67, FBI file on Armand Hammer.
5. Collier with Horowitz, *The Roosevelts*, p. 457.
6. Hammer with Lyndon, *Hammer*, pp. 276–279.
7. Ibid., pp. 280–284.
8. Weinberg, *Armand Hammer*, p. 111.
9. Hammer with Lyndon, *Hammer*, p. 285.
10. *Hammer v. Hammer* (1956).
11. Hammer with Lyndon, *Hammer*, p. 285.

CHAPTER THIRTEEN: THE REINCARNATED MISTRESS

The material about Hammer's second divorce comes from the extensive record of the litigation, *Hammer v. Hammer* (1953–1956).

1. *Hammer v. Hammer* (1953–1956).
2. Murphy interview.

CHAPTER FOURTEEN: LIKE FATHER, LIKE SON

The description of Hammer's private life during this period comes from Julian Hammer (who also supplied photographs, written statements correcting allegations made about him, and a diary of a trip he took with his father) and from Bettye Murphy. Fred Gross, who was Hammer's pilot, corroborated much of Murphy's account.

Julian Hammer's court records are from Superior Court, Los Angeles, California, Criminal Case 173163 (1955).

The material about James Roosevelt comes from Roosevelt's correspondence with Hammer, which I obtained from the Franklin D. Roosevelt Library (hereinafter, James Roosevelt Papers).

1. Julian Hammer interview.
2. Julian Hammer, Caribbean diary, February 1956.
3. *New York Times*, May 11, 1955.

4. Julian Hammer interview.
5. Quoted in Hammer with Lyndon, *Hammer,* p. 288.
6. Gabler, *An Empire of Their Own,* p. 294.
7. Collier with Horowitz, *The Roosevelts,* p. 460.
8. Telegram from Armand Hammer to James Roosevelt, July 2, 1955, James Roosevelt Papers.
9. Telegram from Armand Hammer to James Roosevelt, August 18, 1955, James Roosevelt Papers.
10. Letter from James Roosevelt to Armand Hammer, July 30, 1955, James Roosevelt Papers.
11. Letter from Armand Hammer to James Roosevelt, August 26, 1955, James Roosevelt Papers.

CHAPTER FIFTEEN: THE MARITAL EL DORADO

Joan Weiss, Frances Hammer's niece, provided information about Hammer's relationship with his third wife. Bettye Murphy described to me her own relationship with Hammer. The description of Armasha Hammer comes from Mikhail Bruk's article in *Soviet Life* and from Joseph Finder's *Red Carpet.*

1. Hammer with Lyndon, *Hammer,* p. 290.
2. Tax returns of Armand Hammer, 1948–1955, and affidavits in author's archives.
3. Murphy interview.
4. Weiss interview.
5. Passport-application file on Rose Hammer.
6. Finder, *Red Carpet,* pp. 136–137.

CHAPTER SIXTEEN: THE PATH REOPENED: FROM KENNEDY TO KHRUSHCHEV

During the 1960s, Hammer created a paper trail with his correspondence with State Department and Commerce Department officials, correspondence that attempted to justify his contacts with Soviet, Libyan, and other foreign officials. Although his explanations must be discounted as self-serving, the letters provide an important chronology of his activities. The State Department released its file on Hammer on microfiche in response to FOIA requests (hereinafter referred to as the State Department Files), as did the Commerce Department (hereinafter, Commerce Department Files). The account of Hammer's dealings with James Roosevelt is based on the James Roosevelt Papers.

The information about Occidental Petroleum comes from its annual reports and from 10-K Securities and Exchange Commission statements made between 1960 and 1970. The information about Frances Hammer comes from the previously cited Weiss lawsuit against Armand Hammer.

The description of the CIA's interest in Hammer is based on interviews I conducted with James Angleton and his staff in 1981.

1. Quoted in Schlesinger, *A Thousand Days,* p. 165.
2. Hammer with Lyndon, *Hammer,* p. 314.
3. Correspondence with Armand Hammer, January 1961, Albert Gore Papers, Middle Tennessee State University, Murfreesboro, Tennessee.
4. Gibson interview.
5. Hammer with Lyndon, *Hammer,* p. 314.
6. Quoted in Finder, *Red Carpet,* p. 142.
7. Correspondence with Sam Picione re Occidental Oil Explorers II, 1964–1966, James Roosevelt Papers.
8. Lawrence O'Brien interview.
9. James Roosevelt to O'Brien, 1961, James Roosevelt Papers.
10. Weinberg, *Armand Hammer,* pp. 295–297.
11. Ibid., p. 158.
12. Quoted in Yergin, "The One-Man Flying Circus," p. 43.
13. Letter from Luther Hodges to Dean Rusk, March 3, 1961, State Department Files.
14. Frances Hammer interview, 1981.
15. Hammer with Lyndon, *Hammer,* p. 315.
16. Memorandum from Armand Hammer on his meeting with V. M. Vinogradov and M. N. Gribkov, February 15, 1961, State Department Files.
17. Memorandum from Armand Hammer on his conversation with William N. Morrell, Jr., February 14, 1961, State Department Files.
18. Hammer with Lyndon, *Hammer,* p. 313.
19. Memorandum from Armand Hammer on his conversation with Anastas Mikoyan, February 15, 1961, State Department Files.
20. Quoted in Beschloss, *The Crisis Years,* p. 79.
21. Memorandum from Armand Hammer on his conversation with Nikita Khrushchev, February 17, 1961, State Department Files.
22. Quoted in Beschloss, *The Crisis Years,* pp. 169–172.
23. Hammer with Lyndon, *Hammer,* pp. 323–324.
24. Letter from Armand Hammer to Hodges, February 19, 1961, Commerce Department Files.

25. Memorandum on Armand Hammer's meeting with Hodges, February 27, 1961, Commerce Department Files.

26. Letter from Armand Hammer to Mikhail Menshikov, March 31, 1961, James Roosevelt Papers.

27. Letter to James Roosevelt, May 1961, James Roosevelt Papers.

28. U.S. Senate memorandum, August 16, 1961, James Roosevelt Papers.

29. Letter from Daly to James Roosevelt, April 3, 1962, James Roosevelt Papers.

30. Telegram from Armand Hammer to John F. Kennedy, September 21, 1963, James Roosevelt Papers.

31. Letter from James Roosevelt to Armand Hammer, September 23, 1963, James Roosevelt Papers.

32. Letter from Armand Hammer to Khrushchev, May 8, 1964, Commerce Department Files.

33. Memorandum from Armand Hammer on his conversation with Khrushchev, June 12, 1964, State Department Files.

34. Ibid. See also Finder, *Red Carpet,* p. 149.

35. Hammer, *The Quest of the Romanoff Treasure,* p. 1; Armand Hammer interview.

36. *New York Times,* September 27, 1964.

37. Memorandum from W. A. Brannigyn to William C. Sullivan, February 23, 1961, FBI file on Armand Hammer.

38. Memorandum, July 14, 1961, FBI file on Armand Hammer.

39. Sullivan interview.

40. Angleton interview.

41. FBI file on Armand Hammer, August 4, 1944, p. 15.

CHAPTER SEVENTEEN: THE GEOPOLITICS OF CRUDE

Although Hammer went to great lengths to conceal the secret mechanisms through which Occidental Petroleum received its crucial concessions in Libya, litigation over the commissions brought to light the basic outlines of the scheme. I derived many details, including the dates, the places, and the participants in the meetings, as well as actual documents, from these lawsuits. The suits filed by Allen and Company (U.S. District Court, Southern District of New York, Case 67-4011 [1968]; hereinafter, the Allen lawsuit), the estate of Wendell Phillips (*Wendell Phillips Estate v. Occidental Petroleum,* U.S. District Court, Central District of California, Case 87-1461ER; hereinafter, the Phillips lawsuit), Hans Kunz (*Hans-Albert Kunz v. Occidental Petroleum Corporation, Armand Hammer and Arthur Andersen & Company,* U.S. District Court for the District of Columbia, Civil Action 88-1169 [1988]; hereinafter, the Kunz lawsuit), and Omar Shelhi (Shelhi Amended Complaint, *Omar Ibrahim El Shelhi v. Kemal Zeinal Zade,* Court of First Instance, Case 875 A 1714, Geneva, Switzerland [April 2, 1979], in author's archives; hereinafter, the Shelhi lawsuit) were particularly revealing. The previously cited SEC investigation of Occidental Petroleum and sixteen cartons of back material, which were released under FOIA, including SEC File 1, 520-0407, April 14, 1978 (hereinafter, the SEC Files), also produced important information.

I learned much from G. Henry Schuler, a former State Department official in Libya who gave me his unpublished manuscript, "Uncertain Signals," which both investigates and analyzes economic and political activities in the Middle East. I benefited greatly from interviews of Mustafa Ben Halim (in London in 1995), an influential minister in the Libyan government at the time Hammer went to Libya; Wendell Phillips's sister, Merilyn Phillips Hodgson, and her husband, Gordon Hodgson, the executor of Phillips's estate; Omar Shelhi, a principal intermediary in the Libyan transactions; Dorman Commons, Occidental's chief financial officer; and George Williamson, who became Hammer's chief operating officer in Libya and supplied me with documents from the period.

Much of the picture of Hammer's relationship with President Johnson is contained in the Lyndon Baines Johnson Library in Austin, Texas (hereinafter, the LBJ Papers). The section on Bettye Murphy comes from interviews with her. I also interviewed a number of Hammer's pilots during this period, including Fred Gross.

1. See Epstein, "The Cartel That Never Was," p. 68.
2. Tremlett, *Gadaffi,* p. 76.
3. Ben Halim interview.
4. James Akins, testimony before U.S. Senate Foreign Relations Committee, October 11, 1973.
5. Ben Halim interview.
6. Ibid.
7. Commons interview.
8. Hammer with Lyndon, *Hammer,* pp. 334, 335.
9. Letter from Armand Hammer to Luther Hodges, February 24, 1961, Commerce Department Files.

10. Letter from Armand Hammer, September 18, 1964, Allen lawsuit.
11. Deposition by Armand Hammer, February 7, 1968, Allen lawsuit.
12. Williamson interview.
13. Deposition by Armand Hammer, February 7, 1968, Allen lawsuit.
14. Commons interview.
15. "Oil Millionaire W. Phillips Dies at 54," *Honolulu Advertiser,* December 5, 1975.
16. Merilyn Phillips Hodgson interview; Gordon Hodgson interview.
17. Phillips lawsuit.
18. Shelhi interview.
19. Ibid.
20. Telegram from Armand Hammer to Taber Ogbi, June 19, 1965, Allen lawsuit.
21. Gross interview.
22. Weinberg, *Armand Hammer,* pp. 165–166.
23. Shelhi interview.
24. Hammer with Lyndon, *Hammer,* p. 336.
25. Memorandum by James Murdy on conversation with investigator for U.S. Senate Foreign Relations Committee, November 29, 1973, p. 1, SEC Files.
26. Confidential File FO 5, LBJ Papers.
27. Letter from James Roosevelt to Henry Hall Wilson, Confidential File FO 5, LBJ Papers.
28. Note from Marvin Watson to Lyndon Johnson, Confidential File FO 5, LBJ Papers.
29. Hammer with Lyndon, *Hammer,* p. 365.
30. Murphy interview.
31. Letter from Armand Hammer to Omar Shelhi, May 2, 1966, Phillips lawsuit.
32. Shelhi interview.
33. McCartney, *Friends in High Places,* p. 148.
34. Brown, "Hammer in Libya."
35. Hammer with Lyndon, *Hammer,* p. 343.
36. Shelhi interview.
37. Letter from Hans Kunz to Wendell Phillips, July 31, 1968, Phillips lawsuit.
38. Shelhi interview.
39. Letter from Kunz to Phillips, July 31, 1968, Phillips lawsuit.
40. Letter from Armand Hammer to Kunz and Kemal Zeinal Zade, May 1, 1969, Phillips lawsuit.
41. Williamson interview.

CHAPTER EIGHTEEN: AVOIDING JUDGMENT DAY

The section about the CIA's interest in Hammer comes from interviews with James Angleton and with Angleton's chief of staff, Newton Scot Miler.

1. Tremlett, *Gadaffi,* pp. 65–73.
2. Williamson interview.
3. Schuler interview.
4. Williamson interview.
5. Dunne, "Armand Hammer," p. 18.
6. Memorandum by James Murdy on conversation with investigator for U.S. Senate Foreign Relations Committee, November 29, 1973, p. 1, SEC Files.
7. Shelhi interview.
8. Memorandum by Murdy, p. 1, SEC Files.
9. Commons interview.
10. Letter from Armand Hammer to Hans Kunz, December 5, 1969, Kunz lawsuit.
11. Letter from Kunz and Kemal Zeinal Zade to Armand Hammer, January 7, 1970, Kunz lawsuit.
12. Williamson interview.
13. Alam, *The Shah and I,* p. 63.
14. Hammer with Lyndon, *Hammer,* p. 345.
15. Williamson interview.
16. Ibid.
17. Gross interview.
18. Quoted in Yergin, *The Prize,* p. 580.
19. Schuler interview.
20. Kunz lawsuit.
21. Hammer with Lyndon, *Hammer,* p. 353.

CHAPTER NINETEEN: THE ART OF BRIBERY

My analysis of Hammer's techniques for bribing government officials is based on three principal sources.

First is the source memorandum written by a special committee of Occidental's board of directors. This committee was formed in 1977 to conduct an independent investigation of Occidental's bribes and questionable payments, a response to shareholder and SEC lawsuits. It had no power to compel testimony, but it sent a questionnaire to Occidental executives and, based on their answers, reported thirty-three incidents of illegal or questionable payments. The report, "Investigated Payments and Accounting Practices of Occidental Petroleum Corporation, 1969–1975," was filed with the SEC in 1978 (hereinafter referred to as the Occidental Source Memorandum).

Second is material resulting from three major investigations of Occidental conducted by the SEC. This material, including SEC Investigations HO-494, HO-557, and HO-846, was released in response to FOIA requests. The raw data in Occidental's files that the SEC had subpoenaed was released in 1993 in response to an FOIA request filed by Steve Weinberg eight years earlier (and is hereinafter referred to as the SEC Investigative Files).

Third are cassette and microcassette recordings, now in my possession, that Hammer surreptitiously made between 1969 and 1983 (referred to here as the Hammer Tapes). On these tapes, Hammer often recorded sensitive discussions, including those in which he gave instructions regarding the disbursement of bribes and other secret payments.

I also interviewed a number of Hammer's associates who had peripheral knowledge of some of Hammer's cash transactions, including Sir John Foster, a director of Occidental, and John Burton Tigrett, an adviser to Hammer on the international oil business.

1. Sir John Foster interview.
2. Occidental Source Memorandum.
3. Armand Hammer interview.
4. Commons interview.
5. Foster interview.
6. Occidental Source Memorandum.
7. Commons interview.
8. Commons interview.
9. Letter from Hans Kunz to Wendell Phillips, May 1, 1969, Phillips lawsuit.
10. Conversation between Armand Hammer and John Askew, November 1971, Hammer Tape 4, side 1.
11. Occidental Source Memorandum, p. 20.

CHAPTER TWENTY: TO RUSSIA WITH MONEY

Some of the historical context of this chapter is derived from my interviews with Richard Nixon and Henry Kissinger, and with members of Kissinger's national security staff, including Helmut Sonnenfeldt. The reconstruction of Hammer's return to the Soviet Union is based on interviews with a number of his associates, including Mikhail Bruk, who served as his liaison in Moscow; Dorman Commons; and Zoltan Merszei, who later became president of Occidental. I also consulted the previously cited Hammer Tapes, on which Hammer secretly recorded discussions with his executives about Russian deals. The section on Cyrus Eaton and the Pugwash Conferences comes from Joseph Finder's excellent book, *Red Carpet.*

1. Kissinger, *Diplomacy,* p. 714.
2. Finder, *Red Carpet,* pp. 201–202.
3. Bruk interview.
4. Quoted in Finder, *Red Carpet,* p. 226.
5. Hammer with Lyndon, *Hammer,* p. 402.
6. Ibid., pp. 401–402.
7. Quoted in Finder, *Red Carpet,* p. 93.
8. Bruk interview.
9. Ibid.
10. Khrushchev, *Khrushchev Remembers,* pp. 81, 245.
11. Obituary of Yekaterina Furtseva, *New York Times,* October 25, 1974.
12. Gibson interview.
13. Hammer with Lyndon, *Hammer,* pp. 433–434.
14. Ibid., p. 402.
15. Bruk interview.
16. Ibid. Bruk's reports on Leo Szilard may have been the basis for the claim by Pavel Sudoplatov in 1993 that Szilard was a Soviet source. See Sudoplatov and Sudoplatov, *Special Tasks,* p. 3.
17. Merszei interview.
18. Bruk interview.
19. Ibid.
20. *New York Times,* July 18, 1972, p. 1.
21. Peter Peterson interview; Helmut Sonnenfeldt interview; Kissinger interview.
22. Hammer with Lyndon, *Hammer,* p. 411.
23. Haldeman, *Haldeman Diaries,* p. 484.
24. Ibid.
25. Sonnenfeldt interview.
26. Commons interview.
27. Hammer with Lyndon, *Hammer,* p. 405.
28. "The Russian Connection—Dr. Armand Hammer" (produced by Lucy Jarvis; broadcast on NBC, June 18, 1974).

29. Alam, *The Shah and I,* p. 284.

30. Merszei interview.

31. "Soviet and Occidental in Multi-Billion-Dollar Deal," *New York Times,* April 14, 1973.

32. *Wall Street Journal,* May 22, 1973.

33. Letter from Armand Hammer to Richard Nixon, March 13, 1974, in author's archives.

34. Letter from Nixon to William J. Casey, May 20, 1974, in author's archives.

35. *New York Times,* May 22, 1974, p. 1.

36. Merszei interview.

CHAPTER TWENTY-ONE: WATERGATE CRIMES AND MISDEMEANORS

The unusually detailed record of Armand Hammer's illegal campaign contributions comes from the investigation of Hammer by the Watergate Special Prosecution Force and, particularly, its memorandum of September 16, 1974, in the Summary of Evidence (National Archives, Record Group 460, files on Armand Hammer and Occidental Petroleum). In addition, the FBI investigation, including a summary of an interview with Hammer, is contained in Hammer's previously cited FBI file. The assessment of Hammer's probation officer and the court's reaction to it come from the Probation Report on Armand Hammer (U.S. District Court, Washington, D.C., Case 75-668) and from the hearing before Judge Lawrence Lydick (U.S. District Court, Central District of California, Case 74-727, February 13, 1975).

I also interviewed Hammer's lawyer, Edward Bennett Williams, in 1981, and Hammer's London consultant.

1. Hammer with Lyndon, *Hammer,* p. 414.

2. Hammer interview.

3. Watergate Special Prosecution Force, memorandum of September 16, 1974.

4. Interview with Hammer's London consultant.

5. Summary of interview with Armand Hammer, August 24, 1973, in FBI file on Armand Hammer.

6. Williams interview.

7. Hammer with Lyndon, *Hammer,* p. 414.

8. Ibid.

9. Letter from Armand Hammer to James Walker, Probation Report on Armand Hammer.

10. Hammer with Lyndon, *Hammer,* p. 414.
11. Hearing before Judge Lydick.
12. Letter from Frances Hammer to Victor and Ireene Hammer, April 2, 1976.
13. Julian Hammer interview.
14. Bruk, "Dr. Hammer Gives a Housewarming Party."

CHAPTER TWENTY-TWO: OLD MASTERS AND YOUNG MISTRESSES

This chapter benefited greatly from interviews with Martha Kaufman/ Hilary Gibson in 1992 and from files she made available to me, which include the quoted minutes of the meeting of the Executive Committee of Occidental Petroleum Corporation on December 3, 1980, and Armand Hammer's 1981 correspondence with UCLA. The text is also based on interviews with Jack Tanzer and John Richardson, who were vice presidents of Hammer's Knoedler Galleries, and Victor Hammer and his adopted daughter, Nancy Wicker. Roger Shockley, who served as the chief financial officer of Occidental under Hammer, provided me with some insight into how Hammer justified investing corporate funds in his art ventures.

1. Hammer with Lyndon, *Hammer,* p. 447.
2. Letter from Armand Hammer citing need for approval from an OGPU representative, Umanskii, January 14, 1927, Soviet Archive.
3. Quoted in Ronay, "Framed in a Masterful Swindle," pp. 14–15.
4. Victor Hammer interview.
5. Ibid.
6. Hammer with Lyndon, *Hammer,* pp. 178–180.
7. Ibid., p. 235.
8. Murphy interview.
9. Richardson, "Hammer Nailed," pp. 96–102.
10. Jones, "Battle for the Masterpieces," p. 8.
11. *Washington Post,* March 28, 1970. See also Weinberg, *Armand Hammer,* p. 380.
12. Quoted in Crawford-Mason, "Wheeler Dealer Armand Hammer," p. 54.
13. Weinberg, *Armand Hammer,* p. 380.
14. Walker, *Self Portrait with Donors,* p. 38; Weinberg, *Armand Hammer,* pp. 380–382.
15. Hammer with Lyndon, *Hammer,* p. 442.

16. Tax returns of the Armand Hammer Foundation, 1985.

17. Merszei interview.

18. Richardson, "Hammer Nailed," p. 102.

19. Ibid.

20. Richardson interview.

21. Conversation in which Armand Hammer describes the Goya transaction, January 10, 1978, Hammer Tapes; also, Tanzer interview; Richardson interview.

22. Richardson interview.

23. Gibson interview.

24. Ibid.

25. Shockley interview.

26. *Hilary Gibson v. Musick, Peeler, and Garrett,* Superior Court, Los Angeles, California, Case BC 118 207; also, Gibson interview.

27. Hammer with Lyndon, *Hammer,* p. 444.

28. Gibson interview.

29. Esterow, "Hammer," p. 73.

30. Hammer with Lyndon, *Hammer,* p. 444; Jones, "Battle for the Masterpieces," p. 13.

31. Hammer with Lyndon, *Hammer,* pp. 449–450.

32. Armand Hammer interview.

33. Merszei interview.

34. Occidental Petroleum Corporation, minutes of meeting of December 3, 1980.

35. Armand Hammer correspondence with UCLA, 1981.

36. Hammer with Lyndon, *Hammer,* p. 446.

37. Hammer interview and author's observation of the Codex Hammer.

38. Gibson interview.

39. McGuigan and Wright, "Whose Art Is It, Anyway?" p. 52.

CHAPTER TWENTY-THREE: THE GO-BETWEEN

This chapter is based on my observations of Armand Hammer and on interviews I conducted while traveling with him in 1981 (see Author's Note). The picture of Occidental is drawn from my interviews of its top executives—including Robert Abboud, Zoltan Merszei, Roger Shockley, and James Galvin—and from its annual reports and other documents, which were provided to the SEC. Hammer provided me with his airplane flight records for this period and with other travel data. I also interviewed Richard Allen, President Reagan's national security adviser. I learned additional details about David Karr from Leo Henzel, who was

Hammer and Karr's associate in Soviet deals (and later sued Hammer), and from Jean-Louis Gergeron, a French intelligence expert. I interviewed Ijaz ul-Haq, a son of President Zia, who was killed in an air crash in 1988. Hammer's perspective of his mission comes from tape-recorded notes he dictated between 1978 and 1982 (on the Hammer Tapes).

1. Merszei interview. Merszei was with Hammer at the inauguration.
2. Reagan, *An American Life,* pp. 226–229.
3. Merszei interview.
4. Letter from Armand Hammer to Leonid Brezhnev, January 23, 1980, State Department Files.
5. Galvin interview.
6. Hammer with Lyndon, *Hammer,* p. 424.
7. Ibid., p. 425.
8. Armand Hammer's airplane flight records.
9. Hammer Tapes, April 11, 1980, side 1.
10. Ibid.
11. Hammer Tapes, June 6, 1980, side 2.
12. Zbigniew Brzezinski interview.
13. Hammer Tapes, June 6, 1980, side 2.
14. Ibid.
15. Yousaf and Adkin, *The Bear Trap,* pp. 24–41.
16. Hammer with Lyndon, *Hammer,* p. 426.
17. Interview with ul-Haq.
18. Armand Hammer interview; Allen interview.
19. Armand Hammer interview; Henzel interview.
20. Rowan, "Death of David Karr and Other Mysteries," p. 102.
21. Ibid., p. 96.
22. Gergeron interview.
23. Woodward, *Veil,* p. 40; interview with Arnaud de Borchgrave, who attended the meeting on November 21.
24. Quoted in Woodward, *Veil,* p. 40.
25. Hammer with Lyndon, *Hammer,* pp. 428–429.
26. Weinberg, *Armand Hammer,* p. 392.
27. Author's observations at the 1981 dinner with Prince Charles.
28. Author's observations, 1981.
29. David Murdock interview.
30. Hammer with Lyndon, *Hammer,* p. 376.
31. Murdock interview; Armand Hammer interview.
32. Letter from Armand Hammer to Ronald Reagan, April 23, 1981.
33. Armand Hammer interview and author's observations.

34. Bruk interview.
35. Armand Hammer interview.
36. Hammer with Lyndon, *Hammer,* p. 429; records for 1981 in FBI file on Armand Hammer, which show there was no FBI investigation or clearance.
37. Duncan, "Hammer of the Midas Touch," p. 13.
38. Weinberg, *Armand Hammer,* p. 455.
39. Hammer with Lyndon, *Hammer,* p. 496.
40. Bruk interview.
41. Hammer with Lyndon, *Hammer,* p. 481.
42. Ibid., pp. 495, 499.
43. Bruk interview.
44. Boward, "Dr. Armand Hammer," p. 55.
45. Hammer with Lyndon, *Hammer,* p. 501.

CHAPTER TWENTY-FOUR: BALANCE OF POWER

This and the following chapter are based on my observations of and interviews with Hammer when I traveled with him in 1981 (see Author's Note). I was provided with travel records for this period. The Hammer Tapes, which I acquired later, contain memorandums that Hammer dictated while on his plane and in hotel rooms between 1978 and 1982.

The description of Occidental's activities is again drawn from interviews with the company's top executives—including Robert Abboud, Zoltan Merszei, Roger Shockley, and James Galvin—and from annual reports and 10-K Forms filed with the SEC.

1. Hammer began discussing the Brando character at the opening of the Armand Hammer Collection at the Corcoran Gallery on September 25, 1980 ("Hollywood Formula for Synthetic Fuel," *Newsweek,* October 25, 1980, p. 17), and continued discussing it for at least a year; Armand Hammer interview.
2. Quoted in Crawford-Mason, "Wheeler Dealer Armand Hammer," p. 47.
3. Armand Hammer, speech to the American Petroleum Institute, Bakersfield, California, October 23, 1980.
4. Armand Hammer interview.
5. Murphy interview.
6. Duncan, "Hammer of the Midas Touch," p. 13.
7. For medical offers, see Hammer with Lyndon, *Hammer,* pp. 469–472; information on Libyan bribes is based on Ben Halim interview.

8. Jules Kroll interview. For more on the criminal informant (Herbert Itkin), see Weinberg, *Armand Hammer,* pp. 319, 445.

9. Gibson interview.

10. *Washington Post,* April 7, 1979; *Washington Star,* June 20, 1979.

11. Jerrold L. Schecter interview.

12. Quoted in Crawford-Mason, "Wheeler Dealer Armand Hammer," p. 47.

13. Author's observations; Abboud interview.

14. Julian Hammer interview; Gibson interview.

15. Merszei interview.

16. Kinkead, "Armand Hammer's Costly Dreams," p. 100.

17. Weinberg, *Armand Hammer,* p. 325.

18. Author's observation; Murdock interview.

19. Murdock interview.

20. Kinkead, "Armand Hammer's Costly Dreams," p. 102.

21. Hammer, "On a Vast China Market," p. 23.

22. Hammer with Lyndon, *Hammer,* p. 377.

23. Ibid., p. 378.

24. Gibson interview.

25. Hammer with Lyndon, *Hammer,* p. 398.

26. Gibson interview.

27. Kinkead, "Armand Hammer's Costly Dreams," p. 98.

28. Merszei interview.

29. *Los Angeles Times,* August 25, 1984, p. B1.

30. Hammer interview, *Modern Maturity,* p. 62.

31. Cook, "Armand's New Elephant," p. 67.

32. Shelhi interview.

33. Merszei interview.

34. (Bogotá) *El Tiempo,* November 1, 1986.

35. Sutton sued Occidental in 1988 for wrongful dismissal (*James Sutton v. Occidental Petroleum,* Superior Court, Kern County, California, Case 202003 [1988]); also see *Forbes,* March 18, 1991.

36. Quoted in *Wall Street Journal,* May 13, 1985, p. 1.

37. Shelhi interview; SEC Files.

CHAPTER TWENTY-FIVE: THE QUEST FOR THE NOBEL PRIZE

While traveling with Hammer in 1981, I interviewed a number of his key aides, including Jerrold L. Schecter, William McSweeny, and James Pugash. I later spoke to Theodore Lockwood, who, along with Pugash, helped organize the Armand Hammer United World College of the American West.

I was briefed on the Nobel Peace Prize procedures in Stockholm by Baron Stig Ramel, a director of the Nobel Foundation.

1. Armand Hammer travel records for May 1988; Armand Hammer birthday-celebration guest list; Toy, "Doctor Hammer Is 90," p. 48.
2. Hammer with Lyndon, *Hammer,* p. 468.
3. Erem, interview with Armand Hammer, p. 17.
4. Schecter interview; author's observations and Armand Hammer interview, October 1981; Pugash interview.
5. Blumay with Edwards, *The Dark Side of Power,* p. 344.
6. Schecter interview.
7. Blumay with Edwards, *The Dark Side of Power,* p. 344.
8. Hammer with Lyndon, *Hammer,* p. 394.
9. Ibid., p. 510.
10. Theodore Lockwood interview; Kopp, "United World College," p. 44.
11. *Los Angeles Times,* May 23, 1985.
12. Hunter, "Hammer," p. 4.
13. Ramel interview; interview with Hammer's London consultant.
14. Hammer with Lyndon, *Hammer,* p. 414.
15. Weinberg, *Armand Hammer,* p. 450.
16. Report on Armand Hammer, April 17, 1984, FBI File 73-20241.
17. Report on Armand Hammer, May 12, 1984, FBI File 73-20241.
18. Report on Armand Hammer, January 17, 1985, FBI File 73-20241.
19. Weinberg, *Armand Hammer,* p. 449; *Los Angeles Times,* December 29, 1988.
20. File on pardon of Armand Hammer, 1991, Justice Department; Weinberg, *Armand Hammer,* p. 448; probate file on the estate of Armand Hammer, Superior Court, Los Angeles, California, Case BP004635 (1995).
21. Hammer with Lyndon, *Hammer,* p. 415.
22. File on pardon of Armand Hammer, 1991, Justice Department.
23. Hammer with Lyndon, *Hammer,* p. 430.
24. Ibid.

EPILOGUE: POSTMORTEM

1. Julian Hammer interview.
2. Weinberg, *Armand Hammer,* p. 435.

3. Blumay with Edwards, *The Dark Side of Power,* pp. 426–427.
4. Bruk interview.
5. Letter from Armasha Hammer to Victor Hammer, 1962.
6. Cook, "The High Cost of Hammer," p. 104.
7. Lee, "Occidental Lets Memory of Ex-Chief Fade," p. D1.
8. Ibid.
9. McGuigan and Wright, "Whose Art Is It, Anyway?" p. 52.
10. Gibson interview.
11. Parachini, "Confused Picture at Hammer Museum," p. 1.
12. Muchnik, "The Hammer's New Role," p. 3.
13. Brown, "The Master Cynic," p. 364.
14. Rose, "Occidental to Fulfill Severance Pact."
15. Probate file on the estate of Armand Hammer, Superior Court, Los Angeles, California, Case BP004635 (1995).
16. Casey Hammer interview; Julian Hammer interview.
17. Ashton Hawkins interview.
18. Murphy interview.
19. Casey Hammer interview.

AUTHOR'S NOTE

1. I describe my relations with Angleton in Epstein, *Deception.*
2. Epstein, "The Riddle of Armand Hammer," p. 112.
3. *New York Times,* December 20, 1981.

BIBLIOGRAPHY

Alam, Asadollah. *The Shah and I: The Confidential Diary of Iran's Royal Court, 1969–1977.* Translated by Alinaghi Alikhani and Nicholas Vincent. London: I. B. Tauris, 1991.

Beschloss, Michael R. *The Crisis Years: Kennedy and Khrushchev, 1960–1963.* New York: Edward Burlingame Books, 1991.

Bessedovsky, Grigory. "How Moscow Finances the Communist Movement in the United States." *Jewish Daily Forward,* March 14, 1930.

Blumay, Carl, with Henry Edwards. *The Dark Side of Power: The Real Armand Hammer.* New York: Simon & Schuster, 1992.

Boward, Walter H. "Dr. Armand Hammer." *Palm Springs Life,* November 1985.

Brown, Christie. "The Master Cynic." *Forbes,* October 17, 1994.

Brown, Stanley. "Hammer in Libya." *Fortune,* July 1969.

Bruk, Mikhail. "Dr. Hammer Gives a Housewarming Party." *Soviet Life,* October 1976.

Cave Brown, Anthony, and Charles B. MacDonald, *On a Field of Red: The Communist International and the Coming of World War II.* New York: Putnam, 1981.

Collier, Peter, and David Horowitz. *The Fords: An American Epic.* New York: Summit, 1987.

Collier, Peter, with David Horowitz. *The Roosevelts: An American Saga.* New York: Simon & Schuster, 1994.

Considine, Robert Bernard. *The Remarkable Life of Dr. Armand Hammer*. New York: Harper & Row, 1975.

Cook, James. "Armand's New Elephant." *Forbes,* June 17, 1985.

———. "The High Cost of Hammer." *Forbes,* May 27, 1991.

Corson, William R., and Robert T. Crowley, *The New KGB: Engine of Soviet Power*. New York: Morrow, 1985.

Costello, John. *Mask of Treachery*. New York: Morrow, 1988.

Costello, John, and Oleg Tsarev. *Deadly Illusions: The KGB Orlov Dossier Reveals Stalin's Master Spy*. New York: Crown, 1993.

Crawford-Mason, Claire. "Wheeler Dealer Armand Hammer Pounces on the Main Chance Like a Dog on a Bone." *People,* October 26, 1981.

Duncan, Andrew. "Hammer of the Midas Touch." *Sunday* (London) *Telegraph Magazine,* July 24, 1983.

Dunne, Angela Fox. "Interview, Armand Hammer." *The Executive,* April 1986.

Duranty, Walter. *I Write As I Please*. New York: Halcyon House, 1935.

———. "Soviet Concession to American Firm." *New York Times,* July 10, 1923.

Ellis, Edward Robb. *A Nation in Torment: The Great American Depression, 1929–1939*. New York: Coward-McCann, 1970.

Epstein, Edward Jay. "The Cartel That Never Was." *Atlantic,* March 1983.

———. *Deception: The Invisible War Between the KGB and the CIA*. New York: Simon & Schuster, 1989.

———. "The Riddle of Armand Hammer." *New York Times Magazine,* November 29, 1981.

Erem, Gabriel. Interview with Armand Hammer, *Lifestyles,* Fall 1990.

Esterow, Milton. "Hammer." *ARTnews,* December 1982.

Faberzhe, *Fabergé Eggs: Imperial Russian Fantasies.* New York: Abrams, 1980.

Filene, Peter G. *Americans and the Soviet Experiment, 1917–1933*. Cambridge, Mass.: Harvard University Press, 1967.

Finder, Joseph. *Red Carpet*. New York: Holt, Rinehart and Winston, 1983.

"Forbes Four Hundred." *Forbes,* October 18, 1993.

Freidel, Frank. *Franklin D. Roosevelt: A Rendezvous with Destiny*. Boston: Little, Brown, 1990.

Freund, Gerald. *Unholy Alliance: Russian-German Relations from the Treaty of Brest-Litovsk to the Treaty of Berlin*. New York: Harcourt, Brace, 1957.

Gabler, Neal. *An Empire of Their Own: How the Jews Invented Hollywood.* New York: Crown, 1988.

Gershman, Carl. "Selling Them the Rope." *Commentary,* April 1979.

Gillette, Philip S. "The Political Origins of American-Soviet Trade, 1917–1924." Ph.D. dissertation, Harvard University, 1969.

Gitlow, Benjamin. *I Confess: The Truth About American Communism.* New York: E. P. Dutton, 1940.

Goodwin, Doris Kearns. *No Ordinary Time: Franklin and Eleanor Roosevelt—The Homefront in World War II.* New York: Simon & Schuster, 1994.

Habsburg, Geza von. "When Russia Sold Its Past." *Art & Auction,* March 1995.

Haldeman, H. R. *The Haldeman Diaries: Inside the Nixon White House.* New York: Putnam, 1994.

Hammer, Armand. Interview. *Modern Maturity,* October–November 1980.

———. "On a Vast China Market." *Journal of International Affairs,* Winter 1986.

———. *The Quest of the Romanoff Treasure.* Foreword by Walter Duranty. New York: W. F. Payson, 1932.

Hammer, Armand, with Neil Lyndon. *Hammer.* New York: Putnam, 1987.

Heller, Abraham Aaron. *The Industrial Revival in Soviet Russia.* New York: Thomas Seltzer, 1922.

Heller, Mikhail, and Aleksandr Nekrich. *Utopia in Power: The History of the Soviet Union from 1917 to the Present.* New York: Summit Books, 1986.

Hellman, Geoffrey T. "The Innocents Abroad." *New Yorker,* December 23, 1933.

Howe, Irving. *World of Our Fathers: The Journey of the Eastern European Jews to America and the Life They Made.* New York: Harcourt Brace Jovanovich, 1976.

Hunter, Chris. "Hammer." *Palm Beach* (Florida) *Daily News,* April 22, 1986.

Jones, Robert A. "Battle for the Masterpieces." *Los Angeles Times Magazine,* May 22, 1988.

Khrushchev, Nikita. *Khrushchev Remembers: The Last Testament.* Edited and translated by Strobe Talbott. Boston: Little, Brown, 1974.

Kinkead, Gwen. "Armand Hammer's Costly Dreams." *Fortune,* November 26, 1984.

Kissinger, Henry. *Diplomacy.* New York: Simon & Schuster, 1994.

————. *The White House Years*. Boston: Little, Brown, 1979.

Klehr, Harvey, John Earl Haynes, and Fridrikh Igorevich Firsov. *The Secret World of American Communism*. New Haven: Yale University Press, 1995.

Kopp, April. "United World College." *New Mexico Magazine,* June 1985.

Larsons, M. J. [Moisey Yakovlevich Lazerson]. *An Expert in the Service of the Soviet*. Translated by Angelo S. Rappoport. London: E. Benn, 1929.

Lazitch, Branko, with Milorad M. Drachkovitch. *Biographical Dictionary of the Comintern*. Stanford, Calif.: Hoover Institution Press, 1986.

Lee, Patrick. "Occidental Lets Memory of Ex-Chief Fade." *Los Angeles Times,* March 28, 1991.

Lenin, V. I. *Collected Works*. Moscow: Progress Publishers, 1970.

Liberman, Simon. *Building Lenin's Russia*. Chicago: University of Chicago Press, 1945.

Lyons, Eugene. *Assignment in Utopia*. New York: Harcourt, Brace, 1937.

Martin, David C. *Wilderness of Mirrors*. New York: Harper & Row, 1980.

McCartney, Laton. *Friends in High Places: The Bechtel Story: The Most Secret Corporation and How It Engineered the World*. New York: Simon & Schuster, 1988.

McGuigan, Cathleen, and Lynda Wright. "Whose Art Is It, Anyway?" *Newsweek,* July 30, 1990.

Muchnik, Suzanne. "The Hammer's New Role." *Los Angeles Times,* September 10, 1992.

Nevins, Allan, and Frank Ernest Hill. *Ford: Expansion and Challenge, 1915–1933*. New York: Scribner, 1957.

Nizer, Louis. *Reflections Without Mirrors: An Autobiography of the Mind*. Garden City, N.Y.: Doubleday, 1978.

O'Toole, G.J.A. *Honorable Treachery: A History of U.S. Intelligence, Espionage, and Covert Action from the American Revolution to the CIA*. New York: Atlantic Monthly Press, 1991.

Parachini, Alan. "Confused Picture at Hammer Museum." *Los Angeles Times,* January 25, 1991.

Pyatt, Rudolph A., Jr., *Washington Star,* June 20, 1979.

Reagan, Ronald. *An American Life*. New York: Simon & Schuster, 1990.

Richardson, John. "Hammer Nailed." *Vanity Fair,* March 1991.

Ronay, Gabriel. "Framed in a Masterful Swindle." (London) *Times Saturday Review,* February 16, 1991.

Rose, Frederick. "Occidental to Fulfill Severance Pact." *Wall Street Journal,* November 7, 1991.

Rovere, Richard H. *Senator Joe McCarthy.* New York: Harcourt, Brace, 1959.

Rowan, Roy. "Death of David Karr and Other Mysteries." *Fortune,* December 3, 1979.

Schlesinger, Arthur M., Jr. *A Thousand Days: John F. Kennedy in the White House.* Boston: Houghton Mifflin, 1965.

Seretan, L. Glen. *Daniel De Leon: The Odyssey of an American Marxist.* Cambridge, Mass.: Harvard University Press, 1979.

Sorensen, Theodore. *Kennedy.* New York: Harper & Row, 1965.

Sudoplatov, Pavel, and Anatoli Sudoplatov with Jerrold L. Schecter and Leona Schecter. *Special Tasks: The Memoirs of an Unwanted Witness.* Boston: Little, Brown, 1994.

Taylor, S. J. *Stalin's Apologist: Walter Duranty,* The New York Times*'s Man in Moscow.* New York: Oxford University Press, 1990.

Toy, Stewart. "Dr. Hammer Is 90 and the Road Show Keeps Rolling On." *BusinessWeek,* May 30, 1988.

Tremlett, George. *Gadaffi: The Desert Mystic.* New York: Carroll & Graf, 1993.

U.S. House of Representatives, hearings before the Committee on Armed Services, 82nd Congress, 1st session, October 24, 1951. Washington, D.C.: U.S. Government Printing Office, 1951.

Vincent, Howard P. *Daumier and His World.* Evanston, Ill.: Northwestern University Press, 1968.

Volkogonov, Dmitrii. *Lenin: A New Biography.* Edited and translated by Harold Shukman. New York: Free Press, 1994.

Walker, John. *Self Portrait with Donors: Confessions of an Art Collector.* Boston: Little, Brown, 1974.

Weinberg, Steve. *Armand Hammer: The Untold Story.* London: Abacus, 1992.

Weissman, Benjamin M. *Herbert Hoover and Famine Relief to Soviet Russia, 1921–1923.* Stanford, Calif.: Hoover Institution Press, 1974.

Whaley, Barton. *Codeword BARBAROSSA.* Cambridge, Mass.: MIT Press, 1973.

Wheeler-Bennett, John. *The Nemesis of Power: The German Army in Politics, 1918–1945.* London: Macmillan, 1964.

Wilkins, Mira, and Frank E. Hill. *American Business Abroad: Ford on Six Continents.* Detroit: Wayne State University Press, 1964.

Williams, Robert C. *Russian Art and American Money, 1900–1940.* Cambridge, Mass.: Harvard University Press, 1980.

Wilson, Edmund. *To the Finland Station: A Study in the Writing and Acting of History.* New York: Harcourt, Brace, 1940.

Wixen, Joan Sanders. "The Mogul Who Refuses to Retire." *Modern Maturity,* October–November 1980.

Wolfe, Bertram D. *A Life in Two Centuries: An Autobiography.* New York: Stein & Day, 1981.

Woodward, Bob. *Veil: The Secret Wars of the CIA, 1981–1987.* New York: Simon & Schuster, 1987.

Wright, Peter. *Spycatcher: The Candid Autobiography of a Senior Intelligence Officer.* New York: Viking, 1987.

Yergin, Daniel. "The One-Man Flying Circus." *Atlantic Monthly,* June 1975.

———. *The Prize: The Epic Quest for Oil, Money, and Power.* New York: Simon & Schuster, 1991.

Yousaf, Mohammed, and Mark Adkin. *The Bear Trap: Afghanistan's Untold Story.* London: Leo Cooper, 1992.

Zuckerman, Harriet. *Scientific Elites: Nobel Laureates in the United States.* New York: Free Press, 1977.

AUTHOR'S NOTE

I first met Armand Hammer on February 21, 1981, at his office in the Occidental headquarters in Los Angeles. I had gone there to write a profile of Hammer for *The New York Times Magazine.*

Hammer, who was just beginning his campaign for the Nobel Peace Prize, assumed that I would present him favorably, since he was on friendly terms with Arthur "Punch" Sulzberger, the chairman and publisher of the *Times.* He immediately asked if I knew Punch, and when I said I did not, he offered to take me to dinner with him (as he eventually did). He also told me that he assumed the story would be featured on the cover of the magazine, and he suggested that if I had "any problems" with my editor, he would "call Punch" in my behalf. He clearly liked to believe he was in control—and at the time, I did nothing to disillusion him.

On a personal level, I found Hammer to be a modest and affable man who far more closely resembled a country doctor than a corporate magnate. He invited me to travel with him on his private jetliner, *Oxy One,* on his nonstop business and political trips. The *Oxy One* had been specially designed for intercontinental flight. It had a one-hundred-foot-long cabin configured as a personal salon, with twin beds and a shower and an office. In the course of the next six months, I traveled with Hammer to Paris, London, Ottawa, Chicago, Washington, D.C., and New York. He enjoyed prestigious hotels, in particular Claridge's in London, the Plaza Athénée in Paris, and the Madison in Washington, D.C., and liked it when he was recognized by the hotel employees. (The only time I saw him lose his temper was when the cashier at the Plaza Athénée refused to accept his assistant's credit card—and held up the delivery of baggage to his room.) He had little tolerance for gourmet food, often preferring to order a hamburger.

During these trips, I spent scores of hours discussing his life, achievements, and business strategies. It was not always easy. He was slightly hard of hearing, and he used this infirmity to great effect when he did not want to discuss an issue. When I asked Hammer questions he did not expect or did not want to answer, he simply ignored them. He also wore thick glasses that did not entirely correct his severe myopia, and often, like the Mr. Magoo character in the cartoon series, he did not recognize acquaintances.

When he crossed time zones in *Oxy One,* Hammer had little respect for other people's time. He had no inhibitions about calling subordinates at home in the middle of the night. He kept his own schedule, napping or working to suit his convenience. His wife almost always accompanied him and acted as his helpmate. When the plane landed, he was usually met by a sizable entourage of personal assistants, public relations men, security men, and his personal photographer, who strained to keep up with him as he spryly went about his business.

Throughout the winter and spring of 1981, Hammer invited me to a constant stream of events at which he was the center of attention. I went with him to diplomatic receptions, award ceremonies, museum openings, private parties, press conferences, and charity benefits. He introduced me to such acquaintances as Prince Charles, Nancy Reagan, Bob Hope, Louis Nizer, Senator Charles Percy, Edgar Faure, Sir John Foster, Prince Bandar Bin Sultan of Saudi Arabia, David Murdock, and Pierre Trudeau. His purpose was to provide me with colorful material for a story in which, as he conceived of it, he would be a central actor in a rarefied universe of money, altruism, and power. When by summer I still had not completed the story, he grew somewhat impatient and offered to help me write it. I thanked him for his interest, but I did not tell him what was delaying the completion of my profile.

I was then in the midst of writing a book about Soviet intelligence. One of my sources for this book was James Angleton, the former CIA counterintelligence chief.[1] Angleton had an interest in Hammer that went back to a cryptic tip he had received from a KGB defector almost twenty years before, about the Soviet agent of influence known as the Capitalist Prince. Though Angleton suspected that Hammer might be that agent, he did not tell me about this case—Project Dinosaur—until years later. At the time, he suggested to me in his elliptical way that I might find "another side" of Hammer's activities in the documents seized by British intelligence agents in 1927, when they raided Arcos, the Soviet trade mission in London. Through my very able British researcher, Rebecca Fraser, I managed to obtain the Arcos documents. While there was no smoking gun there, they did show that Hammer was the subject of an intriguing investigation that explored links between his export business and payments to Soviet espionage agents in the 1920s. Without having access to Hammer's FBI file, I was not able to discover the results of this investigation. But as I tried to reconstruct Hammer's past life, the profile took a direction different from the one Hammer had anticipated.

The story appeared in *The New York Times Magazine* in November 1981 under the title "The Riddle of Armand Hammer" and posed the question, Does Hammer merely take advantage of his contacts with the Russians to advance his business interests, or does he take advantage of his business contacts to serve Moscow's interest?[2] Hammer was infuriated and he wrote a twenty-five-page letter to the editor of the *Times,* describing himself in the way that he wanted to be described in the article. He demanded that the editors publish it in full, but they ran a one-page excerpt in the letters-to-the-editor section.[3]

I saw no point in responding or writing further on the subject, since, without access to the Soviet archives and the FBI files on Hammer, there seemed to be no way to resolve the issue I had raised. Then, after Hammer died, the Soviet Union collapsed—a contingency he could not have foreseen—and documents began flowing out of the former U.S.S.R. I retained East View Publications, a company in Minneapolis that specializes in obtaining material in Soviet archives, to acquire the files on Hammer. Through them, I got more than three thousand pages of classified Soviet documents that describe in considerable detail Hammer's relations with the Soviet authorities. I also succeeded in obtaining, under the Freedom of Information Act, most of the material in the previously classified FBI file on Hammer. This information provided a unique opportunity to write a biography from the vantage point of two opposing intelligence services, and I decided to write this book.

ACKNOWLEDGMENTS

I am deeply grateful to Cynthia Anderson, who was my chief researcher on this project, for her assistance in obtaining material through Freedom of Information Act (FOIA) requests and searches of government records stored at the National Archives and other government repositories.

In helping to unearth the Soviet Archive, I am indebted to Kent Lee and Demi Frangala of East View Publications and Oleg Gorelov, who did research for me in Moscow. I also am grateful to Harvey Klehr for the documents that he supplied me from the Comintern Archives. Lisa Svenson did a superb job of translating the Soviet documents.

I also benefited enormously from the investigative work of three other authors who had tackled the problem of Hammer previously: Professor Robert C. Williams, the author of *Russian Art and American Money;* Joseph Finder, the author of *Red Carpet;* and Steve Weinberg, the author of *Armand Hammer.* Weinberg was especially generous in sending me material he assiduously researched.

I am grateful to G. Henry Schuler, the director of the Bartlett Program on Energy Security, for the insights and material he provided on Libya.

I also owe a great debt to Julian Hammer for the time he spent helping me form a picture of his father.

I would like to thank the Lynde and Harry Bradley, and Carthage foundations for providing funds for researching this project and the Center for Social Policy and Philosophy for administrating the research grants. The book benefited greatly from the scrutiny the early drafts received from

Tina Bennett and Ellen Frankel Paul. I owe special debts of gratitude to Thomas Fedorik, Clay Felker, Robert D. Fisher, Rebecca Fraser, Hillel Fradken, Philip S. Gillette, Laura Glaz, Casey Hammer, Jean Hammer, William Hood, Mort Janklow, Michael Joyce, Jules Kroll, Richard Larry, Fred D. Miller, Jr., Bettye Murphy, Jonathan Napack, Dan Nessel, Ann Odom, Jeffrey Paul, Caron Smith, Olivia Snaije, and Katrina Vandenheuval.

Suzanne Jackson rendered invaluable assistance in helping me research and clarify the material.

I would like to thank Joseph Iseman for his legal sagacity and the advice he provided me.

Finally, this book benefited enormously from Sharon DeLano's superb editing skills.

INDEX

ABOUT THE AUTHOR

EDWARD JAY EPSTEIN studied government at Cornell and Harvard, and received a Ph.D. from Harvard in 1973. His master's thesis on the search for political truth (*Inquest: The Warren Commission and the Establishment of Truth*) and his doctoral dissertation on television journalism (*News from Nowhere*) were both published. He taught political science at Harvard, MIT, and UCLA but decided that researching and writing books was a more educational enterprise. *Dossier* is his twelfth book. He lives in New York City.

ABOUT THE TYPE

This book was set in Times Roman, designed by Stanley Morison specifically for *The Times* of London. The typeface was introduced in the newspaper in 1932. Times Roman had its greatest success in the United States as a book and commercial typeface.